DATE DUE

Demco, Inc. 38-293

E

F

an

2001

Copyright © 2001 by the International Bank
for Reconstruction and Development/The World Bank
1818 H Street NW, Washington, DC 20433, USA

This publication has been compiled by the staff of the Development Prospects Group of the World Bank's Development Economics Vice Presidency. The World Bank does not accept responsibility for the accuracy or completeness of this publication. Any judgments expressed are those of World Bank staff or consultants and do not necessarily reflect the views of the Board of Executive Directors or the governments they represent.

ISBN 0-8213-4675-X
ISSN 1014-8906
Library of Congress catalog card number: 91-6-440001 (serial)

Contents

Acknowledgments

This report was prepared by the Development Prospects Group, and drew from resources throughout the Development Economics Vice Presidency, the Poverty Reduction Board, and World Bank operational regions. The principal author of the report was William Shaw, with direction by Uri Dadush. The chapter authors were Hans Timmer (chapter 1), Ataman Aksoy (chapter 2), Dominique van der Mensbrugghe (chapter 3), and William Shaw (chapter 4). The report was prepared under the general direction of Jo Ritzen and Nicholas Stern.

The report drew on inputs by other staff of the Development Economics Vice Presidency and from throughout the Bank. Ibrahim Al-Ghelaiqah, Caroline Farah, Himmat Kalsi, Robert Keyfitz, Annette I. De Kleine, Robert Lynn, Fernando Martel Garcia, Dominique van der Mensbrugghe, Shoko Negishi, and Mick Riordan contributed to the analysis of global economic trends and prospects in chapter 1. Tamar Manuelyan Atinc, Shaohua Chen, Valerie Kozel, Giovanna Prennushi, Martin Ravallion, and Aristomene Varoudakis contributed to the discussion of poverty. Betty Dow, Faezeh Fouraton, Carol Gabyzon, Theresa Goldberg, Dorsati Madani, Donald Mitchell, Ashish Narain, Francis Ng, and Konstantin Senyut contributed to chapter 2. Constantine Michalopoulos and John S. Wilson contributed to chapter 3. Carol Gabyzon, Somik Lall, Ashish Narain, Andrew Sunil Rajkumar, and David Wheeler contributed to chapter 4. And John Baffes, Betty Dow, Donald Mitchell, and Shane Streifel contributed to the analysis of commodity prices in chapter 1 and the annex.

Many others from inside and outside the Bank provided inputs, comments, guidance, and support at various stages of the report's publication. John Beghin, David Rohland-Holst, and Matthew Slaughter wrote background papers on trade issues. Henry Ergas and Iain Little wrote a background paper on electronic commerce. Gary Hufbauer, Arvind Panagariya, Francisco Rodriguez, and Alan Winters served as outside reviewers. Carlos Braga, Shanta Devarajan, Richard Newfarmer, and Gene Tidrik were discussants at the Bankwide review. We would particularly like to thank Gordon Betcherman, Milan Brahmbhatt, Sara Calvo, Richard Eglin, David Ellerman, Michael Finger, Carsten Fink, Andrea Goldstein, Bernard Hoekman, Albert Keidel, Ioannis Kessides, Michael Klein, Amy Luinstra, Will Martin, Aaditya Mattoo, Marcelo Olarreaga, Gary Pursell, David Tarr, and Edith Wilson for their helpful comments. The Development Data Group contributed to the appendix. Betty Sun served as the External Affairs task manager, Robert King managed dissemination from the Development Prospects Group, and Phil Hay managed media arrangements. Sarah Crowe served as the principal assistant to the team and Katherine Rollins assisted with chapter 1. Book design, editing, and production were directed and managed by the Production Services Unit of the World Bank's Office of the Publisher.

Summary

TECHNOLOGICAL INNOVATIONS AND THE dismantling of trade barriers over the past decade have contributed to an acceleration of growth in global trade. This acceleration has been associated with faster growth in developing countries as a group. However, many of the poorest countries have not kept pace. This year's *Global Economic Prospects* focuses on international trade and discusses policies that are required if developing countries are to benefit from global integration.

Prospects for developing countries and world trade

The global economy is likely approaching a cyclical high in 2000, boosted by a further acceleration of growth in the United States, the recovery in Europe and Japan, and the sharp rebound in countries affected by the global financial crisis. World trade volumes are likely to increase by 12.5 percent, the highest rate of growth since before the first oil shock of the 1970s. A moderation of growth in the crisis countries and slower consumption growth in the United States are likely to lead to a deceleration of output growth over the next year.

The apparent shift upward in trend productivity growth in the United States, increased labor market flexibility and product market competition in Europe, and steps toward financial and corporate restructuring in Japan have improved the prospects for long-term growth. The same applies in developing countries, where liberalization of markets, more stable macroeconomic policies, and technological change have promoted integration. Indicators of human capital, including school enrollment and literacy rates, show broad improvement across most developing regions.

However, cyclical and structural aspects of the current boom have increased imbalances and tensions in the global economy. Easier monetary policy in the United States and increased fiscal stimulus in Japan boosted growth from the depths of the financial crisis, but these policies also increased the already large U.S. current account deficit (4.5 percent of GDP) and Japanese government debt (115 percent of GDP). The strong global recovery of 1999–2000, coupled with the sharp reduction in OPEC (Organization of Petroleum Exporting Countries) supply, caused a surge in oil prices. Structural reforms and rapid technological change have also generated political tensions. The fast pace of global economic integration has accentuated competition and increased uncertainty, particularly for firms in declining industries and their workers. Inequality both among and within countries appears to have risen, in part the result of technological progress.

A low-case scenario assumes a less favorable resolution of these imbalances and tensions, marked by continued high oil prices and a reversal of international investment flows from the United States. The resulting recession, coming on the heels of the global financial crisis, may feed "reform fatigue" and thus lower developing countries' long-term growth potential.

Trade policies in the 1990s and the poorest countries

Over the past decade, developing countries reduced the level and dispersion of tariffs, dismantled nontariff trade barriers, and increased reliance on market forces to allocate foreign exchange. These policies, coupled with other market reforms, were associated with an acceleration of output and export growth, except for countries that were affected by conflict or the breakup of the Soviet Union. The per capita income of small, low-income countries (thus excluding China and India) declined during the 1990s, but growth averaged 1 percent a year if countries involved in conflict and countries in transition are excluded. This represents a significant acceleration compared with the 1980s but is still well below the average of middle-income countries.

Weaknesses in trade-related policies continued to impede growth in many of the poorest countries. Appreciated real exchange rates and high real exchange rate volatility have often been associated with a muted export response to trade liberalization; per capita income growth was significantly faster in poor countries with relatively stable real exchange rates. The absence of effective duty exemption/drawback programs, coupled with fiscal reliance on tariffs on intermediate and capital goods, has increased costs for exporters. Finally, weak export infrastructure, inadequate ancillary export services, and high transport costs—often in part the result of policy shortcomings—have left many countries (particularly the landlocked ones) at a competitive disadvantage on international markets.

High trade barriers imposed by industrial countries on agriculture and processed food imports, along with agricultural subsidies, have contributed to the decline in developing countries' share of world trade in these commodities. These trade distortions have particularly affected the poorest countries, because a host of other domestic policy and institutional weaknesses inhibit their diversification into less restricted sectors.

Standards, developing countries, and the global trade system

Product standards (rules governing the characteristics of goods that are generally imposed to protect health and safety) are critical to the effective functioning of markets and provide important support to the trade system. However, many developing countries (particularly the poorest ones) lack the technological and financial resources to develop product standards effectively, meet industrial countries' import requirements, and bring disputes when standards are used to discriminate against their exports.

Adherence to labor and environmental standards (for example, the right to form unions and limits on pollution) is critical to economic efficiency and welfare. However, pressures to use trade sanctions to support labor and environmental standards threaten to restrict developing countries' access to international markets while doing little to improve welfare. Labor and environmental standards generally improve as countries develop, but low labor and environmental standards are not usually a significant source of competitive advantage. The imposition of trade sanctions is vulnerable to capture by protectionist interests and hurts workers by reducing demand for the goods they produce. Even if the threat of sanctions improves conditions for some workers, average working conditions in the economy are unlikely to improve. Similarly, empirical studies show that imposing trade sanctions on exporters can cause considerable output losses while doing little to reduce pollution.

Electronic commerce and developing countries

The Internet will boost efficiency and enhance market integration, particularly in developing countries that are most disadvantaged by poor access to information. The Internet will raise productivity through increased procurement system efficiency, strengthened inventory control, lowered retail transaction costs, and elimination or transformation of intermediaries. The cost of reaching industrial country markets will fall, generating large gains from trade. Developing-country firms that sell labor-intensive, differentiated products (for example, crafts, software, and business services—particularly services involving the remote processing of routine information) will experience increased demand. Developing-country firms also will benefit from the opportunity to leapfrog to the most advanced technologies.

Nevertheless, Internet access is grossly unequal across countries, and the Internet also brings increased danger of economic marginalization to countries that cannot access it effectively. For example, developing-country firms that lack the reputation to bid on the new online exchanges or the technology to interact efficiently with more sophisticated firms could see reduced demand. While the growing use of cell phones and other technologies should increase Internet access rapidly over the next 10 years, access is likely to remain limited in per capita terms, especially in the poorest countries.

Taking advantage of electronic commerce requires an open economy to promote competition and diffusion of Internet technologies; improved international coordination (for example, in confronting challenges to domestic tax and financial systems); and efficient social and infrastructure services, in particular a competitive telecommunications sector and a well-educated labor force. The importance of network effects and first-mover advantages emphasizes the importance of government support for achieving these goals.

Abbreviations, Acronyms, and Data Notes

APEC	Asia Pacific Economic Cooperation
CAP	Common Agricultural Policy
CEE	Central and Eastern Europe (Central and Eastern European countries are CEECs)
CFA	Communauté Financière Africaine
CIS	Commonwealth of Independent States
EBRD	European Bank for Reconstruction and Development
ECA	Europe and Central Asia
EMU	European Monetary Union
EU	European Union
FAO	Food and Agriculture Organization of the United Nations
FDI	Foreign direct investment
GATT	General Agreement on Tariffs and Trade
GDP	Gross domestic product
GSP	Generalized System of Preferences
HIPC	Heavily indebted poor countries
HIV/AIDS	Human immunodeficiency virus/acquired immune deficiency syndrome
ILO	International Labour Organisation
IT	Information technology
LAC	Latin America and the Caribbean
LIBOR	London interbank offered rate
LDC	Least-developed countries
M&A	Mergers and acquisitions
MNA	Middle East and North Africa
Mercosur	Latin America Southern Cone trade bloc (Argentina, Brazil, Paraguay, and Uruguay)
MFN	Most favored nation

MFP	Multifactor productivity
MRA	Mutual recognition agreement
MUV	Manufactures unit value index
NAFTA	North American Free Trade Agreement
NASDAQ	National Association of Securities Dealers Automated Quotation
NIE	Newly industrializing economy
NTBs	Nontariff barriers
OECD	Organisation for Economic Co-operation and Development
OPEC	Organization of Petroleum Exporting Countries
PSE	Producer support estimate
RIA	Regional integration agreement
saar	Seasonally adjusted annualized rate
TBT	Technical barriers to trade
TRIPs	Trade-related intellectual property rights
SPS	Sanitary and Phytosanitary Standards
UNAIDS	Joint United Nations Programme on HIV/AIDS
WTO	World Trade Organization

Data notes

The "classification of economies" tables at the end of this volume classify economies by income, region, export category, and indebtedness. Unless otherwise indicated, the term "developing countries" as used in this volume covers all low- and middle-income countries, including the transition economies.

The following norms are used throughout:

- Billion is 1,000 million.
- All dollar figures are U.S. dollars.
- In general, data for periods through 1998 are actual, data for 1999 are estimated, and data for 2000 onward are projected.

1

Prospects for Developing Countries and World Trade

WORLD ECONOMIC ACTIVITY DURING 2000 is proceeding at the fastest pace in over a decade, with developing-country output growth expected to exceed 5 percent. World trade volumes are expected to rise by a record 12.5 percent in the year. Although oil prices have surged by more than 50 percent, inflation in both industrial and developing countries continues, thus far, to be relatively subdued. But developments in oil markets remain a major uncertainty in the outlook, as do the sustainability of the remarkable non-inflationary U.S. expansion and the general fragility of financial systems in East Asia. This chapter reviews the cyclical and structural factors responsible for the robust economic expansion and discusses the major challenges and risks ahead, in both the short and the medium terms. The main conclusions are:

The world economy recovered remarkably well and is likely approaching a cyclical high in 2000

Many of the developing countries that experienced a sharp rebound after the 1997–98 recession appear to have reached cyclical peaks, with the five East Asian countries hit hardest by the financial crisis the clearest example of this development (figure 1.1). The strength of the recovery in Latin America has been impressive, but momentum appeared to be waning in the second half of the year. And the rebound in the Russian Federation has also been unexpectedly strong, though largely dependent on high oil revenues and more fragile than in East Asia. With oil prices expected to ease in the medium term and the effect of the 1998 ruble devaluation wearing off, the Russian Federation's current GDP growth of about 7.2 percent is expected to slow significantly over the medium term. Sub-Saharan Africa has experienced a less uniform recovery, with oil exporters gaining and commodity-dependent oil-importing nations suffering large terms-of-trade losses. These synchronous recoveries have carried developing-country growth to a peak of 5.3 percent in 2000—0.7 percentage points faster than projected nine months ago in the World Bank's *Global Development Finance 2000*—with a slight slowing to 5.0 percent expected next year (table 1.1). Growth in the industrial countries may also be nearing a turning point; it is expected to slow from this year's rapid 3.7 percent pace to 2.9 percent in 2001. Moderation of consumer demand in the United States, following interest rate increases and stock market declines, is the principal factor behind this modest deceleration.

The current double-digit growth of world trade, the strongest since before the first oil shock of the early 1970s, is clearly a cyclical phenomenon tied to robust world activity levels. During the upswing, as inventories were replenished and investments accelerated, trade expanded much faster than the economy as a whole. Once stocks of durable goods and capital goods have adjusted, growth rates of trade

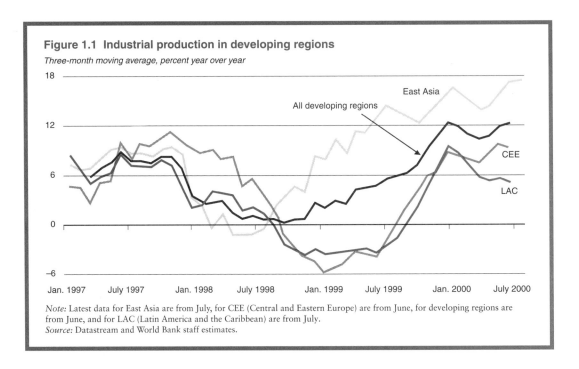

Figure 1.1 Industrial production in developing regions

Three-month moving average, percent year over year

Note: Latest data for East Asia are from July, for CEE (Central and Eastern Europe) are from June, for developing regions are from June, and for LAC (Latin America and the Caribbean) are from July.
Source: Datastream and World Bank staff estimates.

should moderate to around 8 percent, which is still a high level by historical standards.

Foundations for longer-term growth have improved in many industrial and developing regions . . .

Industrial countries have been undergoing a period of accelerated transformation, restructuring, and adjustment that is now starting to pay off. The United States appears to have created an institutional and policy environment that supports the adoption of new information and communications technologies at a rapid pace, contributing to a substantial acceleration in productivity growth. Most European countries have made some progress in rendering labor markets more flexible and exposing product and service markets to greater competition; these processes have been facilitated by regional integration, including, most recently, the introduction of a single currency. The recent decline in Euro Area unemployment rates, and the more than doubled value of merger and acquisitions (M&A) activities and corporate bond issues in 1999, offers some indication of accelerated restructuring and

improved business confidence. And Japan appears to be emerging from a long period of sluggish growth. This follows the initiation of serious efforts toward financial and corporate restructuring, although a lack of self-sustaining effective demand, especially from private consumers, is still a danger.

Liberalization, accompanying policy measures, and technological change in many developing countries have led to a spectacular increase in openness during the 1990s. Foreign direct investment (FDI) flows into developing countries rose from 0.5 percent of developing countries' GDP in 1990 to 2.7 percent at the end of the decade. Despite the financial crisis, exports of goods and services from developing countries increased by 10 percent a year during the 1990s, contrasted with less than 4 percent during the 1980s. Competition from both domestic and foreign sources has increased in this more open environment, and macroeconomic policies have become more prudent, keeping inflation low and reducing some of the larger fiscal deficits. And indicators of human capital, including school enrollment and illiteracy rates, have shown broad improvement across

Table 1.1   Global conditions affecting growth in developing countries and world GDP growth
(percentage change from previous year, except interest rates and oil price)

	Current Estimate	Current Forecasts			March 2000 Forecasts		
	1999	2000	2001	2002	2000	2001	2002
Global Conditions							
World trade (volume)	5.8	12.5	8.0	6.8	8.3	6.9	6.5
Inflation (consumer prices)							
G-7 OECD countries[a,b]	1.2	2.0	1.9	1.9	1.8	1.9	2.0
United States	2.2	3.4	3.0	2.8	2.7	2.5	2.6
Commodity prices (nominal $)							
Commodity prices, except oil ($)	−11.2	−0.8	3.4	4.9	5.6	3.9	3.3
Oil price ($, weighted average), $/bbl	18.1	28.0	25.0	21.0	23.0	19.0	18.0
Oil price, Percent Change	38.3	55.0	−10.7	−16.0	27.3	−17.4	−5.3
Manufactures export unit value ($)[c]	−2.7	−2.3	3.6	3.7	2.5	2.5	2.6
Interest rates							
LIBOR, 6 months (*US$, percent per year*)	5.5	6.7	6.8	6.2	6.5	6.5	5.5
EURIBOR, 6 months (*Euro, percent per year*)	3.0	4.5	5.0	4.6	...	...	...
World GDP growth	2.8	4.1	3.4	3.2	3.5	3.1	3.1
High-income countries	2.7	3.8	3.0	2.8	3.2	2.7	2.6
OECD countries	2.7	3.7	2.9	2.7	3.0	2.6	2.5
United States	4.2	5.1	3.2	2.9	3.8	2.7	2.8
Japan	0.3	2.0	2.1	2.2	1.2	1.4	1.6
Euro Area	2.4	3.4	3.2	2.8	3.4	3.1	2.8
Non-OECD countries	4.2	6.3	5.1	5.1	4.6	4.8	5.1
Developing countries	3.2	5.3	5.0	4.8	4.6	4.8	4.8
East Asia and Pacific	6.9	7.2	6.4	6.0	6.6	6.3	6.1
Europe and Central Asia (ECA)	1.0	5.2	4.3	3.9	2.5	3.4	3.6
Latin America and the Caribbean	0.1	4.0	4.1	4.3	3.6	3.8	4.4
Middle East and North Africa	2.2	3.1	3.8	3.6	3.5	3.6	3.6
South Asia	5.7	6.0	5.5	5.5	5.9	5.8	5.5
Sub-Saharan Africa	2.1	2.7	3.4	3.7	3.2	3.7	3.8
Memorandum items							
East Asia-5 countries[d]	6.7	6.9	5.5	5.1	5.7	5.4	5.1
Transition countries of ECA	2.5	5.0	4.2	3.7	2.1	3.0	3.3
Developing countries							
Excluding the transition countries	3.3	5.3	5.1	5.0	5.0	5.0	5.1
Excluding China and India	2.2	4.7	4.4	4.3	3.8	4.0	4.2

... Not available.
a. Canada, France, Germany, Italy, Japan, the United Kingdom, and the United States.
b. In local currency, aggregated using 1995 GDP weights.
c. Unit value index of manufactures exports from G-5 to developing countries, expressed in U.S. dollars.
d. Indonesia, the Republic of Korea, Malaysia, the Philippines, and Thailand.
Source: Development Prospects Group, baseline, October 2000; and GDF projections of March 2000.

most developing regions. With these structural changes, many countries in Latin America, Central Europe, and Sub-Saharan Africa appear to have considerably improved their growth potential. Assuming continued corporate and financial restructuring to deal with the debt overhang left by the crisis, countries in East Asia should achieve high rates of growth over the next decade.

. . . but these favorable cyclical and structural conditions contain built-in tensions

Developments during the global financial crisis sowed the seeds for some severe imbalances that have remained or become evident during the current boom. The adoption of an easier monetary policy in the United States to avert a global recession in late 1998 contributed to an acceleration of U.S. demand growth and a widening of the current account deficit, which is likely to breach 4.5 percent of GDP in 2000. Fiscal stimulus in Japan, while helping to sustain demand during the worst part of the crisis, has further increased the huge burden of government debt to some 115 percent of GDP. Nonperforming loans in the Asian crisis countries reached 30 to 50 percent of GDP and have been declining only gradually. The financial vulnerabilities translated into an average decline of more than 30 percent in the equity markets in these countries between January and November. The strong global recovery of 1999–2000, coupled with the sharp reduction in OPEC supply (following the plunge in oil prices to $10 per barrel in 1998), caused a surge in oil prices.

Structural reforms and rapid technological change have also generated political tensions. The fast pace of global economic integration has accentuated competition and increased uncertainty, particularly for firms in declining industries and their workers. Inequality, both among and within countries, and in part tied to technological change, appears to have increased. A backlash against globalization could result in a slower pace of reforms, especially if the current expansionary phase is broken.

These tensions could reduce growth in both the short and longer terms

The baseline scenario assumes a soft landing for the U.S. economy, smooth private sector adjustment, and prudent policy reactions to the current oil price shock. However, a less favorable resolution of the tensions now affecting the global economy is possible. Supply interruptions or unexpectedly high demand could lead to a sharper and more protracted spike in oil prices, while uncertainty about future oil prices could severely affect business and consumer confidence. These adverse reactions could be reinforced by a tightening of monetary policies. A reversal of international investment flows to the United States, triggered by increasing current account deficits and a change in sentiment in the stock market, could accentuate the global downturn affecting East

Asia and Latin America more severely. The sharp growth slowdown that would result, coming on the heels of the global financial crisis, may feed "reform fatigue" in developing countries, resulting in low growth. The low-case scenario below illustrates the importance of reducing short-run imbalances to safeguard the long-term prospects for growth.

This chapter is organized as follows. First the cyclical environment and the long-term growth potential in the industrial countries are discussed, and a review of recent developments and prospects for world trade and financial flows to developing countries follows. The section on commodity prices focuses on the sharp hike in oil prices, one of the major threats to the current outlook. And the following two sections summarize the consequences of these trends for developing regions in the short and longer terms, including elaboration of a low-case scenario. Finally, the consequences for poverty alleviation are explored.

Long-term growth in industrial countries is projected to be higher

Growth in the high-income Organisation for Economic Co-operation and Development (OECD) countries may average 3.7 percent in 2000 (the fastest growth recorded in over a decade), driven by a sharp acceleration of exports, strong carryover effects of the U.S. consumer boom of late 1999 to mid-2000, broadening and strengthening of economic activity across the Euro Area, and a pickup in Japanese private and public investment spending. Growth rates in the three major blocs are expected to move toward convergence, yielding OECD growth of 2.9 percent in 2001 and 2.7 percent in 2002 (figure 1.2). But this outlook is subject to important risks, including the potential for a hard landing in the United States because of investor concern over the burgeoning current account deficit, higher inflation and the likelihood of monetary tightening if the present spike in oil prices is sustained, and a disruption of the Japanese recovery because of fragile financial conditions.

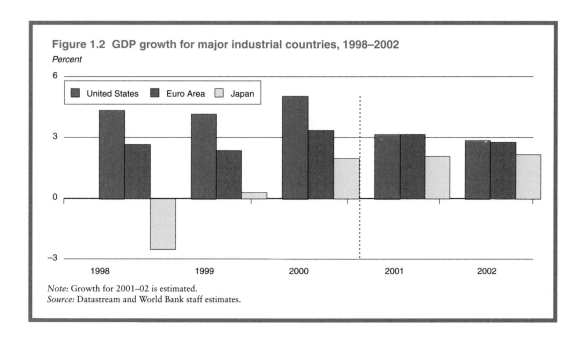

Figure 1.2 GDP growth for major industrial countries, 1998–2002

Percent

Legend: United States, Euro Area, Japan

X-axis: 1998, 1999, 2000, 2001, 2002

Note: Growth for 2001–02 is estimated.
Source: Datastream and World Bank staff estimates.

Structural transformation may lead to stronger long-term growth

Technology-driven productivity growth in the United States, market reforms and adjustment to a common currency in the European Union (EU), and corporate and financial restructuring and deregulation in Japan offer the potential for rapid growth in the long run. However, important challenges remain in reaping the benefits of these new technologies, expanding the EU to the east, and adjusting to slower population growth. Moreover, the huge U.S. external deficit and Japan's rising government debt will continue to pose major risks. Assuming effective policies to confront these challenges, growth for the industrial countries over 2003–10 has been upgraded from earlier forecasts to 2.8 percent.

Cyclical and structural forces are shaping the path of U.S. expansion

United States. The remarkable performance of the U.S. economy since the mid-1990s has its roots in prudent monetary, fiscal, and regulatory policies that encouraged private sector activity. It also stems from the availability of venture capital and a flexible labor force that facilitated productivity-enhancing innovations in information and communications technology (box 1.1). Nevertheless, cyclical factors have played an important role in the boom. Increasing job opportunities, rising incomes and wealth, and strong corporate profits have boosted consumer and business optimism to record levels and encouraged rapid growth in expenditure. Equity price movements have exerted a large impact on consumer behavior (figure 1.3). Over 1995–98, household net wealth grew each year by some 30 percentage points more than disposable incomes.[1] Partly as a result, the personal saving rate dropped from 7.6 percent in the first half of the 1990s to negative territory (–0.2 percent) in the third quarter of 2000.

Consumer price inflation has risen by 1.5 percentage points over the last year, partly in response to the 50 percent rise in oil price. Compensation pressures are rising, as the Employment Cost Index increased by 4.4 percent during the first three quarters of the year. However, the pass-through of rising input costs to core inflation has been limited, in large measure because of strong productivity growth (4.7 percent through the third quarter from a year ago)—suppressing any increase in unit labor costs—and the appreciation of

Box 1.1   U.S. labor productivity and information technology

The rise in U.S. labor productivity growth from 1.5 percent per year in 1980–95 to nearly 2.6 percent per year in the late 1990s was closely tied to innovations in information technology (IT).[a]

There are three principal sources of productivity growth: capital deepening, represented by increases in the amount of plant and equipment per worker; improvements in technology and in the organization of the production process, otherwise known as multifactor productivity, or MFP; and improvements in the quality of the work force tied to advances in education and increased experience. Oliner and Sichel (2000) calculate the contribution of these three sources of growth to the one-percentage-point acceleration of labor productivity growth in the nonfarm business sector between the first half and the second half of the 1990s: increased *use* of IT capital (capital deepening) accounts for 43 percent of the upward shift in productivity growth, and improvements in MFP in the computer industries accounts for another 36 percent. In the *World Economic Outlook* (IMF 2000), the International Monetary Fund cites these sources of productivity growth from computers and IT, in addition to investment spillover effects, such as those tied to gaining Internet access as more consumers and businesses establish Internet capabilities.

Labor productivity growth: nonfarm business sector output per hour

Annual average percentage change

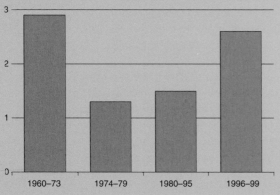

Source: Economic Report of the President, U.S. Council of Economic Advisors, February 2000.

Why now?
Why did it take until the late 1990s for mainframe computers and related IT, which have been widely used over the last quarter century, to have an impact on productivity? The full implementation and widespread adoption of new general purpose technologies usually takes many years, because of both investment and learning costs. Productivity may slow initially because of costs associated with obtaining and implementing the new technology, as well as increased scrap rates, reflecting more rapid obsolescence of old capital. The speed of the recovery in productivity is determined by factors such as the steepness of the learning curve and the time required for the complete replacement of older technologies. Hence, while firms have been investing in computers for many years, associated gains in productivity are only now being realized: managers needed to figure out how to incorporate IT into business processes and staff needed to be trained.

A number of underlying factors contributed to the upswing in productivity growth, including supportive macroeconomic policies and deregulation, the end of the Cold War (allowing resources to be redeployed from the defense sector to the commercial sector), and trade liberalization (resulting in greater cross-border competition). The combination of advances in IT and deregulation may also have helped by providing tools for the unbundling of risks in capital markets through IT and by creating a more competitive market environment.

Will the rebound be sustained?
How long the increase in productivity growth will persist depends critically on the penetration of IT productivity gains into the service sector (which represents close to 80 percent of U.S. GDP); evidence on this issue is lacking or unclear.[b] The extensive research on assessing productivity gains in different sectors of the economy has revealed severe measurement problems.[c] However, Triplett (1999) and Jorgenson and Stiroh (2000) stress the importance of industry-level analysis in examining past trends in U.S. productivity growth. Until these information gaps are addressed, evaluating the spread of IT gains

Box 1.1 (continued)

in productivity to other sectors will remain an open question. To this end, Bosworth and Triplett (2000) make a plea for improving U.S. statistical agencies' methods, which have not kept up with changes in the underlying structure of the U.S. economy.

While the transmission of IT productivity gains to the service sector has not materialized fully in the data, it is clear that the demand for IT goods has remained strong, making it reasonable to expect that gains in IT productivity will continue to contribute

positively to overall productivity growth in the United States for some time. Recent evidence suggests productivity appears to be increasing outside of IT sectors: nonmanufacturing productivity has increased noticeably since mid-1999, and productivity in retail activity has been on the upswing since mid-1997 (Kasman 2000). If these indicators reflect the onset of IT penetration into the production processes of other sectors, then strong productivity growth could continue for some time.

a. In the four quarters through the second quarter of 2000, year-on-year growth in nonfarm business output per hour has averaged 4 percent.

b. Indeed, Gordon (forthcoming) evaluates recent labor productivity growth in the United States, applying cyclical factors, and he argues that the failure itself—of IT productivity gains to penetrate into non-IT sectors—implies that the growth momentum in trend productivity will not be sustained.

c. For a number of service industries (for example, education), the current method for measuring productivity involves assuming that real output and price changes move together—that is to say that there is no labor productivity growth (Bosworth and Triplett 2000).

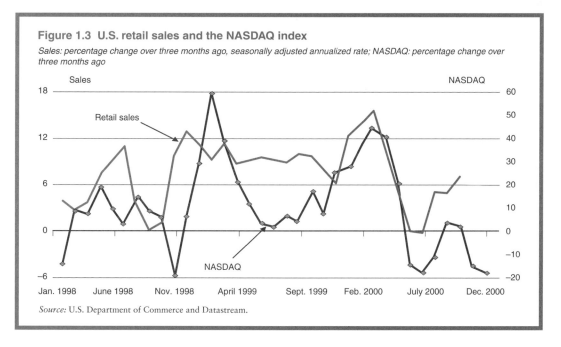

Figure 1.3 U.S. retail sales and the NASDAQ index

Sales: percentage change over three months ago, seasonally adjusted annualized rate; NASDAQ: percentage change over three months ago

Source: U.S. Department of Commerce and Datastream.

the dollar on the heels of massive capital inflows.[2]

The Federal Reserve's increase in the Federal Funds rate (by 175 basis points in six steps from June 1999 to May 2000) reduced the

momentum of consumer demand growth over the course of the first half of the year, with interest-sensitive sectors such as automobiles and housing being particularly affected (figure 1.4). The slowing of consumption growth was

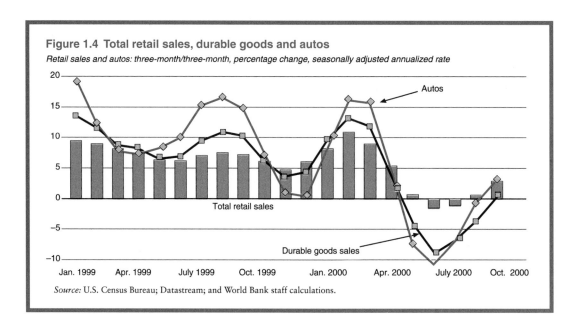

Figure 1.4 Total retail sales, durable goods and autos

Retail sales and autos: three-month/three-month, percentage change, seasonally adjusted annualized rate

Source: U.S. Census Bureau; Datastream; and World Bank staff calculations.

short-lived, however, and third-quarter data revealed a rebound in spending to 4.5 percent growth. Nonetheless, GDP advanced at a 2.7 percent pace in the third quarter representing a dramatic slowing to about one-half the rate of the previous year. A sharp decline in business fixed investment was a major factor in the slowdown, as an unwinding of the high-tech spending boom appears to have begun.

Still, prospects remain favorable for a soft landing and we expect that GDP growth will average 5.1 percent in 2000[3] and about 3 percent on average in 2001–02. The consensus view of financial analysts is that the Federal Reserve is likely to raise interest rates further in 2001 against the background of still rapid domestic demand growth, high oil prices, and continued wage pressures. With a slackening in the pace of economic activity over the course of 2001, policy as well as long-term interest rates should ease moderately in 2002. The underlying risk of a harder landing remains, however, since domestic savings are not expected to recover and the current account deficit is likely to register $450 billion to $475 billion in 2000–02 (4.5 percent of GDP). The possibility of tax cuts following the November elections suggests a reduction of the public sector sur-

plus, which would tend to increase the current account deficit yet further. Current financial tensions in the high-yield sectors may be a first sign that financing of large U.S. private debt is becoming increasingly difficult.

Strong productivity growth is likely to continue over the medium term (box 1.1), as the rapid growth in IT investment (which has risen over the 1990s at four times the rate of other private capital–spending components) despite cyclical up- and downturns is likely to continue at high rates on a secular basis (figure 1.5). With demographic factors likely to slow growth of the labor force to rates below 1 percent per year over the coming decade,[4] long-term potential growth could be as high as 3 or 3.5 percent, without risk of significant inflationary pressure. But achieving this *potential* growth will present policy challenges, as correction of the persistent external deficit will require extended periods of low import demand, a fall in the value of the dollar, or both.

Japan emerges from recession, but its financial underpinnings are fragile

Japan. GDP rose by 10.3 percent (seasonally adjusted annualized rate, or saar) in the first quarter of 2000 and 4.2 percent in the second,

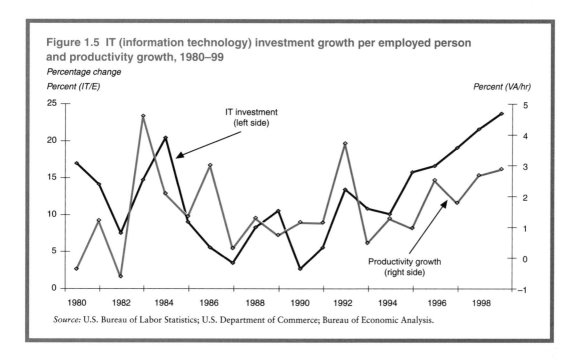

Figure 1.5 IT (information technology) investment growth per employed person and productivity growth, 1980–99

Percentage change

Source: U.S. Bureau of Labor Statistics; U.S. Department of Commerce; Bureau of Economic Analysis.

as public investment increased and a sharp recovery in profits supported private capital spending (figure 1.6). There are now signs that household demand is rising (after a decade of stagnation or decline), grounded in improved labor market conditions. This could give con-

sumer confidence the boost necessary for the recovery to maintain momentum. The Bank of Japan has abandoned its "zero" policy interest stance, suggesting that the pickup in activity is sufficiently grounded to withstand the 25–basis point rise. With evidence that industrial corpo-

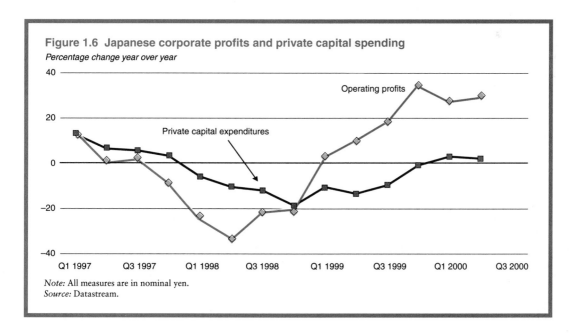

Figure 1.6 Japanese corporate profits and private capital spending

Percentage change year over year

Note: All measures are in nominal yen.
Source: Datastream.

rate recovery is more advanced than anticipated, that public works–related investment is
now filtering through the economy, that a
nascent upturn in consumer demand could
consolidate with rising incomes, and that prospects for Japanese exports remain favorable,
we have upgraded projections for GDP growth
in 2000 to 2 percent, and to a range of 2–2.2
percent over 2001–02.

Recent efforts in the corporate and financial
restructuring required for long-term recovery
from a decade of slow growth show progress.
Announcements of corporate restructuring
plans (mostly by larger firms) surged during
1999 and 2000, and many of these plans contained commitments to refocus on core activities, improve long-term profitability, strengthen
financial control, and forge links with foreign
partners. The government is drafting more
workable insolvency laws to help facilitate
labor mobility and the scrapping of excess capacity, is providing loans and credit insurance
to startups and venture firms, and is easing the
process for mergers and acquisitions and em-
ployee buyouts. Successful restructuring over
the next decade could generate significant gains
in productivity, which together with the expected decline in the labor force would imply
output growth modestly above 2 percent per
year.

Nevertheless, critical challenges remain.
Uneven corporate restructuring continues to
pose a threat to the near-term recovery. The
number of business failures soared to a record
in the first seven months of 2000, and debt associated with the failed firms has skyrocketed.
Events triggered by the still fragile state of
several financial institutions and nonmanufacturing firms could impair consumer and business confidence, as evidenced by the bank-
ruptcy of the Sogo department stores (carrying
$17 billion in debt) after the withdrawal of a
proposed government bailout. And Japan's
general government gross liabilities will reach
115 percent of GDP in 2000; massive expenditure compression and an overhaul of the tax
system will be required to address the debt
overhang in the medium term.

Growth solidifies in the Euro Area, but weak currency is underpinning inflationary pressures

Euro Area. During the second half of 1999,
improvements in world activity, a competitive
exchange rate, and buoyant domestic demand
delivered a rebound for the Euro Area from
the crises of 1998, with GDP growth averaging 3.8 percent on an annualized basis. This
pace of growth continued unabated in the first
quarter of 2000, slowing to an annualized 3.5
percent in the second. A key to the recovery
was the momentum underlying export growth,
which continued to build during the first half
of 2000 toward rates of 10 to 15 percent, with
thickening export order books and rising manufacturing production (figure 1.7 highlights
the case of Germany).

The European Commission's surveys of
consumer and business confidence reached
record highs during the first half of 2000, with
retail sales rising 3.5 percent in the year to
June. Notable after several years of stagnant
employment growth has been the creation of
over one million jobs in 1999, bringing down
Euro Area unemployment to 9 percent from
11 percent in 1998. The economic expansion
has also become more broadly based across
the region, although Italy remains weak in
part because of tightened fiscal policies in
the run-up to the European Monetary Union
(EMU). Preliminary figures for the third quarter point to a slight slowing and stabilization
of activity, partly as a consequence of the oil
related terms-of-trade shock and rising interest rates. Higher oil prices and the weak euro
have boosted the harmonized index of consumer prices by 2.8 percent in the year to
September, well above the European Central
Bank's (ECB) target of 2 percent year-on-year
growth. In response, the ECB has tightened
monetary policy since November 1999, gradually raising the repurchase rate by 225 basis
points to 4.75 percent in October. Further
hikes in policy rates appear likely in order to
prevent a translation of high current inflation
into higher price and wage expectations—or
so-called second-round effects.

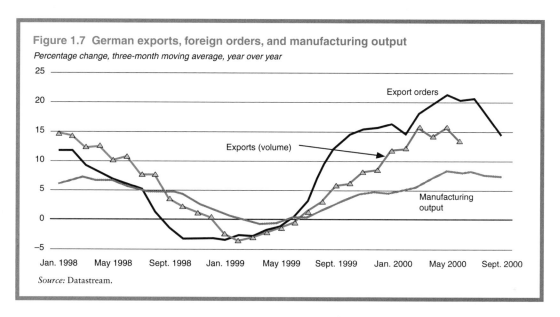

Figure 1.7 German exports, foreign orders, and manufacturing output

Percentage change, three-month moving average, year over year

Source: Datastream.

Recovery in 2000 will likely result in Euro Area growth of 3.4 percent, up from 2.4 percent in 1999. Looking forward, growth should be supported by continued firm consumer demand—bolstered by tax reductions in France, Germany, Italy, and Spain—with stronger spillovers to fixed investment, and the expected unwinding of the terms-of-trade shock as oil prices fall. Yet growth will be restrained by the higher interest rate environment and slowing from exceptionally rapid growth in a number of smaller countries (such as Belgium, the Netherlands, and Spain). These factors suggest a slight moderation in growth toward 3.2 percent in 2001 and further to 2.8 percent in 2002.

Economic performance in the major European countries is expected to improve substantially over the next decade compared with the 1990s, when low productivity growth (1.3 percent during the second half of the decade—figure 1.8), persistent unemployment, and sluggish capital spending limited GDP growth to less than 2 percent per year, compared with more than 3 percent in the United States. Potential growth rates may be as high as 2.8 or 3 percent underpinned among other things, by the introduction of the euro; the growing participation of women in the labor force; and

the possibility of "New Economy" contagion. EMU comes on the heels of increased competition in the financial field stemming from the internal market, deregulation, and rapid technological process, thereby accelerating the move toward integrated and more efficient capital markets. The more than doubling of the value of M&A activities and of corporate bond issues in 1999 is some evidence of the early impact of the EMU. The eastward expansion of the EU could enhance the positive growth scenario outlined above. Alternatively, difficulties in absorbing substantial new population blocs into the union could present risks to future growth.[5] Questions regarding intra-EU labor mobility and especially the Common Agricultural Policy (CAP) will become more pressing as expansion moves forward.

World trade remains on a long-term high-growth path

The 1990s witnessed a dramatic acceleration of world trade, both in comparison with the 1980s and in relation to growth in GDP, driven by technological change and the removal of trade barriers (figure 1.9). World trade is likely to continue to grow strongly, although somewhat below the current record pace.

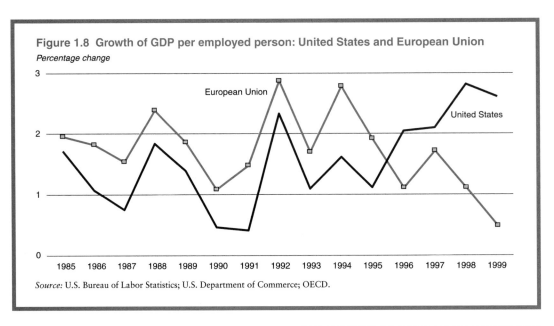

Figure 1.8 Growth of GDP per employed person: United States and European Union

Percentage change

Source: U.S. Bureau of Labor Statistics; U.S. Department of Commerce; OECD.

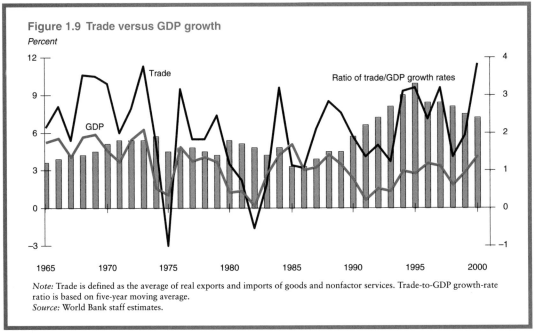

Figure 1.9 Trade versus GDP growth

Percent

Note: Trade is defined as the average of real exports and imports of goods and nonfactor services. Trade-to-GDP growth-rate ratio is based on five-year moving average.
Source: World Bank staff estimates.

Global trade is now at a cyclical high

World trade accelerated in the second half of 1999, peaked at 14 percent (year on year) in the first quarter of 2000, and is expected to average a remarkable 12.5 percent for the year as a whole, the highest annual rate of growth since before the first oil crisis. This robust growth was supported by strong demand growth in industrial countries and the recovering economies of East Asia (which contributed 25 percent of the growth in world demand in 1999). After the financial crisis, industrial production in the crisis countries surged to refill inventories and stocks of capital goods and consumer durable goods

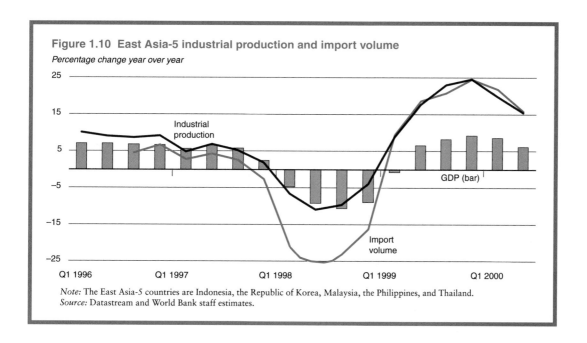

Figure 1.10 East Asia-5 industrial production and import volume

Percentage change year over year

Note: The East Asia-5 countries are Indonesia, the Republic of Korea, Malaysia, the Philippines, and Thailand.
Source: Datastream and World Bank staff estimates.

(figure 1.10). Demand for foreign durable goods and intermediate inputs increased at the same rate. As industrial production will rise faster than GDP only temporarily, the extraordinarily strong import demand is only transitory. Other regions recovering from the crisis showed similar, although weaker, patterns.

In addition, real exchange rate depreciation fueled developing countries' export volumes. East Asian countries' real exchange rates depreciated by an average of 23 percent in 1999 compared with June 1997 levels, resulting in strong gains in market share—though there were short-lived losses in U.S. dollar terms—(figure 1.11, first panel). Brazil, Colombia, Ecuador, and Peru also undertook large exchange rate adjustments in early 1999 (although the average real exchange rate in Latin America in 1999 was only 7 percent below precrisis levels).

Even China, which initially gained export market share in U.S. dollar terms because of its policy decision to hold the renminbi fixed during the crisis period, benefited handsomely from the cyclical upturn with export volumes growing in excess of 35 percent year on year in the first half of 2000. This can be compared with China's record of no growth in this area between October 1998 and April 1999. In contrast, Latin American countries (excluding Mexico) experienced significant losses in market share in 1999 (figure 1.11, second panel), and the rebound witnessed in the first half of 2000 was weak in comparison to that of East Asia. Export volumes continued to grow strongly in Mexico throughout the crisis period of 1997–99 and averaged about 15 percent in the first half of 2000, despite an appreciating real exchange rate, owing to strong links to U.S. manufacturing developed through the globalization of production and cemented by the North American Free Trade Agreement (NAFTA). Similarly, exports from Central European economies benefited from their increasingly close ties to Western Europe (particularly Germany) as they progress toward full accession to the EU (figure 1.11, third panel).

Structural factors boosted trade during the 1990s

Developing countries' exports increased by 10 percent per year during the 1990s, triple the growth rate during the 1980s (figure 1.12). Privatization and more intense competition in

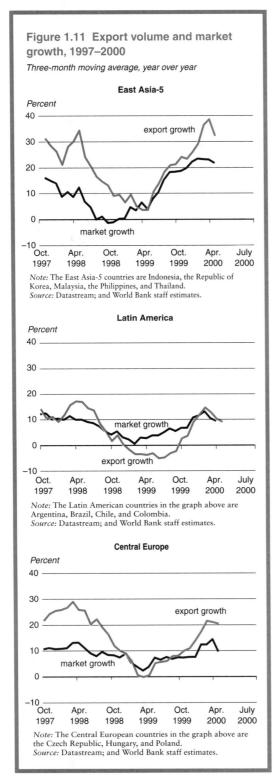

Figure 1.11 Export volume and market growth, 1997–2000

Three-month moving average, year over year

East Asia-5

Note: The East Asia-5 countries are Indonesia, the Republic of Korea, Malaysia, the Philippines, and Thailand.
Source: Datastream; and World Bank staff estimates.

Latin America

Note: The Latin American countries in the graph above are Argentina, Brazil, Chile, and Colombia.
Source: Datastream; and World Bank staff estimates.

Central Europe

Note: The Central European countries in the graph above are the Czech Republic, Hungary, and Poland.
Source: Datastream; and World Bank staff estimates.

domestic markets increased the incentive to find lower-cost intermediate inputs and to search for new export markets. Technological advances reduced communications and transportation costs, greatly facilitating marketing and outsourcing of production (World Bank 1992, 1997). And regional and multilateral agreements have reduced barriers and greatly contributed to the acceleration in trade.

Multilateral agreements. Negotiations under the General Agreement on Tariffs and Trade (GATT) and the World Trade Organization (WTO) have provided an enormous impetus to trade. Multilateral agreements were primarily responsible for the reduction in average tariff rates in industrial countries and the removal of a wide range of nontariff barriers through the mid-1990s, when the Tokyo Round was fully implemented. Further, the GATT negotiations have exerted important influences on other negotiations and trade policy in general. Precedents established under the GATT have guided regional arrangements.[6] The GATT has provided an important venue for many countries to participate in trade negotiations, sometimes for the first time; has established a wide variety of standards (such as tariffication, import valuation, standards for trade in food and animals [SPS agreement], protection of intellectual property [TRIPs agreement], and so forth); has contributed immeasurably to maintaining stable rules of the game in international trade relations, by facilitating dispute settlement and constraining unfair trade practices;[7] and has heightened awareness of the importance of international trade and encouraged significant improvements in countries' capacity for trade administration and negotiation.[8]

Regional agreements. Regional agreements played an increasingly important role in the global trading system during the 1990s (box 1.2). They have often provided opportunities for more comprehensive dismantling of trade barriers and greater harmonization of rules governing trade than can be accomplished under multilateral negotiations. This is particularly true of the EU and NAFTA, both of which developed important precedents for

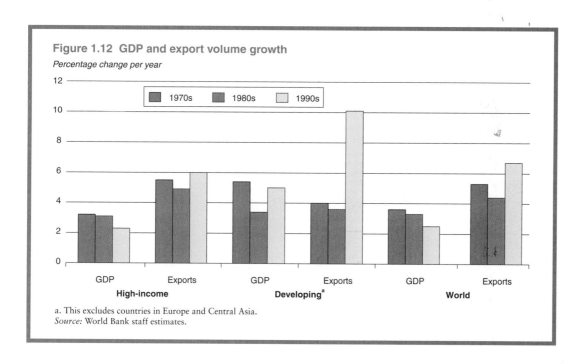

Figure 1.12 GDP and export volume growth

Percentage change per year

a. This excludes countries in Europe and Central Asia.
Source: World Bank staff estimates.

multilateral negotiations and other regional arrangements. There are many reasons for entering regional trade agreements—many of a political economy nature. However, there are significant concerns over their economic benefits. Regional trade agreements shift import supply from external countries to countries within the free trade area. This may lead to reduced efficiency for the countries within the free trade area if external suppliers are lower-cost suppliers. Also, those outside the agreement suffer from lost market share or lower supply prices.

A myriad of other regional integration agreements have evolved (figure 1.13 and the annex).[9] Some of these agreements are designed to address similar leverage and harmonization issues that faced the EU and NAFTA. Some countries have undertaken more ambitious efforts at regionalism—for example, the members of the Association of Southeast Asian Nations and the Asia Pacific Economic Cooperation.

It is extremely difficult to measure the relative importance of regional and multilateral agreements to the expansion of trade. Multi-

lateral agreements that lead to increased growth may spur intraregional exports because of lower transport costs (than outside the region) and other agglomeration effects (for example, greater knowledge of closer markets than of extraregional ones). Conversely, regional arrangements can stimulate global trade through improving the efficiency and hence competitiveness of regional producers and expanding demand for inputs from nonregional sources. Nevertheless, the existing data do indicate that some regional arrangements have been associated with expanded trade. The growth of intraregional trade was significantly greater than the growth of exports outside the region in NAFTA and the EU during the 1980s, and in NAFTA and Mercosur (the Latin America Southern Cone trade bloc) during the first half of the 1990s (table 1.2). The EU during 1990–95 is an exception, owing to the relatively slow growth in Europe following German reunification.[10]

Many of the other regional arrangements lack the economic diversity required to meet the bulk of their trade needs. Only three of the non-NAFTA and EU agreements have more

Box 1.2 North–South regional arrangements

One distinguishing feature of NAFTA, its North-South orientation, is of special relevance to developing countries, and this fact alone makes it likely to influence most regional integration agreements (RIAs) in the future. Motives for North-South agreements are many. Included among these are the usual regional incentives such as shared history, trade, and transport economies. Agreements between industrial and developing countries also imply more extensive shifts in specialization (and thereby greater gains from trade) than regional agreements among developing countries alone. North-South agreements have also encouraged developing countries to lock in domestic economic and other reforms,[a] enhance prospects for market-driven development strategies, and increase the likelihood of lower external tariffs. From the developing-country partner perspective, these include enlargement of export markets, accelerated foreign capital inflows, technology transfer, and possibly enhanced mobility of other factors.

These strategic properties should make North-South agreements more attractive to developing countries than South-South arrangements, since the latter have more limited potential for exploiting comparative advantage or capturing growth externalities and can lead to trade diversion and greater economic divergence. Moreover, North-South RIAs are more likely to foster economic convergence that, if it coincides with accelerated growth, can be beneficial to all partners. Surely this fact explains the willingness of both sides to extend existing successful regional agreements outside their immediate boundaries. The EU is currently expanding trade partnership in two "southern" directions—Eastern Europe and the Maghreb. The NAFTA is also looking as far as the Southern Cone to expand its economic ties.

a. Some authors have argued that North-South conclaves are an important impetus for democratization, and very recent experience with EU enlargement and the NAFTA do not contradict this view.
Source: World Bank 2000d.

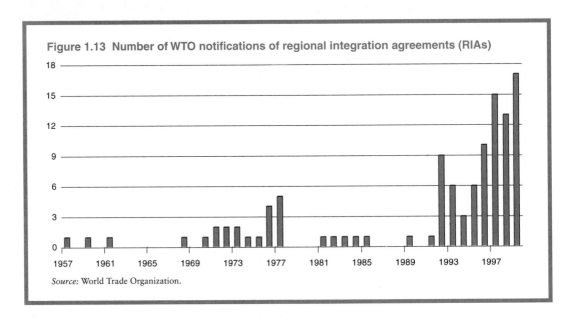

Figure 1.13 Number of WTO notifications of regional integration agreements (RIAs)

Source: World Trade Organization.

than 20 percent of their average trade within their respective regions (figure 1.14). Nonetheless, regional integration arrangements may cover a growing share of trade in the future.

The vast increase in the number of countries participating in the WTO has greatly complicated negotiations, a fact that may lead countries to focus more on regional arrangements

Table 1.2 Intra- and extraregional trade
(annual percentage change in exports)

	1980–90		1990–95	
	Within region	Outside region	Within region	Outside region
NAFTA	15.6	9.8	9.9	5.3
European Union	16.1	10.9	3.2	6.6
Mercosur	4.3	9.3	27.5	4.0

Source: World Bank staff data.

with smaller memberships, where reciprocal concessions can be more transparent and immediate (thus facilitating the negotiating process). Smaller memberships may also make it easier to negotiate the increasingly important issues inherent in product standards (see chapter 3).

Prospects for trade growth
Strong growth momentum in industrial country import demand in the first half of the year will bolster developing-country export volume

growth to 12–13 percent in 2000. However, world trade growth is likely to slow over the course of the year, in line with the expected slowing of world industrial production. Industrial production in key developing regions (such as East Asia and Latin America) had already slowed by the second quarter. While some upturn is likely for these countries in the second half, overall momentum is unlikely to return to the rates experienced in the latter half of 1999 and the first quarter of 2000.

Growth in world trade volumes is projected to slow to 8 percent in 2001 and 6.8 percent in 2002, for a number of reasons. First, the cyclical pattern of world GDP growth is expected to move toward more sustainable long-run rates, thereby reducing import demand. For example, U.S. import growth, which reached 13 percent (year on year) in the first half of 2000, is likely to slow toward 7 or 8 percent in 2001–02, helping to stabilize the widening trend in the current account deficit. This is unlikely to be offset completely by increases in import demand in other major trading coun-

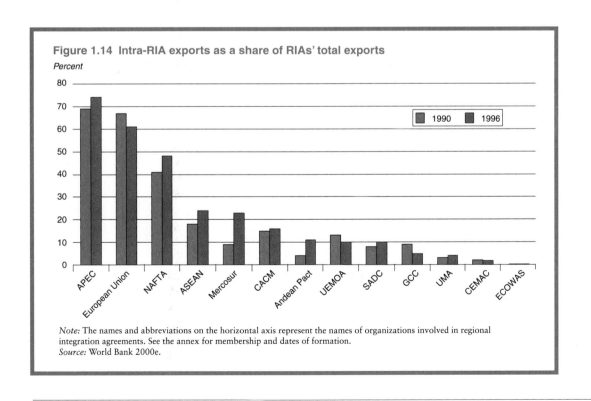

Figure 1.14 Intra-RIA exports as a share of RIAs' total exports

Note: The names and abbreviations on the horizontal axis represent the names of organizations involved in regional integration agreements. See the annex for membership and dates of formation.
Source: World Bank 2000e.

tries. Second, gross private capital flows to developing countries are expected to rise by only 15 to 20 percent over the next two years, well below the rate of increase in 1996–97, when large capital flows permitted some developing regions (such as Latin America) to boost imports. Third, the terms of trade for oil-importing countries are likely to remain soft in the near term, as oil prices stay relatively high and non-oil commodity prices rebound weakly. This, in combination with fairly sluggish private capital flows, would tend to limit the ability of oil-importing countries to sustain rapid import growth for an extended period. However, none of the above factors are expected to cause a massive deterioration in world trade growth in the near term.

In the longer term (2003–10), world trade is projected to grow by 6.8 percent a year. The long-term forecast for trade growth is 2.1 times the projected rate of world GDP growth, lower than what was observed in the 1990s but still much higher than in the 1980s. The very high ratio of the 1990s was in part due to the one-time increases in integration represented by the EU single-market initiative and NAFTA as well as large-scale trade liberalization in a number of developing countries.

While participating countries will continue to benefit from increased integration, it is unlikely that further reductions in trade barriers will be of the same magnitude.

Other forces may boost world trade growth in comparison with the 1990s. For example, there may well be improvements in information technology (see the section on industrial countries and chapter 4), and another round of trade negotiations may be successfully concluded (despite the derailing of the launch of a new round in Seattle in December 1999). While any quantitative comparison of these influences is extremely speculative, on balance we anticipate some decline in the ratio of world trade growth to output growth.

Private capital flows remain volatile

The surge in globalization during the 1990s was even more spectacular in capital flows than in trade flows. Net long-term capital flows to the developing countries surged from $80 billion in 1989 to $344 billion just before the financial crisis, before falling to $280 billion in 1999 (figure 1.15). FDI flows grew steadily to $180 billion in

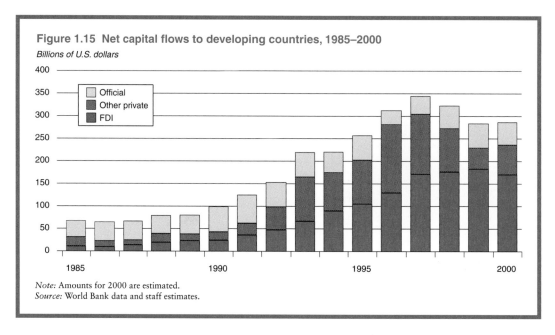

Figure 1.15 Net capital flows to developing countries, 1985–2000

Billions of U.S. dollars

Legend: Official, Other private, FDI

Note: Amounts for 2000 are estimated.
Source: World Bank data and staff estimates.

1999, almost eight times their level at the beginning of the decade. Other private flows

sing ten-
declining
rs of the
d around
996 and
ing gross
zed, with
from its

ital flows
lly driven
rnational
flects im-
d a sharp
ial world.
cial crisis
trol while
ge devalu-
ents, and
modating
stic credit

conditions, combined with large current account surpluses, reduced the need for international financing. At the same time, the current account deficits in the high-income countries increased from $9 billion in 1998 to $175 billion in 1999, and they are expected to reach $250 billion in 2000. With an increased domestic savings shortfall from $218 billion to $435 billion during the last two years, the United States (which saw an investment boom) was the main source of the deterioration of the current account in the industrial world.

Continued uncertainty and risk aversion following the financial crisis constrained market-based flows (bonds, bank loans, and equity) to several of the emerging market economies in 2000. The average risk premium on developing-country secondary market debt remained high. New financing primarily targeted less risky borrowers: 60 percent of total developing-country bond issuance came from sovereign borrowers (compared with 55 percent in 1999), and the share of private borrowers remained low (figure 1.16). Moreover, a substantial proportion of bank lending (55 percent) went to finance the rollover of upcoming liabilities or

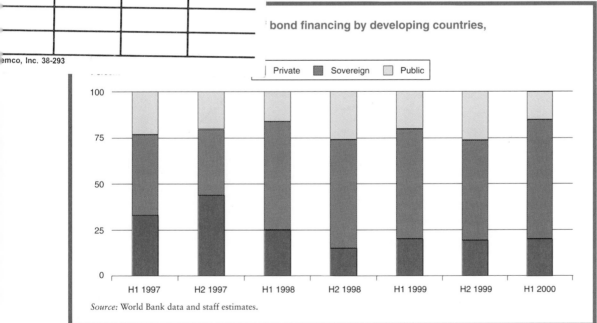

bond financing by developing countries,

Private   Sovereign   Public

Source: World Bank data and staff estimates.

took the form of less risky lending, such as trade finance or securitized lending.

The volatility of capital flows in the second quarter underlined the continued vulnerability of developing countries to shifts in investor sentiment. A sharp correction in the U.S. NASDAQ market was associated with a jump in volatility in developing-country stock markets,[11] and the risk premium on developing-country external debt rose to 850 basis points (compared with 760 basis points at the start of the year). In April, the volume of capital flows to developing countries dropped by 75 percent over March, and it declined marginally further in May before recovering in June to almost the March level.

For the first time in over a decade, preliminary data suggest a contraction in FDI flows to developing countries in 2000 from the $180 billion recorded in 1999[12] (figure 1.17). The downturn in FDI was brought about by reduced commitments for new projects in major recipient countries, combined with a slowdown in M&A activity, and completion of large-scale privatization projects. China, the largest recipient of FDI, experienced a substantial reduction in the value of new commitments during the past years, from $111 billion in 1993 to $52 billion in 1998 and $41 billion in 1999.[13]

In the long term, capital flows should regain momentum

FDI flows to developing countries are likely to rise over the long term, as rapid international integration continues (witness the recent wave of cross-border mergers and acquisitions among corporations in the industrial countries),[14] and developing countries' growth rates continue to exceed growth rates in the industrial world. Renewed cross-border M&A activity in Korea and in other East Asian countries could raise FDI inflows to the region. And political commitment to removing obstacles to privatization may accelerate postponed projects in a number of Central and Eastern European economies. However, the growth of FDI is unlikely to be as spectacular as it was in the 1990s.

Other private capital flows are expected to regain some momentum from their current depressed levels. A narrowing of current account imbalances may increase demand in some developing countries, and further progress in financial reforms should go some way toward

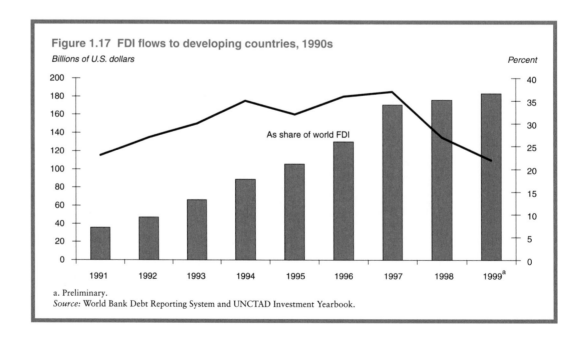

Figure 1.17 FDI flows to developing countries, 1990s

Billions of U.S. dollars

Percent

As share of world FDI

1991 1992 1993 1994 1995 1996 1997 1998 1999[a]

a. Preliminary.
Source: World Bank Debt Reporting System and UNCTAD Investment Yearbook.

restoring the confidence of international investors. However, capital market flows will remain volatile, in turn contributing to the uncertainty in the real economy. For that reason, FDI flows are likely to continue as the primary source of international funding for developing countries, in the process helping to reduce vulnerability to financial shocks.

Commodity prices exhibit divergent recoveries

Oil prices. The present oil price shock is expected to be temporary, since it was generated by the confluence of a number of unexpected short-term factors. The spike in oil prices has its roots in the reaction to the 1998 price decline in the wake of the financial crisis—a decline that in real terms placed the oil price at one-quarter of its peak level of 1980. OPEC members, along with some nonmembers, agreed on production cuts in 1999 to boost prices, while low prices also led to a slowdown in the growth of non-OPEC production and in investment in the oil sector. The drop in production coincided with the unexpectedly strong rebound in world economic activity in 1999, and hence in oil demand. Oil

inventories fell dramatically, and prices skyrocketed (figure 1.18). OPEC has responded to the near-term shortage in the market by raising its production ceiling back to the levels of early 1998. A combination of supply increases and some decline in demand (from higher prices) should reduce oil prices from an average of $28 per barrel in 2000 to $25 per barrel in 2001 and $21 per barrel in 2002.

Plausible worst-case scenarios (for example, an unusually cold winter or unanticipated supply disruptions) could see prices averaging $30 a barrel in 2000 and 2001, with temporary spikes running to $50 or more. Depending on policy and private sector reactions, such higher prices could pose a substantial threat to global expansion, particularly if the shock contributes to steep declines in the several highly valued industrial country equity markets (the implications are explored in the low-case scenario—see below). However, it is difficult to see significantly higher prices being sustained for more than a year or two, given that non-OPEC production would increase in response. Prices are expected to average about $18 to $19 per barrel for the rest of the decade, as technological improvements (for instance, better methods of locating and recov-

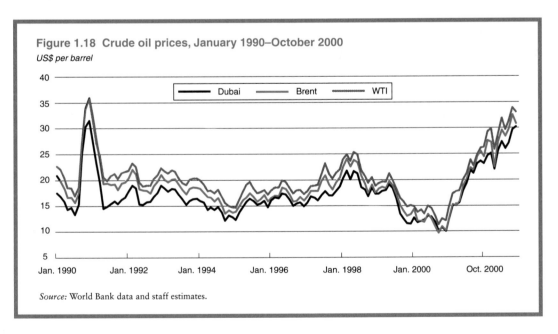

Figure 1.18 Crude oil prices, January 1990–October 2000

Source: World Bank data and staff estimates.

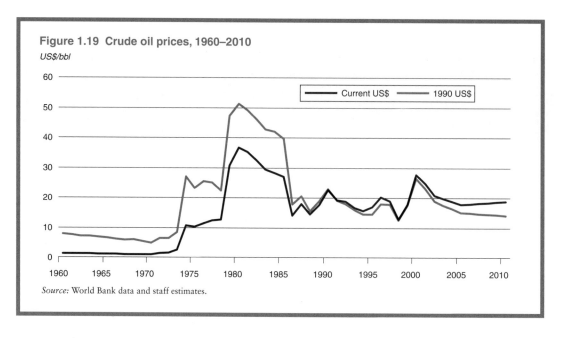

Figure 1.19 Crude oil prices, 1960–2010

US$/bbl

Source: World Bank data and staff estimates.

ering crude oil) boost energy production and conservation efforts continue.

The impact of the current oil price rise on industrial countries has been less than the impact of price rises during the oil price shocks of 1973–74 and 1979–80, because the current increase is smaller and output is much less dependent on oil than before. Oil prices in 2000 should average about half the level of the 1979–80 oil shock in real terms (figure 1.19).[15] Nevertheless, the oil price rise has increased inflationary pressures and trade deficits in some of the industrial countries, as well as exacerbating tensions over the level of gasoline taxes.

Oil-importing developing countries have been more severely affected than industrial countries, because they consume more energy per unit of output and have less access to the external financing required to sustain expenditure levels until oil prices decline. Moreover, prices for their primary commodity exports (especially tropical beverages and other agricultural goods) have continued to drop over the course of 1999 and 2000, so their terms of trade have fallen precipitously.

To illustrate the effects of higher crude oil (and natural gas) prices on developing coun-

tries, table 1.3 presents the impact of a $10 per barrel increase in price (the average increase anticipated in the baseline for 2000) on current account positions for a sample of 92 countries. While the current account balance of oil-exporting developing countries is expected to improve by about $135 billion (at unchanged oil trade volumes) as a result of the oil price increase, that of oil-importing developing countries is expected to deteriorate by about $40 billion, or a little over 1 percent of GDP.

Because the oil shock is expected to be temporary, there is a good economic case for oil-importing countries to meet higher bills for oil and gas imports through temporary balance of payments deficits and external financing rather than through adjustment. However, there is a good deal of uncertainty about how high prices will go and for how long, and even a temporary shock could make international lenders jittery about the sustainability of countries' external debt. This uncertainty increases the risk of a sudden withdrawal of external finance. It is thus likely that risk-averse policymakers in oil-importing countries will undertake some degree of prudent adjustment.

The oil-importing emerging market economies should be able to smooth the impact of

Table 1.3   Current account effects for a sample of developing countries from a $10 increase in oil prices

	Oil importers			Oil exporters			All developing countries		
	Number in sample	$US bln.	as % GDP	Number in sample	$US bln.	as % GDP	Number in sample	$US bln.	as % GDP
East Asia and Pacific	7	–16	–1.0	3	7	2.0	10	–9	–0.7
South Asia	5	–5	–0.9	0	0	0.0	5	–5	–0.9
Latin America	15	–4	–0.7	7	22	2.0	22	18	0.8
Sub-Saharan Africa	13	–2	–0.7	5	13	19.5	18	11	3.2
Europe and Central Asia	18	–14	–1.7	3	27	10.3	21	13	1.5
Middle East and North Africa	6	–2	–1.1	10	66	11.4	16	64	8.6
Total developing countries	64	–43	–1.1	28	135	5.7	92	92	1.5
Memo item: HIPC	13	–2	–1.4	6	5	19.0	19	3	1.7

Note: The table shows the direct current account impact (keeping volumes constant) of a $10/bbl increase in crude oil and refined products and a (similar) 54 percent increase in the gas price.
Source: World Bank staff estimates.

the shock with private finance, though some with already large current account deficits will have to proceed with caution. Oil-importing developing countries without access to private capital markets will face an additional official financing need of about $18 billion (without adjustment). Since countries will be undertaking some degree of adjustment (leading to a lower financing need), and the need for official aid flows to oil exporters may be much less for a time, the net additional call on international donors does not appear insurmountable.

Non-oil commodity prices. Non-oil commodity prices began to decline in early 1997 and then plummeted with the East Asian crisis (figure 1.20). While the global economic recovery has led to some recovery of metals and minerals prices, agricultural prices continue to languish near their cyclical troughs. This divergent recovery is not surprising, since met-

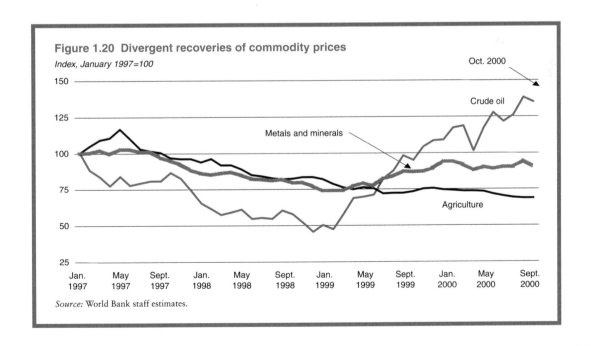

Figure 1.20 Divergent recoveries of commodity prices

Index, January 1997=100

Source: World Bank staff estimates.

23

als, which are used as inputs to industrial production, have higher short-run income elasticities than food and beverages.

After the price declines in 1998, metals and minerals producers cut production at high-cost mines and smelters, leading to some slow-down in production growth. For example, copper production slowed to 3 percent growth in 1999, from 4 percent in 1998. At the same time, the strong global economic recovery boosted demand for metals. Consumption of copper rose 4 percent in 1999 and will rise an expected 6 percent in 2000, while aluminum consumption rose 6 percent in 1999 and is up 5 percent in 2000. Slower production growth and accelerating demand have reduced stocks, and metals and minerals prices are estimated to have risen above 14 percent in 2000, to a level about 20 percent above the cyclical trough.

In contrast, agricultural prices remained stagnant for most of this year. Despite this, the United Nations' Food and Agriculture Organization's index of global agricultural production rose by 1.6 percent in 1999 (slightly below the 30-year trend growth rate of 2.2 percent), which contributed to further stock buildups. Consequently, world stocks of most agricultural commodities remain high—and in some cases stocks have continued to increase. Sugar stocks, for example, rose for the fifth consecutive year in 1999, while cocoa stocks reached the same levels as in 1990–91, when the International Cocoa Organization was operating a buffer stock mechanism. An exception to this trend is cotton, for which production is expected to decline by 2 percent, contributing to a 15 percent reduction in stocks. Moreover, recovery in demand has been weaker than in metals. Grain consumption is expected to be roughly unchanged in 2000; but consumption of raw materials is recovering, led by cotton, which is expected to increase 2 percent next year.

Recent trends in commodity prices have obviously favored food importers (particularly the oil-exporting countries, which simultaneously have benefited from higher oil revenues), while net agricultural exporters, such as many countries in Latin America and Sub-Saharan Africa, have seen substantial deterioration in their commodity terms of trade. Côte d'Ivoire, Ghana, Kenya, and Uganda all receive 40 to 60 percent of export earnings from agriculture (mainly coffee and cocoa), and fuel imports constitute 20 to 30 percent of import costs. Most Asian countries have been less affected, since they are less dependent on agricultural exports and fuels are a smaller share of total imports.

Non-oil commodity prices are expected to increase in the near term, gradually aligning with the continued expansion of the global economy (table 1.4). Metals and minerals prices, which rose about 14 percent in 2000, are expected to increase about 2 percent per year in nominal terms over the next several years, but more rapid increases are possible if global economic growth is higher than anticipated.

The recovery in agricultural prices is expected to remain slow, as supplies continue to increase at nearly the same pace as consumption. But experience shows that current low prices in agriculture could give way to a surge in the near to medium term. While it is difficult to predict when such an event might occur, historical evidence indicates that it could begin about two to three years after the cyclical low.

Over the longer term, non-oil commodity prices are likely to decline in real terms, continuing the trend over the past 100 years (real non-oil commodity prices fell by nearly two-thirds during the twentieth century, and by half over the last two decades—[figure 1.21]). There appears to be no letup in the improvements in technology that boost commodity supplies at lower cost. Crop yields continue to increase along historical trends, and new plant-breeding techniques offer the prospect of further increases. Improved mining and refining techniques reduce the cost of recovering ore and producing metals. On the demand side, population growth is projected to slow from 1.4 percent during the 1990s to 1.1 percent during the first decade of the 21st century and 0.9 percent during the second decade. In Asia, where the demand for commodities has

Table 1.4   Annual percentage change in nominal oil and non-oil commodity prices, 1981–2010

Commodity	1981–90	1991–97	1998	1999	Forecasts 2000	2001	2002–10
Oil	−4.7	−2.5	−31.8	38.3	55.0	−10.7	−3.0
Non-oil	−2.2	2.3	−15.7	−11.2	−0.8	3.4	2.8
Agriculture	−3.2	3.7	−16.3	−13.9	−5.2	3.9	3.3
Food	−3.3	2.2	−9.8	−16.5	−3.9	5.1	2.4
Grains	−2.9	1.6	−9.7	−14.7	−9.4	7.5	3.8
Beverages	−5.8	7.9	−17.7	−23.4	−16.9	1.5	4.3
Raw materials	−0.4	1.9	−23.2	1.4	3.7	4.2	3.5
Metals and minerals	0.6	−1.5	−16.2	−2.3	13.6	2.2	1.6
Fertilizers	−2.5	2.6	2.0	−6.6	−6.3	4.7	1.1
Memorandum item							
G-5 manufactures unit value	3.3	1.1	−1.9	−2.7	−2.3	3.6	2.2

Note: The G-5 countries are France, Germany, Japan, the United Kingdom, and the United States.
Source: World Bank data and projections update, November 2000.

grown most rapidly, population growth will be even slower. This may be partially offset by faster growth of world real incomes (projected at 3.4 percent over 2000–10 compared to 2.7 percent during the 1990s). However, since income elasticities of demand for commodities are low, the overall impact of more rapid income growth on commodities will be small.

Developing countries' recovery is unexpectedly rapid, and prospects for long-term growth have improved

Developing countries' recovery from the 1997–98 financial crisis at 5.3 percent growth has been faster and much stronger than anticipated.[16] All regions have experienced

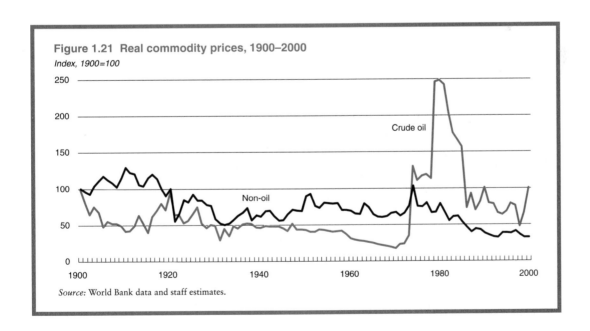

Figure 1.21 Real commodity prices, 1900–2000

Index, 1900=100

Source: World Bank data and staff estimates.

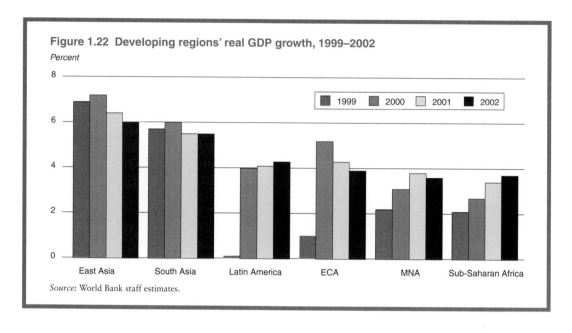

Figure 1.22 Developing regions' real GDP growth, 1999–2002

Percent

Legend: 1999 | 2000 | 2001 | 2002

Regions (x-axis): East Asia, South Asia, Latin America, ECA, MNA, Sub-Saharan Africa

Source: World Bank staff estimates.

stronger growth in 2000, although there has been diversity across regions. Contributing factors include easier monetary policies in the industrial countries and in East Asia, which lowered interest rates and stimulated domestic demand; the depreciation of many developing countries' currencies, which boosted exports; and more recently the rise in oil prices, which has supported economic activity in some of the economies hit by the crisis or in those near crisis (such as Indonesia, Nigeria, and the Russian Federation). Industrial production in most of the crisis-affected countries of East Asia rebounded at double-digit growth rates in late 1999 and into 2000. Latin America also is recovering sharply, albeit at a slower rate than in the wake of the Mexican peso crisis. And Russian growth (a large segment of the growth in the Europe and Central Asia region) was unexpectedly strong, boosted by oil revenues (figure 1.22 and table 1.5). China and India continue to exhibit sustained rapid growth, and Middle Eastern countries are benefiting from high oil prices and recovery in the Euro Area. Even the non-oil exporters in Sub-Saharan Africa increased GDP by 3.2 percent, despite low non-oil commodity prices. Altogether, developing countries' GDP is expected to increase

by 5.3 percent in 2000, matching peak years 1983 and 1997. Inflation came down quickly following the crisis (when sharp exchange rate depreciations led to rapid price rises in several countries) and remains moderate despite the spike in oil prices. Despite this favorable picture, financial tensions are building up once again in East Asia and Latin America. The decline in stock markets and the recent increase in spreads make several countries vulnerable in the short run. The risks associated with these vulnerabilities are explored later in this chapter where the possibilities of a strong global downturn are discussed. The baseline forecast, however, features a moderate slowdown from the cyclical peak in early 2000. With this moderate deceleration, all developing regions are expected to enjoy near-term increases in per capita income, ranging from nearly 6 percent in East Asia to about 1.5 percent in the Middle East and North Africa and Sub-Saharan Africa.

Payoffs to domestic reforms and improved external conditions favor long-term growth
The cyclical recovery is expected to be followed by an acceleration of long-term growth, although the outlook varies considerably across regions (figure 1.23). Population growth in the

Table 1.5   Growth of world GDP, 1998–2002

(percentage change in real GDP)

	1998	1999	Forecast		
			2000	2001	2002
World total	1.9	2.8	4.1	3.4	3.2
High-income countries	2.1	2.7	3.8	3.0	2.8
OECD	2.1	2.7	3.7	2.9	2.7
United States	4.4	4.2	5.1	3.2	2.9
Japan	–2.5	0.3	2.0	2.1	2.2
Euro Area	2.7	2.4	3.4	3.2	2.8
Non-OECD countries	0.7	4.2	6.3	5.1	5.1
Developing countries	1.0	3.2	5.3	5.0	4.8
East Asia and Pacific	–1.4	6.9	7.2	6.4	6.0
Europe and Central Asia (ECA)	0.0	1.0	5.2	4.3	3.9
Latin America and the Caribbean	2.0	0.1	4.0	4.1	4.3
Middle East and North Africa	3.3	2.2	3.1	3.8	3.6
South Asia	5.6	5.7	6.0	5.5	5.5
Sub-Saharan Africa	2.0	2.1	2.7	3.4	3.7
Memorandum items					
East Asia-5 countries[a]	–8.2	6.7	6.9	5.5	5.1
Transition countries of ECA	–0.7	2.5	5.0	4.2	3.7
Developing countries					
Excluding the transition countries	1.2	3.3	5.3	5.1	5.0
Excluding China and India	–0.6	2.2	4.7	4.4	4.5

Note: All countries listed in the "classification of economies" section at the end of this volume are included as components of the regions presented in tables 1.5 and 1.6 (as well as the world summary table [table 1.1]). Exceptions for which sufficient historical data or projections are unavailable include: 11 low-income countries (among which are Armenia, Honduras and Nicaragua); seven middle-income countries (among which are Iraq, Georgia, and Guyana); and two high-income countries (Cyprus and Iceland).
a. Indonesia, the Republic of Korea, Malaysia, the Philippines, and Thailand.
Source: Development Prospects Group, baseline, October 2000.

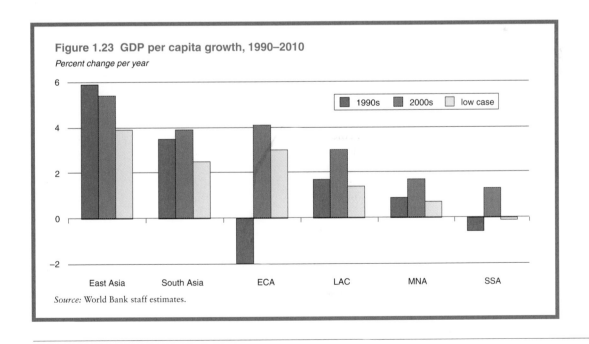

Figure 1.23 GDP per capita growth, 1990–2010

Percent change per year

Legend: 1990s | 2000s | low case

Source: World Bank staff estimates.

developing world is slated to slow from 1.6 percent annually in the 1990s to 1.3 percent during 2000–10. And output per capita in developing countries is projected to rise by 3.7 percent per year over the next decade, more than double the 1990s rate, in large part reflecting the turnaround from output declines in the transition economies (table 1.6). Other developing regions are expected to achieve more modest increases in growth rates. External conditions are assumed to be more favorable than during the 1990s, as higher productivity–led per capita growth in industrial countries (2.6 percent versus 1.9 percent, respectively) and further progress in trade liberalization should support the growth of demand for developing-country exports at high levels. And capital flows to developing countries should resume within an environment of low inflation and low interest rates.

It is important to note that developing countries all over the world are expected to

reap the benefits of reforms carried out over the past decade (selected indicators are highlighted in table 1.7). In effect, these factors constitute the initial conditions from which longer-term prospects may be drawn. A number of clear improvements can be discerned. Median inflation rates have been halved, and central government budget deficits are lower now than in the late 1980s, contributing to improved investor confidence. And developing countries are much more open now than they were 10 years ago, as trade liberalization and stronger trade growth have helped raise trade to GDP ratios by 50 percent on average. In addition, better policies have attracted FDI (which increased from 0.5 percent of developing countries' GDP in 1988–90 to 2.7 percent in 1998–2000). Moreover, rapid growth in exports facilitated a significant decline in debt-to-export ratios compared with the late 1980s.

Many developing countries have made substantial investments in human capital. For ex-

Table 1.6 Growth of world GDP per capita, 1980s through 2010
(annual average percentage change)

			Forecast Baseline	Low case	Difference in growth rates
	1980s	1990s	2000–10	2000–10	
World total	1.3	1.3	2.3	1.3	−1.0
High-income countries	2.4	1.9	2.7	1.7	−1.0
OECD	2.4	1.9	2.6	1.6	−1.0
United States	2.2	2.3	2.5	1.2	−1.3
Japan	3.4	1.1	2.3	1.0	−1.3
Euro Area	2.1	1.9	3.0	2.4	−0.6
Non-OECD countries	3.7	3.7	4.1	2.3	−1.8
Developing countries	0.8	1.8	3.7	2.3	−1.4
East Asia and Pacific	5.6	5.9	5.4	3.9	−1.5
Europe and Central Asia (ECA)	0.4	−2.0	4.1	3.0	−1.1
Latin America and the Caribbean	−0.9	1.7	3.0	1.4	−1.6
Middle East and North Africa	−0.6	0.9	1.7	0.7	−1.0
South Asia	3.5	3.5	3.9	2.5	−1.4
Sub-Saharan Africa	−1.2	−0.6	1.3	−0.1	−1.4
Memorandum items					
East Asia-5 countries[a]	4.4	3.5	4.2	2.9	−1.3
Transition countries of ECA	0.3	−2.6	4.1	3.1	−1.0
Developing countries					
Excluding the transition countries	1.3	3.0	3.7	2.2	−1.5
Excluding China and India	0.0	0.5	2.9	1.6	−1.3

a. Indonesia, the Republic of Korea, Malaysia, the Philippines, and Thailand.
Source: Development Prospects Group, baseline and low-case, October 2000.

Table 1.7 Forecast assumptions: developing countries

Initial conditions	1988–90	1998–2000
1. Ratio of real GDP per capita: industrial / developing countries	19.5	20.5
2. Trade (X+M) / GDP ratio (real)	29.0	43.5
3. Median inflation rate	12.6	6.1
4 Median fiscal balance / GDP	–2.7	–1.8
5. Investment / GDP (real)	23.1	24.3
6. Investment / GDP (nominal)	25.6	24.3
7. Gross national savings / GDP	25.2	23.3
7a. Gross domestic savings / GDP	27.1	25.1
8. Current account balance / GDP	–0.7	–0.8
9. FDI / GDP	0.5	2.7
10. External DOD / exports*	172.6	142.2
11. School enrollment rates		
Primary	78.0	82.0
Secondary	56.0	63.0
12. Illiteracy rate	31.0	26.0
13. Under-5 mortality rate	91.0	79.0
14. Life expectancy	63.0	65.0

Exogenous assumptions	1990s	2001–10
1. Population growth	1.6	1.3
2. OECD GDP growth	2.4	2.9
3. Oil price $ per barrel (avg.)	18.2	20.2
4. World trade growth	6.5	6.8

*Exports of goods and services plus workers remittances.
Note: Real indicators use 1995 as base year.
Source: World Bank database, World Bank staff estimates.

ample, school enrollment rates are substantially higher than in the late 1980s, and illiteracy rates fell from 31 percent in 1990 to 26 percent in 1998. And health indicators show improvement: under-five mortality rates dropped from 91 per 1,000 live births to 79, and life expectancy has increased from 63 years to 65 years. These developments suggest that newcomers to the labor force should be better educated and more capable of working than those who retire—a positive development for absorption of new technologies and for innovation. With real per capita incomes today still only one-twentieth that of the industrial countries, developing countries that remain open to trade and FDI can achieve higher rates of growth through maximizing the new technology and skills embodied in these flows.

East Asia. On average, output in the five countries most affected by the financial crisis (Indonesia, the Republic of Korea, Malaysia, the Philippines, and Thailand) recovered smartly in 1999 at a rate of 6.7 percent in contrast with their 1998 crisis decline of 8.2 percent. They consolidated further with growth near 7 percent in 2000. A low-inflation, low-interest-rate environment has been particularly beneficial to the process of unwinding the domestic debt problems faced by firms and consumers in these crisis countries. Corporate and financial restructuring and rehabilitation of the financial sectors are being pursued, though perhaps at a slower pace than warranted. The slow pace could be a detrimental factor to near-term growth, if interest rates rise rapidly or demand falters leading to diminished cash flow. Robust export growth and firming export prices have helped maintain a positive current account balance. Though the recovery of imports and higher oil prices have narrowed the balance in many countries, rising reserves and the improved term structure of foreign debt have strengthened external positions vis-à-vis precrisis levels.

Growth in China during the postcrisis period has ranged between 7 and 8 percent. A falloff in export growth, combined with the short-term impact of reform programs for the state enterprises and the financial system, led initially to a drop in domestic demand and a period of deflation. The real depreciation of the yuan, coupled with the global recovery, eventually led to a resurgence of exports. Combined with fiscal pump priming, and an incipient increase in FDI, export growth has produced improving conditions in China, with GDP growth accelerating in the first half of 2000 and the deflationary cycle ending. In 2001–02, output for the East Asia region is likely to begin a general process of moderating and converging toward longer-term growth paths. The two most vulnerable countries are Indonesia and the Philippines. These countries also suffer from political weaknesses, civil disturbances, and a perception (from the point of view of investors) that business operating practices have not changed substantially from less than transparent modes.

East Asia should continue to achieve the most rapid rates of growth over the longer term, although some deceleration from the last decade's pace is likely. Growth in the region's higher-income economies is expected to converge toward more moderate OECD average rates. Lower-income countries that have achieved high growth rates through strong reform programs may find the future reform agenda (particularly strengthening the financial sector) more difficult to implement.

South Asia. GDP growth in South Asia has risen to 5.7 percent in 1999 and is likely to register 6 percent in 2000, owing to better than expected agricultural sector performance in Bangladesh, India, and Pakistan, as well as an acceleration of India's industrial production to double-digit rates and strong advances in services output. Burgeoning foreign demand for IT-related services from Bangalore and a pickup of FDI inflows ($2.2 billion in 1999) are major factors underlying India's improved export performance. To facilitate the growth of Indian services exports, legislation has been introduced to support the IT sector and develop electronic business infrastructure. Average growth for the region is expected to slow to 5.5 percent in 2001–02. Financial difficulties are likely to restrain growth in Pakistan. In addition, the region is heavily dependent on energy imports and (especially in the case of the smaller countries) on agricultural exports such as cotton, tea, and rubber. The necessity of adjusting to terms-of-trade losses from the recent, adverse movements in primary commodity prices may dampen growth in the near term. By contrast, South Asian economies may raise per capita growth rates in the long term if they can manage to reduce fiscal deficits (while still maintaining growth-enhancing expenditures) and make necessary progress in trade liberalization. For example, India's average tariff for all goods, while considerably reduced from that of 10 years ago, remains at 40 percent.

Latin America's GDP is expected to rise by 4 percent in 2000, although the dispersion of growth across the region is wide, ranging from over 6 percent in Mexico and Chile to nearly 2 percent in Colombia and Uruguay, and to little growth in Argentina, Ecuador, and Jamaica. Stabilization of global financial markets and the surge of world trade growth have supported a broad resumption of economic activity across the region. At the same time, inflation eased or held steady in most countries, allowing interest rates to continue on a general declining trend. Exchange rates stabilized in several countries that experienced periods of free fall during 1999 (for example, Brazil and Ecuador), improving the outlook for domestic demand growth, especially in Brazil.

Global conditions are expected to be more supportive of growth in the region over the next two years. However, recent experience suggests that volatility in financial markets and primary commodity prices remains a substantial threat to near-term recovery. Private capital inflows fell dramatically in the second quarter of 2000, tied to the worldwide decline in equity markets, and the recovery in industrial production among the large countries of the region appeared to have faltered. The surge in the price of oil, concomitant with weakness in commodity prices of critical importance to the region (particularly the prices of coffee, grains, and soybeans) produced terms-of-trade losses for a large number of countries. Nonetheless, consolidation of the region's recovery in 2001–02 is likely, as adjustment in Brazil has been impressive so far, and new governments in Argentina and Mexico appear set to embark on a path of deepened reforms. Regional output growth is expected to reach 4.1 percent in 2001 and to rise further to 4.3 percent in 2002.

Latin America is poised to enter a phase of sustained moderate growth over the next decade that is due to the past trend toward market-friendly policies in the larger countries; relatively strong banking and financial sectors; potential for technology spillovers from the United States; the largest rise in FDI among developing regions (much of which went into infrastructure such as telecommunications, utilities, ports, and so forth); and the potential strengthening of Mercosur through trade links with Europe and NAFTA. But low national savings and large debt overhangs that will need to be rolled over on a continuing basis make the region vulnerable to swings in external financing and are likely to constrain growth below the rates expected in Asia.

Europe and Central Asia. Average GDP growth is expected to rise to 5.2 percent in 2000, significantly above the 1 percent advance of 1999. The 50 percent rise in oil and gas prices has transformed the Russian primary fiscal position from deep deficit to surplus, allowing reductions in government wage arrears and contributing to higher disposable incomes.[17] Moreover, Russian industry continues to benefit from the sharp devaluation of August 1998, although import-substitution effects are diminishing with the recent real appreciation of the ruble. Higher energy prices and economic spillovers from the Russian Federation are contributing to stronger output growth among hydrocarbon-rich members of the Commonwealth of Independent States (CIS). The Central and Eastern European countries (CEECs) and the Baltic countries are benefiting from growing demand from Western Europe and to a lesser degree from the Russian Federation.[18] Growth in Turkey is approaching 6 percent in 2000, up from the sharp 5.1 percent contraction in 1999, principally because of a rebound domestic demand linked to declines in real interest rates.

Growth performance for the region through 2002 is expected to remain relatively strong in aggregate, stabilizing at around 4 percent. Developments in the EU export market, policy implementation related to EU accession for the CEECs, and the path of the oil price will be critical factors in shaping the outlook. The Russian Federation and other hydrocarbon exporters of the CIS may experience a slowing of growth beginning in 2001, as oil prices retreat from current high levels. The region's longer-term prospects have improved considerably after the difficulties experienced during the initial period of transition to market economies in the 1990s. Countries anchored by the EU accession process have strong incentives to implement reforms and are positioned for stronger growth than other countries in the region. The baseline assumes improved economic management and some progress in implementing recently proposed social and economic reforms in the Rus-

sian Federation, while the trajectory of growth in world trade and output should support steady gains in other CIS states.

Sub-Saharan Africa. Fallout from the 1997–99 crisis continued to exert a depressing effect on the region in 2000, as non-oil commodity prices remained near cyclical lows. But higher oil revenues boosted growth for the region's oil exporters, and output in South Africa strengthened moderately to 2.2 percent growth following several years of subdued performance. On average, the region experienced an acceleration of growth to 2.7 percent from 2.1 percent in 1999, and per capita income gained an average of 0.2 percent. Countries with better policy environments—Botswana, Uganda, and several countries of the Communauté Financière Africaine (CFA) zone—tended to perform better than average, with GDP gains of 4.4 percent. Countries experiencing civil strife or major political disruption—Angola, the Democratic Republic of Congo, Ethiopia, Sierra Leone, and Zimbabwe—registered the weakest performances, averaging a decline of 1.5 percent during the year.

Growth is projected to accelerate to 3.4 percent in 2001 and 3.7 percent in 2002. Oil producers, including Angola, Nigeria, and Sudan, are scheduled to bring further supply onstream, while continued high prices through 2001 should abet revenue growth. The terms of trade for commodity exporters should stabilize or improve moderately from their current low levels as non-oil commodity prices firm. The HIPC (Heavily Indebted Poor Countries) Initiative is gaining momentum, with nine African countries—Benin, Burkina Faso, Cameroon, Mali, Mauritania, Mozambique, Senegal, Tanzania, and Uganda—now having qualified for a total of close to $9 billion (net present value) of relief. And several more countries are expected to reach completion points in the near term. The enhanced HIPC Initiative is worth nearly $30 billion in net present value terms, with some 80 percent of the program earmarked for Sub-Saharan Africa.

Progress in reform programs and in debt–relief has improved the prospects for growth. Per capita income is projected to rise by 1.3

percent per year over the next decade. This prospect is far better than the decline that continued over the 1990s, but the increase is only one-third the average rate of Asian economies. Economies in Sub-Saharan Africa will continue to confront the severe problems of poor transport and communications infrastructures, a lack of investor confidence that encourages capital flight and constrains private investment rates, and continued low levels of official assistance. It is important to realize that HIV/AIDS will have a substantial negative impact on a number of countries. According to estimates by UNAIDS (2000), Sub-Saharan Africa contains 24.5 million (or 70 percent) of the 34.3 million existing cases worldwide and 12.1 million of a total of 13.2 million AIDS orphans. In the longer term, lower human capital accumulation may well emerge as the biggest cost, and in the worst-affected countries, labor force growth could slow by 1 or 2 percentage points, with a depressing effect on growth.

Middle East and North Africa. Developments for both oil exporters and diversified exporters in the region have been quite favorable, with GDP growth of 2.2 percent reported in 1999 and growth of 3.1 percent anticipated for 2000. Many of the major oil producers had formulated budgets around an assumed oil price of $22 per barrel, and higher revenues have contributed to lower borrowing requirements, lower deficits, and a decline in domestic arrears. Strong growth in Western Europe has fueled a boom in tourism, with record numbers of tourist arrivals in many North African and Mediterranean countries. The economic revival in Europe has also led to stronger gains in non-oil exports and workers' remittances. For example, remittance flows to Tunisia rose by 75 percent during 1999. And the ending of drought conditions in many countries boosted agricultural incomes and exports and led to declines in required food imports.

Activity is expected to pick up moderately to 3.8 percent in 2001 and 3.6 percent in 2002. With an average oil price of $25 per barrel for 2001 and $21 in 2002, export revenues should continue to support income

growth in the oil exporters. For the diversified exporters, the positive effects of higher external demand are being counterbalanced by relatively strong currencies, high fiscal deficits in Egypt and Lebanon, as well as recent declines in stock markets. Moreover, the ongoing nature of recent conflict in the Levant may also have dampening effects on confidence in the rest of the MNA region.

Progress in structural reforms and improved fiscal behavior with respect to commodity price booms and busts should support some acceleration of per capita growth over the next decade. However, large and inefficient public sectors, a shortage of social safety nets, and low savings and private investment rates should limit growth rates to well below those of most other regions. Moreover, without more substantial diversification of production, these economies will remain exposed to unfavorable terms-of-trade shocks.

Vulnerabilities are significant

While the baseline scenario of solid growth in all regions is realistic and achievable, history cautions that cyclical downturns or crises induced by commodity or financial shocks are difficult to anticipate. To explore the implications of less favorable outcomes, a low-case scenario has been developed that combines a downturn of the global economy in the short run with lower potential growth rates in the long run. In the short run, continued high oil prices especially characterized by short-lived "spikes," contribute to inflationary pressures and increased uncertainty, triggering serious cuts in demand and restrictive monetary policies. Additionally, investor concern over the high U.S. current account deficit leads to a rapid reversal of foreign funds and a large stock market correction, while the associated fall in demand, depreciation of the dollar, and rise in interest rates have significant spillovers to other regions through trade, capital flows, and debt service. The East Asian countries, in process of financial restructuring, would be particularly affected. The ensuing global recession exacerbates the strains inherent in rapid globalization and structural adjustment, leading to a hold on reform programs that slows expected gains in productivity leading to long-term growth. On average, these elements bring down the potential growth rate of the developing countries as a group by almost 1.5 percentage points over the period to 2010 (table 1.6 and figure 1.24).

The implications of the short-term global recession differ greatly across developing regions. Latin America, with high levels of debt and relatively high dependence on exports to the United States, is hit hardest by the global downturn and the higher interest rates. East Asia, which has a similar export orientation toward the United States, is directly hurt by the fall in U.S. demand, the depreciation of the dollar, and mounting domestic financial difficulties. Central and Eastern Europe, the Middle East and North Africa, and Sub-Saharan Africa, all with a stronger focus on Europe, experience a more moderate downturn in the short run, as the growth slowdown in Europe is not as severe as in the United States. In South Asia, the impact of the global downturn is diverse. As during earlier crises, India exhibits some resilience to less favorable external de-

velopments, while for Pakistan the worsening of international financial conditions has very severe consequences.

Since the structural risks are mainly of domestic origin, they are by nature quite differentiated across countries. Nevertheless, there are some common elements that follow from past trends in the regions. Sub-Saharan Africa and the Middle East and North Africa are at the end of two decades of stagnation or decline, while growth in Latin America has picked up from the "lost decade" of the 1980s (figure 1.25). Reform programs in many of these countries have greatly improved the conditions for growth. However, high indebtedness and the fragility of the reforms make these regions very vulnerable to adverse global conditions, especially a rapid rise in interest rates. The main risk for the oil-importing countries in these regions is that a global downturn, combined with a deterioration of the terms of trade and a lack of immediate improvements, could bring about social unrest and "reform fatigue." For oil exporters, the danger is that the temporary surge in oil revenues might suggest that reform is not urgent anymore. Such a reversal of the reform momentum in both oil-exporting and oil-importing countries could reduce the growth

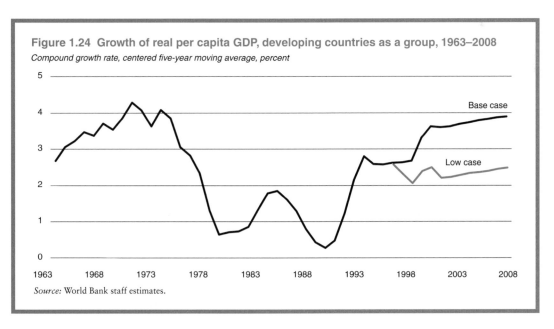

Figure 1.24 Growth of real per capita GDP, developing countries as a group, 1963–2008

Compound growth rate, centered five-year moving average, percent

Base case

Low case

Source: World Bank staff estimates.

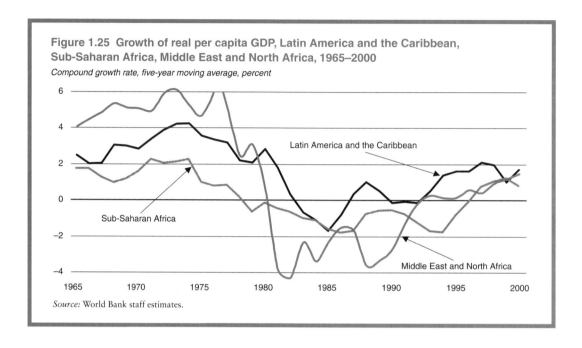

Figure 1.25 Growth of real per capita GDP, Latin America and the Caribbean, Sub-Saharan Africa, Middle East and North Africa, 1965–2000

Compound growth rate, five-year moving average, percent

Source: World Bank staff estimates.

potential for the coming decade. And in Sub-Saharan Africa, diminished government revenues tied to terms-of-trade losses could make HIV/AIDS prevention and alleviation campaigns more difficult, further increasing economic losses associated with the epidemic.

In Asia, by contrast, many countries achieved rapid rates of growth through strong reform programs during the 1980s and 1990s. Nevertheless, continued rapid growth in the larger countries requires further reforms, including trade liberalization (in China measures related to WTO accession, in India reduction of high existing tariffs), strengthening of the financial sector (through much of East Asia)—(figure 1.26) and strengthening of the fiscal position in India. In the alternative scenario, a backlash to reform programs reduces the long-term growth potential in Asia by about 1.5 percentage points a year.

The transition economies experience some weakening of reform momentum that lowers long-term productivity, without repeating the disastrous experience of the 1990s. Central European countries' accession to the European Union is postponed because the global downturn reduces growth in Europe and increases the perceived costs of accession. For Central

Europe, this increases domestic tensions and reduces FDI flows, bringing down trend growth. The oil-exporting countries in the CIS experience a delay of necessary reforms, similar to the delay in the Middle Eastern and North African oil exporters. When, ultimately, the oil price declines quickly as a result of the economic downturn, the lack of reforms translates into lower potential growth.

Recent trends and prospects for poverty reduction

Poverty trends during the 1990s. Our estimates for poverty in developing countries have changed slightly since last year's *Global Economic Prospects* because of the availability of new information from household surveys. These revisions do not affect the major conclusions about poverty trends. Extreme poverty declined only slowly in developing countries during the 1990s: the share of the population living on less than $1 a day fell from 28 percent in 1987 to 23 percent in 1998, and the number of poor people remained roughly constant as the population increased.[19] The share and number of people living on less than

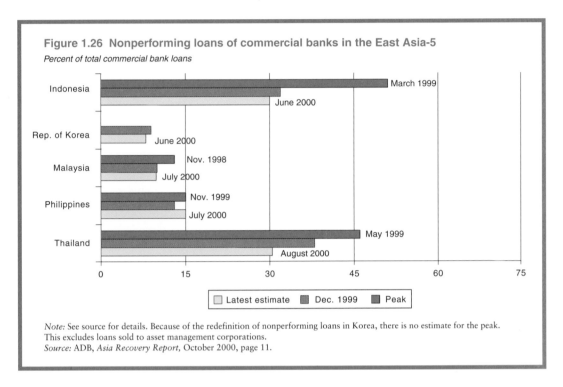

Figure 1.26 Nonperforming loans of commercial banks in the East Asia-5

Percent of total commercial bank loans

Note: See source for details. Because of the redefinition of nonperforming loans in Korea, there is no estimate for the peak. This excludes loans sold to asset management corporations.
Source: ADB, *Asia Recovery Report,* October 2000, page 11.

$2 per day—a more relevant threshold for middle-income economies such as those of East Asia and Latin America—showed roughly similar trends (tables 1.8 and 1.9).

It should be emphasized that these historical estimates are subject to some uncertainty. Up-to-date survey and price data are not available for all countries, and the quality of household surveys can vary considerably among countries and over time. Some country surveys yield income measures of living standards, while others yield consumption measures, and these two sources are likely to give different poverty estimates for the same underlying population.[20] Further, the international measure of poverty used here is subject to error because of the difficulties involved in estimating purchasing power parity exchange rates. Despite these weaknesses, the estimates provide a fairly reliable view of poverty trends at the aggregate level, because of the substantial increases in the coverage of household surveys and in data accuracy over the past few years.

In general, poverty declined in countries that achieved rapid growth, and increased in countries that experienced stagnation or contraction. Indeed, the overall decline in extreme poverty during the 1990s was driven by high rates of growth in countries with large numbers of poor people. For example, China accounted for a fourth of the total number of poor at the start of the decade, and per capita GDP during the 1990s rose by 9 percent per year, so by 1998 China's share of the world's poor was less than one-fifth. Nevertheless, the decline in poverty in rapidly growing countries was slowed by increases in inequality in a number of countries with large numbers of poor, in particular in China, Bangladesh, India, and Nigeria.[21] Income inequality is an important factor in determining poverty outcomes (box 1.3).

In **East Asia**, poverty declined most rapidly during the 1990s, falling sharply in China. However, growth in China's poorer and more rural western provinces was much slower than in the more industrialized east. This divergence reflects slow growth in rural incomes related to declining prices for agricultural products and reduced opportunities for off-

Table 1.8   Population living on less than $1 per day and head count index in developing countries, 1987, 1990, and 1998

Region	Population covered by at least one survey (percent)	Number of people living on less than $1 a day (millions)			
		1987	1990	1998 new	1998 (GEP 2000)
East Asia and Pacific	90.8	417.5	452.4	267.1	278.3
Excluding China	71.1	114.1	92.0	53.7	65.1
Europe and Central Asia	81.7	1.1	7.1	17.6	24.0
Latin America and the Caribbean	88.0	63.7	73.8	60.7	78.2
Middle East and North Africa	52.5	9.3	5.7	6.0	5.5
South Asia	97.9	474.4	495.1	521.8	522.0
Sub-Saharan Africa	72.9	217.2	242.3	301.6	290.9
Total	88.1	1,183.2	1,276.4	1,174.9	1,198.9
Excluding China	84.2	879.8	915.9	961.4	985.7

Region	Population covered by at least one survey (percent)	Head count index (percent)			
		1987	1990	1998 new	1998 (GEP 2000)
East Asia and Pacific	90.8	26.6	27.6	14.7	15.3
Excluding China	71.1	23.9	18.5	9.4	11.3
Europe and Central Asia	81.7	0.2	1.6	3.7	5.1
Latin America and the Caribbean	88.0	15.3	16.8	12.1	15.6
Middle East and North Africa	52.5	4.3	2.4	2.1	1.9
South Asia	97.9	44.9	44.0	40.0	40.0
Sub-Saharan Africa	72.9	46.6	47.7	48.1	46.3
Total	88.1	28.3	29.0	23.4	24.0
Excluding China	84.2	28.5	28.1	25.6	26.2

Note: The $1 a day is in 1993 purchasing power parity terms. The numbers are estimated from those countries in each region for which at least one survey was available during the period 1985–98. The proportion of the population covered by such surveys is given in column 1. Survey dates often do not coincide with the dates in the above table. To line up with the above dates, the survey estimates were adjusted using the closest available survey for each country and applying the consumption growth rate from national accounts. Using the assumption that the sample of countries covered by surveys is representative of the region as a whole, the numbers of poor are then estimated by region. This assumption is obviously less robust in the regions with the lowest survey coverage. The head count index is the percentage of the population below the poverty line. Further details on data and methodology can be found in Chen and Ravallion 2000.
Source: World Bank staff estimates.

farm employment. This widening of income inequality slowed the rate of poverty reduction for the country as a whole.[22] Elsewhere in the region, poverty increased in the aftermath of the 1997–98 financial crisis. In Indonesia, the government responded to the crisis by strengthening safety nets, which helped cushion the impact of the crisis. However, the incidence of poverty still increased substantially, doubling from its precrisis level. Since early 1999, there have been indications that poverty has declined significantly as rice prices have fallen, and real wages are starting to recover (Suryahadi and others 2000).

In **South Asia,** the share of the population living in poverty declined moderately through the 1990s, but not sufficiently to reduce the absolute number of poor. Household survey data indicate limited growth in average consumption in rural areas, reflecting slow growth in agriculture.[23] Urban poverty appears to have declined at twice the rate of poverty in rural areas. However, the Indian poverty data are subject to considerable uncertainty. In particular, private consumption as measured in the national accounts has grown about three times faster over the 1990s than household consumption as measured by the National

Table 1.9 Population living on less than $2 per day and head count index in developing countries, 1987, 1990, and 1998

Region	Population covered by at least one survey (percent)	Number of people living on less than $2 a day (millions)			
		1987	1990	1998 new	1998 (*GEP 2000*)
East Asia and Pacific	90.8	1,052.3	1,084.4	884.9	892.2
Excluding China	71.1	299.9	284.9	252.1	260.1
Europe and Central Asia	81.7	16.3	43.8	98.2	92.9
Latin America and the Caribbean	88.0	147.6	167.2	159.0	182.9
Middle East and North Africa	52.5	65.1	58.7	85.4	62.4
South Asia	97.9	911.0	976.0	1,094.6	1,095.9
Sub-Saharan Africa	72.9	356.6	388.2	489.3	474.8
Total	88.1	2,549.0	2,718.4	2,811.5	2,801.0
(excluding China)	84.2	1,796.6	1,918.8	2,178.7	2,168.9

Region	Population covered by at least one survey (percent)	Head count index (percent)			
		1987	1990	1998 new	1998 (*GEP 2000*)
East Asia and Pacific	90.8	67.0	66.1	48.7	49.1
Excluding China	71.1	62.9	57.3	44.3	45.0
Europe and Central Asia	81.7	3.6	9.6	20.7	19.9
Latin America and the Caribbean	88.0	35.5	38.1	31.7	36.4
Middle East and North Africa	52.5	30.0	24.8	29.9	21.9
South Asia	97.9	86.3	86.8	83.9	84.0
Sub-Saharan Africa	72.9	76.5	76.4	78.0	75.6
Total	88.1	61.0	61.7	56.1	56.0
Excluding China	84.2	58.2	58.8	57.9	57.6

Note: The $2 a day is in 1993 purchasing power parity terms. See the note to table 1.8.
Source: World Bank staff estimates.

Sample Survey. Discrepancies are to be expected, as the two sources track different aggregates.[24] Moreover, the survey data tend to understate the consumption of high-income households. Nevertheless, the size of this difference and the slowness of poverty reduction revealed in the survey data are difficult to account for, particularly given the improvement in human development indicators. Thus more accurate data could indicate more rapid poverty reduction than our current estimates. In Bangladesh, steady growth reduced the incidence of poverty during the 1990s, in contrast to the relative stagnation experienced in the 1980s. Poverty in urban areas fell at a considerably faster rate than rural poverty, partly reflecting slower growth in rural wages and higher rural unemployment. Landlessness has

been key in holding back the reduction of poverty in rural areas.[25]

In **Latin America,** both the share and the number of poor declined between 1990 and 1998. In Brazil, successful stabilization has stepped up the reduction of poverty, with the poor gaining from stronger growth and the decrease in inflation. Nonetheless, their livelihoods remain vulnerable. Evidence from employment surveys in metropolitan areas shows large swings in poverty, with an upturn in the poverty rate in the wake of the 1997–99 crisis and a decrease since late 1999, thanks to the rebound in growth. Low educational attainment has helped to perpetuate income inequality and poverty by preventing the poor from taking advantage of opportunities created by growth (World Bank 2000a).

Box 1.3 Trends in inequality

Countries with high levels of initial inequality have reduced poverty less for given rates of growth than countries with low initial inequality (World Bank 2000d), and if growth is accompanied by increasing inequality, its impact on poverty will be reduced. However, our understanding of long-term trends in inequality is limited, partly because of weaknesses in the data.[a] Trends in inequality have been extremely diverse. For example, Malaysia saw declines in inequality (as measured by the Gini coefficient) during the 1980s, but this trend was reversed in the 1990s. Korea and Indonesia experienced rapid growth during the 1980s with little change in inequality, while China and Russia experienced large increases in inequality over the same period.

The available data show no stable relationship between growth and inequality.[b] On average, income inequality within countries has neither decreased nor increased over the last 30 years. However, since within-country inequality has increased in some populous countries, overall more people have been affected by increases in inequality than by decreases.

What drives inequality? Here, too, our knowledge is limited. Nevertheless, both cross-country analyses and case studies have generated insights into the link between inequality and several policy and institutional factors.

- Policies fostering stable macroeconomic conditions, openness to trade, and moderate size of government tend to stimulate growth but have been found in one study not to systematically affect the distribution of income (Dollar and Kraay 2000). However, policies that reduce inflation from very high levels appear to benefit the poor more than the average.
- If growth is strong in areas where the poor live and sectors where they are employed (for example,

smallholder agriculture), they benefit more; if growth takes place in areas or sectors that are not accessible to the poor, inequality can increase. Domestic policy distortions that hinder agriculture (along with international trade barriers) have restrained growth in rural incomes in many countries. This has also been reflected in rising regional inequality, as in poor regions farming is often the dominant sector of activity.[c]

- Changes in income inequality reflect changes in the distribution of assets (for example, education) and in the return to these assets. In some countries, such as Mexico, more educated workers saw larger increases in earnings than did others workers, and these gains contributed to increasing income inequality.
- Gender bias and other forms of discrimination have led to increasing inequality where the groups that are discriminated against are poorer than others to start with. For example, discrimination led to lower returns to education and lower overall incomes for ethnic minorities in Vietnam and indigenous groups in Latin America.
- The impact of liberalization programs on inequality has differed among countries. If prereform controls benefit higher-income groups disproportionately, reforms can narrow inequality. If, on the other hand, prereform controls favor the poor, liberalization can have the opposite effect (Ravallion 2000). For example, in the transition to an open trade regime, the poor may suffer if sectors where they have a stake are subjected to competition. This may happen especially in middle-income developing economies with intermediate skill endowments. These economies may have a comparative advantage regarding goods that require medium-intensity skills. These countries are likely to protect sectors intensive in unskilled labor where low-paid workers can be found.[d]

a. Inequality is estimated with a certain degree of uncertainty, as it is based on sample surveys. Thus changes over time need to be considered carefully to assess whether they are significant to a certain degree or whether they fall within the margin of error. The estimation of standard errors is complex, and work on this is just beginning.

b. See for example Deininger and Squire 1996; Ravallion and Chen 1997; Bruno, Ravallion, and Squire 1998; Dollar and Kraay 2000.

c. For example, in the Indian state of Uttar Pradesh—which has a population of 160 million and a poverty rate of about 40 percent—agriculture accounts for 40 percent of GDP and provides 75 percent of employment.

d. For example, in Mexico, a country that implemented one of the most ambitious trade policy reform programs from 1985 to 1988, the nominal tariff and import license coverage in apparel and footwear were among the highest in manufacturing (Revenga 1995). A similar preform pattern of protection was also found in Morocco (Currie and Harrison 1997).

In **Africa,** slow growth increased both the share and the number of the poor over the 1990s; Africa is now the region with the largest share of people living on less than $1 per day. In Nigeria, the number of people living in extreme poverty rose steeply following the reversal of the 1985–92 reforms, reaching an estimated 70 million (66 percent of the population) based on the national definition (rather than the international $1-a-day definition used here). Nigeria now accounts for nearly one-fourth of Sub-Saharan Africa's poor. Urban poverty has grown faster than rural poverty, owing to massive migration from rural areas to the cities, with the incidence of urban poverty now matching that of rural poverty. By contrast, the rural poverty rate fell in Ethiopia, Sub-Saharan Africa's second most populous country and one of the poorest. The reforms implemented after the end of the civil war in the early 1990s spurred a strong recovery, ending a two-decade slump. The benefits of agricultural price liberalization have spread quickly, boosting growth of rural incomes. Urban poverty, on the other hand, has been stagnant. Urban inequality has risen, in part because of large population movements resulting from the civil war, and in part as a result of economic reform, as agricultural price liberalization raised consumer prices in urban areas and civil service rationalization reduced urban employment. Unfortunately, progress is likely to have been slowed by the border conflict.

In the **Middle East and North Africa,** the percentage of people living on less than $1 per day declined slightly, but the proportion living below $2 per day increased, from 25 to 30 percent of the population, because of increases in Egypt, Morocco, and Yemen.

Poverty also rose markedly in the **transition economies** during the 1990s. In the Russian Federation, the breakup of the central planning system was accompanied by a steep fall in output and a sharp increase in inflation. Poverty as measured by the national definition had jumped from an estimated 11 percent during the Soviet period to 43 percent by 1996, and probably increased further with the 1998 crisis. Inequality widened dramatically during the transition, with the Gini coefficient of consumption expenditure rising from an estimated 0.24 in 1988 to about 0.49 in 1998. Increasing disparities in poverty across regions have also surfaced, exacerbated by a inefficient system of fiscal decentralization that left the more backward regions short of resources to assist the poor.

Prospects for poverty. As noted above, progress in reducing extreme poverty during the 1990s was constrained by increasing inequality in a few countries that accounted for a large share of the world's poor. As in last year's *Global Economic Prospects,* this year's poverty scenarios show that continued increases in inequality, coupled with less than robust growth, would imply failure to reach the poverty target for developing countries as a group; in particular, the scenarios indicate substantial increases in the number of poor in Sub-Saharan Africa. Given the uncertainty surrounding the historical estimates for poverty and the risks associated with long-term growth projections, these scenarios should not be viewed as presenting the full range of poverty rates that are likely to occur.

The three poverty scenarios outlined below require a projection of growth of the economy as a whole (and of population growth), a projection of the average growth rate in per capita consumption for the household sector (measured by household surveys)[26]; and a projection of changes in the distribution of per capita consumption.

Income growth. The three scenarios differ only in terms of the assumed growth rate for the economy as a whole. Scenario A reflects the base case growth rates, and scenario B reflects the low case growth rates described above. A third scenario assumes that the growth rate of each developing-country region is reduced proportionally from the low-case forecast, so that the average growth for developing countries as a group is equal to that experienced in the 1990s (1.7 percent in per capita terms).

Consumption trends. In previous poverty forecasts, the projected growth rate of per capita consumption for households was taken from forecasts of private consumption from the national income accounts. By contrast, the scenarios outlined below take account of recent research that shows that the growth in household consumption from survey data has been lower on average than private consumption growth as measured by the national income accounts. Data for 142 time periods (during the 1980s and 1990s) for 60 countries suggest that the growth of per capita consumption from household surveys was an estimated 87 percent of the growth rate in private consumption from the national accounts.[27] The most likely explanation for this discrepancy is that the surveys do not pick up fully the growth in living standards of the rich.[28] As the poverty estimates are based on consumption from household surveys, we assume in poverty forecasts for most developing countries that the growth rate of this variable will equal 87 percent of the growth rate of private consumption from the national income accounts. The failure to adjust the forecast of household consumption growth to reflect the historical divergence from the national income accounts has resulted in substantial overestimation of the rate of poverty reduction in past forecasting exercises.

The discrepancy between consumption growth from the household surveys and the national accounts is larger in China and India (which together account for more than half of the world's poor) and in the Europe and Central Asia region. For China, the time series evidence indicates that 72 percent of a gain in private consumption is reflected in household consumption, and this adjustment is used in the projections. For India, only 28 percent of an increase in private consumption is reflected in the household consumption, and in Europe and Central Asia the time series evidence for the 1990s suggests virtually no correlation between the two consumption aggregates. It is difficult to understand these unusually large discrepancies, which probably reflect serious data problems, as well as the failure to capture the consumption levels of the rich. Thus, the projections for India and the ECA region assume that the share of national accounts growth reflected in the survey mean will equal 51 percent over the forecast period, the lower bound of the 95 percent confidence interval for the estimate for the developing world as a whole (excluding China, India, and Europe and Central Asia).[29]

Distribution. The other determinant of the incidence of poverty is in the distribution of household consumption. Long-term cross-country evidence suggests that most countries have not experienced a systematic trend in household consumption inequality as measured using household survey data. Thus, the assumption for the bulk of the developing countries is that inequality will not change over the forecast period.

However, there are exceptions. The 1990s did witness a dramatic rise in inequality in the Europe and Central Asia region. We assume that this was a transitional phenomenon and will not continue. Further, the available data do indicate a rise in inequality in China and India over the past decade,[30] in part because of slower growth in rural areas, where the majority of the poor live, than in urban areas. We assume that inequality will continue to rise in both countries over the forecast period. In China, the liberalization of trade in agricultural commodities and land markets is likely to allow a shift to more remunerative crops and larger landholdings. Since good quality land is scarce, the consolidation of landholdings and higher returns to good quality land are likely to lead to higher levels of inequality in rural areas. Moreover, continued integration with the world economy will increase the demand for skilled labor. Inequality within urban areas may rise, as wages increase rapidly for skilled workers in manufacturing and some services while low-skill service workers experience lagging wages under the twin pressures of migrant laborers and laid-off workers from the state enterprises. Rising demand for skilled labor may also increase inequality between urban and rural areas, as the gap in educational attainment between the two is high. Thus, both scenarios assume that urban incomes will increase more rapidly than rural incomes, and that inequality within both the rural and the urban sectors will increase slightly, in the form of a 10 percent higher Gini coefficient in each sector by 2015.

In India, rising inequality during the 1990s appears to have slowed the rate of poverty reduction relative to that of the previous decade. So far, reforms have largely bypassed the economy in rural areas, where the majority of the poor live, leading to a wide divergence of growth between urban and rural areas. Weak infrastructure services, limited education, and inadequate health care have made it difficult for the poor to share equally in the country's rapid growth. For example, the liberalization process is increasing returns to education, while education is inequitably distributed (one-third of men, and 60 percent of women, over the age of 15 are illiterate). The forecasts assume that the divergence in consumption growth between rural and urban areas will continue along past trends.

Scenarios. In scenario A, with base case growth (adjusted for historical differences between household survey and national income accounts consumption) and rising household consumption inequality in China and India, the world as a whole would be on track to reach the International Development Goal of reducing the share of people living on less than $1 per day by 2015 to half of what it was in 1990. The total number of poor people would decline to about 800 million (see table 1.10 for the forecasts of total population in developing countries). But not all regions would be on track: Africa would be far from reaching the goal even under this favorable growth scenario. With low case growth rates (scenario B), the world as a whole would not reach the target. Only the countries of East Asia would be able to reduce poverty beyond the target of half the 1990 incidence. The total number of poor people in the world (excluding China) would remain unchanged from the 1990 level

Table 1.10 Population estimates and projections, developing countries, 1998–2015
(millions of people)

Region	1998	2015
East Asia and Pacific	1,817	2,099
Excluding China	569	708
Eastern Europe and Central Asia	475	483
Latin America and the Caribbean	502	623
Middle East and North Africa	286	390
South Asia	1,305	1,676
Sub-Saharan Africa	627	914
Total	5,011	6,185
Excluding China	3,763	4,794

Source: World Bank staff estimates.

of about 1 billion.[31] Finally, if aggregate GDP growth in developing countries over the next 15 years were to equal the average of the 1990s, then progress in poverty reduction would be even slower than in scenario B, and the number of people living on less than $1 a day at the end of the forecast period would be only marginally lower than in 1998. The number of poor based on the $2 per day level would actually increase. Table 1.11 provides a summary of the poverty forecasts, and tables 1.12 and 1.13 give regional details for the two scenarios that use the base case and low case growth rates.

The preceding scenarios highlight the importance of achieving fast growth and distributing the benefits of growth equitably. Without macroeconomic stability, sustained structural reforms, prudent and transparent use of public resources, improvements in the provision of public services and infrastructure to the poor, and actions to reduce vulnerability and give the poor more voice in development choices, the pattern of sustained, inclusive growth that underlies the best scenario will not be realized and millions more people will remain enslaved in poverty. Achieving the poverty reduction targets also will require an increase in aid flows to the poorest countries.

Table 1.11 Poverty in developing countries under scenarios of base case growth (scenario A); low case growth (scenario B); and 1990s average growth, 1990, 1998, 2015

	$1 a day		$2 a day	
	Head count ratio (percent)	Number of poor (million)	Head count ratio (percent)	Number of poor (millions)
1990	29.0	1,276	61.7	2,718
1998	23.4	1,175	56.1	2,812
2015: scenario A (base case growth)	12.6	777	36.7	2,272
2015: scenario B (low case growth)	16.4	1,011	43.2	2,672
2015: growth as in 1990s	18.7	1,157	47.5	2,938

Source: World Bank staff estimates.

Table 1.12 Regional breakdown of number of people living on less than $1 per day and head count index in developing countries, under scenarios of base case growth (scenario A) and low case growth (scenario B), 1990, 1998, and 2015

Region	Number of people living on less than $1 per day			
	1990	1998	2015 low case	2015 base case
East Asia and Pacific	452.4	267.1	100.7	65.1
Excluding China	92.0	53.7	20.1	9.4
Europe and Central Asia	7.1	17.6	9.0	6.3
Latin America and the Caribbean	73.8	60.7	58.3	42.8
Middle East and North Africa	5.7	6.0	6.2	5.1
South Asia	495.1	521.8	410.7	296.7
Sub-Saharan Africa	242.3	301.6	426.2	360.6
Total	1,276.4	1,174.9	1,011.2	776.5
Excluding China	915.9	961.4	930.6	720.9

Region	Head count index (percent)			
	1990	1998	2015 low case	2015 base case
East Asia and Pacific	27.6	14.7	4.8	3.1
Excluding China	18.5	9.4	2.8	1.3
Europe and Central Asia	1.6	3.7	1.9	1.3
Latin America and the Caribbean	16.8	12.1	9.4	6.9
Middle East and North Africa	2.4	2.1	1.6	1.3
South Asia	44.0	40.0	24.5	17.7
Sub-Saharan Africa	47.7	48.1	46.7	39.5
Total	29.0	23.4	16.4	12.6
Excluding China	28.1	25.6	19.4	15.0

Source: World Bank staff estimates.

With slow growth and increases in inequality, progress would be much slower everywhere, the target would be out of reach for all regions apart from East Asia, and more than 200 mil-lion more people worldwide would remain mired in poverty. If policies are inadequate to achieve more than the slow growth of the 1990s, then the number of people living in ex-

Table 1.13   Regional breakdown of number of people living on less than $2 per day and head count index in developing countries, under scenarios of base case growth (scenario A) and low case growth (scenario B), 1990, 1998, and 2015

Region	Number of people living on less than $2 per day			
	1990	1998	2015 low case	2015 base case
East Asia and Pacific	1,084.4	884.9	472.2	323.2
Excluding China	284.9	252.1	187.2	114.6
Europe and Central Asia	43.8	98.2	57.6	46.9
Latin America and the Caribbean	167.2	159.0	161.6	132.9
Middle East and North Africa	58.7	85.4	79.7	57.5
South Asia	976.0	1,094.6	1,213.6	1,077.8
Sub-Saharan Africa	388.2	489.3	690.3	636.7
Total	2,718.4	2,811.5	2,675.0	2,275.1
Excluding China	1,918.8	2,178.7	2,390.0	2,066.5

Region	Head count index (percent)			
	1990	1998	2015 low case	2015 base case
East Asia and Pacific	66.1	48.7	22.5	15.4
Excluding China	57.3	44.3	26.4	16.2
Europe and Central Asia	9.6	20.7	11.9	9.7
Latin America and the Caribbean	38.1	31.7	25.9	21.3
Middle East and North Africa	24.8	29.9	20.4	14.7
South Asia	86.8	83.9	72.4	64.3
Sub-Saharan Africa	76.4	78.0	75.6	69.7
Total	61.7	56.1	43.3	36.8
Excluding China	58.8	57.9	49.9	43.1

Source: World Bank staff estimates.

treme poverty would remain near current levels for the next 15 years.

In Africa, the number of people living in poverty would increase under all scenarios. If the lack of progress observed over the last decade with respect to other dimensions of poverty—life expectancy, school enrollment, and child mortality—continues, as may well be the case if the AIDS epidemic is not stemmed, then the gap between the region and the rest of the world could widen significantly. This would be a grim outlook, not just for Africa but for the whole world, and efforts are needed in the region and elsewhere to break with the recent pattern of conflict and crisis, and to deal with the AIDS epidemic.

Even if the most optimistic scenario is achieved, 2.3 billion people would still be liv-ing on less than $2 per day in 2015. Thus, the global war on poverty is likely to be with us well into the twenty-first century.

In closing, it is important to note that these projections have some serious limitations. First, despite enormous progress in measuring poverty over the past 10 years, the database has significant weaknesses: recent data are missing for a number of countries, especially in Africa, where renewed efforts are needed to institutionalize survey work that began in the 1990s. Major questions remain as to the trends for India. In addition, our understanding of trends in inequality and the divergence between national accounts and household-based measures of private consumption is limited. Research to address some of these limitations, including further analysis of the data for India, is underway.

Notes

1. See Gale and Sabelhous 1999.

2. Gross capital inflows (largely portfolio flows) exceeded $750 billion in 1999. See U.S. Department of Commerce, *Survey of Current Business,* various issues.

3. This figure is strongly influenced by large carry-over in GDP levels from late 1999 and first-half 2000; growth on an annualized basis is anticipated to fall within a range of 3 percent during the second half of the year.

4. This assumes little or no increase in participation rates from the average of the 1990s.

5. The total population of the EU, assuming all countries now under consideration (excluding Turkey) join, will be close to 500 million in 2010, with the new members representing close to 25 percent of the total.

6. There is an entire literature on strategic linkages between multilateral and regional integration agreements. See World Bank 1999, Section 5, for more detailed discussion.

7. For more discussion, see Hoekman and Kostecki 1995.

8. Nonetheless, many developing-country members of the WTO—particularly the least developed—still face significant impediments in being able to participate fully in the workings of the WTO and other international bodies related to international trade (see chapter 3). Capacity building, technical assistance, and financial resources to help developing countries improve their presence in Geneva are major items on their agenda for the new post–Uruguay Round negotiations.

9. Forty-two of the 108 notifications listed in figure 1.13 represent extensions of the EU or NAFTA.

10. Since intraregional trade is usually among closer substitutes than extraregional trade, the former can be more vulnerable to the business cycle.

11. The performance of stock markets in developing countries was heavily influenced by the technology and telecommunications sectors, which accounted for some 65 percent of total equity placements in the first half of 2000.

12. The 1999 figure of $180 billion reflects a revision from the estimate of $192 billion presented in *Global Development Finance 2000* because of lower levels of inflows to China and Saudi Arabia during the year.

13. However, the recent downtrend in FDI to China may be reversed, as the value of approved projects rose 25 percent year on year during the first five months of 2000.

14. Global crossborder acquisitions of a more than 10 percent–stake reached $720 billion in 1999, up 35 percent from 1998.

15. Oil prices deflated by the U.S. Dollar Manufactured Export Unit Value (MUV) index for France, Germany, Japan, the United Kingdom, and the United States. The latter index has been essentially flat over the 1990s.

16. See appendix 1, Regional Economic Prospects, for further details.

17. The percentage of the population on wages "below subsistence" remains high at 27.6 percent, according to official estimates as of June 2000. However, it has declined significantly from the 34 percent average of 1999.

18. The EU market now accounts for 60 to 80 percent of Central and Eastern European countries' exports.

19. Figures for 1998 were updated in September 2000 using data from surveys that have become available only recently, and they differ slightly from the preliminary estimates included in last year's *Global Economic Prospects.*

20. The estimates of global poverty given here are based on consumption, and income data are adjusted accordingly.

21. A common way to measure inequality is to calculate the Gini coefficient. The Gini coefficient would be equal to 0 if all had the same income and to 1 if one person had all the income and everybody else had none. We observe Gini coefficients for income in the range of 0.2 to 0.6 (the Slovak Republic has the lowest Gini, 0.195, while Swaziland and Brazil have the highest (0.6); among OECD countries, Austria has the lowest Gini at 0.23 and New Zealand the highest at 0.44 (World Bank 2000c).

22. The data for China pose several problems. First, consumption per capita, as estimated by surveys, has been growing less rapidly than estimates of private consumption from the national accounts would suggest. Second, urban household surveys do not include rural migrants. Third, savings rates are very high in China, even among the poor, so poverty estimates based on consumption measures yield a higher poverty incidence than those based on income. Moreover, it appears that savings rates increased among the poor over this period. The estimates above differ from official estimates, and new survey work will be needed to reconcile the differences (work on urban surveys is under way). These discrepancies cast doubt on the estimates for China and therefore on the global estimates, given the size of the country.

23. Unfavorable trends in agriculture partly reflect inefficiencies in public support to farming, as well as limited reform, in contrast to the deregulation of the urban sector.

24. The major differences are that consumption measures from household surveys sometimes do not include imputed housing, and private consumption in the

national accounts typically includes spending by non-profit enterprises (nongovernmental organizations, political parties, churches, charities, and so on) as well as households.

25. For example, a household with at least 2.5 acres enjoyed 43 percent higher per capita consumption in 1995–96 than did a landless rural household (World Bank 1999).

26. This excludes consumption by other private entities such as nonprofit organizations, political parties, unincorporated enterprises and so forth that are often included in the national accounts estimate of private consumption.

27. See Ravallion 2000. India, China, and Europe and Central Asia are excluded from this estimation.

28. There is a presumption that higher-income groups tend to underreport consumption. Moreover, consumption measures from household surveys sometimes do not include imputed housing expenditures, which, in fast-growing economies, are likely to grow rapidly in the higher-income groups. There are other explanations for the divergence between survey mean household consumption growth rates and those from the national accounts, including the fact that (for most countries) private consumption in the national accounts includes spending by nonprofit enterprises (such as churches and charities and so on) as well as households, and the share of the nonprofit sector is probably rising.

29. This assumption has an important impact on the forecasts. For example, if in India consumption were assumed to rise at 87 percent (rather than 51 percent) of the national income accounts growth rate, then by 2015 the forecast (using base case growth rates) for extreme poverty in South Asia would be only about half the 22 percent rate shown for scenario A.

30. For example, the per capita consumption (as measured in the household survey) of the bottom 10 percent of China's population increased by 2.5 percent per year during 1990–98, while per capita consumption of the top 10 percent increased by 11 percent per year. In India, per capita consumption of the bottom 10 percent did not increase at all during 1985–97, while the top 10 percent saw a rise of 4.7 percent per year.

31. These results are roughly similar to the poverty forecasts in *Global Economic Prospects 2000*. In scenario A, the head count poverty index is 15.9 percent in 2008 (the last year of the *GEP 2000* forecasts), compared with 12.3 percent in *GEP 2000*. This year's forecast is more pessimistic because we assume that growth in household consumption will be slower than in private consumption in the national income accounts. Conversely, the *GEP 2000* forecast for scenario B was more pessimistic (head count index of 21.9 percent compared with 19.5 percent now), because last year we assumed a rise in inequality in all regions.

References

Bosworth, Barry P., and Jack E. Triplett. 2000. "Numbers Matter." Brookings Institution Policy Brief 63 (July). Washington, D.C.

Bruno, Michael, Martin Ravallion, and Lyn Squire. 1998. "Equity and Growth in Developing Countries: Old and New Perspectives on the Policy Issues." Policy Research Working Paper 1563. World Bank, Washington, D.C.

Chen, Shaohua, and Martin Ravallion. 2000. "How Did the World's Poorest Fare in the 1990s?" Policy Research Working Paper 2409. World Bank, Washington, D.C.

Council of Economic Advisors. 2000. "Economic Report of the President." Washington, D.C., GOP. Available at http://w3.access.gpo.gov/usbudget/fy2001/pdf/2000 erp.pdf.

Currie, Janet, and Ann Harrison. 1997. "Sharing the Costs: the Impact of Trade Reform on Capital and Labor in Morocco." Journal of Labor Economics (U.S.) 15:S44–S71.

Deininger, Klaus, and Lynn Squire. 1996. "A New Data Set Measuring Income Inequality." The World Bank Economic Review 10(3):565–91 (September). Data available at http://www.worldbank.org/research/growth/dddeisgu.htm

Dollar, David, and Aart C. Kraay. 2000. "Growth Is Good for the Poor." Policy Research Working Paper (forthcoming). World Bank, Washington, D.C. Available at http://www.worldbank.org/research/growth/pdfiles/growthgoodforpoorpdf.

Gale, William G., and John Sabelhaus. 1999. "Perspectives on the Household Saving Rate." *Brookings Papers on Economic Activity* (1):181–224.

Gordon, Robert J. Forthcoming. "Does the 'New' Economy Measure up to the Great Inventions of the Past?" Draft for *Journal of Economic Perspectives.*

IMF (International Monetary Fund). 2000. *World Economic Outlook: 2000.* Preliminary edition, September. Washington, D.C.

Jorgenson, Dale W., and Kevin J. Stiroh. 2000. "Industry-level Productivity and Competitiveness between Canada and the United States: U.S. Economic Growth at the Industry Level." *American Economic Review* 90 (2): 161–7.

Kasman, Bruce. 2000. "U.S. productivity growth: It's breadth that matters." J. P. Morgan Global Data Watch. 18 August, 7–10. Available online to subscribers at http://www/morganmarkets.com.

Kotlikoff, Laurence J., and others. 2000.

OECD (Organisation for Economic Co-operation and Development). 1999. *Economic Survey of Japan.* November. Paris.

Oliner, Stephen D., and Daniel E. Sichel. 2000. "The Resurgence of Growth in the Late 1990s: Is Information Technology the Story?" Federal Reserve Board. May. Washington, D.C.

Ravallion, Martin. 2000. "A Note on Forecasting Poverty Using National Accounts Growth Rates." A background paper for *Global Economics Prospects and the Developing Countries 2000*.

Ravallion, Martin, and Shaohua Chen. 1997. "What Can New Survey Data Tell Us about Recent Changes in Distribution and Poverty?" *World Bank Economic Review* 11(2):357–82.

Revenga Ana. 1995. "Employment and Wage Effects of Trade Liberalization: The Case of Mexican Manufacturing." Policy Research Working Paper 1524 World Bank, Washington, D.C.

Shah, Shekhar, Martin Ravallion, and Quentin Wodon. 1999. Bangladesh: from Counting the Poor to Making the Poor Count. A World Bank country study. Washington, D.C.

Suryahadi, Asep, and others. 2000. "The Evolution of Poverty during the Crisis in Indonesia, 1996 to 1999 (Using Full Susenas Sample)." Social Monitoring and Early Response Unit Working Paper. Jakarta. Available at http://www.smeru.or.id/data/ report/evolpov2.pdf.

Triplett, Jack E. 1999. "Economic Statistics, the New Economy, and the Productivity Slowdown." *Business Economics*, April 1999. 34(2):13–17. Also available at http://www.brook.edu/es/research/ areas/productivity/papers/trip4 99.pdf.

U.S. Department of Commerce. 1996. "Prospects for Growth in Japan in the 21st Century." Office of the Chief Economist Economics and Statistics Administration Research Series: OMA 2-96, November. Washington DC.

———. Various years. *Survey of Current Business*. Washington, D.C.

UNAIDS (United Nations 2000. *Report on the Global HIV/AIDS Epidemic*. Geneva: Joint United Nations Programme on HIV/AIDS), http://www.unaids. org/epidemic_update/report/Epi_report.pdf.

World Bank. 1999.

World Bank. 2000a. *Attacking Brazil's Poverty: A Framework for Sustainable Poverty Reduction— with a Focus on Urban Areas*. Forthcoming. Washington, D.C.

———. 2000b. Global Economic Prospects and the Developing Countries 2000. Washington, D.C.

———. 2000c. *World Development Indicators 2000*. Washington, D.C.

———. 2000d. *World Development Report 2000/01*. Washington, D.C.

———. 2000e. *Trade Blocs*. New York: Oxford University Press.

Annex 1 Membership of selected major regional integration agreements (RIAs) and dates of formation

INDUSTRIAL AND DEVELOPING ECONOMIES

European Union (EU): formerly European Economic Community (EEC) and European Community (EC), **1957:** Belgium, France, Germany, Italy, Luxembourg, Netherlands; **1973:** Denmark, Ireland, United Kingdom; **1981:** Greece; **1986:** Portugal, Spain; **1995:** Austria, Finland, Sweden.

European Economic Area (EEA): 1994: EU, Iceland, Liechtenstein, Norway.

Euro-Mediterranean Economic Area (Euro-Maghreb): Bilateral agreements, **1995:** EU and Tunisia; **1996:** EU and Morocco.

EU bilateral agreements with Eastern Europe: 1994: EC and Hungary, Poland, **1995:** EC and Bulgaria, Romania, Estonia, Latvia, Lithuania, Czech Republic, Slovak Republic, Slovenia.

Canada-US Free Trade Area (CUSFTA): 1988: Canada, United States.

North American Free Trade Area (NAFTA): 1994: Canada, Mexico, United States.

Asia Pacific Economic Cooperation (APEC): 1989: Australia, Brunei Darussalam, Canada, Indonesia, Japan, the Republic of Korea, Malaysia, New Zealand, Philippines, Singapore, Thailand, United States; **1991:** China, Taiwan (China), Hong Kong (China); **1993:** Mexico, Papua New Guinea; **1994:** Chile; **1998:** Peru, the Russian Federation, Vietnam.

LATIN AMERICA AND THE CARIBBEAN

Andean Pact: 1969: revived in 1991, Bolivia, Colombia, Ecuador, Peru, Republica Bolivariana de Venezuela.

Central American Common Market (CACM): 1960: revived in 1993, El Salvador, Guatemala, Honduras, Nicaragua; **1962:** Costa Rica.

Southern Cone Common Market, Mercado Común del Sur (Mercosur): 1991: Argentina, Brazil, Paraguay, Uruguay.

Group of Three (G-3): 1995: Colombia, Mexico, Republica Bolivariana de Venezuela.

Latin American Integration Association (LAIA): formerly Latin American Free Trade Area (LAFTA), **1960:** revived 1980, Argentina, Bolivia, Brazil, Chile, Colombia, Ecuador, Mexico, Paraguay, Peru, Uruguay, Venezuela.

Caribbean Community and Common Market (CARICOM): 1973: Antigua and Barbuda, Barbados, Jamaica, St. Kitts and Nevis, Trinidad and Tobago; **1974:** Belize, Dominica, Grenada, Montserrat, St. Lucia, St. Vincent and the Grenadines; **1983:** The Bahamas (part of the Caribbean Community but not of the Common Market).

MIDDLE EAST AND ASIA

Association of Southeast Asian Nations (ASEAN): 1967: ASEAN Free Trade Area or AFTA was created in 1992, Indonesia, Malaysia, Philippines, Singapore, Thailand; **1984:** Brunei Darussalam; **1995:** Vietnam; **1997:** Myanmar, Lao People's Democratic Republic; **1999:** Cambodia.

Gulf Cooperation Council (GCC): 1981: Bahrain, Kuwait, Oman, Qatar, Saudi Arabia, the United Arab Emirates.

South Asian Association for Regional Cooperation (SAARC): 1985: Bangladesh, Bhutan, India, Maldives, Nepal, Pakistan, Sri Lanka.

AFRICA

Cross-Border Initiative (CBI): 1992: Burundi, Comoros, Kenya, Madagascar, Malawi, Mauritius, Namibia, Rwanda, Seychelles, Swaziland, Tanzania, Uganda, Zambia, Zimbabwe.

East African Cooperation (EAC): 1967: formerly East African Community (EAC), broke up in 1977 and recently revived, Kenya, Tanzania, Uganda.

Economic and Monetary Community of Central Africa (CEMAC): 1994: formerly Union Douanière et Economique de l'Afrique Centrale (UDEAC), **1966:** Cameroon, Central African Republic, Chad, Congo, Gabon; **1989:** Equatorial Guinea.

Economic Community of West African States (ECOWAS): 1975: Benin, Burkina Faso, Cape Verde, Côte d'Ivoire, Gambia, Ghana, Guinea, Guinea-Bissau, Liberia, Mali, Mauritania, Niger, Nigeria, Senegal, Sierra Leone, Togo.

Common Market for Eastern and Southern Africa (COMESA): 1993: Angola, Burundi, Comoros, Djibouti, Egypt, Ethiopia, Kenya, Lesotho, Malawi, Mauritius, Mozambique, Rwanda, Somalia, Sudan, Swaziland, Tanzania, Uganda, Zambia, Zimbabwe.

Indian Ocean Commission (IOC): 1984: Comoros, Madagascar, Mauritius, Seychelles.

Southern African Development Community (SADC): 1980: formerly known as the Southern African Development Coordination Conference (SADCC), Angola, Botswana, Lesotho, Malawi, Mozambique, Swaziland, Tanzania, Zambia, Zimbabwe; **1990:** Namibia; **1994:** South Africa; **1995:** Mauritius; **1998:** Democratic Republic of the Congo, Seychelles.

Economic Community of West Africa (CEAO): 1973: revived in 1994 as UEMOA, Benin, Burkina Faso, Côte d'Ivoire, Mali, Mauritania, Niger, Senegal.

West African Economic and Monetary Union (UEMOA or WAEMU): 1994: Benin, Burkina Faso, Côte d'Ivoire, Mali, Niger, Senegal, Togo, **1997:** Guinea-Bissau.

Southern African Customs Union (SACU): 1910: Botswana, Lesotho, Namibia, South Africa, Swaziland.

Economic Community of the Countries of the Great Lakes (CEPGL): 1976: Burundi, Rwanda, Democratic Republic of the Congo.

Source: World Bank 1999.

2

Trade Policies in the 1990s and the Poorest Countries

URING THE 1960S AND 1970S, DEVELOP-
ing economies exhibited severe trade-
related distortions, including quantitative restrictions on imports and exports, very
high tariffs, overvalued exchange rates, and
administrative controls on foreign exchange
allocation. Although growth remained rapid
against a background of a favorable external
environment up to the first oil shock in 1973,
policies of import control and substitution induced inefficiencies as well as rigidities in economic structure. Often, they resulted in peri-
odic balance of payments crises. Subsequently,
the failure of many countries to adjust adequately to the external shocks of the 1970s
and early 1980s underlined the importance of
reforms designed to encourage responsiveness
to market signals, improve the investment climate, and to enhance export diversification.

One result was that most developing countries implemented significant liberalization of
their trade regimes during the late 1980s and
the 1990s. Their export growth accelerated
during the 1990s, and kept pace with the 6
percent per year expansion of world trade
in volume terms. However, average per capita
growth rates in developing countries as a group
remained well below those of the rich countries
in the 1990s. Though the giant low-income
countries China and India embarked on market
reforms and grew rapidly, growth in a large
number of small, poor countries was disappointing. This led many observers to question
the success of liberalization programs.

This chapter reviews the export and
growth performance of developing countries
in the 1990s, giving special attention to the
poorest economies. It reviews the decline in
trade barriers during the 1990s, examines output and export trends, and analyzes domestic
trade-policy constraints. Finally, it considers
external barriers to developing countries' efforts to accelerate their export growth.

The chapter reaches the following conclusions:

- Trade regimes were significantly liberalized during the late 1980s and 1990s. Developing countries cut the average tariff
rate by half, narrowed tariff dispersion in
many instances, and greatly reduced the
incidence of nontariff barriers to trade.
Most countries now rely on market forces
rather than administrative fiat to allocate
foreign exchange, and black market premiums have declined significantly. Although the degree of trade protection is
still high in many developing countries,
gross distortions in trade regimes have
been greatly reduced.

- Despite the reforms and improved global
economic conditions, developing countries' average real per capita incomes increased by less than 1 percent per year
during the 1990s, compared with more
than 2 percent in industrial countries.
This outcome is partially affected by the
political shocks and various foreign and

civil conflicts. Eighteen developing countries were severely affected by conflict, and as a group they suffered declines in per capita income of more than 1 percent per year. Incomes also fell in most transition economies following the breakup of the Soviet Union. Excluding countries hit by these severe political shocks, developing countries saw per capita incomes rise by 1.5 percent a year, about 1 per cent faster than in the 1980s.

- These countries also saw merchandise export growth of 6.4 percent per year during the 1990s, about 2 percent faster than during the 1980s. Export outcomes were very uneven, however. Regions that saw the largest declines in trade barriers, including East Asia, South Asia, and Latin America also saw the largest acceleration in exports. By contrast, growth in export volumes in Sub-Saharan Africa averaged only 2 percent per year, in part because world trade of the products Africa exports grew at half the rate of growth of world trade. Countries in Sub-Saharan Africa and in the Middle East and North Africa also saw market share decline in their traditional exports.

- The poorest countries were those most affected by conflict and political shocks. Ten of the 32 low-income countries were affected by conflict. Average per capita income of the low-income, small countries declined during the 1990s, but averaged 1 percent a year in real terms if countries involved in conflict are excluded. This represents a significant acceleration compared with the 1980s, but is still well below the average of middle-income countries. Exports also accelerated in the small low-income countries not involved in conflict, but grew about 3.5 percent slower than in the middle-income countries in the 1990s.

- Despite significant progress, many of the poorest countries have not put in place the policies necessary to raise living standards by improving (or even maintaining) export shares in traditional markets and en-

couraging rapid diversification. Appreciated real exchange rates and high real exchange rate volatility have often been associated with a muted export response to trade liberalization and other reform measures. Per capita income growth was significantly faster in countries with relatively stable real exchange rates. Additionally, institutional weaknesses, such as the absence of effective duty exemption/ drawback programs, coupled with the need to use revenues from tariffs on intermediate and capital goods as a revenue source, have acted as an effective tax on exports in many of the poorest developing countries. Finally, weak export infrastructure, inadequate ancillary export services, and high transport costs—often in part the result of policy shortcomings—have left many of the poorest countries (particularly the landlocked ones) at a competitive disadvantage on international markets.

- External barriers to exports from developing countries, especially agricultural and labor-intensive products, continue to impede the integration of the poorest economies into the world market. While the share of developing countries in world trade of manufactures rose sharply in the 1990s, their share of world trade in agricultural products and processed foods has declined. In part this development is the result of domestic policies that restrain agricultural exports. But high trade barriers imposed by industrial countries on agriculture and processed food imports, and agricultural subsidies in industrial countries, are also important and have become even more important with the domestic policy reforms in developing countries. These barriers particularly penalize rural areas where the majority of the poor in developing countries reside, and impede growth in the poorest countries in areas of their comparative advantage. Various restrictions and subsidies in industrial countries also hamper the poorest countries' efforts to diversify into downstream processing, higher value added, and faster-growing products. The poorest countries are the least equipped to deal with these external barriers because a host of other domestic policy and institutional weaknesses inhibit their diversification into less restricted sectors.

Reductions in barriers to trade

Developing countries made substantial progress in reforming their trade and exchange rate policies during the 1990s. Tariffs were cut, their dispersion declined in many countries, fewer products were covered by quantitative restrictions (QRs), the number of countries allocating foreign exchange through administrative means (as measured by the International Monetary Fund) dwindled, and the black market premium narrowed. Although any one of these measures is an imperfect guide to the restrictiveness of the trade regime,[1] taken together they show enormous progress in opening the developing economies to international trade. Several studies have found that increased openness is associated with economic growth (box 2.1).

Tariffs. The average tariff rate in developing countries has been cut by at least half in the last 20 years, from 32 percent in the first half of the 1980s to 15.6 percent in the second half of the 1990s. Tariff reductions have been significant in most regions (figure 2.1), but have been largest in South Asia (where, however, they remain the highest of any region), Latin America, and East Asia. In many developing countries, the degree of tariff dispersion has also declined (table 2.1). Despite this progress, tariffs remain high in many countries, averaging more than 15 percent in three of the six geographical regions in 1996–98.

Latin American countries reduced tariffs substantially during the 1990s. Colombia, for example, slashed import tariffs by 65 percent in just one year in 1991, while Argentina and Nicaragua reduced them from an average of 110 percent to 15 percent in one bold move in 1992 (Dornbusch and Edwards 1995). India

reduced its average tariff from 100 percent in 1986 to around 33 percent in 1998, and Bangladesh's average tariff fell from 82 percent to 24 percent during the same period.

Tariffs in Africa have also been reduced, though more moderately: the average unweighted tariff remains at almost 20 percent. Some countries have embarked on rapid reforms, however. Tariffs fell in Kenya from 41 percent in 1980–85 to 13.5 percent in 1996–99 and in Guinea from 76.4 percent in 1978–80 to 10.8 percent in 1990–95. A few countries, such as Zimbabwe, increased their average tariffs (from 10 percent in 1980–85 to 22.7 percent in 1996–99), reflecting in part the conversion of an import surcharge into tariffs.[3] The Middle East and North Africa region has seen little reduction in average tariffs, although the signing of trade agreements with the European Union in recent years by several countries in the region should eventually pave the way for significant reductions.

Nontariff barriers (NTBs). Developing countries in all regions have substantially reduced the coverage of NTBs (such as licensing, prohibitions, quotas, and administered pricing) during the 1990s (table 2.2).[4] In many countries where NTBs remain more or less prevalent (for example, India and Korea), commitments have been made to liberalize them in the future (Michalopoulos 1999). NTB coverage has been reduced significantly in a number of Latin American countries, with the remaining NTBs mainly on agricultural products (Dornbusch and Edwards 1995). Most countries in South Asia have reduced NTBs significantly, though India still has restrictions on a relatively large number of imports.

Exchange rate regimes. The 1990s also saw a general move toward market-based foreign exchange regimes. In 1991, 66 countries had restrictions on payments for current account transactions, but by 1995 only 28 did (table 2.3). Many countries also undertook significant exchange rate reforms. The average black market premium for developing countries, one indicator of the restrictiveness of foreign exchange allocations as well as of macro-

Box 2.1   Openness and growth—evidence, old and new

A large number of cross-country empirical studies have documented a strong relationship between trade and growth.[2] Dollar (1992) finds that two separate measures of trade restrictions (an index of real exchange rate distortion and an index of real exchange rate variability) are negatively correlated with growth in developing countries. Sachs and Warner (1995) find that an openness index reflecting tariff and nontariff barriers, the black market premium, and the existence of commodity marketing boards has a high and robust negative coefficient in growth equations. Ben David (1993) finds that income levels in countries that joined the European Common Market have tended to converge toward the level of the richest partners. Similar studies have documented income convergence among states within the United States. Edwards (1997) finds a significant, positive relationship between openness and productivity growth, which is robust to several different measures of openness. In a recent study designed to identify measures of openness that cannot be said to be affected by economic growth, Frankel and Romer (1998) find that countries that are geographically closest to centers of demand have grown faster.

The positive relationship between openness and growth has also been supported by numerous case studies (Bhagwati 1978; Little, David, Scitovsky, and Scott 1970; and Papageorgiou, Choksi, and Michaely 1991), firm-level analyses (Bigsten and others 1998; Clerides, Lach, and Tybout forthcoming; and Kraay 1997), as well as a combination of economic theory and anecdotal evidence dating back at

least to Adam Smith. But the statistical relationship identified by cross-country studies is still occasionally challenged by researchers. For example, a recent analysis (Rodriguez and Rodrik 1999) raises several questions about the findings, and argues that the advocates of trade liberalization claim too much. In some cases the indicators of openness that researchers use as measures of trade barriers are highly correlated with other sources of poor economic performance, including macroeconomic policy, or they imperfectly reflect a country's trade policy regime. For example, most of the explanatory power of the Sachs and Warner index is derived from just two indicators—the black market premium and state monopoly over major exports. These two indicators are correlated with a wide range of macroeconomic policy and institutional factors other than trade openness, and thus yield an upward bias in the estimation of trade restriction effects. Rodriguez and Rodrik (1999) underline that tariff and nontariff barriers, two variables that directly measure trade openness, have little explanatory power when considered separately in the cross-country regression studies.

It is perhaps not surprising that the effects of trade reform are difficult to isolate statistically, since trade liberalization is rarely implemented as a stand-alone policy measure, nor is such a course recommended. It has long been accepted that trade liberalization needs companion policies to be successful, often including other market reforms, macroeconomic stabilization, exchange rate adjustment, and adequate safety nets. (See, for example, World Bank 1997b.)

economic imbalances, fell almost 70 percent between the 1980s and the 1990s.[5]

The average black market premium has remained low or fallen further in all regions. East Asian countries have had low black market premiums in recent years because they were early adopters of an outward-oriented development strategy. Latin America also achieved impressive gains in the late 1980s, as did South Asia in the first half of the 1990s. In Sub-Saharan Africa and in the Middle East

and North Africa, the considerable reductions in black market premiums in many countries are masked by two outliers (table 2.4).

Reforms by income group. The trend toward lowering tariffs and eliminating foreign exchange restrictions is evident in both low-income and middle-income countries. The average tariff rate for low-income countries fell from almost 45 percent in the early 1980s to 20 percent in the late 1990s, only slightly above the average rate for middle-income

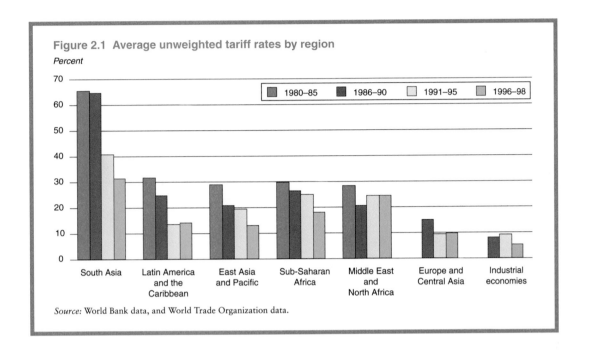

Figure 2.1 Average unweighted tariff rates by region

Percent

Legend: 1980–85, 1986–90, 1991–95, 1996–98

X-axis regions: South Asia, Latin America and the Caribbean, East Asia and Pacific, Sub-Saharan Africa, Middle East and North Africa, Europe and Central Asia, Industrial economies

Source: World Bank data, and World Trade Organization data.

Table 2.1 Standard deviation of tariff rates

	1990–94	1995–98
South Asia		
Bangladesh	114.0	14.6
India	39.4	12.7
Sri Lanka	18.1	15.4
Sub-Saharan Africa		
South Africa	11.3	7.2
Malawi	15.5	11.6
Zimbabwe	6.4	17.8
East Asia and Pacific		
Philippines	28.2	10.2
Thailand	25.0	8.9
Indonesia	16.1	16.6
China	29.9	13.0
Latin America and the Caribbean		
Argentina	5.0	6.9
Brazil	17.3	7.3
Colombia	8.3	6.2
Mexico	4.4	13.5
Middle East and North Africa		
Egypt, Arab Rep. of	425.8	28.9
Tunisia	37.4	11.7
Turkey	35.7	5.7

Notes: Country observations are for one year in the time period noted above.
Source: World Bank, *World Development Indicators* 1998; 2000; WTO, *Trade Policy Reviews.*

countries (figure 2.2). By the late 1990s, most of the low-income countries had eliminated current account restrictions and reduced the black market premium to negligible levels.

Trends in trade and economic growth

The lowering of trade barriers and widespread adoption of market-based foreign exchange regimes during the 1990s was ac-

Table 2.2 Frequency of total core nontariff measures for developing countries, 1989–98

Region	1989–94	1995–98
East Asia and Pacific (7)	30.1	16.3
Latin America and the Caribbean (13)	18.3	8.0
Middle East and North Africa (4)	43.8	16.6
South Asia (4)	57.0	58.3
Sub-Saharan Africa (12)	26.0	10.4

Notes: Average number of commodities subject to nontariff measures as a percentage of total. Figures in parentheses are the number of countries in each region for which data are available.
Source: Michalopoulos 1999.

Table 2.3 Countries imposing restrictions on payments for current account transactions
(percent)

Region	1980	1991	1995
East Asia and Pacific (9)	33	33	22
South Asia (5)	100	100	40
Middle East and North America (6)	67	67	33
Sub-Saharan Africa (23)	85	83	39
Latin America and the Caribbean (30)	44	60	17
Europe and Central Asia (17)	. . .	94	47
Industrialized economies (12)	17	8	0
Total (102)	55	65	27

Notes: Figures in parentheses are the number of countries in each regional grouping.
Source: IMF, *Exchange Arrangements and Exchange Restrictions,* 1981, 1992, 1996.

Table 2.4 Average black market premium
(percent)

Region	1980–89	1990–93	1994–97
Total[a]	82.0	78.2	20.3
East Asia and Pacific	3.6	3.6	3.2
Middle East and North Africa	165.6	351.6	46.5
Excluding outliers[b]	7.1	8.8	1.4
Latin America and the Caribbean	48.7	13.1	4.4
South Asia	40.8	45.1	10.1
Sub-Saharan Africa	116.5	28.6	32.2
Excluding Nigeria	112.1	25.8	9.6

a. Sample of 41 developing countries.
b. Algeria and the Islamic Republic of Iran.
Source: World Bank data.

companied by an acceleration of trade in developing countries. The improvement in the international environment in the 1990s, marked by lower interest rates and inflation but higher world trade growth and non-oil commodity prices than in the 1980s, also contributed to the acceleration of exports (table 2.5). Moreover, developing countries faced a more stable global economy in the 1990s, as the volatility of these key indicators declined. The growth of developing-country exports almost doubled in real terms, to 6.2 percent a year in the 1990s, compared to 3.7 percent a year in the 1980s.[6] Per capita income also accelerated, though more modestly, from no growth in real terms in the 1980s to 0.7 percent in the 1990s.

The observation that developing countries as a group continued to exhibit relatively slow growth in per capita income in the 1990s—about one-third the rate of advance in the rich countries, despite large-scale liberalization and

export expansion—has sometimes been cited as evidence that increased integration with the global economy has not helped developing countries, particularly the poorest. In fact, output declines in countries that were hit by severe political shocks, including the breakup of the Soviet Union and various external or internal conflicts, had a large effect on the developing-country aggregates, and the rise of incomes in countries that did not suffer these calamities was considerable (table 2.6). Excluding the transition economies and countries involved in conflict, per capita GDP growth rates in developing countries averaged 1.5 percent per year during the 1990s, versus 0.4 percent in the 1980s, and export growth rates averaged 6.4 percent in the 1990s, compared with 4.3 percent in the 1980s. Furthermore, while developing countries became more open during the 1990s, volatility declined in most countries (see box 2.2).

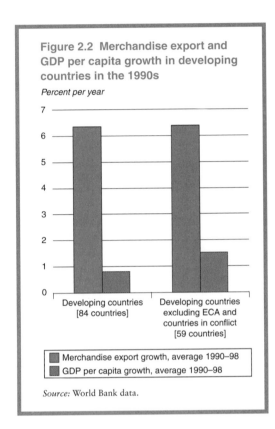

Figure 2.2 Merchandise export and GDP per capita growth in developing countries in the 1990s

Percent per year

Source: World Bank data.

Table 2.5 The international environment

	1980–89	1990–98
U.S. real LIBOR	4.8	2.4
G-7 CPI (percent per year)	5.3	2.7
G-7 real GDP growth (percent per year)	2.8	2.1
World export growth (percent per year)	4.4	6.4
Oil price (index, 1987 = 100)	138.4	113.1
Non-oil commodities price (index, 1987=100)	115.6	123.0

Note: The G-7 countries are Canada, France, Germany, Italy, Japan, the United Kingdom, and the United States.
Source: World Bank data.

in tariffs during the 1990s also saw the most rapid increases in GDP and exports.[7] GDP and export growth rates more than doubled in Latin America in the late 1980s and 1990s (table 2.7), a period that followed large advances in trade liberalization as well as the adoption of important macroeconomic reforms and widespread privatization. South Asia and East Asia also saw very sharp increases in export growth rates and continued high GDP growth. By contrast, countries in Sub-Saharan Africa and in the Middle East and North Africa made relatively less progress in reducing tariffs, and both GDP and export growth was considerably slower than in the other regions.

Factors affecting developing country exports. The acceleration of exports of developing countries in the 1990s reflected higher growth of world trade (itself a reflection in part of the increased integration of developing

With the exception of the countries in transition and conflict, there is little evidence that developing regions that engaged in rapid trade liberalization and companion reforms saw a deterioration in performance. In fact, developing regions that saw the largest reductions

Table 2.6 GDP and merchandise export growth rates

(percent per year, in constant prices; group simple average)[a]

	GDP per capita		Merchandise exports[b]		Number of countries
	1980–89	1990–98	1980–89	1990–98	
World	0.6	1.2	4.1	6.4	133
Industrial countries	2.1	2.2	5.6	6.8	30
Countries that lack consistent data	–0.4	1.8	3.6	6.4	20
Developing countries (*excluding those that lack consistent data*)	0.3	0.7	3.7	6.2	83
Europe and Central Asia[c]	2.6	–1.1	0.4	7.6	6
Countries in conflict	–1.1	–1.3	3.0	5.0	18
Developing countries excluding ECA and countries in conflict	0.4	1.5	4.3	6.4	59

a. All growth rates are estimated using least squares for the sample periods.
b. Merchandise exports are deflated by constant 1987 U.S. dollar export prices.
c. To give comparable data over 1980s and 1990s, the republics of the former Soviet Union are treated as one country.
Source: World Bank data.

Box 2.2   Trends in volatility

The increase in openness and acceleration of growth during the 1990s were associated with a small decline, and not an increase, in the volatility of output and export growth in developing countries (see table). Output volatility increased significantly in countries affected by conflict and in Europe and Central Asia (ECA), but fell for other developing countries as a group and in three of the five geographic regions. Although open economies are more vulnerable to external shocks, especially when they are reliant on short-term capital flows (Easterly, Islam, and Stiglitz 2000), lower volatility in the 1990s may have resulted from less severe global economic shocks than in the 1980s. The 1990s were, of course, not tranquil for developing countries: they saw the breakup of the Soviet Union, the Gulf War followed by a global recession, the Tequila crisis, and

the global financial crisis of 1998–99. But the decade of the 1980s was characterized by much larger oil shocks that contributed to two global recessions and dramatically affected economic volatility of oil exporters. Partly reflecting the oil shocks, the industrial countries saw high inflation and international interest rates rose to high levels. The buildup of oil-related debts in the 1970s contributed to a massive debt crisis in developing countries that lasted most of the decade.

Policies, as well as luck, may have contributed to the modest reduction in volatility in the 1990s, especially lower inflation in both industrial and developing countries reflecting sounder macroeconomic policies. Increased integration with world markets may also have contributed to reduced volatility in countries where shocks originated domestically.

Volatility of growth rates

	GDP per capita (1987 US$)[a]		Merchandise exports (1987 US$)[a]		Merchandise exports (import prices deflator)[b]	
	1980s	1990s	1980s	1990s	1980s	1990s
All countries	4.5	4.2	15.2	14.1	17.9	15.2
Industrial	2.9	3.4	7.3	8.1	8.5	8.9
Developing	5.0	4.4	17.6	16.0	20.8	17.1
Conflicts	6.3	7.3	21.3	28.9	25.6	30.0
Europe and Central Asia	4.1	7.0	10.6	17.7	12.2	17.5
Other countries	6.4	4.1	24.8	19.6	28.0	18.1
Developing excluding ECA and countries in conflict	4.8	3.6	17.3	13.2	20.3	14.4
Sample	4.3	3.5	15.1	11.2	18.0	13.2
East Asia	3.8	4.6	10.4	10.8	12.8	9.1
Middle East and North Africa	5.0	3.6	15.4	7.7	21.7	14.0
Latin America and the Caribbean	4.3	2.7	12.6	13.0	15.6	14.6
South Asia	2.1	2.6	11.8	8.2	14.0	10.0
Sub-Saharan Africa	4.6	3.7	18.4	12.3	20.2	14.0

a. Standard deviation of growth rates expressed as a percentage in constant U. S. dollars.
b. Standard deviation of growth rates of merchandise exports, deflated by import prices and expressed as a percentage.
Source: World Bank data.

countries), as well as greater diversification of their export base and, for some developing regions, improved market share in traditional markets (table 2.8).[8] While South Asia, East Asia, and Latin America saw both increases in market share in traditional markets and some

diversification, countries in the Middle East and North Africa and Sub-Saharan Africa saw some diversification, but a large decline in market share in traditional markets.

Sub-Saharan Africa stands out because the region experienced much slower growth of world

Table 2.7 GDP, services, and merchandise export growth rates

(percent per year, in constant prices; group simple average)

| | GDP[a] | | Exports | | | | Purchasing power of GNFS exports[c] | | Number of countries |
| | | | Merchandise[a] | | Goods and services[a] | | | | |
	1980–89	1990–98	1980–89	1990–98	1980–89	1990–98	1980–89	1990–98	
Total[b]	3.1	3.8	4.3	6.4	4.5	6.3	2.2	6.2	59
East Asia and Pacific	5.4	6.3	5.7	14.5	5.9	14.3	4.1	13.7	7
Middle East and North Africa	3.6	3.4	5.3	6.0	5.5	5.0	0.2	3.3	9
Latin America and the Caribbean	1.8	3.6	3.9	9.1	4.8	8.1	1.6	8.8	14
South Asia	4.9	5.2	5.8	9.3	5.0	10.3	5.3	10.7	5
Sub-Saharan Africa	2.5	2.9	3.5	2.0	3.4	2.6	2.0	2.7	24

a. All growth rates are simple arithmetic averages of individual rates computed using least squares. Nonfactor services are deflated by constant 1987 GDP deflator; other series are expressed in constant U.S. dollars.
b. Refers to a sample of 59 developing countries.
c. Denotes average annual growth rate of GNFS export deflated by merchandise import prices.
Source: World Bank data.

Table 2.8 Decomposition of merchandise export growth for the sample countries

(percent per year, current U.S. dollars)

| | 1980/81–1989/90 | | | | 1989/90–1997/98 | | | |
	Total Exports	World Trade Growth	Market Share	Diversification	Total Exports	World Trade Growth	Market Share	Diversification
Total	3.9	4.1	–1.0	0.8	5.9	5.4	0.0	0.6
East Asia and Pacific	8.5	5.2	2.1	0.9	11.9	6.5	4.9	0.1
Middle East and North Africa	2.4	3.1	–1.3	0.6	3.0	6.2	–3.5	0.5
Latin America and the Caribbean	3.9	5.4	–2.2	0.8	8.3	6.7	0.6	0.9
South Asia	8.9	5.9	1.5	1.5	10.0	6.4	2.8	0.6
Sub-Saharan Africa	1.0	2.9	–1.6	0.8	3.0	3.8	–1.2	0.6

Source: COMTRADE database, and authors' calculations.

trade in its export basket in both decades than other developing regions. Reflecting the continued decline in primary commodity prices and low-income elasticities of demand, world trade growth rates during the 1990s were less than 2 percent annually for exports of some of the poorest African countries, including Benin, Chad, Mali, and Mauritania, among others.

Trends in the poorest developing countries. Excluding China and India, which saw

significant increases in per capita incomes in the 1990s, per capita income declined in the 1990s in the poorest developing countries as a group (figure 2.3). Since 1980, 10 of the 32 low-income countries with consistent data have been involved in foreign or civil wars (see box 2.3). In 1999, one African in five lived in a country severely disrupted by conflict (World Bank 2000a). Excluding countries affected by conflict, per capita GDP growth rates in small

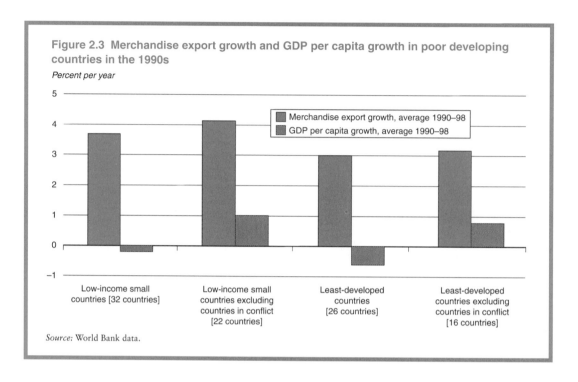

Figure 2.3 Merchandise export growth and GDP per capita growth in poor developing countries in the 1990s

Percent per year

Legend:
- Merchandise export growth, average 1990–98
- GDP per capita growth, average 1990–98

Categories:
- Low-income small countries [32 countries]
- Low-income small countries excluding countries in conflict [22 countries]
- Least-developed countries [26 countries]
- Least-developed countries excluding countries in conflict [16 countries]

Source: World Bank data.

low-income countries averaged 1 percent per year during the 1990s, well below the 1.5 percent rate of growth achieved by middle-income countries (table 2.9).

Merchandise export volume growth rates in the 22 small, low-income countries (exclud-

ing countries affected by conflict) averaged only 4.1 percent per year during the 1990s, up from 2.9 percent in the 1980s but still well below performance in the middle-income countries. More than two-thirds of these small low-income countries (16 of 22) are in Sub-Saharan

Box 2.3   Economic factors contributing to conflict

There is a large body of literature documenting the negative impact of wars and rebellions on a country's growth performance, and there is also evidence that economic factors also contribute to conflict. Using a panel data set for 161 countries, Collier and Hoeffler (1999) find that, among other factors, the risk of civil war is significantly and negatively related to growth in per capita income. A reliance on exports of primary commodities is positively related to civil conflict. For a country with a primary commodity export share of around 0.26, the risk of a civil war is around 23 percent (compared with 0.5 percent for countries with no natural resource exports), in part because the capture of resources either

motivated or made possible several rebellions. Diamonds in Angola and Sierra Leone and drugs in Colombia are some obvious examples.

Countries that are commodity-dependent are subject to larger external shocks. Rodrik (1998) argues that while external shocks can lead to distributional conflicts, societies that are cohesive and have strong institutions can adjust more easily to such shocks and avoid conflict. He compares Brazil, Korea, and Turkey, all of which suffered sharp trade declines during the 1970s. Korea was the hardest hit, as it was more open than either of the other two, but it recovered much faster. Adjustment was delayed in both Turkey and Brazil, and they witnessed considerable turmoil.

Table 2.9 Growth rates by income level for the sample countries
(percent per year)

	GDP		Merchandise exports		GDP per capita		Number of countries
	1980s	1990s	1980s	1990s	1980s	1990s	
Total	3.1	3.8	4.3	6.4	0.4	1.5	59
Low income (large countries)	7.9	8.4	6.7	14.1	6.1	6.9	2
Low income (small countries)	2.7	3.6	2.9	4.1	–0.1	1.0	22
Least developed	2.2	3.5	2.9	3.2	–0.6	0.8	16
Middle income	3.0	3.6	5.1	7.4	0.5	1.5	35

Note: The sample (59 developing countries) excludes countries in conflict, transition economies, and those with limited data.
Source: World Bank.

Africa. An important factor accounting for the slow growth of the poor countries' exports was slow growth of world trade in their traditional export baskets. Several of the poorest developing countries lost market share in traditional exports and were unable to diversify rapidly enough into new products.

Summarizing, developing countries not in conflict and not in transition saw significant acceleration in incomes and exports in the 1990s, following adoption of trade and companion reforms. The poorest small countries were among those most affected by conflicts and political shocks. The poorest small countries that avoided these calamities performed better, but still not as well as the middle-income countries, on average. Thus, despite significant progress, it appears that policy regimes in many of the poorest countries are still inadequate to improve or even maintain export competitiveness in traditional markets or to encourage rapid diversification. The next two sections will discuss the key trade-related policy impediments to rapid integration of the poorest countries in the world economy, including trade barriers to their exports in industrial countries.

Weaknesses in domestic trade-related policies

Domestic policies that directly restrict exports or deter investment in the export sector remain important in most of the poorest developing countries (Yeats and others 1997). Policies that tend to discourage investment in the export sector include overvalued real exchange rates, inconsistent or erratic macroeconomic policies, a high share of government spending in aggregate expenditure, excessive reliance on tariff revenues and on taxes on agriculture, and a variety of direct public interventions in product and factor markets, especially price controls and requirements that bank credit be allocated to the public sector (World Bank 1989, 1994, 2000a). Weak infrastructure and inadequate provision of ancillary services to exports also severely constrain export performance in many countries. As discussed in previous sections, some of the most severe policy distortions present in developing countries in the 1980s are being alleviated: average inflation and fiscal deficits have declined significantly (Easterly 2000); real exchange rates have been adjusted in many cases; tariffs and quotas have been cut; and export taxes and restrictions on agriculture have been reduced or eliminated in many countries.

This section examines three aspects of trade-related domestic policies that remain important impediments to integration of many of the poorest developing countries into the global economy: overvalued and unstable real exchange rates, high cost of imported inputs for exporters, and the higher costs of transportation and other trade-supporting infrastructure.

Exchange rate management. A competitive and stable real exchange rate ensures that producing tradable goods is profitable, and to underpin investor confidence in the export sector. In many of the poorest countries, protracted episodes of real exchange rate overvaluation have impaired the competitive position of local firms. At different times, they have contributed to unsustainable trade deficits, and prompted increased tariffs, quantitative restrictions, and foreign exchange controls in futile attempts to contain these deficits. Episodes of overvaluation have also resulted in foreign exchange crises, economic instability, and the deterioration of growth over the long run. At the same time, unsustainable macroeconomic policies have also contributed to the overvaluation of real exchange rates (Bhagwati 1978; Krueger 1978; Papageorgiou, Choksi, and Michaely 1991; and Rodrik 1996).

The effects of real exchange rate overvaluation have been studied extensively. Dollar (1992) shows that Africa and Latin America had relatively overvalued exchange rates and large real exchange volatility, while East Asia had relatively undervalued exchange rates lower real exchange rate volatility, and more rapid growth. Using a wide variety of measurements and techniques, econometric studies have fairly uniformly found that overvaluation and associated real exchange rate volatility are negatively correlated with both export and GDP growth.[9]

The factors that lie behind protracted episodes of real exchange rate overvaluation, despite awareness of their adverse implications for growth, are varied. They include use of the exchange rate as a nominal anchor for the stabilization program and difficulties in exiting from the peg; rigid exchange rate regimes that fail to accommodate secular deterioration in the terms of trade and adjust to widening productivity differentials; disproportionate influence of urban elites who are consumers of imported consumer goods; concerns about the effect on the urban poor dependent on imported food staples or energy; and aversion to incur the immediate fiscal costs revaluating foreign currency liabilities.

Perhaps because of increased openness, in recent years policymakers appear to have become more aware of the need to maintain competitive and stable real exchange rates. The average exchange rate of developing coun-

tries depreciated during the 1990s (Easterly 2000), and many countries adopted more flexible nominal exchange rate arrangements.[10] In some cases, for example the CFA countries (see box 2.4), these efforts resulted in a sharp turnaround in economic performance.

Several of the poorest countries failed to achieve stable and competitive real exchange rates during the 1990s. Overall, the average volatility of real exchange rates in the small, low-income countries increased. High exchange rate volatility was associated with weak economic performance. Among the countries in our sample (excluding countries affected by conflict), the poor countries that exhibited low exchange rate volatility saw exports rise at over 6 percent a year and per capita incomes rise at nearly 2 percent a year, much faster than countries with high exchange rate volatility (figure 2.4).

As countries became more open to international trade, the adverse effects of real exchange rate volatility on stability and growth may have become even more severe. In some cases, trade liberalization combined with sharp real exchange appreciation severely impaired the profitability of domestic firms.[11] Exchange rate overvaluation and high volatility also has a negative effect on investor confidence and can delay the supply response to liberalization.[12] Figure 2.5 shows six countries in Africa that moved to flexible exchange rates and liberalized their trade regimes during the early 1990s. These countries subsequently experienced appreciation and high volatility of the real exchange rates and low rates of growth. Per capita income growth in these six countries averaged only 0.5 percent a year in the 1990s, and their export effort (changes in market share and diversification) fell by 2.3 percent a year.

The causes of high real exchange rate volatility have been widely explored. They include unstable or inconsistent macroeconomic policies, which result in inflationary pressures and high fiscal and current account deficits. Many countries have tried to maintain stable nominal exchange rates, despite the formal

Box 2.4   Exchange rate overvaluation in the CFA countries

The CFA countries provide one of the most striking examples of the impact of exchange rate overvaluation on growth and the gains from improved exchange rate policies. The currencies of these countries are tied to the French franc, and at various times the appreciation of the franc, deterioration in the terms of trade, and higher inflation in CFA countries contributed to a highly appreciated currency that tended to depress export and GDP growth, the latter to less than 1 percent per year for 1986 to 1993 (see box table). The CFA franc was devalued in 1994, and GDP growth accelerated to 5 percent per year from 1994 to 1998. Export growth also accelerated, reflecting improved market share in traditional products and greater diversification, as well as acceleration of world trade in the CFA countries' export products: export effort, which measures the annual rate of increase in exports due to rising market shares and diversification, rose from –4.8 percent per year in 1986–93 to 7.8 percent per year in 1994–98.

Exchange rates and CFA countries

	1986–93	1994–98
Average GDP growth	0.7	4.7
Average REER index	99.4	63.0
Export effort[a]	–4.8	7.8

Note: The countries included are Burkina Faso, Cameroon, Central African Republic, Chad, Côte d'Ivoire, Gabon, Mali, Niger, Senegal, and Togo.
a. The merchandise export growth rate achieved through changes in market share and export diversification.
Source: IMF, *International Financial Statistics.*

adoption of more flexible exchange rate regimes during the 1990s (Calvo and Reinhart 2000).[13] However, attempts to maintain nominal exchange rate stability in the face of high and variable inflation rates or various domestic or foreign shocks imply that the real exchange rate will be volatile. For example, 17 of the 26 countries that exhibited high real exchange rate volatility were also rated by the World Bank as exhibiting relatively unstable macroeconomic policies.[14] Among the 22 low-income countries in our sample, only two managed to achieve both macroeconomic stability and low real exchange rate volatility.

In addition, terms-of-trade shocks are an important factor contributing to high real exchange rate volatility in commodity-dependent countries. Hausman and others (1999) cite the volatility of capital flows as a driving force behind the volatility of exchange rates in many middle-income countries, particularly in conjunction with large debts denominated in foreign currency.

Thus, the record of the 1990s underlines the difficulties that poor countries face in maintaining a stable and competitive real exchange rate, reflecting their thin foreign exchange markets, their vulnerability to weather-related shocks, and their dependence on primary commodity exports that are subject to sharp changes in price.[15]

Exchange rate policies are hampered by the lack of clear signposts as to the exchange rate regime that minimizes real exchange rate volatility. The choice of exchange rate regime will depend on many factors, including the currency composition of public and private external debt and domestic financial assets, the track record and credibility of the monetary authorities, and the nature of external and internal shocks.[16]

Free trade status for exporters. High tariffs coupled with inefficiencies in customs and tax administration have increased the costs of exporting from many developing countries. Access to inputs at world prices is critical to

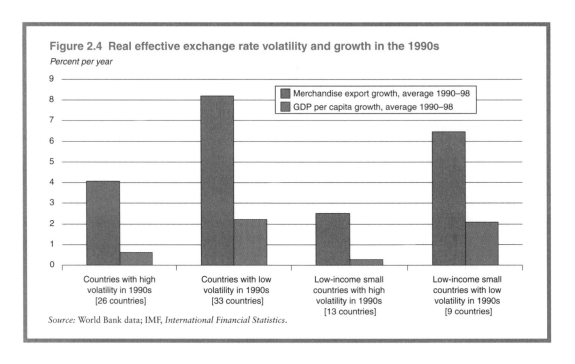

Figure 2.4 Real effective exchange rate volatility and growth in the 1990s

Percent per year

Legend:
- Merchandise export growth, average 1990–98
- GDP per capita growth, average 1990–98

Categories:
- Countries with high volatility in 1990s [26 countries]
- Countries with low volatility in 1990s [33 countries]
- Low-income small countries with high volatility in 1990s [13 countries]
- Low-income small countries with low volatility in 1990s [9 countries]

Source: World Bank data; IMF, *International Financial Statistics.*

export competitiveness, so that high tariffs on intermediate and capital goods can reduce exports, particularly of processed goods that require substantial intermediate inputs. At the same time, many developing countries depend on tariffs for an important share of government revenues. Thus governments often face a difficult tradeoff between the desire to encourage export production through low tariffs on imported inputs and the need to generate sufficient revenues.

Successful exporters such as the Asian newly industrializing countries, in the early stages of their export drive, have enabled export firms to obtain their inputs at world market prices through reimbursing tariff duties on inputs (duty drawback systems), providing exemptions on duties for exporters (duty exemption systems), and setting up export processing zones where intermediate inputs can enter the country free of duty.[17] These systems have been effective in reducing or eliminating tariffs on exporters' inputs, while maintaining a tariff structure that meets the revenue needs of the government. These systems, however, require considerable administrative resources to

ensure that reimbursement or exemption is granted quickly and fairly.

By contrast, the poorest developing countries have faced severe difficulties in ensuring duty-free access to inputs by exporters, for two reasons. First, a substantial share of government revenues in many of these countries is generated from taxes on international trade. To reduce distortions affecting domestic production and to simplify administration, tariff reform in many poor countries involves increasing low tariffs while reducing peak tariffs (Falvey and Kim 2000; Harberger 1988). As a result, many of the poor countries have significant tariffs on intermediate and capital goods (table 2.10). Although the average tariff rates for this sample of 15 African countries are not high compared with those of many other developing countries (figure 2.1), the duties on capital and intermediate goods do represent a considerable tax on export production.[18] These duties are essentially designed to collect revenues, rather than to protect domestic production.[19]

Second, most of the poorer countries lack the administrative resources required to establish effective drawback/exemption schemes.

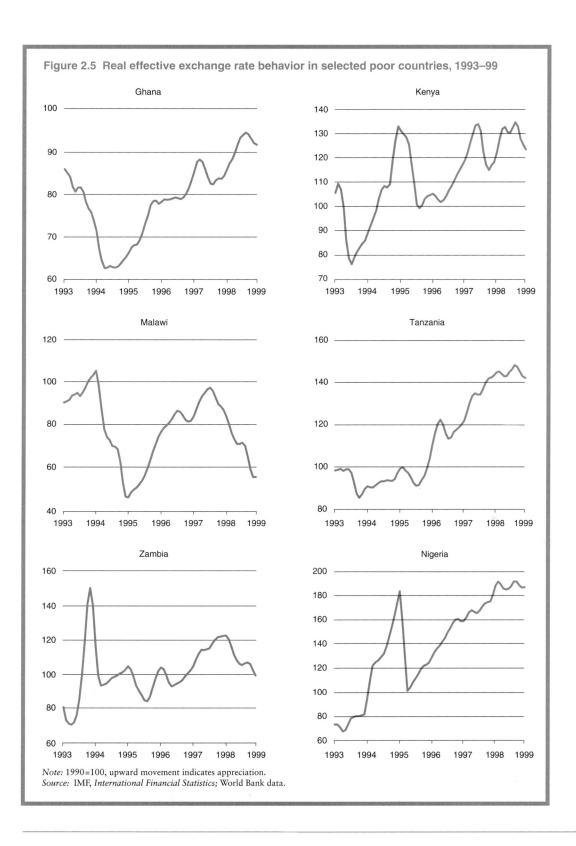

Figure 2.5 Real effective exchange rate behavior in selected poor countries, 1993–99

Note: 1990=100, upward movement indicates appreciation.
Source: IMF, *International Financial Statistics;* World Bank data.

Table 2.10 Tariffs in selected African countries

	Average nominal tariff	Trade weighted average	Collection Rate	Share of tariff revenues
All goods	19.8	16.2	10.3	100.0
Capital goods	13.7	13.2	7.8	12.9
Intermediate goods	16.9	14.2	8.1	42.4
Consumer goods	23.6	15.3	10.9	22.4

Note: Textiles, energy, and passenger cars are not included in capital, intermediate, and consumer goods. Data are for 1996 for Benin, Burkina Faso, Cameroon, Cape Verde, Côte d'Ivoire, Ghana, Malawi, Mauritius, Senegal, South African Customs Union, Tanzania, Uganda, Zambia, and Zimbabwe; data for Mali are for 1997.
Source: World Bank data.

Attempts to establish such systems during the 1990s were generally not successful. The requirement of examining individual import transactions imposed a substantial administrative burden on exporters and the government. In many countries, the government failed to provide (or significantly delayed) promised reimbursements of duties paid on imported inputs.[20] Even exporters' value added taxes were not reimbursed consistently. Ongoing work on 15 reforming Sub-Saharan African countries shows that none had a working duty drawback system. Mauritius operated a successful export processing zone program, while Cape Verde and South Africa had low duties on intermediate goods. The 12 other countries imposed significant duties on inputs to export production without effective means of compensating exporters.

There is no easy solution for poor countries attempting to ensure duty-free access to inputs by exporters.[21] Further efforts are required to strengthen the administration of customs and to increase reliance on other sources of revenues such as income taxes. However, such efforts take time. In the short term, depending on the structure of export activity (for example, degree of processing) and the level of institutional development, governments need to decide whether drawback/exemption systems or free trade zones are feasible, or alternatively whether reductions in intermediate and capital goods tariffs are necessary to encourage export production. Since all but five of the countries in table 2.10 have total collection rates of less than 10 percent it is possible to move to a tariff structure that has zero or very low rates for capital and intermediate goods along with much lower rates for consumer goods (coupled with reduced exemptions).

Infrastructure for trade expansion. Weak infrastructure constrains economic growth in many of the poorest countries and has a severe impact on trade performance. A firm's ability to compete in the world economy depends in part on the cost and availability of supporting services, such as transport, communications, and finance. While some of the problems these countries face in providing adequate infrastructure and other services are to some extent the result of location, technological deficiencies, and a lack of capital, many of these problems result from restrictive regulatory policies that limit competition.[22]

Many of the least-developed countries have weak and expensive service suppliers. Amjadi, Reincke, and Yeats (1996) conclude that high transport costs in low-income African countries are a more important trade barrier than tariffs.[23] These high costs add to the cost of exporting, and (other things being equal) lower its profitability in many of these countries. Countries in Africa normally absorb all, or most, of the transport charges for penetrating external markets. Africa's net freight and insurance payments in 1990/91 were about $3.9 billion, approximately 15 percent of the total value of the region's exports. For developing countries as a whole similar payments averaged 5.8 percent, about one-third of Africa's ratio. Thus, in order to be competitive, an average producer in Africa has to be 10 percent more efficient than firms in other developing countries. For the 10 landlocked countries in Africa, average net freight and insurance payments in 1990 were 42 percent of their total exports, eight times the average for other developing countries.

Limão and Venables (1999) also find that higher transport costs and weak infrastructure explain a significant portion of Africa's poor trade performance. This is especially true for landlocked countries. Exporters from landlocked economies face final city destinations that are on average four times further from the sea than that of exporters from coastal economies. The median transport cost for landlocked countries is 58 percent higher than the median for coastal countries. Delays and coordination problems at the border, higher insurance costs due to uncertainty and delays, and direct charges made by transit countries also add to the transport costs of landlocked countries. Improving transport infrastructure in landlocked countries and their transit countries can dramatically reduce costs and increase trade flows. Improving a country's worldwide rank from the 75th percentile to the 50th percentile in the distribution of infrastructure quality would double the volume of trade.

Poor availability of communications and energy can also constrain exports. Unreliable service can be even more damaging to competitiveness than high costs. Production stoppages, missed delivery dates, and lack of reliable communications make it difficult to compete and become part of global production networks. Despite liberalization of the financial systems in many countries, access to credit is limited, interest rate spreads are high, and in many countries weakness in regulatory institutions have kept financial sector reforms from having their anticipated benefits.

Reforms are being undertaken in many developing countries to liberalize the policy regimes for these sectors. Foreign participation is being allowed to improve the level of technology and efficiency, and also to generate the financing for the required investments. The potential gains from these reforms and resulting investments are very large. For example, allowing exporters to charter their own vessels in Côte d'Ivoire halved the costs of shipping bananas to the United States, and reduced cocoa freight costs one-quarter (World Bank 2000a). Improving the operating efficiency of the Nacala rail line through Mozambique, with little new investment, would increase the GDP of Malawi by 3 percent. These efforts may have a significant role in improving export performance over the next decade (AfDB 1999). Donors also are engaged in the efforts to help the low-income countries to overcome the major institutional impediments that inhibit their integration into the world economy (see box 2.5).

Protection in industrial countries

Import restrictions and subsidies in industrial countries limit the growth of developing countries' exports by supporting less efficient production in industrial countries. Export subsidies to industrial country producers further limit the expansion of developing-country exports to third markets. Moreover, these policies make it difficult for developing countries to diversify into products for which world demand is high or increasing, and in line with their evolving competitive advantage.

Industrial-country import restrictions. Although the average tariffs in the Quad (Canada, European Union, Japan, and the United States) countries range from only 4.3 percent in Japan to 8.3 percent in Canada, their tariffs and trade barriers remain much higher on many products exported by developing countries (Finger and Laird 1987). The Uruguay Round contributed to a sharp decline in the use of nontariff barriers (NTBs) in the OECD. In the Quad, only 1.2 percent of tariff lines are subject to NTBs. However, most of the NTBs are found in agriculture (tariff quotas, for example)[25] and textiles and clothing (Multifiber Arrangement), where developing countries have a comparative advantage (Finger and Schuknecht 1999).

Products with high tariffs in Quad countries include (1) major agricultural staple food

Box 2.5 The integrated framework for least-developed countries

The least-developed countries (LDCs) are particularly disadvantaged by a lack of capacity to provide the minimal public and private trade facilitation services and infrastructure required to support international trade.[24] The Uruguay Round agreement included promises by industrial countries to provide technical assistance to help developing countries strengthen their trade services, but these promises were not binding, and the reality has been disappointing (Michalopoulos 1999; Wang and Winters 2000).

The Integrated Framework (IF) was established in 1996 to increase the effectiveness and efficiency of trade-related technical assistance to the LDCs, in part by strengthening coordination among participating agencies and ensuring that technical assistance is demand driven. Participating agencies are the World Trade Organization, the International Monetary Fund, the International Trade Center, the United Nations Development Programme, the United Nations Conference on Trade and Development, and the World Bank.

By the summer of 2000, 40 LDCs had completed the first step of the IF process (a needs assessment). The six international agencies responded, indicating areas in which they could assist. This process revealed little overlap in the activities of the agencies and substantial needs that required additional financing. Progress in organizing IF roundtables to mobilize donor resources proved difficult; by

August 2000 only five roundtables had taken place. In only one case (Uganda) did the roundtable lead to the commitment of new funds from donors.

An independent review of the IF, completed in June 2000, highlighted that recipients expected additional funding, while donors were hoping to increase the effectiveness of technical assistance through improved coordination among agencies. The report noted a lack of clear priorities, weak administration, and a lack of donor resources. The review recommended that trade needs be better integrated in national development strategies, that steps be taken to strengthen the secretariat and coordination functions, and that a trust fund be established for IF activities. Although the memberships and governing bodies of the core IF agencies broadly support the first four suggestions, to date there has been little concrete support for the trust fund proposal. Efforts are ongoing to mobilize the required resources.

The six agencies are committed to continue to deliver trade-related technical assistance to least-developed countries within their existing resource constraints, pursuant to their mandates and competence. The World Bank's activities in trade policy, trade facilitation, and export development are primarily undertaken at the country level and based on the country's development strategy. Consequently, the Bank's efforts in mainstreaming trade will be driven by the priorities identified by each country's government.

products, such as meat, sugar, milk, dairy products, and chocolate, where tariff rates frequently exceed 100 percent; (2) tobacco and some alcoholic beverages; (3) fruits and vegetables—including 180 percent for above-quota bananas in the European Union and 550 percent and 132 percent for shelled groundnuts in Japan and the United States, respectively; (4) food industry products, including fruit juices, canned meat, peanut butter, and sugar confectionery, with rates exceeding 30 percent in several markets; and (5) textiles, clothing, and footwear, where tariff rates are in the 15 to 30

percent range for a large number of products. These are sectors in which developing countries have a comparative advantage.

For example, in the United States only 311 of 5,000 tariff lines are above 15 percent.[26] Yet 15 percent of exports from least-developed countries to the United States face these tariffs (Hoekman, Ng, and Olarreaga 2000). Thus, there might be considerable potential for the least-developed countries to increase their exports if U.S. tariffs were reduced.

Some of the highest tariff rates in industrial countries are applied to products that are

Table 2.11 Developing-country exports to Quad countries facing tariffs of more than 50 percent

Average most favored nation tariff (%)	113
Range of tariffs (%)	50–343
Exports to Quad (billion US$)	5.0
Share of developing countries in total imports of Quad (%)	10
Exports to the world (billion US$)	26.6

Source: OECD, 2000b; UN COMTRADE; and staff calculations.

typically exported by developing countries. For example, almost $26 billion of exports from developing countries in 1999 to the world were products that would have faced tariffs above 50 percent in the Quad countries. Only about $5 billion of that sum was actually exported to the Quad countries. On the other hand, Quad countries imported about $50 billion of the same goods, most of it from other industrial countries.[27] This suggests some potential for developing countries to expand exports of these products to the Quad if the tariffs were lowered. Although $26 billion is only about 2 percent of total developing-country exports, individual developing countries (including among the least-developed countries in the above example) may be more affected.

The tariff rates in table 2.11 do not reflect the Generalized System of Preferences (GSP) and other preferential schemes operated by Quad countries. These schemes tend to reduce the tariff rates applicable to imports of these products from some developing countries. North-South preferential trade agreements such as NAFTA or the Euro-Mediterranean Agreements also provide duty-free entry for some developing countries.[28] However, in most cases where tariff peaks are present, the sensitivity of domestic industry to imports exclude various products from preferential schemes limit the amount that can be imported under the preferential rates, or restricts the number of countries that are eligible. For example, the United States has no GSP or least-developed country preference for products facing tariffs of more than 50 percent.[29] The EU limits pref-

erential margins and imposes country or sector quotas, or both (Michalopoulos 1999).

The potential for growing exports in the restricted categories is illustrated by those developing countries that have managed to accelerate their agricultural exports through free trade arrangements with industrial countries (see chapter 1 for a discussion of the benefits of North-South regional trade agreements). For example, since Mexico joined NAFTA in 1994, the value of its agricultural exports has increased by 15 percent per year—twice the rate of the previous five years. After joining the EU in 1986, Portugal's agricultural exports grew by 9.2 percent per year in nominal U.S. dollars, and Spain's exports grew by 10.9 percent. In the prior five years, both Portugal and Spain had seen declining export earnings from agriculture. These experiences suggest that further trade liberalization in agriculture is likely to have a major effect on developing countries' abilities to increase agricultural exports.

Developing-country trade barriers. Developing countries' exports are subject to much higher trade barriers in other developing countries than in industrial countries. The average tariff developing countries face in their exports of manufactures to other developing countries is 12.8 percent, more than three times the average tariff on their manufactured exports to industrial countries (table 2.12) (Hertel and Martin 1999). Tariffs in developing countries

Table 2.12 Average tariff rates by importing and exporting region
(percent)

	Importing region	
Exporting region	High-income countries	Developing countries
Manufactures		
High-income	0.8	10.9
Developing	3.4	12.8
World	1.5	11.5
Agriculture		
High-income	15.9	21.5
Developing	15.1	18.3
World	15.6	20.1

Source: Hertel and Martin 2000.

Table 2.13 Producer support estimates for OECD countries

	Percent		US$ billion	
	1986–88	1997–99	1986–88	1997–99
Lower-income OECD countries	37.5	28.7	28.8	39.4
Australia, New Zealand	9.5	4.5	1.8	1.4
Canada, United States	29.5	18.5	47.5	47.8
European Union	44.0	44.0	95.2	116.6
Other non-EU OECD countries	71.0	66.7	7.8	7.8
Japan	67.0	61.0	53.6	53.1
OECD	41.8	34.9	234.8	266.2

Source: OECD 2000a.

are somewhat higher in agricultural markets as well. These high tariffs are becoming all the more important to developing countries, as the share of South-South trade in their exports has risen from about 26 percent in 1980 to 40 percent in 1999.

Industrial-country agricultural subsidies. Agricultural subsidies in industrial countries limit the growth of developing countries' agricultural exports by supporting inefficient producers. Furthermore, surplus agricultural products have been exported at a loss, further reducing the opportunities for many developing-country producers in third markets. Estimates of agricultural producer support declined as a share of gross farm receipts between the mid-1980s and the mid-1990s. Over the past few years, however, when agricultural prices have declined, subsidies have actually increased.[30] By 1999 the average producer support estimate reached 40 percent, almost equal to the average of 1986–88 (table 2.13). Virtually all OECD countries, except New Zealand and Australia, have increased their support levels. The biggest increases in the rate of protection took place in lower-income OECD countries, but the largest subsidy in absolute terms was given by the EU. During 1997–99, the average annual value of subsidies was about 60 percent of total world trade in agriculture, and almost twice the value of agricultural exports from developing countries.[31]

The impact of trade restrictions on diversification and trade growth. The lowering of industrial country trade barriers has combined with improved efficiency in developing countries to spur rapid export growth. The more successful middle-income countries have achieved rapid progress by increasing exports of labor-intensive manufactures, in part replacing production in industrial countries. This deceleration or decline in industrial countries' share in labor-intensive manufactures has allowed developing countries to increase their exports at a much higher rate than the growth of world income.[32] By allowing the least-cost producers to capture a greater share of demand, the efficiency of global production has increased. Despite remaining quotas and other restrictions on many labor-intensive products (such as textiles), the shares of developing countries' manufacturing exports in world trade (figure 2.6) and in the consumption of the Quad countries have increased. But even in 1995 the shares were not high—ranging from 6.8 percent of consumption in Canada and the United States to only 3.4 percent in Japan.

Tariff escalation in industrial-country markets has restricted the market access of developing-country producers of finished goods, thus hampering industrialization.[33] The Uruguay Round has made some progress in reducing the degree of overall tariff escalation. Yet, in a number of sectors (such as food processing) that are of particular interest to developing countries, high levels of tariff escalation are still present (box 2.6). Many products are also protected by some form of quota. As some of these quotas are allocated on the basis of historical trade shares, new and more efficient countries cannot enter these markets.

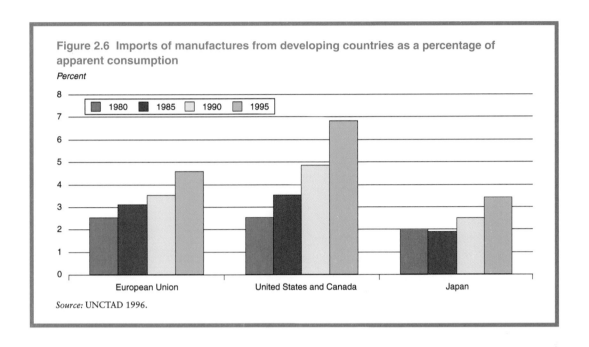

Figure 2.6 Imports of manufactures from developing countries as a percentage of apparent consumption

Percent

Legend: 1980 1985 1990 1995

Source: UNCTAD 1996.

Developing-country exporters of agricultural products have not achieved even the limited penetration of industrial-country markets that occurred in manufactures. The share of developing countries' agricultural exports in world trade have actually decreased (figure 2.7). The relatively low level of developing-country agricultural exports can be attributed in part to greater protection and subsidies in agriculture than in manufacturing. Higher protection allows only the most efficient agricultural producers in developing countries to enter industrial country markets and relatively more inefficient producers in industrial countries to maintain their market share. The success of many developing countries in products that face lower protection and subsidies, such as cut flowers from Africa, and more stable trade shares in fruits and vegetables also suggest that if protection in agriculture is lowered, many of the poorest countries could expand their exports.[34]

Implications for the poorest countries. While external constraints are not the primary reason for slow export growth and declining terms of trade of the poorest countries,[35] nevertheless, industrial-country trade restrictions and subsidies are having an adverse impact on

growth and poverty reduction. Many of the poorest countries are still primarily agricultural exporters, 40 to 60 percent of their population (and the majority of the poor—World Bank 2000c) lives in rural areas, and expansion of agricultural exports is one of their few avenues to accelerating growth (at least in the medium term), given their level of technology and human capital base. Many of the poorest countries made progress during the 1990s in removing domestic policy constraints on agricultural exports; however, policy reforms and investments in rural areas, which are necessary for poverty alleviation, are unlikely to yield significant improvements unless the demand for many of these products can be expanded through exports to world markets.

Numerical estimates of gains from reduced agricultural protection vary considerably, but reducing protection could have a particularly important impact on the poorest countries. Ianchovichina, Mattoo, and Olarreaga (2000) show that if all the Quad countries gave free trade access to the low-income African countries, their net exports would increase about 6 percent. The negative impact of this expansion on other developing

Box 2.6 Food processing

Food manufacturing products are subject to high tariff levels and a high degree of escalation. In the European Union and Japan, fully processed manufacturing food products face tariffs almost twice as high as tariffs on products in the first stage of processing. In Canada, tariffs on fully processed food products are 13 times higher than for products in the first stage of processing. High nominal tariffs on goods with high degrees of processing imply even higher rates of effective protection (because the tariff rate is a relatively large percentage of value added).

Partly because of these trade restrictions, the penetration of developing-country food exports has been limited, is much lower than average manufacturing, and has been declining in some markets.

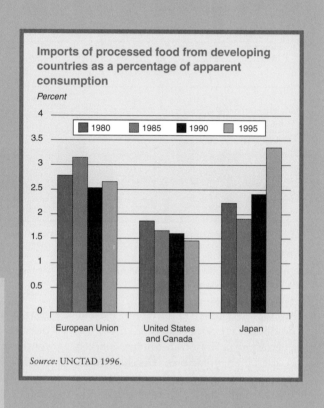

Imports of processed food from developing countries as a percentage of apparent consumption

Source: UNCTAD 1996.

Tariff escalation in food manufacturing
(percent)

	Canada	EU	Japan
First stage	3	15	35
Semiprocessed	8	18	36
Fully processed	42	24	65

Source: WTO (several years), *Trade Policy Review—Quad Countries.*

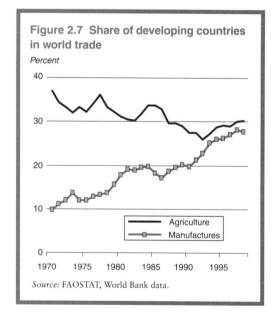

Figure 2.7 Share of developing countries in world trade

Source: FAOSTAT, World Bank data.

countries and on industrial countries would be negligible, because the absolute size of the increase is very small in comparison to the world trade.[36] Almost all the gains come from the expansion of agricultural trade. Hertel, Hoekman, and Martin (2000) report that a 40 percent reduction in industrial countries' agricultural tariffs and export subsidies by 2005 (a less radical assumption than in the paper cited above) would increase income in most developing regions by less than 1 percent.

However, one point needs to be underlined when discussing the trade barriers facing the exports of the poorest counties. Most of these countries have weak export-supporting infrastructure and skills that make it difficult to switch from domestic markets to exporting, and vice versa, in response to changes in relative prices, or to diversify out of traditional commodities facing artificially constrained markets. These weaknesses are reflected in little export-market diversification, imperfect capital markets that do not provide adequate and timely credit, low capitalization of many enterprises, small numbers of firms, and a very difficult environment for transactions. The fact that many of these countries have a history of policy reversals and mismanagement implies that the credibility that must underpin investment is lacking. Thus they are in a much weaker position than some of the more successful countries to overcome industrial countries' barriers to their traditional exports through diversification.

Notes

1. For example, import-weighted calculations of average tariffs may understate the importance of very high rates that block all imports, while the number of QRs may not accurately reflect their impact on trade. Moreover, data availability for these series is uneven both over time and across countries. Nevertheless, they are preferable indicators of trade policy than many used in the literature (see Edwards 1997). Some of them (such as share of trade to GDP, or growth of exports) are endogenous variables that depend on location, country size, and other policies; some rank trade regimes as perceived by users (the Heritage index), while others measure the degree of trade distortions only at one point in time (the Sachs-Warner index). Most of these measures have even more limited country and time period coverage.

2. See Barro and Sala-i Martin 1995 for a review of the econometric literature. Sensitivity of results to both variables and specifications are highlighted by Levine and Renelt 1992 and Sala-i Martin 1997a, 1997b.

3. One concern is that in many developing countries tariff bindings have been applied to only a small percentage of tariff lines, and wherever applied, these ceilings in general have been higher than the actual applied tariffs. In a sample of 42 countries, the bound ceilings were 49 percent, while the average applied rate was only 18 percent. The large gap between tariff bindings and actual levels may make the government susceptible to protectionist pressures and creates uncertainty about the future direction of reforms.

4. These averages need to be used with caution, as data are available for only a few countries in each region and may not exist for both the time periods under consideration.

5. The black market premium is used here to measure the administrative allocation of foreign exchange for trade purposes. However, a large black market premium may also reflect the degree of overvaluation as well as capital account restrictions.

6. This chapter uses simple averages, which give equal weight to individual countries regardless of size. These figures differ from the weighted average growth rates reported in chapter 1 and annex 1, which give greater weight to bigger countries. China and India in Asia, and South Africa and Nigeria in Africa, dominate the regional averages. Weighted averages are appropriate for measuring the total regional increase in GDP or exports, while simple averages are appropriate in analyzing the impact of policy on growth (since the relationship between policy and performance is just as relevant for a small country as for a large one).

7. Tariff reductions are clearly not the only determinant of export growth rates, and some regions with relatively high tariff rates (such as South Asia) had rapid growth in exports. Nevertheless, the reductions in tariff rates during the 1990s were, on average, associated with rapid export growth.

8. To measure the role of world trade conditions as opposed to other factors that determine export performance, export growth (in nominal dollars) is decomposed into three components using COMTRADE data: (a) growth caused by the expansion of world trade for products defined as traditional exports in the initial period, (b) gains in the share of individual countries in world trade in these commodities, and (c) growth attributable to diversification. COMTRADE data are not identical to the trade data used in the rest of the report. They are based on the reported imports from OECD and other reporting countries and cover about 90 percent of world trade. Because most countries in Sub-Saharan Africa and the Commonwealth of Independent States (CIS) do not report their imports fully, they underestimate intra-African and intra-CIS trade. The decomposition into growth in traditional markets, increased market share, and diversification depend on the definition of the traditional or initial export basket. In table 2.8 the export baskets of 1979–80 and 1989–90 were taken and all exports above US$5 million were classified as major. Growth of new exports and exports that were less than $5 million during the initial period are classified as diversified. (See Yeats 1998, and Ng and Yeats 2000 for a similar exercise.)

9. See Dollar 1992; Elbadawi 1998; Ghura and Grenness 1993; Razin and Collins 1997; and Sekkat and Varoudakis 2000. Edwards and Savastano (1999) have a critical review of the measures of exchange rate misalignment. See also Hinkle and Montiel 1999 and Williamson 1994 for a detailed analysis of the measurement issues and economic implications of exchange rate misalignment.

10. According to IMF, 97 percent of its members in 1970 were classified as having a pegged exchange rate; by 1999, this share had come down to very low levels

(Calvo and Reinhart 2000). As of 1999, of the 185 countries reporting their exchange rate arrangements, 84 had pegged regimes, 75 had floating rates, and 26 managed a system of limited flexibility. Of the countries with floating rates, 27 maintained a managed float, and 48 had an independent float (Shatz and Tarr 2000).

11. The fears of deindustrialization by many African countries are usually attributed to trade reform, while the exchange rate behavior probably played an even more important role.

12. Some studies have found a negative relationship between indicators of real exchange rate volatility and private investment (Aizenman and Marion 1995, 1996). Similar results were obtained by Darby and others 1998 for a group of five OECD countries and by Serven 1998 for developing countries. Other studies have found no relationship between real exchange rate volatility and aggregate investment (Bleaney 1996; Goldberg 1993; Ramey and Ramey 1995).

13. They cite various evidence, including the lower volatility of nominal exchange rates in developing countries than in several industrial countries, higher volatility of foreign exchange reserves than would be expected under floating rates, that countries use nominal interest rates to smooth exchange rate fluctuations, and that exchange rate rigidity occurs in the face of commodity price shocks.

14. The World Bank prepares ratings of developing countries' macroeconomic policy stances using a consistent framework, for the purpose of cross-country comparisons. Although exchange rate volatility macroeconomic stability ratings are highly correlated, the relationship is not perfect. There are 21 countries which either had high exchange rate volatility and were rated as having stable macroeconomic policies or vice versa. Only 16 countries managed to achieve both macroeconomic stability and low real exchange volatility. These countries also achieved much higher per capita GDP growth rates than other countries.

15. Thin markets lead to large changes in exchange rates due to small changes in demand and supply of foreign exchange.

16. A recent IMF study on exchange rate regimes comes to the same conclusions (Mussa and others 2000).

17. In many countries, initial policies did not include broad trade liberalization, but what can be called "compensatory" policies for exports. These range from elaborate input coefficients for duty exemption systems in Korea and duty drawback systems in Taiwan to export processing zones, and so on, which gradually gave way to elimination of NTBs, lower tariffs, and opening up of the domestic economy. Mauritius relied on an effective free trade zone, while the success of Bangladesh garments is due to a well-working bonded warehouse scheme, which is a form of duty exemption system.

18. There has been significant tariff reduction since 1996 in most of these countries. Also, there are large differences among the countries included (the trade-weighted tariff ranges from 25 percent in Zimbabwe to about 7 percent in the South African Customs Union).

19. Many of these products do not have local substitutes, and it is unlikely that they will be produced in these countries over the medium term. In that sense, they are pure revenue tariffs.

20. See Nash and Fourotan 1997 for the experiences in Africa, and Rajapatirana 1997 for Latin America and the Caribbean.

21. Just lowering tariffs on intermediate and capital goods without corresponding reductions in tariffs on consumer goods will increase the effective rate of protection for domestic producers, and thus may impair the efficiency of resource allocation.

22. Most infrastructure services in developing countries are supplied by governments or public departments with administrative barriers to entry. This lack of competition leads to higher costs, poor maintenance, and a lack of investment for technological upgrading. Opening up many of these services to competition under a transparent regulatory environment will lower costs, attract foreign and private capital, and improve delivery of services. For examples of recent privatization and demonopolization efforts and their positive impact on performance, see AfDB 1999.

23. In a sense these high costs act as an export tax, increasing the costs of production over those of suppliers that do not pay these duties.

24. See various needs assessment papers issued through the Integrated Framework for Trade-Related Technical Assistance to Least-Developed Countries process. They include references to the state of standards and conformity assessment systems and infrastructure needs in these countries (www.ldcs.org/index.htm).

25. Under tariff quotas, a fixed quantity of products from specified countries can be imported at a lower tariff and anything above that level is subject to the normal tariff.

26. The average most favored nation (MFN) tariff for these 311 lines is 21 percent; for the least-developed countries it is 18 percent.

27. It is not clear why so few of these products are imported into Quad countries. But the significant difference between the United States' (86 percent) and the European Union's (9 percent) share of developing countries' exports suggest that intra-EU trade makes up the difference.

28. Note that GSP and North-South free trade arrangements imply some trade diversion that will benefit some developing countries, but hurt others. Forthcoming work by Hoekman, Ng, and Olareaga (2000) argues that these preferences are not very extensive.

29. The NAFTA preference is 50 percent for these tariffs.

30. The producer support estimate (percent PSE) is calculated as the annual monetary value of production-related support to agricultural producers as a share of gross farms receipts (OECD 2000a).

31. The recent proposal by the EU to grant duty-free access to all exports from least-developed countries and the move to income support rather than direct support to production should improve market access for developing countries.

32. UNCTAD (TDR 1999) has shown that in low- and medium-skill manufactures, small changes in import penetration ratios significantly increase the export growth rates for these products from developing countries.

33. Tariff escalation means that the tariff rate rises with the level of processing.

34. For example, developing countries' share in fruits and vegetables trade, which is less protected, has not declined over this period.

35. Previous sections described the impact of conflicts and trade-related policies on developing countries' performance. In addition, expansion of agricultural exports (such as tropical commodities) that are subject to few trade restrictions in industrial countries tends to reduce prices and hence the terms of trade.

36. The effect on agricultural exports is much greater. The model reduces the exports of other products that faced lower tariffs because of factors moving to the expanding agricultural sector.

References

AfDB (African Development Bank). 1999. *African Development Report 1999: Infrastructure Development in Africa.* New York: Oxford University Press.

Aizenman, Joshua, and Nancy Marion. 1995. "Volatility, Investment and Disappointment Aversion." Working Paper 5386. National Bureau of Economic Research, Cambridge, Mass.

———. 1996. "Volatility and the Investment Response." Working Paper 5841. National Bureau of Economic Research, Cambridge, Mass.

Amjadi, Azita, Ulrich Reincke, and Alexander Yeats. 1996. "Did External Barriers Cause the Marginalization of Sub-Saharan Africa in World Trade?" World Bank Discussion Paper 348. World Bank, Washington, D.C. March.

Barro, Robert J., and Xavier Sala-i Martin. 1995. *Economic Growth.* Cambridge, Mass.: MIT Press, McGraw Hill.

Ben David, Dan. 1993. "Equalizing Exchange: Trade Liberalization and Income Convergence." *Quarterly Journal of Economics* 108(3).

Bhagwati, Jagdish. 1978. *Foreign Trade Regimes and Economic Development: Anatomy and Consequences of Exchange Control Regimes.* Cambridge, Mass.: Ballinger.

Bigsten, Arne, and others. 1998. "Exporting and Efficiency in African Manufacturing." (Paper presented for the Conference on Policies for Competitiveness in Manufacturing in Sub-Saharan Africa, Johannesburg, South Africa. 6–7 November.)

Bleaney, Michael. 1996. "Macroeconomic Stability, Investment and Growth in Developing Countries." *Journal of Development Economics* 48: 461–77.

Calvo, Guillermo A., and Carmen Reinhart. 2000. "Fear of Floating." University of Maryland, College Park, Md., and National Bureau of Economic Research, Cambridge, Mass. Draft. May.

Clerides, Sofronis, Saul Lach, and James Tybout. Forthcoming. "Is Learning by Exporting Important? Micro-Dynamic Evidence from Colombia, Mexico, and Morocco." *Quarterly Journal of Economics.*

Collier, Paul, and Anke Hoeffler. 1999. "Greed and Grievance in Civil War." Working Paper 2355. World Bank, Washington, D.C.

Darby, Julia, and others. 1998. "The Impact of Exchange Rate Uncertainty on the Level of investment." Discussion Paper 1896. Centre for Economic Policy Research, London.

Dollar, David. 1992. "Outward-Oriented Developing Economies Really Do Grow More Rapidly: Evidence from 95 LDCs, 1976–85." *Economic Development and Cultural Change* 40: 523–44. April.

Dornbusch, Rudiger, and Sebastian Edwards, eds. 1995. *Reform, Recovery and Growth. Latin America and the Middle East.* Cambridge, Mass.: National Bureau of Economic Research.

Easterly, William. 2000. "The Lost Decades . . . and the Coming Boom? Policies, Shocks, and Developing Countries" Stagnation 1980–1998." World Bank, Washington, D.C. May.

Easterly, William, Roumeen Islam, and Joseph E. Stiglitz. 2000. "Explaining Growth Volatility." World Bank, Washington, D.C. January. Processed.

Edwards, Sebastian. 1997. "Openness, Productivity and Growth: What Do We Really Know?" Working Paper 5978. National Bureau of Economic Research, Cambridge, Mass. March.

Edwards, Sebastian, and Miguel A. Savastano. 1999. "Exchange Rates in Emerging Economies: What Do We Know? What Do We Need to Know." Working Paper 7228. National Bureau of Economic Research, Cambridge, Mass. July.

Elbadawi, Ibrahim. 1998. "Real Exchange Rate Policy and Non-Traditional Exports in Developing Countries." Research for Action 46. UNU World Institute for Development Economics Research (UNU/ WIDER), The United Nations University, Helsinki.

Falvey, Rod, and Cha Dong Kim. 2000."Timing and Sequencing Issues for Trade Liberalization in Africa." In *Trade and Fiscal Adjustment in Africa*, edited by David Bevan, Paul Collier, Norman Gemmell, and David Greenaway. Great Britain: Macmillan Press Ltd.

Finger, J. Michael, and Sam Laird. 1987. "Protection in Developed and Developing Countries: An Overview." *Journal of World Trade Law* 21 (6).

Finger, J. Michael, and Ludger Schuknecht. 1999. "Market Access Advances and Retreats: the Uruguay Round and Beyond." Policy Research Working Paper. World Bank, Washington, D.C.

Frankel, Jeffrey A., and David Romer. 1999. "Does Trade Cause Growth?" *The American Economic Review* 89 (3): 379–99. June.

Ghura, Dhaneshwar, and Thomas J. Grenness. 1993. "The Real Exchange Rate and Macroeconomic Performance in Sub-Saharan Africa." *Journal of Development Economics* 42: 155–74.

Goldberg, Linda S. 1993. "Exchange Rates and Investment in United States Industry." *Review of Economics and Statistics* 75: 575–88.

Harberger, Arnold C. 1988. *Reflections on Uniform Taxation*. Processed.

Hausman and others. 1999. "Financial Turmoil and the Choice of Exchange Rate Regime." Working Paper, Inter-American Development Bank, Washington, D.C.

Hertel, Thomas, Bernard Hoekman, and Will Martin. 2000. "Towards a new round of WTO negotiations: issues and implementation for developing countries." (Paper presented at the ABCDE meeting. World Bank, Washington D.C. April.)

Hertel, Thomas, and Will Martin. 1999. "Would Developing Countries Gain From Inclusion of Manufactures Trade in the WTO 2000 Negotiations?" (World Bank Paper presented at the Conference on the Millennium Round, WTO, Geneva. September 20–21.)

——. 2000. "Liberalising Agriculture and Manufacturers." *The World Economy* 23 (4): 455–69. April.

Hinkle, Lawrence E., and Peter J. Montiel. 1999. *Exchange rate misalignment: Concepts and Measurement for Developing Countries*. Washington, D.C.: World Bank.

Hoekman, Bernard, Francis Ng, and Marcelo Olarreaga. 2000. "Problems Created by Protection in the Markets for Developing Country Exports." World Bank, Washington, D.C. July.

Ianchovichina, Elena, Aaditya Mattoo, and Marcelo Olarreaga. 2000. "Duty-Free Access for LDCs' Exports: How Much Is It Worth and Who Pays?" World Bank, Washington, D.C. June.

IMF (International Monetary Fund). 1981. *Exchange Arrangements and Exchange Restrictions*. Washington, D.C.

——. 1992. *Exchange Arrangements and Exchange Restrictions*. Washington, D.C.

——. 1996. *Exchange Arrangements and Exchange Restrictions*. Washington, D.C.

——. 1998. *Trade Liberalization in IMF-Supported Programs*. February 1998. IMF, Washington, D.C.

——. *International Financial Statistics*. Washington, D.C.

Kraay, Aart C. 1997. "Exports and Economic Performance: Evidence from a Panel of Chinese Enterprises." Development Research Group, World Bank, Washington, D.C. Processed.

Krueger, Anne O. 1978. *Liberalization Attempts and Consequences*. A Special Conference Series on Foreign Trade Regimes and Economic Development. Volume X. Cambridge, Mass.: National Bureau of Economic Research; New York: Ballinger Pub. Co.

Levine, Ross, and David Renelt. 1992. "A Sensitivity Analysis of Cross-Country Growth Regressions." *American Economic Review* 82: 942–63.

Limão, Nuno, and Anthony Venables. 1999. "Infrastructure, geographical disadvantage and transport costs." Policy Research Working Paper 2257. Development Research Group—Trade, World Bank, Washington, D.C. December.

Little, Iain, Malcolm David, Tibor Scitovsky, and Maurice Fitzgerald Scott. 1970. *Industry and Trade in Some Developing Countries*. Oxford, U.K.: Oxford University Press.

Michalopoulos, Constantine. 1999. "Trade Policy and Market Access Issues for Developing Countries: Implications for the New Millennium Round." Policy Research Working Paper 2214. World Bank, Washington, D.C.

Mussa, Michael, and others. 2000. "Exchange rate regimes in an increasingly integrated World Economy." Occasional Paper 193. International Monetary Fund, Washington, D.C. Also available on (http://www.imf.org/EXTERNAL/PUBS/CAT/lon gres.cfm?sk&sk=3518.0).

Nash, John, and Faezeh Foroutan, eds. 1997. *Trade Policy and Exchange Rate Reform in Sub-Saharan Africa*. National Centre for Development Studies, The Australian National University.

Ng, Francis. 1997. "A Profile of Tariffs, Para-tariffs, Non-Tariff Measures, and Economic Growth in Developing Countries." World Bank, Washington, D.C.

Ng, Francis, and Alexander Yeats. Forthcoming. "On the Recent Trade Performance of Sub-Saharan African Countries: Cause for Hope or More of the Same?" Africa Region Technical Paper, World Bank, Washington, D.C.

Organisation for Economic Co-Operation and Development (OECD). 1996. "Indicators of Tariff and Non-Tariff Trade Barriers."

——. 2000a. "Agricultural Policies in OECD Countries: Monitoring and evaluation 2000." Agriculture and Food, Paris.

——. 2000b. "Tariffs and Trade: OECD Query and Reporting System." CD Rom. Paris.

Papageorgiou, Demetrios, Armeane M. Choksi, and Michael Michaely, eds. 1991. *Liberalizing Foreign Trade in Developing Countries—The Lessons of Experience.* Washington, D.C.: World Bank; Oxford: Blackwell.

Rajapatirana, Sarath. 1997. *Trade Policies in Latin America and the Caribbean: Priorities, Progress and Prospects.* San Francisco, Calif.: International Center for Economic Growth.

Ramey, George J., and Valerie A. Ramey. 1995. "Cross-Country Evidence on the Link between Volatility and Growth." *American Economic Review* 1138–51.

Razin, Offair, and Susan M. Collins. 1997. "Real Exchange Rate Misalignments and Growth." Working Paper 6174, National Bureau of Economic Research, Cambridge, Mass. September.

Rodriguez, F., and Dani Rodrik. 1999. "Trade Policy and Economic Growth: A Skeptic's Guide to the Cross-national Evidence." May, Discussion Paper. Centre for Economic Policy Research, London.

Rodrik, Dani. 1996. "Understanding Economic Policy Reform." *Journal of Economic Literature* 24 (1). March.

——. 1998. "Where did all the Growth Go? External Shocks, Social Conflict and Growth Collapses." Working Paper 6350, National Bureau of Economic Research, Cambridge, Mass.

Sachs, Jeffrey D., and A. Warner. 1995. "Economic Reforms and the Process of Global Integration." *Brookings Papers on Economic Activity* 1–118.

Sala-i-Martin, Xavier. 1997a. "I Just Ran Four Million Regressions." Working Paper 6252. National Bureau of Economic Research, Cambridge, Mass.

——. 1997b. "I Just Ran Two Million Regressions." *American Economic Review, Papers and Proceedings* 87 (2): 178–83.

Sekkat, Khalid, and Aristomene Varoudakis. 2000. "Exchange Rate Management and Manufactured Exports in Sub-Saharan Africa." *Journal of Development Economics* 61 (1). February.

Serven, Luis. 1998. "Macroeconomic Uncertainty and Private Investment in LDCs: An Empirical Investigation." Washington, D.C. World Bank. Processed. September.

Shatz, Howard J., and David G. Tarr. 2000. "Exchange Rate Overvaluation and Trade Protection: Lessons from Experience." Policy Research Working Paper 2289, World Bank, Washington, D.C. February.

——. 1996. "Handbook of International Trade and Development Statistics." Geneva.

UNCTAD, 1999. Trade and Development Report, Geneva.

Wang, Zhen Kun, and L. Alan Winters. 2000. "Putting 'Humpty' Together Again: Including Developing Countries in a Consensus for the WTO." Policy Paper 4. Centre for Economic Policy Research, London.

Williamson, John (ed). 1994. *Estimating Equilibrium Exchange Rates.* Washington, D.C: Institute for International Economics.

World Bank. 1989. *Sub-Saharan Africa: From Crisis to Sustainable Growth. A Long-Term Perspective Study.* Washington, D.C.: World Bank.

——. 1994. *Adjustment in Africa: Reforms, Results, and Road Ahead.* World Bank Policy Research Report. New York: Oxford University Press.

——. 1995. *Global Economic Prospects and the Developing Countries.* Washington, D.C.: World Bank.

——. 1996. "Trade Policy Reform in Developing Countries since 1985." Discussion Paper 267. Washington, D.C.

——. 1997a. *Global Economic Prospects and the Developing Countries.* Washington, D.C.: World Bank.

——. 1997b. *World Development Indicators.* Washington, D.C.

——. 1998. *World Development Indicators.* Washington, D.C.

——. 2000a. *Can Africa Claim the 21st Century?* Washington, D.C.: World Bank.

——. 2000b. *Trade Blocs: A World Bank Policy Research Report.* New York: Oxford University Press.

——. 2000c. *World Development Report: Poverty and Development.* Washington, D.C.

——. 2000d. *World Development Indicators.* Washington, D.C.: World Bank.

WTO (World Trade Organization). *Trade Policy Reviews—Quad Countries.* Geneva.

——. 1998. *Trade Policy Reviews for 31 Developing Countries 1995–98.* Geneva.

Yeats, Alexander. 1998. "Have Policy Reforms Influenced the Trade Performance of Sub-Saharan African Countries." Trade Research Team. World Bank. Washington, D.C.

Yeats, Alexander J., with Azita Amjadi, Ulrich Reincke, and Francis Ng. 1997. *Did Domestic Policies Marginalize Africa in International Trade?* Directions in Development, World Bank, Washington, D.C.

Annex 2   Sample countries in various charts and tables

No.	Region	All developing countries [105]	Countries in conflict [19]	ECA countries (excluding Yugoslavia) [6]	Core sample [59]	Within core sample			
						Least-developed countries [16]	Low-income small countries [22]	Countries with high REER volatility in 1990s [26]	Countries with low REER volatility in 1990s [33]
1	Africa	Angola	Angola						
2	Africa	Burundi	Burundi						
3	Africa	Benin			Benin	Benin	Benin	Benin	
4	Africa	Burkina Faso			Burkina Faso	Burkina Faso	Burkina Faso	Burkina Faso	
5	Africa	Botswana			Botswana				Botswana
6	Africa	Central African Republic			Central African Republic	Central African Republic	Central African Republic	Central African Republic	
7	Africa	Côte d'Ivoire			Côte d'Ivoire			Côte d'Ivoire	
8	Africa	Cameroon			Cameroon			Cameroon	
9	Africa	Congo	Congo						
10	Africa	Comoros							
11	Africa	Cape Verde							
12	Africa	Djibouti							
13	Africa	Ethiopia	Ethiopia						
14	Africa	Gabon			Gabon			Gabon	
15	Africa	Ghana			Ghana		Ghana		Ghana
16	Africa	Guinea							
17	Africa	Gambia			Gambia	Gambia	Gambia		Gambia
18	Africa	Guinea-Bissau							
19	Africa	Equatorial Guinea							
20	Africa	Kenya			Kenya		Kenya	Kenya	
21	Africa	Liberia	Liberia						
22	Africa	Lesotho							
23	Africa	Madagascar			Madagascar	Madagascar	Madagascar	Madagascar	
24	Africa	Mali			Mali	Mali	Mali	Mali	
25	Africa	Mauritania			Mauritania	Mauritania	Mauritania		Mauritania
26	Africa	Mauritius			Mauritius				Mauritius
27	Africa	Malawi			Malawi	Malawi	Malawi	Malawi	
28	Africa	Namibia							
29	Africa	Niger			Niger	Niger	Niger	Niger	
30	Africa	Nigeria			Nigeria		Nigeria	Nigeria	
31	Africa	Rwanda	Rwanda						
32	Africa	Sudan							
33	Africa	Senegal			Senegal			Senegal	
34	Africa	Sierra Leone	Sierra Leone						
35	Africa	São Tomé and Principe							
36	Africa	Swaziland							
37	Africa	Seychelles Islands							
38	Africa	Chad			Chad	Chad	Chad	Chad	
39	Africa	Togo			Togo	Togo	Togo	Togo	
40	Africa	Tanzania			Tanzania	Tanzania	Tanzania		Tanzania
41	Africa	Uganda	Uganda						
42	Africa	South Africa			South Africa				South Africa
43	Africa	Democratic Republic of the Congo	Democratic Republic of the Congo						
44	Africa	Zambia			Zambia	Zambia	Zambia	Zambia	
45	Africa	Zimbabwe			Zimbabwe		Zimbabwe	Zimbabwe	
46	East Asia	China			China				China
47	East Asia	Fiji							
48	East Asia	Indonesia			Indonesia		Indonesia	Indonesia	

Annex 2   Sample countries in various charts and tables (continued)

No.	Region	All developing countries [105]	Countries in conflict [19]	ECA countries (excluding Yugoslavia) [6]	Core sample [59]	Within core sample			
						Least-developed countries [16]	Low-income small countries [22]	Countries with high REER volatility in 1990s [26]	Countries with low REER volatility in 1990s [33]
49	East Asia	Republic of Korea			Republic of Korea			Republic of Korea	
50	East Asia	Malaysia			Malaysia				Malaysia
51	East Asia	Philippines			Philippines				Philippines
52	East Asia	Papua New Guinea							
53	East Asia	Thailand			Thailand				Thailand
54	East Asia	Myanmar			Myanmar	Myanmar	Myanmar		Myanmar
55	ECA	Former Soviet Union		Former Soviet Union					
56	ECA	Bulgaria		Bulgaria					
57	ECA	Former Czechoslovakia		Former Czechoslovakia					
58	ECA	Hungary		Hungary					
59	ECA	Poland		Poland					
60	ECA	Romania		Romania					
61	ECA	Yugoslavia, Federal Republic of (Serbia/Montenegro)	Yugoslavia, Federal Republic of (Serbia/Montenegro)						
62	LAC	Argentina			Argentina			Argentina	
63	LAC	Bolivia			Bolivia				Bolivia
64	LAC	Brazil			Brazil			Brazil	
65	LAC	Barbados							
66	LAC	Chile			Chile				Chile
67	LAC	Colombia			Colombia				Colombia
68	LAC	Costa Rica			Costa Rica				Costa Rica
69	LAC	Dominican Republic			Dominican Republic				Dominican Republic
70	LAC	Ecuador			Ecuador				Ecuador
71	LAC	Guatemala	Guatemala						
72	LAC	Guyana							
73	LAC	Honduras			Honduras			Honduras	
74	LAC	Haiti	Haiti						
75	LAC	Jamaica			Jamaica				Jamaica
76	LAC	Mexico			Mexico			Mexico	
77	LAC	Nicaragua	Nicaragua						
78	LAC	Panama							
79	LAC	Peru	Peru						
80	LAC	Paraguay			Paraguay				Paraguay
81	LAC	El Salvador	El Salvador						
82	LAC	Suriname							
83	LAC	Trinidad and Tobago							
84	LAC	Uruguay			Uruguay				Uruguay
85	LAC	Venezuela, Rep. Bol. de			Venezuela, Rep. Bol. de			Venezuela, Rep. Bol. de	
86	MNA	Turkey			Turkey				Turkey
87	MNA	United Arab Emirates							
88	MNA	Kuwait	Kuwait						
89	MNA	Morocco			Morocco				Morocco
90	MNA	Bahrain							
91	MNA	Algeria			Algeria			Algeria	

Annex 2   Sample countries in various charts and tables (continued)

No.	Region	All developing countries [105]	Countries in conflict [19]	ECA countries (excluding Yugoslavia) [6]	Core sample [59]	Within core sample			
						Least-developed countries [16]	Low-income small countries [22]	Countries with high REER volatility in 1990s [26]	Countries with low REER volatility in 1990s [33]
92	MNA	Egypt, Arab Rep. of			Egypt, Arab Rep. of				Egypt, Arab Rep. of
93	MNA	Iran, Islamic Rep. of			Iran, Islamic Rep. of			Iran, Islamic Rep. of	
94	MNA	Iraq	Iraq						
95	MNA	Jordan			Jordan				Jordan
96	MNA	Oman			Oman				Oman
97	MNA	Saudi Arabia			Saudi Arabia				Saudi Arabia
98	MNA	Syrian Arab Republic	Syrian Arab Republic						
99	MNA	Tunisia			Tunisia				Tunisia
100	MNA	Yemen, Rep. of	Yemen, Rep. of						
101	South Asia	Bangladesh			Bangladesh	Bangladesh	Bangladesh		Bangladesh
102	South Asia	India			India				India
103	South Asia	Sri Lanka			Sri Lanka		Sri Lanka		Sri Lanka
104	South Asia	Nepal			Nepal	Nepal	Nepal		Nepal
105	South Asia	Pakistan			Pakistan		Pakistan		Pakistan

3

Standards, Developing Countries, and the Global Trade System

PRODUCT STANDARDS, OR RULES GOVERN-ing the characteristics of goods, are critical to the effective functioning of markets and provide important support to the trade system. For example, government testing and certification of the bacteria content of imported beef safeguards health and increases consumer acceptance of imported products. Product standards in the international trade system do, however, raise difficult issues for developing countries. These countries' limited technical capability and financial resources make it hard for them to participate effectively in negotiations governing standards or to bring disputes. In addition, pressures sometimes exerted to use trade sanctions in support of labor and environmental standards—legitimate and desirable as these standards may be intrinsically—threaten to restrict developing countries' access to international markets without achieving their professed goals.

The rapid growth of international trade has greatly increased the importance of effective regulation of standards at the international level. This chapter examines how standards imposed by governments in importing countries affect developing-country exporters and discusses the international regulation of some of the more prominent standards addressed in global trade negotiations.[1] Its main messages are as follows:

- Insufficient technical and financial resources limit developing countries' abilities

to play an effective role in the design and implementation of product standards and thus constrain their access to some markets. Many developing countries, particularly the poorest ones, lack the technological capabilities and financial resources to participate effectively in the development of product standards, to meet industrial countries' import requirements, and to bring disputes when standards are used to discriminate against their exports. For example, the European Union (EU) is harmonizing standards for levels of aflatoxin, a substance that may cause liver cancer, in food products. The new standard, which is more stringent than would be suggested by internationally accepted standards, would lower risks by approximately 1.4 cancer deaths per billion per year.[2] The new standard has the potential for substantially reducing exports of cereals from developing countries into Europe (Otsuki, Wilson, and Sewadeh 2000). Few developing countries have the technology to evaluate the dangers of aflatoxin, nor do they have the capabilities in scientific analysis to address the new EU standard. Furthermore, considerable legal and financial resources are needed to initiate a review under the World Trade Organization's (WTO's) dispute resolution mechanism. One achievement of the Uruguay Round agreement was to strengthen international rules governing product standards in order to minimize their use for protectionist purposes and to create a level playing field. Nonetheless, the lack of capacity in developing countries, particularly the poorest, limits the ability of these countries to benefit from the new rules (Wilson 2000b).

- The adoption and respect of core labor standards—including freedom from discrimination, from exploitative child labor, forced labor, and the freedom to associate and bargain collectively—are desirable and essential. However, the threat of trade sanctions or the imposition of trade barriers are likely to be excessively costly instruments for raising labor standards, and could even be counter-productive in some cases. Barriers to a country's exports hurt workers by reducing demand for the country's products. Even if sanctions force improvements in some sectors, they are unlikely to improve average working conditions in the economy. For example, the result of foreign pressure to reduce the use of child labor in the production and export of garments in Bangladesh was that many of the laid-off children were employed in more harmful occupations, such as prostitution or brick-breaking, and in factories that did not produce for export (*Financial Times,* August 24, 1999). The imposition of trade barriers to improve labor standards is vulnerable to capture by well-organized interests in domestic markets that would benefit from limiting imports. Similarly, trade sanctions are usually ineffective in addressing environmental degradation. Empirical studies show that imposing trade sanctions on exporters can cause considerable losses in output while doing little to reduce pollution.

- Although labor and environmental standards generally improve as countries develop, low labor and environmental standards are not usually a significant source of competitive advantage. Labor and environmental standards are positively correlated with income, both because higher incomes stimulate demand for better standards and because better standards tend to encourage technological change to economize on inputs. Studies have found only limited evidence that low environmental standards increase competitiveness or attract more foreign direct investment. Experience in both industrial and developing countries shows that the cost of appropriately designed environmental protection is often low in terms of both forgone growth and the capital cost of abatement. Keeping labor standards low is not an effective way of gaining a competitive advantage over trading partners. Indeed, low labor standards are likely to erode competitiveness over time because they reduce incentives for workers to improve skills and for firms to introduce labor-saving technology.

- The international community has more effective means than trade sanctions to encourage improved environmental and labor standards in developing countries. Efforts to support development, such as increasing assistance to countries with good policies, will raise standards. Encouraging greater openness to trade and to foreign direct investment (FDI) will facilitate the diffusion of cleaner technology that can reduce environmental degradation and improve worker productivity, thereby promoting better labor standards. Regional collaboration is appropriate for addressing environmental issues that have a clear regional component, such as transboundary emissions and shared water resources.

The regulation of standards: setting the stage

In the broadest sense, regulations are established because of perceived market failures, when reliance on voluntary market transactions is not efficient from the standpoint of society.[3] For example, market prices may not reflect the full cost of production because firms use public waterways to dispose of waste; consumers may lack information about product defects that can have serious consequences (unsafe automobiles, for example); and collusion and monopoly may mean increased costs for consumers. Establishment of regulatory standards is appropriate when the benefits of correcting these market failures exceed the costs. For example, current auto safety standards have significantly reduced the chances of injury and death but have not eliminated them, presumably because the cost of doing so is too high. Costs include not only the direct costs facing the regulated firm but also the costs of monitoring compliance and of any potential spillovers in other areas. (Taxing gasoline at the pump to limit pollution imposes a direct cost on consumers, but it also imposes a cost on filling stations and refineries as a result of lower demand.) The more detailed the rules are in defining what goods are produced and consumed, and how, the greater the costs in terms of stifling innovation, reducing choice, and monitoring compliance. Thus, regulatory instruments should use the market as much as possible to encourage flexibility and choice of products and of production techniques. For example, taxes and tradable permits have proved to be an effective and efficient means of controlling air and water emissions in certain circumstances and to be less onerous than traditional regulations that specify maximum levels of pollution.

Because preferences and policy options differ from country to country, regulatory regimes should be determined as much as possible by the communities to which they apply, unless there are spillovers to other communities. Given different preferences and different access to information, regulation that is accountable to the community and meets locally defined needs is likely to be more efficient and legitimate than regulation imposed from afar. In an international context, it is important to ensure that regulation (a) does not discriminate between domestic and foreign producers, (b) relates to products or activities that impose costs on domestic markets, (c) is restricted geographically to the markets affected, and (d) is implemented locally.

These simple principles have powerful implications for the appropriateness of different kinds of standards. Briefly put, product standards are necessary to support markets and must be applied in a nondiscriminatory fashion. Environmental standards should be addressed by the community affected by the relevant market failure. The impact of pollution is normally limited to domestic or, sometimes, regional markets, although some issues, such as those related to global warming and deep-sea fishing, require global action. Differences in labor standards do not impose costs on foreign markets and hence are not an appropriate area for international trade negotiations.

Product standards and regulatory barriers to trade

Ensuring that imported products meet appropriate standards for protecting health and safety has become increasingly important with the rapid expansion of trade over the past decade. Discriminatory regulations imposed at the border can disadvantage foreign producers and distort commercial markets. The reduction of tariffs and quotas through multilateral trade negotiations has highlighted the use of product standards as trade barriers. Tariffs, quotas, and subsidies continue to restrict trade in several sectors (see chapter 2), but other barriers—technical requirements, testing, certification, and labeling that affect imports—have emerged as important new issues for liberalization efforts (World Bank 2000b). Two significant achievements of the Uruguay Round, the agreement on Technical Barriers to Trade (TBT) and the agreement on Sanitary and Phytosanitary Standards (SPS), were designed to address some of these issues. The TBT agreement essentially relates to manufactured goods; the SPS agreement applies to food (sanitary standards) and animals and plants (phytosanitary standards).

The role of product standards

Product standards are critical to the effective functioning of markets and play an important role in supporting international trade. For consumers, standards provide information and help ensure quality. (For example, food labeling requirements allow easier comparison across products, and regulations increase consumer confidence that electrical fixtures are safe.)[4] Standards are critical for "component" goods such as consumer electronics and computers, where the ability to mix and match components is important. They also help achieve public objectives such as cleaner air; auto emissions standards and fuel economy regulations are examples. Because the export of goods that are physically dangerous or of agricultural products that are harmful to human health obviously damages the exporting country's (and the firm's) credibility and the acceptance of its products in the international trade system, there are important incentives for self-regulation.

For producers, standards can facilitate scale economies and the efficient combination of parts and components in production. Standards can also be used to gain access to intellectual property and technology. For example, the European Union's (EU's) licensing of technology based on European Telecommunication Standards Institute (ETSI) standards facilitated the spread of wireless telephones in the European market, highlighting the importance of the relationships between standards and trade in goods and services (Wilson 1997). Standards can facilitate coordination of production that might not be achieved through market forces. For example, countries can improve their integration into global information and telecommunication networks by adhering to international compatibility requirements for electrical products. Shared standards can reduce entry barriers by lowering inspection and testing costs that typically arise from imperfect information concerning the quality of traded goods (Moenius 2000).

Standards as barriers to trade

Mandatory standards can also act as nontariff barriers to trade, whether or not the intent is discriminatory; regulatory requirements may raise foreign firms' costs relative to those of domestic firms even if both are subject to the same requirements in the domestic market.[5]

Health and safety standards typically require testing and conformity assessment for all producers, but costs will be greater for exporters than for domestic producers if the exporters must conform to standards different from those in their own market or if they are subject to duplicative tests (Hoekman and Konan 1998). For example, an EU regulation requires that dairy products be manufactured from milk produced by cows kept on farms and milked mechanically. This rule precludes imports from many developing countries, particularly those with many small producers for whom mechanization is not cost-effective (Henson and others 2000). A country may have relatively stringent regulatory requirements owing to a different view of the tradeoff between risks and price. Such requirements may pose a significant compliance cost for exporters but would not be viewed as discriminatory, since they apply to both domestic and foreign producers.

The need to comply with varying standards can raise entry barriers in the form of increased one-time costs of product redesign and creation of an administrative system. For example, manufacturers may need to keep redesigning automobile seat belts to meet changing standards for multiple export markets. Standards may also diminish the ability to compete, owing to the recurrent costs of maintaining quality control, testing, and certification. Often, firms must decide whether to establish a costly platform design that can easily accommodate small modifications—for example, a car chassis that can serve multiple markets—or to design a product solely for the home market, even though costly modifications are required for export. A classic example of the latter is the right-hand or left-hand placement of car steering wheels.

Costs also may be incurred in meeting precise technical regulations and carrying out conformity assessment—that is, in evaluating whether a product "conforms" to a regulatory requirement. These requirements present the largest potential technical barrier to future trade. Governments in importing countries may refuse to recognize tests performed in foreign laboratories or by foreign public authorities and may not accept declarations of conformity by a foreign manufacturer. For example, Mexico used to allow only Mexican organizations and laboratories to test products subject to Mexican regulations. (Under the North American Free Trade Agreement, or NAFTA, Mexico agreed to allow U.S. and Canadian firms to perform testing and certification.) Such requirements may represent legitimate concerns regarding the quality of administration in the exporting countries, or they may result from administrative shortcomings in the importing country (delays, arbitrary inspections, redundant tests, and the like) that affect both foreign and domestic firms.

The use of product standards for protectionist purposes is a clear threat to an open trade regime. In principle, it is possible to distinguish between the "normal" costs of trade (the kinds of frictional costs described above) and barriers that are designed to limit competition from imports. The SPS agreement provides that trade restrictions can be imposed only to the extent necessary to protect life or health, that they must be based on scientific principles, and that they cannot be maintained if scientific evidence is lacking. Where the weight of scientific evidence is clear and well-accepted, this approach has helped to resolve disputes. For example, the United States successfully challenged Japanese technical regulations on the ground that there was no evidence that costly fumigation tests were necessary for each new variety of fruit imported into Japan. At times, the scientific community is unable to assess risks because the damages are only evident ex post (as was the case with asbestos), or the relative newness of the technology may call for caution in accepting existing evidence, as is happening with genetically modified organisms (Messerlin and Zarrouk 2000).

Given differences in historical experiences, levels of development, and risk preferences, differences in product standards among countries will remain an important feature of the trade system. Over time, the accumulation of case law through the WTO dispute settlement mechanism should help establish precedents for determining what is acceptable under WTO disciplines. This should help resolve disputes earlier and restrain discriminatory government initiatives that clearly conflict with principles of nondiscrimination. In addition, greater reliance on private initiatives, as opposed to government fiat, in designing product standards is desirable. For example, whereas voluntary agreements account for a large proportion of the standards (except for those related to health or the environment) in industrial countries, in developing and transition countries such as China, Russia, and Ukraine standards in important areas of economic activity continue to be developed and promulgated by governments. Reliance on private norms in developing countries would reduce the use of standards as trade barriers (industry-based standards may have protectionist intent but can be difficult to enforce unless backed up by government regulations), and they can help ensure appropriate expertise in designing standards.

Empirical evidence on standards as trade barriers

A large proportion of internationally traded goods is subject to standards, including about 60 percent of U.S. exports and 75 percent of intra-EU trade (Wilson 1997). The coverage of standards has increased significantly in the past few years (Hoekman and Konan 1998). Few attempts have been made to measure the general impact of product standards on traded goods.[6] The Organisation for Economic Cooperation and Development found that differing standards and technical regulations, along with costs of testing and certification, can represent between 2 and 10 percent of overall product costs, and the European Commission (1996) found that the average frictional costs of differing standards among EU countries prior to the single-market initiative ranged between 2 and 3 percent of the value of trade. The U.S.-EU mutual recognition agreement on telecommunications and information technology products, if fully implemented, could reduce costs by 5 percent of the value of goods traded (Wilson 1997). These costs are greater than the average tariff on intra-OECD manufacturing trade (less than 1 percent in 1995) and on developing countries' manufactured exports to industrial countries, which was 3.4 percent (Hertel, Hoekman, and Martin 2000).

There is some evidence that the adoption of common standards tends to reduce imports from other sources. Sectors of EU economies for which common trade regulations were adopted as part of the move to the single market represent one-third of EU value added and one-third of intra-EU trade, but only one-fourth of EU imports from the rest of the world. Conversely, sectors in which the establishment of common trade regulations was less successful represent one-third of both intra-EU trade and EU imports from the rest of the world (Messerlin 1998). Surveys and simulation exercises confirm the role of standards in increasing costs. An OECD (1999) survey of 55 firms in Germany, Japan, the United Kingdom, and the United States found that technical standards and conformity assessment procedures imposed significant costs on dairy products, auto parts, and telecommunications. Typical problems included requirements for testing of each product consignment both before shipping and at the port of entry and for frequent tests following design changes. Simulations with a computable general equilibrium (CGE) model found that a 2.5 percentage point decrease in border costs within the EU (the estimated result of adoption of uniform standards) would generate a short-term welfare gain of up to 0.5 percent of the gross domestic product (GDP) of EU countries (Harrison, Rutherford, and Tarr 1996), in part because of scale economies and increasing competition.[7] The benefit could reach 2.4 percent of GDP over the long term as investment increases as a result of a rise in the real return to capital.

Trade disputes on product standards

One indication of the importance of standards in restricting trade is the marked increase in the number of trade disputes over standards and technical barriers during the past five years. (The increase is evident in the U.S. annual reports in the National Trade Estimates series and the EU's annual reports on trade barriers.) In addition, most countries' submissions for the 1999 ministerial conference of the WTO in Seattle stressed the need to address technical barriers in the context of new trade talks (Wilson 1999). The most prominent standards cases in recent years have been in agriculture, such as the dispute between the EU and United States over hormone-treated beef.[8] The use of genetically modified organisms (GMOs) in agriculture is also generating trade tensions. By the end of January 1999, the WTO Dispute Settlement Body had considered 25 disputes that referenced either the SPS or the TBT (Wilson 1999). Nine of the disputes centered on food safety regulations, five involved technical regulations tied to customs requirements, and the remainder were in areas such as quotas, import bans, and disputes over environmental laws. Most of the complaints brought to the WTO are from industrial countries; of the 25 complaints considered by the WTO through January 1999, 16 were brought by industrial countries against other industrial countries, 3 were brought by industrial countries against developing countries, and 6 were brought by developing countries against industrial countries. No low-income country other than India has brought cases to the WTO under the TBT or the SPS or has been challenged under these agreements.[9] Pursuing a case through WTO procedures is expensive and resource-intensive, which may explain in part why many developing countries have not done so.

One indication of the increased focus on WTO dispute settlement—including cases related to standards—by members is the investment by the United States in new staff in the office of the U.S. Trade Representative (USTR). The budget request for fiscal 2001 includes an increase of 14 percent for additional staff, all of whom would focus on dispute settlement case work at the WTO (Hufbauer, Kotschwar, and Wilson 2000).[10] The least-developed countries (a UN-designated group of 48 developing countries) are likely to find it difficult to match this type of investment in WTO dispute settlement processes.

Disputes over standards as barriers to trade will undoubtedly become more important as (a) the share of trade in world output increases and developing countries' weight in world trade rises, (b) exports of finished goods by developing countries grow, and (c) large developing and transition countries, such as China, Russia, and Ukraine, whose domestic regulatory systems and import rules require deep reform, join the WTO. A recent review of Ukraine's standards and regulatory system commissioned by the World Bank, for example, reveals serious economic distortions in the design of the government's standards, testing, and certification systems (World Bank 2000a).

Capacity in developing countries

Product standards may work to the disadvantage of developing countries, where capacity to engage in standards development and to comply with standards in export markets is limited. Because of lack of resources, many developing countries find it difficult to diffuse best-practice information on quality standards such as those in the International Organization for Standardization (ISO) 9000 series and to adopt appropriate process and production methods (World Bank 2000b). Certification costs can be particularly significant for small firms. ISO 9000 certification for a single plant can cost up to $250,000, with additional auditing costs after initial approval. Limits on capacity are particularly important for the least-developed countries.

Developing countries lag behind industrial countries in their capacity for effective certification and accreditation of testing facilities (Stephenson 1997), and authorities in industrial countries may not trust developing countries' inspection procedures (Baldwin 2000). Developing countries thus find it difficult to develop standards based on international norms and to reach mutual recognition agreements (MRAs) with other nations. Their pro-

ducers may thus confront higher costs of entry in markets than do producers from countries that can certify compliance through an MRA (see box 3.1). Furthermore, governments and firms in more advanced countries can establish strategic standards that shut out developing-country firms or that alter the terms of competition or the terms of trade in favor of domestic firms (Fischer and Serra 2000; Gandal and Shy 1999; Matutes and Regibeau 1996).

Full implementation of the commitments made in the SPS and TBT agreements will benefit both developing and industrial countries and will strengthen the multilateral system. There have, however, been reservations about developing countries' abilities to meet specific provisions of these agreements. The SPS agreement, for example, encourages the use of relevant international standards; although a country may apply other standards at the border, it has the burden of demonstrating their scientific merit. Since most standards were designed by industrial countries, they may not be appropriate for the technology mix or preferences in developing countries. "Thus for a country to effectively use the WTO agreement to defend its export rights or justify its import restrictions, it will have to upgrade its SPS system to international standards" (Finger and Schuler 2000). Upgrading standards and providing risk assessments for proposed standards can be costly. There are similar questions regarding requirements in the TBT agreement which embody the concept that trade is best facilitated by harmonizing international standards.

Effective compliance with requirements for WTO enquiry points (offices that provide information regarding national technical regulations) can involve substantial costs, including the costs of establishing governmentwide information systems to report regulatory changes and respond to requests.[11] Formal compliance with enquiry point requirements has improved in developing countries, but it remains less than 60 percent for the SPS agreement and 75 percent for the TBT agreement (figure 3.1). It is not clear whether these enquiry points meet all the provisions of the agreements. The num-

Box 3.1   Mutual recognition agreements

Mutual recognition agreements (MRAs) are specifically encouraged as part of the Technical Barriers to Trade (TBT) agreement. Discussions of MRAs have dominated trade policy discourse since the early 1990s, in part because of internal market harmonization in the European Union (National Research Council 1995). Several bilateral MRAs have been completed among industrial countries, including four between the EU and its trading partners. The EU is pursuing negotiations with other countries. Regional talks on MRAs are also underway among, for example, members of the Asia Pacific Economic Cooperation (APEC). APEC has concluded model MRAs on food, electrical products, and exchange of information on toy safety. There is little quantitative evidence on the economic or trade facilitation benefits of MRAs, although in areas of deep regulatory intervention market expansion may be achieved through convergence in standards over time, if MRAs are fully implemented.

Developing countries find it difficult to participate in MRAs, in particular because more-developed trading partners often are less than confident in their testing and certification procedures. Negotiating MRAs is time- and resource-intensive (as came out in discussions at the WTO Symposium on Conformity Assessment Procedures, June 8–9, 1999). Moreover, the lack of modern technical infrastructure to support an MRA in developing countries poses clear obstacles to implementation. Thus, developing-country firms are likely to be at a competitive disadvantage in exporting to markets covered by MRAs. How MRAs relate to WTO obligations on the most favored nation (MFN) commitment—that is, nondiscrimination—remains unclear. It is unlikely that access to the benefits of an MRA could be offered on a nondiscriminatory basis to developing countries.

Other tools exist to facilitate trade in goods subject to mandatory regulation. For example, manufacturers' declarations of conformity avoid duplicative government or third-party product testing and have been employed for products that pose limited health, safety, or environmental risk. Innovative regional use of declarations of conformity, with countries pooling their resources, could be explored as a way of facilitating developing countries' trade.

ber of notifications by developing countries of new technical regulations and certification rules, as required by TBT and SPS agreements, has grown (figures 3.2 and 3.3), although the increase may not reflect a greater ability to meet product standards for export goods.

All in all, the costs involved in complying with TBT and SPS requirements are substantial and are likely to be equal to an entire year's development budget in some least-developed countries. (This calculation includes the costs of meeting trade-related aspects of intellectual property rights, or TRIPs, requirements; see (Finger and Schuler 2000).)[12] Such expenditures can improve a country's capacity to participate in international trade, but they must be evaluated in light of other development priorities.[13]

Many developing countries have recommended a targeted review of TBT and SPS requirements in light of development needs, including extension of the time frame for complying with some provisions and modification of the rules governing notification of new technical regulations. (Providing 60 days to comment on new regulations is of questionable value to developing countries that lack the capacity to analyze and formulate positions on technical requirements quickly.)[14] A serious and thorough use of the results of the Second Triennial Review of the TBT agreement, scheduled to conclude in November 2000, would help address developing countries' concerns.

Labor standards and trade sanctions

Adoption and compliance with core labor standards is desirable on moral grounds, and necessary for promoting broad-based and

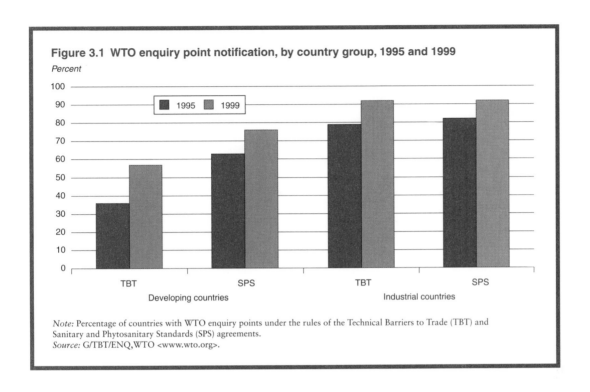

Figure 3.1 WTO enquiry point notification, by country group, 1995 and 1999

Percent

Note: Percentage of countries with WTO enquiry points under the rules of the Technical Barriers to Trade (TBT) and Sanitary and Phytosanitary Standards (SPS) agreements.
Source: G/TBT/ENQ, WTO <www.wto.org>.

inclusive economic development (World Bank 1995 and Aidt and others 2000). However, imposing trade sanctions to bring about improved labor standards is unlikely to enhance either global welfare or the welfare of developing countries. In terms of the criteria for regulatory decisionmaking outlined in the beginning of the chapter, labor standards should not be the subject of trade negotiations because the level of standards in one country does not affect the welfare of its trading partners, and the workers whom trade sanctions are designed to protect have no role in deciding whether sanctions are imposed. Although higher labor standards are associated with improved living conditions and development, the imposition of trade sanctions is a remarkably costly mechanism. Furthermore, trade sanctions are vulnerable to capture by domestic interests, and are likely to hurt the workers the sanctions are designed to assist. Lower labor standards abroad are not a serious threat to the livelihoods of workers in industrial countries; neither theory nor evidence suggests that

lower labor standards generally provide a competitive advantage.

Core labor standards and their relationship to development

Core labor standards are commonly defined to include freedom of association and collective bargaining; nondiscrimination in employment; no exploitative child labor; and no forced labor (for example, slavery).[15] Each of these core standards is covered by at least one International Labour Organisation (ILO) convention. By the mid-1990s, only 27 countries worldwide and only 10 OECD countries had ratified all core ILO conventions, although ratifications increased in the second half of the 1990s (OECD 2000). Several countries that have not ratified some of these standards are regarded as being in compliance with them in practice. Their reasons for nonratification appear not to relate to objections on principle, but rather to specific details of the conventions or their interpretations by ILO bodies (OECD 1996).[16] Of course, ratification does

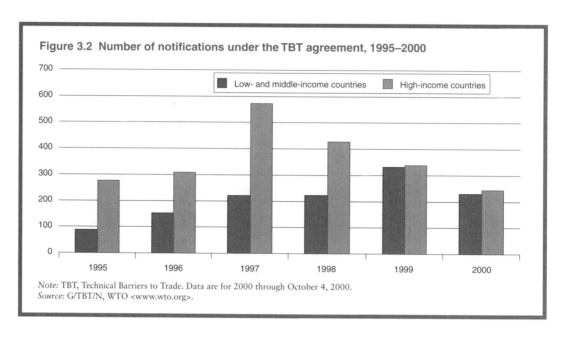

Figure 3.2 Number of notifications under the TBT agreement, 1995–2000

Note: TBT, Technical Barriers to Trade. Data are for 2000 through October 4, 2000.
Source: G/TBT/N, WTO <www.wto.org>.

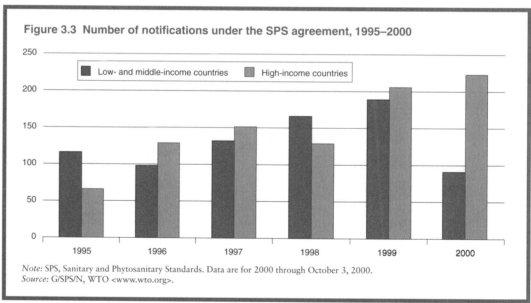

Figure 3.3 Number of notifications under the SPS agreement, 1995–2000

Note: SPS, Sanitary and Phytosanitary Standards. Data are for 2000 through October 3, 2000.
Source: G/SPS/N, WTO <www.wto.org>.

not necessarily imply that core labor standards will be observed, which requires legislative and regulatory changes, as well as monitoring and enforcement to stop abuses.

Adherence to core labor standards, as measured by freedom of association, is weakly correlated with both higher levels, and higher growth rates, of GDP per capita.[17] (Freedom of association is used because it is easier to measure than some of the other standards.) On average, more-developed countries have better-than-average compliance, while compliance in many of the poorest countries is inadequate. Higher income levels stimulate demand for better standards, and higher standards contribute to growth by increasing work effort and stimulating innovation, in order to economize on labor.

There is less evidence that adherence to labor standards is correlated with other measures of economic development, such as real wages. In the newly industrializing countries of East Asia, rising real wages have been associated with improved bargaining rights (Maskus 1997). In a larger sample of countries, however, there is no clear correlation between freedom of association and changes in real wages or changes in manufacturing output per worker for the period 1973–92. In a sample of 17 countries that had recorded discrete improvements in legislation and practice regarding freedom of association, there was no uniform tendency for growth to accelerate after the changes (OECD 1996).

Labor standards and economic welfare

Adherence to core labor standards can make important contributions to improving welfare. The welfare impact depends on the structure of domestic institutions and policies. For example, if monopsonist firms hire workers below their marginal revenue product, allowing worker association and collective bargaining could raise both worker wages and efficiency by boosting employment.[18] Moreover, organized labor can contribute to raising efficiency and welfare in ways that go beyond the adjudication of wages. For example, unions can contribute to firm-specific knowledge and organizational capital, thus raising productivity, and can help improve domestic labor standards by overcoming a "prisoner's dilemma" low-standards equilibrium (Stiglitz 2000).[19] But if the economy starts from a competitive equilibrium, collective bargaining that raises wages above their marginal revenue product may lower efficiency. If collective bargaining is supported by measures to restrict entry (and in competitive conditions, collective bargaining is not likely to have a long-term impact on wage levels otherwise), the excluded workers are clear losers. Thus, evaluating policies for inducing higher labor standards requires detailed knowledge of the competitive conditions in the affected labor markets.

In some cases, improvements in labor standards may have unintended consequences and not necessarily improve the welfare of workers. In several countries, labor standards are lower in export-processing zones (EPZs) than in the rest of the country, mainly because of bans on unions or restrictions on strikes (OECD 1996).[20] Workers in most EPZs, however, earn higher wages and enjoy better working conditions than their counterparts elsewhere in the country (ILO 1993; Maskus 1997).[21] It is not clear what effect better labor standards would have on investors the EPZs are designed to attract. Advocates of improving labor standards in EPZs must understand not only the domestic labor market but also the negotiating position of the developing country relative to investors.

Labor standards and competitiveness

It is often argued that low labor standards impose low wages and thus enhance domestic competitiveness at the expense of trading partners' workers. In some cases, employer collusion, in the absence of collective bargaining rights for workers, may reduce wages below what they would be with effective labor standards, thus potentially raising production.[22] Such an outcome would require nationwide collusion since if a firm pays below the prevailing wage, it will eventually lose its employees to other sectors.[23] The key point in this discussion is that standards need to be ratcheted up in a coordinated and economywide fashion; a sectoral or partial approach will have spillover effects which could in many cases be detrimental to a broad group of workers.

Over time, artificially imposed low labor standards are likely to erode competitiveness because they reduce incentives for workers to improve their skills; the earnings gain that can be achieved by upgrading skills is limited by labor market conditions. Similarly, low labor standards reduce incentives for firms to introduce labor-saving technology, because the savings are worth less if wages are low.

The data do not indicate that core labor standards play a significant role in shaping trade performance (OECD 1996). Countries with higher labor standards had higher growth rates in their share of world manufacturing exports from 1980 to 1990, but it is not possible to infer the direction of causality from these results. Of six countries that achieved significant improvements in labor standards, half saw a decrease in the growth of their share in world manufactures, while half saw an increase. Differences in endowments and technology are much more important than labor standards in determining patterns of comparative advantage.

The OECD study (1996) also examined the relationship between labor standards and FDI. Most world FDI flows from OECD countries into other OECD countries, which generally have high labor standards. As for the inflows of FDI to non-OECD countries, it is not clear that countries with low standards are the primary destinations.[24]

Effectiveness of trade sanctions in improving labor standards

Even where low labor standards reduce economic efficiency and welfare, sanctions are unlikely to improve workers' welfare. It is a familiar principle of economics that the most efficient way to remove a distortion is to address it directly. For example, setting a tariff is an inefficient way to encourage domestic production of a good. Imposing trade sanctions is a vastly inefficient way to encourage better labor standards.

Take a favorable (to those advocating trade sanctions) case, in which government-supported barriers to entry enable monopsonist employers to pay workers below their marginal revenue product. Both employment and wage rates are lower than if the market were competitive. Assume that the rest of the world imposes a tariff on exports of the product, thus reducing the export price. The monopsonist's response to any reduction in demand under this market structure would be to reduce fur-

ther employment and wages in the sector. If the monopsonist were large, that would lead to pressures to reduce wages in the economy as a whole (Maskus 1997).

Trade sanctions on particular export goods are unlikely to improve labor standards for the economy as a whole, even if the sanctions change the behavior of particular firms. For example, barring child labor in one firm or sector without addressing the fundamental causes of child labor is likely to shift children to less-remunerative and perhaps more dangerous occupations in other sectors. In Bangladesh in 1993, the threat of U.S. sanctions led owners of garment factories in Dhaka to dismiss all children under age 16. Anecdotal evidence suggests that many of these children found employment in workshops and factories not producing for export, or as prostitutes, brick-breakers, or street vendors (Panagariya 1999a). There are effective measures for combating abusive child employment, including income-support programs and subsidies for education, but trade sanctions are not among them.

The political-economy arguments against imposing trade sanctions on countries with low labor standards are even more compelling. As discussed above, determining whether particular improvements in labor standards would raise welfare requires considerable information on labor and product market conditions. Determining whether labor arrangements in exporting countries will affect wage rates in importing countries is even more complicated, requiring estimates of various parameters such as demand and supply elasticities in different markets and factor intensities of goods (Maskus 1997). The complexity of these issues, and the decentralized nature of the costs of protection to consumers, increase the potential for decisions to be captured by well-organized domestic interests that would benefit from trade barriers. The fact that labor unions and producers in some protected industries in industrial countries favor using the WTO system to improve labor standards underlines this concern.

While adherence to core labor standards improves welfare, integrating labor standards into the WTO is contentious. Under traditional criteria, which focus on *product* standards, not *process* standards, labor standards would not be considered for trade discussions. The TRIPs agreement has, however, widened the scope for broadening the traditional criteria (see box 3.2).

Inadequate labor standards and poor working conditions are, first and foremost, a development challenge that affects sizable populations, whether or not they are involved in trading activities.[25] It may be easy to identify some blatant abuses linked with goods that enter industrial markets, but the large majority of workers in developing countries may suffer from even worse conditions than workers employed in export activities. The keys to improving workers conditions—beyond development itself—lie in assisting countries with the development of domestic institutions to support workers' rights and improve working conditions, and coordinating policies across developing countries to ratchet up standards and escape a low-standard equilibrium.

The ILO has been actively pursuing these activities since its creation in 1919. The ILO regularly monitors working conditions in its member countries, and traditionally provides incentives (such as technical assistance) to encourage improved compliance with ILO conventions. However, it is able to invoke economic sanctions (Article 33 of the ILO Constitution) and did so for the first time in 2000 (against Myanmar), although implementation of the sanctions was postponed to allow the country time to comply.[26] Strengthening the ILO and enhancing its cooperation with other international organizations would be an effective step toward ameliorating working conditions around the world. The private sector, particularly multinational firms, should also play a more active role by promoting uniform corporate codes of conduct and using best-practice production methods in all countries where they or their affiliates operate.

Environmental standards and trade

The past decade has seen increasing debate over the contribution of trade to environmental degradation. In part, this debate has reflected concern about the role of growth in depleting cross-border public goods; specific issues include the dangers of global warming and the unsustainable pace of fishing and water use in some regions (Nordström and Vaughan 1999). Workers and firms in industrial countries fear that their competitive position is being undermined by environmental regulations that force pollution-intensive industries to move to developing economies. Greater trade integration and access to information, while boosting global welfare, are increasing the intensity of disputes and the potential for domestic interests to be injured by the actions of foreigners.

Although environmental concerns are clearly legitimate, the trade system is rarely the appropriate instrument for addressing them, given the principles outlined at the beginning of this chapter. Only a limited set of environmental issues affect more than one country. To the extent that environmental damage is limited to a single country, decisions on whether to restrict production for environmental reasons should not be imposed through trade negotiations. Imposing trade sanctions to achieve environmental goals is likely to be inefficient and perhaps counterproductive. Countries have different priorities, which are in large part a reflection of different levels of development. Poorer countries are likely to make different choices in facing tradeoffs between growth and environmental goals than do industrial countries—today's industrial countries did the same when they were developing. It is important that developing countries retain access to the international trade system, even if their domestic environmental policies are not those preferred by richer countries. Several international institutions—such as the Joint United Nations Environment Programme (UNEP)—and the international environmental summits, have an environmental mandate and should be the

Box 3.2 The Trade-Related Intellectual Property Agreement (TRIPs) and developing countries

TRIPs requires all WTO members to set minimum standards for protecting intellectual property rights (including patents, copyright, and trademarks) and to establish obligations regarding the enforcement of rights. Disputes under TRIPs are subject to the WTO's integrated dispute settlement system.[27] Industrial countries were strong advocates of TRIPs, and developing countries may have acceded to it to achieve progress in sectors of importance to them, such as agriculture and textiles.

TRIPs makes significant demand for changes in intellectual property regimes, particularly in many developing countries in which protection of intellectual property does not meet minimum TRIPs standards. Changes in legal systems are underway in many countries. However, there is a concern that the tendency to copy intellectual property regimes from industrial countries in order to comply with TRIPs requirements may be inappropriate for many developing countries. For example, these regimes may not adequately protect traditional knowledge, particularly given that the appropriate form of such protection is unknown and will require experience to develop (Finger and Schuler 1999).

Implementation of the TRIPs agreement could have a significant financial impact on developing countries. TRIPs will transfer rents from developing to industrial countries, which hold the overwhelming bulk of patents and copyrights. It is impossible to predict the size of these transfers. Some insight into the orders of magnitude involved can be found in a study by Maskus (2000b). He estimates that, had the TRIPs agreement been in place in 1988, transfers could have amounted to $8.3 billion (in 1995 dollars) to the top six industrial countries, with slightly less than half this amount coming from the developing countries in his sample.[28] A second area of concern regarding the financial impact of the TRIPs agreement is the considerable cost of administering intellectual property rights, particularly for the poorer developing countries. In addition, developing countries may not benefit from the most advanced technologies, due to the costs involved. Beyond pure economic costs, there is concern that TRIPs may constrain countries' access to critical drugs such as those for treating AIDS or malaria. Some of the relatively advanced developing countries may be able to produce these drugs domestically. To do so, they could invoke an exception in the TRIPs agreement to grant compulsory licenses for the domestic production of drugs. (The agreement allows for compulsory licensing under certain conditions, one being bona fide negotiations between the local government and the foreign manufacturer regarding the terms on which the manufacturer would be willing to supply the domestic market. In either case, compensation is due the foreign patent holder.) Less-advanced countries may have difficulties in producing or importing cheaper drugs because, although TRIPs does not entirely foreclose the possibility of exporting drugs produced under compulsory licenses, it does limit it (Subramanian 1999).

The negative impacts of TRIPs for developing countries were intended to be mitigated by several factors. First, they had longer transition periods for implementation, though these have largely expired except for least-developed countries (which have until January 2005). Second the TRIPs obligations do not apply to products and processes that were already on the market before TRIPs took effect. The net impact will eventually depend on the existence or development of substitutes, which could reduce the market power of patent or copyright holders, and the price elasticity of consumer demand.

In the long run, stronger protection of intellectual property in developing countries may contribute to growth by removing a disincentive for owners of technology to export and license, encouraging foreign investment, and by stimulating both domestic and foreign research and development. Such benefits are likely to be greatest for the larger and richer developing countries, which can enforce patent protection and imitate technology (Maskus 2000b). In addition, to counter some of the perceived imbalance in the initial agreement, developing countries have made various proposals to ensure that indigenous culture, knowledge, and genetic resources are protected and remunerated.

forums for discussing environmental goals. In addition, donor countries and international agencies can and do condition their assistance on achievement of environmental goals, including those that affect important aspects of the global commons.

The impact of trade integration on the environment

Trade integration influences growth, the technology mix, and the composition of output. Increased openness will raise economic growth and living standards, which, other things being equal, will increase environmental degradation. This *scale effect* is empirically important, especially for countries that are specialized in environment-intensive activities, such as mining, fisheries, and forestry, as in Chile, and wood and wood products, industrial chemicals, and petroleum, as in Indonesia (Lee and Roland-Holst 1997).

Although the scale effect is always positive (as long as trade integration induces growth), it can be counterbalanced by two other effects: the technique effect and the composition effect.[29] Trade integration changes access to technology (through, for example, capital goods imports), and this *technique effect* may have a positive or negative impact on environmental degradation. New technology may result in savings on energy and other inputs, reducing the pollution intensity of growth. The *composition effect* may also have a positive or negative impact on environmental degradation. Trade integration and growth affect the composition of output, owing to changes in the relative endowments of factors, the increasing consumption of (relatively cleaner) services that accompanies higher incomes, and the increased affordability and desirability of pollution reduction, which indirectly lead to better environmental protection.[30]

The impact of trade integration on the environment has varied considerably, depending on the nature and strength of these three effects, but outward orientation has reduced the pollution intensity of output in several countries (Birdsall and Wheeler 1992), and

outward-oriented economies have lower pollution intensity of aggregate output than inward-oriented ones. During the 1980s outward-oriented growth was associated with declining pollution intensity because the industrial activities of outward-oriented economies became more diversified, shifting away from heavy manufacturing (Lucas, Wheeler, and Hettige 1992).[31] FDI and the use of technology-laden imported inputs have helped transmit cleaner technologies from the regulated industrial-country market to developing countries—for example, in the paper and pulp industry (Wheeler and Martin 1992) and the steel industry (Reppelin-Hill 1999).

Conversely, in many countries import-substitution strategies have been pollution- and resource-intensive because of price distortions and lack of competitive discipline. There is strong evidence that under an import-substitution strategy, countries have specialized in pollution-intensive manufacturing activities in which they are not truly competitive. The resource content of goods in such countries is much higher than that of comparable goods in open economies (Jha, Markandya, and Vossenaar 1999; Vukina, Beghin, and Solakoglu 1999). Some distortions have stronger environmental consequences than others. For example, subsidized energy usually implies a more resource-intensive economy and therefore more emissions.

Trade liberalization and other reforms have helped correct policy distortions that subsidize environmental degradation. For example, energy use per unit of aggregate product in 12 former centrally planned economies declined drastically with market reform, in part because of the rise in domestic oil prices and the cleaner composition of manufacturing output following trade and price liberalization. Energy intensity in China fell by 30 percent between 1985 and 1997 as market-oriented reforms were introduced (Vukina, Beghin, and Solakoglu 1999; World Bank 1997). Similar findings emerge for use of natural resources. For example, in Sri Lanka, trade liberalization increased the demand for land to be planted in tea, which is less erosive than other crops, thus generating both environmental and economic benefits (Bandara and Coxhead 1999).

Some countries do show increased pollution following trade liberalization, owing to both scale and composition effects. Beghin and Potier (1997) suggest that some countries faced more domestic pollution following trade liberalization because their aggregate activities expanded, not necessarily because they specialized in "dirty" activities. Several countries, however, did see increased specialization in dirty activities following trade liberalization because they happened to be competitive in these activities. In this category are Indonesia (Lee and Roland-Holst 1997; Strutt and Anderson 1999); China (Dean 1999; Dessus, Roland-Holst, and van der Mensbrugghe 1999; Jha, Markandya, and Vossenaar 1999); Costa Rica (Abler, Rodriguez, and Shortle 1999; Dessus and Bussolo 1998); and Turkey (Jha, Markandya, and Vossenaar 1999). Ferrantino and Linkins (1999), using simulations with a CGE model to estimate the effects of trade liberalization on output of toxic emissions, suggest that specialization is more important than scale in determining the impact of trade liberalization on pollution. Table 3.1 summarizes the evidence from economywide studies on the relationship between trade liberalization and pollution. Panel studies found a mixed effect of outward orientation. Rock (1996) found that the composition effect of outward orientation was positive or ambiguous. Lucas, Wheeler, and Hettige (1992) found a negative composition effect. Negative results in a study by Vukina, Beghin, and Solakoglu (1999) were robust.

One concern about trade and financial integration is that countries with relatively weak environmental regulations will attract dirty industries away from countries with stronger regulations, and that because of competitiveness concerns integration will inhibit the imposition of strong environmental regulations ("regulatory chill"). A related conjecture is that states could strategically decrease environmental protection to attract new indus-

tries, setting off a "race to the bottom." The emergence of such a race is theoretically possible (Klevorick 1997; Wilson 1997), particularly in political and regulatory environments that are not transparent and are vulnerable to capture by dirty-industry interests. (Capture by "green" interests is also possible—environmental protection would exceed public preferences.) The several methodological approaches used to study this question generally find mixed evidence as to whether environmental regulation is eroding competitiveness in relatively "clean" countries (see table 3.2 and box 3.3).

The cost of environmental protection

One reason for the paucity of evidence that environmental regulations impair competitiveness is that the cost of environmental protection is often low, as measured by forgone growth or the capital cost of abatement. Despite the inefficiency of the command-and-control approach that most OECD countries have used in addressing pollution, the cost of compliance to industries has been surprisingly small, and abatement has been significant (Jaffe and others 1995). Simulations using applied general equilibrium models of developing economies have found that the cost of abatement for most types of emissions is modest in terms of forgone GDP growth. This finding was robust, having been generated from models of seven developing economies with different assumptions on abatement possibilities and for 13 types of pollution. The only type of pollution that was found to be expensive to abate was bioaccumulative toxic releases in water (Beghin, Roland-Holst, and van der Mensbrugghe forthcoming). Detailed qualitative case studies of individual industries undertaken by the United Nations Conference on Trade and Development (UNCTAD) confirm these findings (Jha, Markandya, and Vossenaar 1999).

Malaysia provides an interesting case of specialization in resource-intensive activities accompanied by environmental protection (Jha, Markandya, and Vossenaar 1999). The palm oil industry adapted to a rapidly imple-

Table 3.1 Summary of economywide studies assessing the impacts of trade liberalization on pollution

	Policy change	Scale	Composition	Technique	Total pollution
Mexico[a]	Trade liberalization	+	–	. . .	Small decrease
United States[a]	with NAFTA	+	+	. . .	Increase
Canada[a]		+	+	. . .	Increase
Mexico[a]	Trade liberalization	+	+	. . .	Increase
United States[a]	with NAFTA plus	+	+	. . .	Increase
Canada[a]	investment liberalization	+	+	. . .	Increase
Mexico[b]	Trade liberalization, better terms of trade with United States and Canada	+2.8 to 3.7%	–4.3 to 2.6%	–0.7 to 3.5%	–0.2 to 6.4%
Costa Rica[c]	Trade liberalization	9.4%	5.6 to 10.6%	+ but small	15 to 20%
Vietnam[d]	Trade liberalization	5 to 8.8%	–6.3 to 8%	1.1 to 7.5%	0.8 to 23.1%
Indonesia[e]	Trade liberalization with Japan	0.87%	–.36 to 2.86%	. . .	0.51 to 3.73%
Japan[e]	Trade liberalization with Indonesia	0%	–0.09 to –0.02%	. . .	–0.09 to –0.02%
Global[f]	Multilateral liberalization	. . .	. . .	–0.02 to 0%	–4.32 to 0%

. . . Not available.
Note: NAFTA, North American Free Trade Agreement. The data cited in notes a–f are reproduced from Beghin and Potier 1997.
a. Grossman and Krueger 1992; percentages not available.
b. Beghin, Roland-Holst and van der Mensbrugghe 1995. The scale effect range refers to production and absorption. The ranges for composition and technique effects refer to 13 measures of pollution emissions.
c. Dessus and Bussolo 1998. The scale effect is the increase in output. The composition effect is the difference between total and scale effects.
d. Dessus and van der Mensbrugghe 1996.
e. Lee and Roland-Holst 1997. The range of composition effects refers to 10 pollutant types. The authors also report a human toxicity index.
f. Ferrantino and Linkins 1999, tables 7 and 9. Scale and composition figures are not disaggregated.

mented set of environmental regulations and taxes. Compliance is high, and exports are stable, even though opportunities to pass the cost increase on to consumers were limited by the highly competitive nature of the industry. State-funded research helped develop commercial by-products from palm meal, reducing the cost of compliance by generating revenues from the by-products instead of treating them or dumping them and paying fines and fees (Jha, Markandya, and Vossenaar 1999; Khalid and Braden 1993). The Malaysian electronics industry also continued to grow despite tighter environmental regulations, in part because the strong FDI presence facilitated the introduc-

tion of the latest technology (Jha, Markandya, and Vossenaar 1999).

Trade policy and environmental protection

Tariffs are usually ineffectual instruments for tackling pollution and environmental degradation. Only when the externality originates in trade are trade taxes effective in addressing the problem (Subramanian 1992). A ranking of instruments for addressing pollution emissions follows the targeting principle (Bhagwati and Srinivasan 1997), which, broadly, says "the closer, the better." Hence, emissions taxes are the best instrument for dealing with pollu-

Table 3.2 **Evidence on international competitiveness and environmental regulation**

Approach	Study	Conclusion
Cross-sectional Heckscher-Ohlin (H-O) model	Kalt 1988	U.S. manufacturing exports negatively affected by environmental regulation
	Tobey 1990	World trade in dirty commodities not affected by environmental regulation
	Han 1996	Small negative impact of regulation, decreasing over time
	Valluru and Peterson 1997	Grain trade not affected by environmental regulation
	Diakosauvas 1994	Exports of the five most polluting crops negatively affected by regulation
	Xu 1999	Environmentally sensitive exports of 34 countries not influenced by regulation
Investigations of FDI flows	Albrecht 1998	United States found to import pollution-intensive industries more than it exports them
	Eskeland and Harrison 1997	No pollution-intensive bias in French and U.S. FDI in developing economies
	Xing and Kolstad 1995	U.S. FDI influenced by weak regulation only in chemical industries
Plant location: firm surveys	UNCTAD 1993	Negative effects of environmental policy on location
	Levinson 1997a, summary	Marginal impact of compliance cost except for self-declared U.S. dirty industries
Plant location: econometric approach	Levinson 1997a	No effect
	Bartik 1989	Small and negative effect
	Mani, Pargal, and Huq 1997	Positive effect of one measure of environmental stringency on plant location
	Metcalfe 2000	Negative effect of regulatory stringency on small U.S. livestock operators

tion emissions and minimizing distortionary effects elsewhere in the economy. If emissions taxes are not feasible, input taxes are preferable to production taxes, which in turn are preferable to tariffs (Beghin, Roland-Holst, and van der Mensbrugghe 1997; Lloyd 1992; Ulph 1999). This point has been documented empirically in the case of forestry products (Barbier and Rauscher 1994), as well as for the Indonesian economy (Lee and Roland-Holst 1997). With increasing economic integration, Indonesia is tending to specialize in resource- and pollution-intensive activities. Pollution emissions at the national level (as distinguished from the sector level), however, cannot be decreased even modestly by using tariffs. By contrast, production taxes proportional to the pollution content of output make the targeted pollution abatement feasible at a reasonable cost in forgone growth.

There have been few trade disputes over technical requirements related to the environment. Whalley and Hamilton (1996) report only a limited number of environment-related trade disputes for the period 1982–96, and very few such disputes have been brought to the WTO since 1995 (WTO website). Only two of the 43 requests from developing countries— concerning reformulated U.S. gasoline and the U.S. ban on certain seafood products—involve environmental objectives. Of 300 cases of trade impediments to U.S. agricultural exports, only one was based on environmental goals; most involved food safety and protection of crops and livestock from pests and disease. It is not clear whether the paucity of environment-related disputes reflects the limited impact of environmental regulations on traded goods, the high costs of litigation, or the scope of disputes provided for under WTO rules.

Box 3.3   Evidence on the "race to the bottom"

Empirical studies of the pattern of trade, the allocation of FDI, plant location, and profitability have found limited or no evidence that environmental regulations have reduced investment or lowered competitiveness. As might be expected, evidence for a race to the bottom is somewhat stronger for the dirtiest industries, although even here there are conflicting results. There is no evidence that intracountry differences in environmental regulations affect investment. Large firms appear better-able to accommodate environmental regulations than smaller firms.

Studies of the *patterns of trade* have used the cross-sectional Heckscher-Ohlin (H-O) model, which explains specialization on the basis of environmental abundance, to examine indirectly the effects of environmental regulation on international competitiveness. The results are mixed. Using 1977 data, Kalt (1988) found that U.S. environmental regulation had a significantly negative effect on competitiveness, as measured by net exports of manufacturing goods. Tobey (1990), using 1975 data, found no evidence that increased regulation affected output in pollution-intensive industries. Han (1996) tested the environmental H-O model using panel data (across industries and over time) and actual expenditure data on pollution abatement as a measure of the environmental input. He found that increased environmental regulation has had a significantly negative effect on competitiveness, but that this effect has decreased over time as many countries tightened their regulations and as abatement costs fell with new capital vintages, learning by doing, and new technologies. Valluru and Peterson (1997) and Diakosauvas (1994) found little evidence that environmental regulations have had a significant negative economic effect on agricultural trade except for the most-polluting commodities such as cotton and tobacco. Xu (1999) found that the export performance of environmentally sensitive industries in 34 countries was unchanged between the 1960s and the 1990s despite the emergence of environmental standards in most industrial countries since 1970.

The evidence on the *allocation of FDI* provides little support for the existence of pollution havens. The United States is importing more pollution-intensive industries than it is exporting, and dirty industries are no more likely to invest abroad than other industries (Albrecht 1998, cited in Nordström and Vaughan 1999; Eskeland and Harrison 1997). Eskeland and Harrison (1997) find no evidence of pollution-intensive bias in the allocation of French and U.S. FDI flows going into manufacturing industries in Côte d'Ivoire, Mexico, Morocco, and the Republica Bolivariana de Venezuela. Xing and Kolstad (1995) find that U.S. FDI in chemical industries seems to be influenced by weak environmental regulation, as proxied by sulfur dioxide emissions, but they also find that FDI in cleaner industries was not influenced by environmental stringency.

Studies have found only limited evidence that environmental regulation has a significant effect on *plant location*. Surveys of the relocation of transnational corporations provide some support for the notion of a race to the bottom (Runge 1994; UNCTAD 1993). Surveys, however, tend to be less reliable than actual data because they report what is said rather than what is done (Levinson 1997a). Levinson finds, for many industries and measures of stringency, that interstate differences in environmental regulations do not systematically affect the location choices of most manufacturing plants in the United States. Mani, Pargal, and Huq (1997) find, surprisingly, that a proxy for different levels of enforcement of federal environmental policy in Indian states is positively related to decisions on the location of new manufacturing plants for a wide range of manufacturing industries and for the smaller subset of pollution-intensive industries. It is possible that the proxy for stringency (the share of the state budget spent on environmental programs) measures the efficiency of state administration, which induces firms to locate in states with higher environmental expenditures.

Several other studies have looked at the impact of environmental regulation in agriculture, but mostly in OECD countries. Metcalfe (2000) finds that stringency had little impact on the location of U.S. hog production across states and over time. Stringency did have a negative impact on small operators but not on large, modern, confinement livestock producers. Hettige and others (1996) found evidence of economies of scale in environmental compliance for many other industries in several countries.

Finally, studies have found a positive relationship between environmental performance and the profitability of U.S. firms (Cohen and Fenn 1997; Repetto 1995). Although environmental compliance is not free, it creates new market opportunities and may induce further efficiency gains that may offset its (small) cost. Environmental performance appears to be systematically associated with higher profitability.

Several global environmental treaties have been concluded over the last 25 years, notably the Convention on International Trade in Endangered Species of Wild Fauna and Flora (CITES)[32] protecting trade in endangered species, and the Montreal Protocol[33] banning the use of ozone-depleting chemicals (for example CFCs, widely used as a coolant in refrigerators and air conditioners). These agreements typically provide incentives for compliance through both technical and financial assistance. In addition, many also provide for trade sanctions to enforce compliance. The compatibility with WTO rules-of-trade sanctions potentially allowed by such treaties has not been tested.

Alternative policies for environmental protection

Although trade sanctions are not effective means of inducing environmental protection, foreigners can affect environmental choices in other ways. In some cases, foreign countries could provide subsidies to encourage better environmental practices. For example, in the U.S.-Mexican dispute over protecting dolphins, an alternative policy would have been for the United States to equip Mexican fishermen with improved nets.[34] The cost of this option would have to be compared with the overall losses resulting from trade restrictions. This is to some extent an empirical issue, but the option would at least reduce dolphin kill, which neither trade sanctions nor a consumer boycott is likely to do.

Ecolabeling schemes enable foreign consumers to choose goods produced in an environmentally benign way. These schemes can be a source of trade friction, even though the markets they cover are still relatively small, because of the increased production costs involved in the certification process. For example, ecolabeling schemes in textiles require multiple production standards for dyes, fibers, and bleaching chemicals (OECD 1997a). In addition, most schemes impose fees. Canada's Environmental Choice Program imposes a 0.5 percent charge, based on the price of the good, on sales up to Canadian $1,000,000. Certifi-

cation under industrial-country labeling schemes may be difficult for developing countries to obtain (Jha, Markandya, and Vossenaar 1999; Jha and Zarrilli 1994; OECD 1997a; Zarsky 1994). For example, none of the 48 licenses granted under the EU Commission's ecolabel went to a developing-economy firm, although it is not clear whether any of these firms applied (Nimon and Beghin 1999). Ecolabeling schemes can be used in a discriminatory way, especially in markets dominated by developing economies, such as textiles. Domestic industries have more say in defining ecostandards than do foreign competitors. The standards are likely to favor technologies that are feasible in industrial countries rather than the input mix and technology set of developing countries.

Local ecolabels are emerging in developing countries, especially in timber-based products, but also in textiles, to promote better practice and preempt discriminatory labeling in industrial countries. For example, Malaysia supports ecolabels and standards that apply to all types of timber and are based on internationally agreed standards, not merely on standards developed by one or a few countries (Jha, Markandya, and Vossenaar 1999).

Another approach is to help trading partners implement market-based environmental policies that have proved effective in tackling environmental problems in developing countries. Reducing subsidies on pollution-intensive activities or raising taxes on polluting activities, through discharge, input, or output taxes, has reduced pollution and increased tax revenues in Bangladesh, Brazil, Indonesia, and other countries (World Bank 1997). Market-based instruments also provide incentives to save on the taxed resource and become more resource-efficient. The more targeted the instrument, the better. Some countries, such as China and Malaysia, have used emissions charges with some success. When the cost of monitoring is not prohibitive, the market instrument can be very targeted; for example, many countries use stumpage fees to foster sustainable forest management (World Bank

1997). China has been successfully abating pollution for the past 20 years by using levies (Wang and Wheeler 2000).

Privatization and competition, or incremental reform in this direction, can promote better resource management. Several studies identify state firms as worse polluters than firms in the private sector (Pargal and Wheeler 1996) or centrally planned economies as worse than market economies (Vukina, Beghin, and Solakoglu 1999). Incentives to economize, combined with increased resources for better management, have improved the performance of public entities in many countries. For example, in several countries, water-user associations have been substituting for the government in allocating irrigation water.

Engagement of the public is essential to successful environmental protection. This process can foster partnership among the public, firms, and authorities. The government can be a facilitator for private industry by disseminating information on new technology and environmental regulations. Alternatively, the process can be coercive, relying on disclosure of violation of environmental regulations, such as illegal discharges. The coercive approach has been effective in developing economies such as China (Dasgupta and Wheeler 1997), although complaints tend to be positively associated with higher income and greater human capital.

Regional approaches to environmental standards may prove more effective than global approaches, particularly on issues with a clear regional component such as transboundary emissions and shared water resources. A regional approach does not imply uniform standards for domestic environmental problems; the case against harmonization of policies is overwhelming in most settings because of different valuations of the marginal benefits of environmental protection.

Notes

1. The regulation of standards in a local or national economy, particularly with respect to appropriateness and efficiency impacts, is another important topic for many developing countries, but it is not the main subject of this chapter. The effects of voluntary product standards are touched on summarily.

2. Many international food standards are set by the Codex Alimentarius Commission, which is based in Rome and is a joint commission of the Food and Agriculture Organization of the United Nations (FAO) and the World Health Organization (WHO).

3. This framework is taken, in part, from Rollo and Winters 2000.

4. For a primer on standards and trade, see National Research Council 1995.

5. This section draws on Maskus and Wilson forthcoming.

6. The Development Economics Research Group of the World Bank is carrying out a major project on trade and standards that includes construction of a new global database on standards barriers to support future empirical and policy research in this area.

7. The estimate of the decrease in costs attributable to the adoption of uniform standards is taken from Gasiorek, Smith, and Venables 1992.

8. An overview of all WTO dispute settlement cases may be accessed through the WTO website at <www.wto.org/wto/dispute/bulletin.htm> and the WTO document distribution facility at <www.wto. org/ddf>. The U.S.-EU case on hormone-treated beef is cataloged under WT/DS26 and WT/DS48.

9. WTO cases involving only industrial countries may have implications for developing-country exporters' market access. For example, the EU's restrictions on U.S. exports of genetically modified grains could have major implications for the exports of similar products from countries, such as Argentina and Brazil, where varieties of genetically modified organisms have been widely planted.

10. The budget of the office of the USTR in fiscal 2000 was $25.5 million, and the office had 178 (full-time equivalent) staff members; see <http://www.ustr. gov/reports/spy.pdf>.

11. For additional background, see Wilson 2000a and 2000b.

12. The (unweighted) average development assistance budget as a share of GDP for low-income countries was 11.2 percent in 1998.

13. The World Bank has an active program to assist developing countries in improving their standards infrastructure. Further information is available at <http:// www1.worldbank.org/wbiep/trade/Standards.html>.

14. This discussion is taken from formal positions submitted to WTO General Council, January–November 1999.

15. These core labor standards were enunciated in the June 1998 ILO Declaration on Fundamental Principles and Rights at Work.

16. The 1996 OECD study was updated in a more recent report (OECD 2000), reaching broadly the same conclusions as the earlier study.

17. This analysis should be viewed with some caution, for several reasons: simple correlations provide no information on the direction of causality; the lack of a theoretical model of the determinants of growth means that the measured correlations between standards and growth may be misleading; and it is difficult to construct adequate quantitative measures of the extent of adherence to core labor standards.

18. Alternatively, the worker association could restrict entry of workers and enable them to bargain for a higher wage, improving the welfare of workers in the association at the expense of excluded workers. The outcome would depend on the goals of the association and the relative bargaining power of workers and capital (Maskus 1997).

19. The "prisoner's dilemma" in this context refers to the fact that if a country attempts to improve standards it will lose a competitive edge if it acts alone. As a result, in the absence of coordination, no country will attempt to improve standards.

20. Maskus (1997) points out, however, that labor turnover in EPZs is rapid, in part because assembly employment is dominated by women, who leave to marry. In any event, high labor turnover results in low unionization rates, even in EPZs in which union organization and the right to strike are protected.

21. Firms in EPZs may pay higher wages than other domestic firms for several reasons: they benefit from less burdensome regulations and can operate more flexibly; they tend to be larger and thus enjoy scale economies; they are governed by the policies of foreign-owned firms that are bound by their headquarters' best practices in labor standards; they need to attract labor to move to the area; or pressures to maintain quality to satisfy export requirements may encourage them to pay higher wages to induce greater effort (Maskus 1997).

22. Even here, the impact of higher exports on wages in importing countries is likely to be small, particularly in the familiar case of highly labor intensive goods such as apparel, footwear, and electronics (Maskus 1997).

23. This analysis depends on the structure of labor market conditions. For example, employers who collude to reduce labor standards can benefit if there are effective barriers to labor mobility.

24. In the 1990s China, whose labor standards have been criticized, was the largest beneficiary of FDI flows among developing countries. Significant anecdotal evidence indicates, however, that U.S. FDI in China is establishing above-market-wage, high-standards operations. Clearly, firms are investing in China for many

reasons, but the attraction of a large and rapidly growing market is the most significant motive.

25. Labor markets in developing countries have been a subject of increasing involvement by the World Bank—including the seminal 1995 World Development Report on "Workers in an Integrating World"—in large part because of the recognition that they play a key role in poverty reduction and economic development. Bank projects with a labor market component have increased dramatically since the early 1990s. Efforts are also underway to enhance dialogue with NGOs and other external partners, including regular consultations with representatives from the International Confederation of Free Trade Unions (ICFTU) to discuss areas of mutual concern.

26. For more information, see http://www.ilo.org/public/english/bureau/inf/pr/2000/27.htm.

27. To date, six cases against developing countries have been initiated, all by the EU and the United States. Four cases deal with pharmaceuticals and agricultural chemicals and two concern compatibility of domestic regulations with TRIPs obligations. The countries involved are Argentina, Brazil, India, and Pakistan; see http://www.wto.org/english/tratop_e/dispu_e/stplay_e.doc.

28. The transfers refer to the net present value of payments from 1988 on, based on the 1988 structure of patents.

29. The scale effect, almost by definition, has an elasticity of one with respect to growth. Thus, if an economy grows by x percent, all else being equal, emissions will also increase by x percent.

30. A significant body of literature on the "environmental Kuznets curve" (EKC) posits that pollution intensity follows an inverse-U-shaped curve with respect to income. At low levels of development, pollution tends to increase with economic growth; above a certain income level, it declines. There is evidence, at least for some types of pollutants, that the turning point in some developing countries is occurring at lower levels of income than was witnessed in industrial countries earlier. If this tentative evidence is borne out, it suggests that several factors are working in favor of a more rapid transformation to a cleaner environment in developing countries. These factors include technological diffusion of both cleaner production processes and abatement technologies and greater awareness of the costs of environmental damage on the part of both officials and the general public. This literature is summarized succinctly in Nordström and Vaughan 1999.

31. See Rock 1996, however, for a critique of the measurement of openness and market integration.

32. For more information see http://www.wcmc.org.uk/CITES/index.shtml.

33. For more information on the Montreal Protocol, see http://www.unep.org/ozone/montreal.htm.

34. The United States placed trade restrictions on the import of Mexican tuna because Mexican tuna fishing techniques led to the indiscriminate killing of dolphins.

References

Abler, D. G., A. G. Rodriguez, and J. S. Shortle. 1999. "Trade Liberalization and the Environment in Costa Rica." *Environment and Development Economics* 4 (3): 357–73.

Albrecht, J. 1998. "Environmental Policy and Inward Investment Position of U.S. Dirty Industries." *Intereconomics* (July–August): 186–94.

Anderson, K. 1992. "The Standard Welfare Economics of Policies Affecting Trade and the Environment." In *The Greening of World Trade Issues*, edited by K. Anderson and R. Blackhurst. Chapter 2. Ann Arbor: University of Michigan Press.

Anderson, K., and R. Blackhurst, eds. 1992. *The Greening of World Trade Issues*. Ann Arbor: University of Michigan Press.

Bailey, R., ed. 1995. *The True State of the Planet*. New York: Free Press.

Baldwin, Richard E. 1992. "Are Economists' Traditional Trade Policy Views Still Valid?" *Journal of Economic Literature* 30: 804–29.

———. 2000. "Regulatory Protectionism, Developing Nations and a Two-Tier World Trade System." Discussion Paper 2574. Centre for Economic Policy Research, London.

Baldwin, Robert E., and Anthony J. Venables. 1997. "International Economic Integration." In *Handbook of International Economics,* edited by G. Grossman and K. Rogoff. Vol. 3. Amsterdam: North-Holland.

Bandara, J. S., and I. Coxhead. 1999. "Can Trade Liberalization Have Environmental Benefits in Developing Country Agriculture? A Sri Lankan Case Study." *Journal of Policy Modeling* 21 (3): 349–74.

Barbier, E. B., and M. Rauscher. 1994. "Trade, Tropical Deforestation and Policy Interventions." *Environment and Resource Economics* 4: 75–90.

Barrett, S. 1994. "Strategic Environmental Policy and International Trade." *Journal of Public Economics* 54: 325–38.

Bartik, Timothy J. 1989. "Small Business Start-Ups in the United States: Estimates of the Effects of Characteristics of States." *Southern Economic Journal* 55 (4, April): 1004–18.

Basu, Kaushik. 1999. "International Labor Standards and Child Labor." *Challenge* 42 (5, September–October): 80–93.

Beghin J., and M. Potier. 1997. "Effects of Trade Liberalisation on the Environment in the Manufacturing Sector." *World Economy* 20 (4): 435–56.

Beghin J., B. Bowland, S. Dessus, D. Roland-Holst, and D. van der Mensbrugghe. 1999. "Trade, Environment, and Public Health in Chile. Evidence from an Economywide Model." In Per G. Fredriksson, ed., *Trade, Global Policy, and the Environment*, 35–54. Discussion Paper 402. World Bank, Washington, D.C.

Beghin, John, David Roland-Holst, and Dominique van der Mensbrugghe. 1995. "Trade Liberalization and the Environment in the Pacific Basin: Coordinated Approaches to Mexican Trade and Environment Policy." *American Journal of Agricultural Economics* 10 Aug 1995. 77(3):778.

———. 1997. "Trade and Environment Linkages: Piecemeal Reform and Optimal Intervention." *Canadian Journal of Economics* 30: 442–55.

———, eds. Forthcoming. *Trade and Environment in General Equilibrium: Evidence from Developing Economies*. Dordrecht, the Netherlands: Kluwer Academic Publishers.

Benjamin, Dwayne, Loren Brandt, Paul Glewwe, and Guo Li. 1999. "Markets, Human Capital, and Inequality: Evidence from Rural China." Development Research Group, World Bank, Washington, D.C. Processed.

Bhagwati, J. N. 1997. "The Demands to Reduce Diversity among Trading Nations." In *Fair Trade and Harmonization: Prerequisites for Free Trade?* edited by J. N. Bhagwati and R. E. Hudec. Cambridge, Mass.: MIT Press.

Bhagwati, J. N. and T. N. Srinivasan. 1997. "Trade and the Environment: Does Environmental Diversity Detract from the Case for Free Trade?" In *Fair Trade and Harmonization: Prerequisites for Free Trade?* edited by J. N. Bhagwati and R. E. Hudec. Cambridge, Mass.: MIT Press.

Bhagwati, J. N., and R. E. Hudec, eds. 1997. *Fair Trade and Harmonization: Prerequisites for Free Trade?* Cambridge, Mass.: MIT Press.

Birdsall, N., and D. Wheeler. 1992. "Trade Policy and Industrial Pollution in Latin America: Where Are the Pollution Havens?" In Patrick Low, ed., *International Trade and the Environment*, 159–67. Discussion Paper 159. World Bank, Washington, D.C.

Brainerd, Elizabeth. 1998. "Winners and Losers in Russia's Economic Transition." *American Economic Review* 88 (5): 1094–1116.

Brander, J., and B. J. Spencer. 1985. "Export Subsidies and International Market Share Rivalry." *Journal of International Economics* 18: 83–100.

Brander, J., and S. M. Taylor. 1997. "International Trade between Consumer and Conservationist Countries." Working Paper 6006. National Bureau for Economic Research, Cambridge, Mass.

Brown, Drusilla K., Alan V. Deardorff, and Robert M. Stern. 2000. "U.S. Trade and Other Policy Options and Programs to Deter Foreign Exploitation of Child Labor." In *Topics in Empirical International Economics: A Festschrift in Honor of Robert E. Lipsey*, edited by Magnus Blomstrπm and Linda S. Goldberg. Chicago: University of Chicago Press

Carruth, Alan A., and Andrew J. Oswald. 1981. "The Determination of Union and Non-Union Wage Rates." *European Economic Review* 16: 285–302.

Chang, Seung Wha. 1997. "GATTing a Green Trade Barrier: Eco-Labelling and the WTO Agreement on Technical Barriers to Trade." *Journal of World Trade* 31 (1): 137–159.

Chichilinsky, G. 1994. "North-South Trade and the Global Environment." *American Economic Review* 84: 851–74.

Choksi, A., M. Michaely, and D. Papageorgiu. 1991. "The Design of Successful Trade Liberalization Policies." In *Foreign Economic Liberalization*, edited by A. Koves and P. Marer. Boulder, Colo.: Westview Press.

Cohen, M., and S. Fenn. 1997. "Environmental and Financial Performance: Are They Related?" Vanderbilt University, Department of Economics, Nashville, Tenn..

Copeland, B. R. "International Trade and the Environment: Policy Reform in a Polluted Small Open Economy." *Journal of Environmental Economics and Management* 26: 44–65.

Copeland, B. R., and S. M. Taylor. 1995. "North-South Trade and the Environment." *Quarterly Journal of Economics* 109: 755–87.

Currie, Janet, and Ann Harrison. 1997. "Trade Reform and Labor Market Adjustment in Morocco." *Journal of Labor Economics* 15 (3): S44–S72.

Dasgupta, Susmita, and David Wheeler. 1997. "Citizen Complaints as Environmental Indicators: Evidence from China." Policy Research Working Paper 1704. World Bank, Washington, D.C.

Dasgupta, Susmita, Hua Wang, and David Wheeler. 1997. "Surviving Success: Policy Reform and the Future of Industrial Pollution in China." Policy Research Working Paper 1856. World Bank, Washington, D.C.

Davis, Donald R. 1996. "Trade Liberalization and Income Distribution." Working Paper 5693. National Bureau of Economic Research, Cambridge, Mass.

Dean, J. M. 1999."Testing the Impact of Trade Liberalization on the Environment. Theory and Evidence." In Per G. Fredriksson, ed., *Trade, Global Policy, and the Environment,* 55–63. Discussion Paper 402. World Bank, Washington, D.C.

Deininger, Klaus, and Lyn Squire. 1996. "A New Data Set Measuring Income Inequality." *The World Bank Economic Review* 10 (3): 565–91.

Dessus, S. and D. van der Mensbrugghe. 1997. "Trade Reform and the Environment: The Case of Vietnam." OECD Development Centre, Paris. Processed.

Dessus, S., and M. Bussolo. 1998. "Is There a Trade-off between Trade Liberalization and Pollution Abatement? A Computable General Equilibrium Assessment Applied to Costa Rica." *Journal of Policy Modeling* 20 (February): 11–31.

Dessus, S., and D. van der Mensbrugghe (1996). "Trade Liberalization and the Environment in Vietnam," OECD Development Centre, Paris, mimeo.

Dessus, Sebastien, David Roland-Holst, and Dominique van der Mensbrugghe. 1999 (in preparation or forthcoming) "Trade and Environment in China," in Beghin et al. (eds.), *op citum.*

————. Forthcoming. "Trade and Environment in China." In *Trade and Environment in General Equilibrium: Evidence from Developing Economies*, edited by J. Beghin, D. Roland-Holst, and D. van der Mensbrugghe. Dordrecht, the Netherlands: Kluwer Academic Publishers.

Diakosauvas, D. 1994. "The Impact of Environmental Policies on Agricultural Trade." *Journal of International Development* 6 (2): 207–18.

Eskeland, Gunnar S., and Ann E. Harrison. 1997. "Moving to Greener Pastures? Multinationals and the Pollution Haven Hypothesis." Policy Research Working Paper 1744. World Bank, Washington, D.C.

European Commission. 1996.

Feenstra, Robert C., and Gordon H. Hanson. 1997. "Foreign Direct Investment and Relative Wages: Evidence from Mexico's Maquiladoras." *Journal of International Economics* 42 (3–4): 371–93.

Ferrantino, M. J., and L. A. Linkins. 1999. "The Effect of Global Trade Liberalization on Toxic Emissions in Industry." *Weltwirtschaftliches Archiv/Review of World Economics* 135 (1): 128–55.

Finger, J. Michael and Philip Shuler. 2000. Developing Countries and the Millennium Round. Mimeo.

Finger, J. Michael, and Philip Schuler. 1999. "Implementation of Uruguay Round Commitments: The Development Challenge." Policy Research Working Paper 2215. Trade Development Research Group, World Bank, Washington, D.C.

———. 2000. "Developing Countries and the Millennium Round." Processed.

Fink, Carsten. 2000. "How Stronger Patent Protection in India Might Affect the Behavior of Transnational Pharmaceutical Industries." Policy Research Working Paper 2352. Trade, Development Research Group, World Bank, Washington, D.C.

Fischer, Ronald and Serra, Pablo. 2000. "Standards and protection." Journal of International Economics. 01 Dec 2000. 52(2):377.

Fischer, Ronald. *The New Protectionism and Latin America. Introduction Chapter.*

Freeman, Richard B., and David L. Lindauer. 1999. "Why Not Africa?" Working Paper 6942. National Bureau of Economic Research, Cambridge, Mass.

Gandal, Neil, and Oz Shy. 1996. "Standardization Policy and International Trade." Working Paper 12-96. Sackler Institute for Economic Studies, Tel Aviv.

Gasiorek, Michael, Alasdair Smith, and Anthony J. Venables. 1992. "1992: Trade and Welfare—A General Equilibrium Model." In *Trade Flows and Trade Policy after 1992*, edited by L. A. Winters. Cambridge, U.K.: Cambridge University Press.

Gottschalk, Peter, and Timothy M. Smeeding. 1997. "Cross-National Comparisons of Earnings and Income Inequality." *Journal of Economic Literature* 35 (June): 633–87.

Grossman, G. M., and A. B. Krueger. 1992. "Environmental Impacts of a North American Free Trade Agreement." Discussion Paper 644. Centre for Economic Policy Research, London.

Han, K. 1996. Dissertation on U.S. Manufacturing and Environmental Regulation. University of Illinois, Urbana-Champaign, Ill.

Hanson, Gordon H., and Ann Harrison. 1999. "Trade Liberalization and Wage Inequality in Mexico." *Industrial and Labor Relations Review* 52: 271–88.

Harrison, Glenn W., Thomas F. Rutherford, and David G. Tarr, 1996. "Increased Competition and Completion of the Market in the European Union: Static and Steady State Effects." *Journal of Economic Integration* 11 (3): 332–65.

Hartman, Raymond S., Mainul Huq, and David Wheeler. 1997. "Why Paper Mills Clean Up: Determinants of Pollution Abatements in Four Asian Countries." Policy Research Working Paper 1710. World Bank, Washington D.C.

Haskel, Jonathan, and Matthew J. Slaughter. 2000. "Have Falling Tariffs and Transportation Costs Raised U.S. Wage Inequality?" Working Paper 7539. National Bureau of Economic Research, Cambridge, Mass.

Henson, Spencer, Rupert Loader, Alan Swinbank, Maury Bredahl, and Nicole Lux. 2000. "Impact of Sanitary and Phytosanitary Measures on Developing Countries." Centre for Food Economics Research, Department of Agricultural and Food Economics, University of Reading, Reading, U.K.

Hertel, Thomas W., and Will Martin. 1999. "Developing Country Interests in Liberalizing Manufactures Trade." Background research paper for Seattle Ministerial Meeting of the WTO. World Bank Institute, Washington, D.C.

Hertel, Thomas W., Bernard M. Hoekman, and Will Martin. 2000. "Developing Countries and a New Round of WTO Negotiations." World Bank Institute, World Bank, Washington D.C.

Hettige, H., M. Huq, S. Pargal, and D. Wheeler. 1996. "Determinants of Pollution Abatement in Developing Countries: Evidence from South and Southeast Asia." *World Development* 24: 1891–1904.

Hoekman, Bernard, and Denise Eby Konan. 1998.

Hoekman, Bernard M., and Denise Eby Konan. 1999. "Deep Integration, Nondiscrimination, and Euro-Mediterranean Trade." Policy Research Working Paper 2130. Development Research Group, World Bank, Washington, D.C.

Hufbauer, Gary, Barbara Kotschwar, and John S. Wilson. 2000. "Trade Policy, Standards, and Development in Central America." Paper prepared for a World Bank Institute seminar, Panama City, June 27–29. World Bank Institute, Washington, D.C.

ILO (International Labour Organisation). 1993. *Multinationals and Employment.* Geneva.

———. 2000. *Review of Annual Reports under the Follow-Up to the ILO Declaration on Fundamental Principles and Rights at Work.* Geneva.

Jaffe, A., S. Peterson, P. Portney, and R. Stavins. 1995. "Environmental Regulation and the Competitiveness of U.S. Manufacturing: What Does the Evidence Tell Us?" *Journal of Economic Literature* 33: 132–63.

Jha, V., A. Markandya, and R. Vossenaar. 1999. *Reconciling Trade and the Environment: Lessons from Case Studies in Developing Countries.* Cheltenham, U.K.: Edward Elgar.

Jha, V., and S. Zarrilli. 1994. "Eco-labeling Initiatives as Potential Barriers to Trade." In *Life-Cycle*

Management and Trade, 64–73. OECD Documents. Paris.

Jian, Tianlun, Jeffrey D. Sachs, and Andrew M. Warner. 1996. "Trends in Regional Inequality in China." Working Paper 5412. National Bureau of Economic Research, Cambridge, Mass.

Johnson, George. 1997. "Changes in Earnings Inequality: The Role of Demand Shifts." *Journal of Economic Perspectives* 11 (2): 41–54.

Johnson, Harry G., and Peter Mieszkowski. 1970. "The Effects of Unionization on the Distribution of Income." *Quarterly Journal of Economics* 84 (4): 539–61.

Jones, Ronald W. 1971. "Distortions in Factor Markets and the General Equilibrium Model of Production." *Journal of Political Economy* 79: 437–59.

Kalt, J. P. 1988. "The Impact of Domestic Environmental Regulatory Policies on U.S. International Competitiveness." In *International Competitiveness,* edited by A. M. Spence and H. A. Hazard. Cambridge, Mass.: Ballinger.

Katz, Lawrence F., and Kevin M. Murphy. 1992. "Changes in Relative Wages, 1963–1987: Supply and Demand Factors." *Quarterly Journal of Economics* (February): 35–78.

Khalid, R., and J. B. Braden. 1993. "Welfare Effects of Environmental Regulation in an Open Economy: The Case of Malaysian Palm Oil." *Journal of Agricultural Economics* 44 (January): 25–37.

Klevorick, Alvin. 1997. "Reflections on the Race to the Bottom." In *Fair Trade and Harmonization: Prerequisites for Free Trade?* edited by J. N. Bhagwati and R. E. Hudec. Cambridge, Mass.: MIT Press.

Leamer, Edward E. 1984. *Sources of International Comparative Advantage.* Cambridge, Mass.: MIT Press.

———. 1998. "In Search of Stolper-Samuelson Linkages between International Trade and Lower Wages." In *Imports, Exports, and the American Worker,* edited by Susan M. Collins. Pp. 141–202. Washington, D.C.: Brookings Institution Press.

Lee, H., and D. Roland-Holst. 1997. "The Environment and Welfare Implications of Trade and Tax Policy." *Journal of Development Economics* 52: 65–82.

Levinson, A. 1997a. "Environmental Regulations and Industry Location: International and Domestic Evidence." In *Fair Trade and Harmonization: Prerequisites for Free Trade?* edited by J. N. Bhagwati and R. E. Hudec. Cambridge, Mass.: MIT Press.

———. 1997b. "NIMBY Taxes Matter: States Taxes and Interstate Hazardous Waste Shipments." University of Wisconsin, Madison, Wis.

Li, Hongyi, Lyn Squire, and Heng-fu Zou. 1998. "Explaining International and Intertemporal Variations in Income Inequality." *Economic Journal* 108 (January): 26–43.

Lister, Bruce A. 1987. "Comparison of U.S. Laws and Regulations Concerning Labeling of Prepackaged Foods with the Codex Alimentarius Draft General Standard for Labeling of Prepackaged Foods." *Food, Drug, and Cosmetic Law Journal* 42: 175–83.

Lloyd, P. J. 1992. "The Problem of Optimal Environmental Policy Choice." In *The Greening of World Trade Issues,* edited by K. Anderson and R. Blackhurst. Chap. 2. Ann Arbor: University of Michigan Press.

Lucas, R. E .B., D. Wheeler, and H. Hettige. 1992. "Economic Development, Environment Regulation and the International Migration of Toxic Industrial Pollution: 1960–1988." In Patrick Low, ed., *International Trade and the Environment,* 67–86. Discussion Paper 159. World Bank, Washington, D.C.

Mani, Muthukumara, and David Wheeler. 1998. "In Search of Pollution Havens? Dirty Industry in the World Economy 1960–1995." *Journal of Environment and Development* 7 (3).

Mani, Muthukumara, Sheoli Pargal, and Mainul Huq. 1997. "Does Environmental Regulation Matter? Determinants of the Location of New Manufacturing Plants in India 1994." Policy Research Working Paper 1718. World Bank, Washington, D.C.

Martin, Will, and Keith E. Maskus. 1999. "Core Labor Standards and Competitiveness: Implications for Global Trade Policy." World Bank, Washington, D.C. Processed.

Maskus, Keith E. 1997. "Should Core Labor Standards Be Imposed through International Trade Policy?" Policy Research Working Paper 1817. Development Research Group, World Bank, Washington, D.C.

———. 2000a. "Regulatory Standards in the WTO: Comparing Intellectual Property Rights with Competition Policy, Environmental Protection, and Core Labor Standards." World Bank, Washington, D.C. Processed.

———. 2000b. "Intellectual Property Rights in the Global Economy." Processed.

Maskus, Keith E., and John S. Wilson, eds. Forthcoming. *Quantifying the Impact of Technical Barriers* to Trade: Can It Be Done? Ann Arbor: University of Michigan Press.

Matutes, C., and P. Regibeau. 1996. "A Selective Review of the Economics of Standardization: Entry Deterrence, Technological Progress and International Competition." *European Journal of Political Economy* 12.(2): 183–209.

Messerlin, Patrick A., and Jamel Zarrouk. 2000. "Trade Facilitation: Technical Regulations and Customs Procedures." *World Economy* 23 (4): 577–93.

Metcalfe, M. R. 2000. "Environmental Regulation and Implications for the U.S. Hog and Pork Industries." Ph.D. dissertation. North Carolina State University, Raleigh, N.C.

Michaely, M., D. Papageorgiu, and A. Choksi. 1991. *Liberalizing Foreign Trade: Lessons of Experience in the Developing World.* Cambridge, Mass.: Basil Blackwell.

Moenius, Johannes. 2000. "Information versus Product Adaptation: The Role of Standards in Trade." Northwestern University, Kellogg Graduate School of Management, Evanston, Ill. Processed.

National Research Council. 1995. *Standards, Conformity Assessment, and Trade: Into the 21st Century.* Washington, D.C.: National Academy Press.

Nimon W., and J. Beghin. 1999."Ecolabels and International Trade in the Textile and Apparel Market." *American Journal of Agricultural Economics* 81: 1078–84.

Nordström, H., and S. Vaughan. 1999. *Trade and Environment.* Special Studies 4. Geneva: World Trade Organization.

O'Connor, D. 1994. *Managing the Environment with Rapid Industrialisation: Lessons from the East Asian Experience.* Paris: Development Centre Studies.

OECD (Organisation for Economic Co-operation and Development) 1996. *Trade, Employment and Labour Standards.* Paris.

———. 1997a. "Eco-Labeling: Actual Effects of Selected Programmes." (97)105. Paris.

———. 1997b. *Regionalism and Its Place in the Multilateral Trading System.* Paris.

———. 1999. *An Assessment of the Costs for International Trade in Meeting Regulatory Requirements.* Paris.

———. 2000. *International Trade and Core Labour Standards.* Paris.

Otsuki, Tsunehiro, John S. Wilson, and Mirvat Sewadeh. 2000. "Saving Two in a Billion: A Case Study to Quantify the Trade Effect of European Food Safety Standards on African Exports." World Bank, Washington, D.C. Processed.

Panagariya, Arvind. 1999a. "Labor Standards in the WTO and Developing Countries: Trading Rights at Risk." University of Maryland, College Park, Md.

———. 1999b. "TRIPs and the WTO: An Uneasy Marriage." University of Maryland, College Park, Md.

Pargal, Sheoli, and David Wheeler. 1996. "Informal Regulation of Industrial Pollution in Developing Countries: Evidence from Indonesia." *Journal of Political Economy* 104 (December): 1314–27.

Repetto, Robert. 1995. *Jobs, Competitiveness and Environmental Regulation: What Are the Real Issues?* Washington, D.C.: World Resources Institute.

Reppelin-Hill, V. 1999. "Trade and Environment: An Empirical Analysis of the Technology Effect in the Steel Industry." *Journal of Environmental Economics and Management* 38 (3): 283–301.

Richardson, J. David. 2000. "The WTO and Market-Supportive Regulation: A Way Forward on New Competition, Technological, and Labor Issues." *Review* (Federal Reserve Bank of St. Louis) 82 (4): 115–26.

Robbins, Donald J. 1996. "Evidence on Trade and Wages in the Developing World." Technical Paper 119. OECD Development Center, Paris.

Roberts, Donna. 1998. "Implementation of the WTO Agreement on the Application of Sanitary and Phytosanitary Measures: The First Two Years." IATRC Working Paper 98-4. International Agricultural Trade Research Consortium. Available at <http://www1.umn.edu/iatrc/workpap.html>.

Rock, M. T. 1996. "Pollution Intensity of GDP and Trade Policy: Can the World Bank Be Wrong?" *World Development* 24 (3): 471–79.

Rollo, Jim, and L. Alan Winters. 2000. "Subsidiarity and Governance Challenges for the WTO: Environmental and Labor Standards." *World Economy* (4): 561–76.

Runge, C. F., with F. Ortalo-Magne and P. Van de Kamp. 1994. *Freer Trade, Protected Environment: Balancing Trade Liberalization and Environmental Success.* New York: Council on Foreign Relations Press.

Slaughter, Matthew J. 1999. "Globalization and Wages: A Tale of Two Perspectives." *World Economy* 22 (5): 609–30.

———. Forthcoming. "Trade Liberalization and Per Capita Income Convergence: A Difference-in-Differences Analysis." *Journal of International Economics.*

Stephenson, Sherry M. 1997. "Standards and Conformity Assessment as Nontariff Barriers to Trade." Policy Research Working Paper 1826. Development Research Group, World Bank, Washington, D.C.

Stiglitz, Joseph E. 2000. "Democratic Development as the Fruits of Labor." Keynote address to the Industrial Relations Research Association, Boston, January. Processed.

Strutt, A., and K. Anderson. 1999. "Will Trade Liberalization Harm the Environment? The Case of Indonesia to 2020." In Per G. Fredriksson, ed., *Trade, Global Policy, and the Environment*, 13–34. Discussion Paper 402. World Bank, Washington, D.C.

Subramanian, Arvind. 1992. "Trade Measures for Environment: A Nearly Empty Box?" *World Economy* 15: 135–52.

————. 1999. "TRIPs and Developing Countries: The Seattle Round and Beyond." Paper presented to the Conference on Developing Countries and the New Multilateral Round of Trade Negotiations, Harvard University, Cambridge, Mass. November.

Sykes, Alan O. 1995. *Product Standards for Internationally Integrated Goods Markets*. Washington, D.C.: Brookings Institution.

Szekely, Miguel, and Marianne Hilgert. 1999. "Inequality in Latin America during the 1990s." Inter-American Development Bank, Washington, D.C. Processed.

Tiebout, C. M. 1956. "A Pure Theory of Local Expenditures." *Journal of Political Economy* 64: 416–24.

Tobey, J. A. 1990. "The Effects of Domestic Environmental Policies on Patterns of World Trade: An Empirical Test." *Kyklos* 43: 191–209.

Ulph, A. M. 1999. *Trade and the Environment: Selected Essays of A. M. Ulph*. Cheltenham, U.K.: Edward Elgar.

UNCTAD (United Nations Conference on Trade and Development). 1993. Program on Transnational Corporations. *Environmental Management in Transnational Corporations: Report on the Benchmark Environmental Survey*. Geneva.

Valluru, S. R. K., and E. W. F. Peterson. 1997. "The Impact of Environmental Regulations on World Grain Trade." *Agribusiness* 13 (3): 261–72.

Vukina, T., J. C. Beghin, and E. G. Solakoglu. 1999. "Transition to Markets and the Environment: Effects of the Change in the Composition of Manufacturing Output." *Environment and Development Economics* 4 (4): 582–98.

Wang, Hua, and David Wheeler. 2000. "Endogenous Enforcement and Effectiveness of China's Pollu-

tion Levy System." Policy Research Paper 2336. Infrastructure and Environment, Development Research Group, World Bank, Washington D.C.

Wang, Zhen Kun, and L. Alan Winters. 2000. "Putting 'Humpty' Together Again: Including Developing Countries in a Consensus for the WTO." Policy Paper 4. Centre for Economic Policy Research, London.

Whalley, John, and Colleen Hamilton. 1996. *The Trading System after the Uruguay Round*. Washington, D.C.: Institute for International Economics.

Wheeler, D., and P. Martin (1992). "Price, Policies, and the International Diffusion of Clean Technology: The Case of Wood Pulp Production," in P. Low Ed., *International Trade and the Environment*, World Bank Discussion Papers 159, Washington, D.C., The World Bank: 197–224.

Wilson, J. D. 1997. "Capital Mobility and Environmental Standards: Is There a Theoretical Basis for a Race to the Bottom?" In *Fair Trade and Harmonization. Prerequisites for Free Trade?* edited by J. N. Bhagwati and R. E. Hudec. Pp. 393–428. Cambridge, Mass.: MIT Press.

Wilson, John S. 1999. "The Post-Seattle Agenda of the WTO in Standards and Technical Barriers to Trade: Issues for the Developing Countries." Development Research Group, World Bank, Washington D.C.

————. 2000a. "The Development Challenge in Trade: Sanitary and Phytosanitary Standards." Paper prepared for the WTO Sanitary and Phytosanitary Standards Committee. Development Research Group, World Bank, Washington, D.C.

————. 2000b. "Technical Barriers to Trade and Standards: Challenges and Opportunities for Developing Countries presented by the World Bank." Paper submitted to the Technical Barriers to Trade Committee Meeting, World Trade Organization. Development Research Group, World Bank, Washington, D.C.

Wood, Adrian. 1997. "Openness and Wage Inequality in Developing Countries: The Latin American Challenge to East Asian Conventional Wisdom." *The World Bank Economic Review* 11 (1): 33–58.

World Bank. 1997. "Five Years after Rio. Innovations in Environmental Policy." Environment Department, Washington, D.C.

————. 2000a. "Report on Standardization and Conformity Assessment in Ukraine." Washington, D.C.

————. 2000b. *Trade Blocs. Policy Research Report*. New York: Oxford University Press.

WTO (World Trade Organization) "Overview of the State-of-Play of WTO Disputes." Geneva. Available at <http://www.wto.org/english/tratop_e/dispu_e/dispu_e.htm>.

Xing, Y., and C. Kolstad. 1995. "Do Lax Environmental Regulations Attract Foreign Investments?" Working Papers in Economics 06/95. University of California, Santa Barbara.

Xu, X. 1999. "Do Stringent Environmental Regulations Reduce the International Competitiveness of Environmentally Sensitive Goods? A Global Perspective." *World Development* 27 (7): 1215–26.

Zarsky, L. 1994. "Towards an International Ecolabelling Framework." In *Life-Cycle Management and Trade,* pp. 194–205. OECD: Paris.

4

Electronic Commerce and Developing Countries

THE INTERNET IS GLOBALIZATION ON STER-oids. It will boost efficiency and enhance market integration domestically and internationally, particularly in developing countries that are most disadvantaged by poor access to information. Although the Internet should enhance global growth, it also brings increased danger of economic marginalization to countries that cannot access it effectively. Taking advantage of electronic commerce requires policies similar to those needed to capitalize on the opportunities for trade: improved international coordination, for example in ensuring interoperability of communications technology and confronting challenges to domestic tax and financial systems; an open economy promoting competition and diffusion of Internet technologies; and efficient social and infrastructure services, in particular a competitive telecommunications sector and a well-educated labor force.

Despite the obvious benefits of the Internet, uncertainty exists about the implications of this technology and its likely rate of diffusion. This chapter provides a tentative view of the implications of electronic commerce for developing countries, based on the theoretical literature, inferences from experience in industrial countries, and anecdotal evidence. The discussion is inevitably somewhat more speculative than in other chapters. The evidence, however, warrants four broad conclusions:

Firms in developing countries should enjoy productivity gains and expanded demand with the spread of electronic commerce.

The Internet will boost productivity in developing countries by increasing the efficiency of the procurement system, strengthening inventory control, lowering retail transaction costs, and eliminating or transforming intermediaries. Virtual proximity to industrial country markets will increase as the Internet reduces the costs inherent in operating at a distance. Given the wide differences in returns to factors in developing versus industrial countries, this increased proximity will generate large gains from trade in sectors that lend themselves to electronic commerce.

Consumers will benefit from increased competition and market transparency, but the benefits to firms will vary greatly, depending on the sector, degree of product differentiation, and level of technological sophistication.

Developing-country firms that sell labor-intensive, differentiated products (such as crafts, software, or business services—particularly services involving the remote processing of routine information) will experience increased demand. These firms also will benefit from the opportunity to leapfrog to the most advanced technologies and from easier access to advertising on global markets.

The impact of electronic commerce on developing countries' sales to global supply chains is uncertain. Reduced transactions costs should provide greater interaction among multinationals and technologically sophisticated firms in developing countries. Many developing-country firms may lack the reputation required to bid on the newly created online exchanges, however. Industrial-country multinationals also may prefer integrating their operations more closely with a reduced number of the most advanced firms, given the opportunities for managing tightly linked production processes through the Internet.

Government action is critical to removing impediments to electronic commerce.

Network externalities imply that market prices may not fully reflect the gains to the society from increased levels of Internet access; hence the government has a role in speeding Internet diffusion. Complementary inputs, including telecommunications, transport and power infrastructure, and a well-educated labor force are critical to exploiting the Internet's potential. Governments have also encouraged the expansion of the Internet by subsidizing Internet connections and investing directly in infrastructure, although such investments can crowd out private initiatives and may quickly become obsolete due to rapid changes in technology.

Other policies can also contribute to boosting Internet use. An open foreign direct investment regime is necessary to promote dissemination of information technology and training. Governments can help facilitate services that evaluate and attest to the quality of output from domestic firms, which could support their access to global Internet exchanges. Governments must provide a supportive legal framework for electronic transactions, such as recognition of digital signatures and legal admissibility of electronic documentation. Governments can also encourage Internet expansion by moving procurement and administrative requirements (tax forms and permits, for example) online. Finally, it is desirable to avoid high levels of taxation on critical inputs to electronic commerce such as personal computers and telecommunications equipment.

The gap in Internet access between industrial and developing countries will persist through the next decade.

Access to the Internet is grossly unequal, with 30 percent of the U.S. population online compared with an average of 0.6 percent in developing countries. Access, supported by the growing use of cell phones as a major link to the Internet, is expected to rise at a faster rate in developing countries than in industrial countries during the next 10 years. Internet access is likely, nonetheless, to remain limited in per capita terms, especially in the poorest countries, and to remain well below levels already achieved in industrial countries. Access by firms in developing countries may increase significantly, but the poorest developing countries may still see their competitiveness impaired because of a lack of human capital and complementary services required for effective participation in electronic commerce.

Emergence of electronic commerce

Transacting business using electronic aids is as old as the telegraph, which was introduced in the mid-nineteenth century. More recently, electronic data interchange (EDI) systems not residing on the Internet have facilitated business transactions worth trillions of dollars. This chapter, however, explores how the relatively new phenomenon of the Internet is likely to affect commerce. Several definitions of electronic commerce exist, including transactions where the Internet is used to gather information, to order goods or services, and to make payments. A reasonable definition of electronic commerce would include commercial operations in which two of these three steps are taken electronically.[1]

Although the chapter focuses on electronic commerce (in keeping with the overall theme on trade), this is by no means the only, or necessarily the most important, way the Internet will affect developing countries. Increased access to information holds enormous promise for bettering noncommercial aspects of the lives of people in the developing world—providing health and education services from a distance, and more efficient government administration are but two examples. At the same time, the growth of the Internet will increase the exposure of developing countries to material, such as pornography, that may be viewed as undesirable.

Electronic commerce in industrial countries has grown rapidly, from next to nothing in the mid-1990s to $100 to $200 billion in 1999–2000 (figure 4.1). Nevertheless, the dollar value of electronic commerce transactions is less than 1 percent of the total U.S. gross domestic product (GDP) of $23 trillion (and the business-to-business data refer to total turnover, not just value added). Consumer Internet purchases equal about two-thirds of 1 percent of retail sales of goods in the United States (U.S. Department of Commerce 1999), excluding services such as travel, tickets, and financial brokers, and about one-third of 1 percent in the United Kingdom and Germany (OECD 2000a).[2]

The importance of electronic commerce rests not in its current size but in the likely speed of its establishment as a significant vehicle for commerce and the potential for future growth. Electronic commerce is projected to reach $4 trillion to $6 trillion in the United States alone within the next three to four years (Bermudez and others 2000; *Economist* 1999).[3] Electronic commerce may account for as much as 25 percent of world trade by 2005 (UNCTAD 1999).

The digital divide

The distribution of Internet access among countries is severely unequal. Despite rapid growth in Internet access in developing countries, industrial countries still account for the majority of Internet subscribers (figure 4.2). More than 30 percent of U.S. residents had access to the Internet in 1999, compared with 0.5 percent in Sub-Saharan Africa (figure 4.3). Electronic commerce is also relatively small in most developing countries. In Latin America, for example, electronic commerce is estimated at $459 million in 1999 (Lapper 2000), compared with a GDP of about $2 trillion.

Internet access in the developing world varies greatly. Some countries, particularly in East Asia, have achieved impressive penetration rates. For example, the share of Internet subscribers in Korea has grown rapidly and is estimated at 20 percent of the population in 2000, above rates in most European countries (Grebb 2000). Although per capita subscriber rates in China and India remain low, these countries are so large that they have a critical mass of subscribers ready to benefit from the

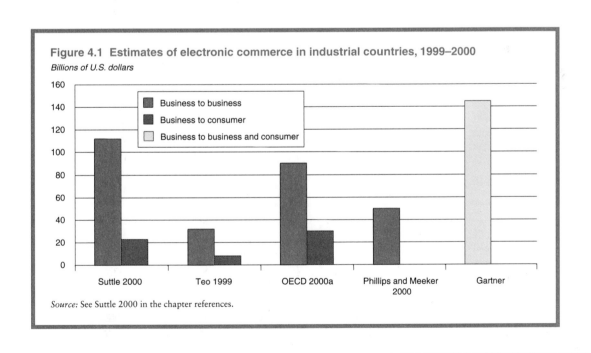

Figure 4.1 Estimates of electronic commerce in industrial countries, 1999–2000

Billions of U.S. dollars

Legend:
- Business to business
- Business to consumer
- Business to business and consumer

Source: See Suttle 2000 in the chapter references.

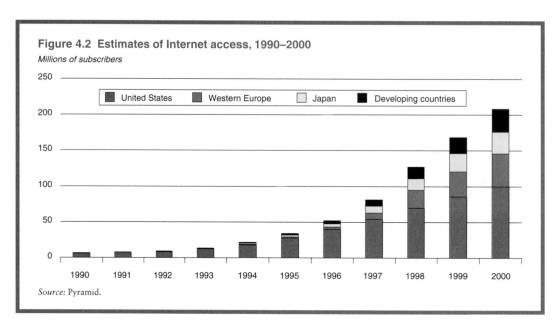

Figure 4.2 Estimates of Internet access, 1990–2000

Millions of subscribers

Source: Pyramid.

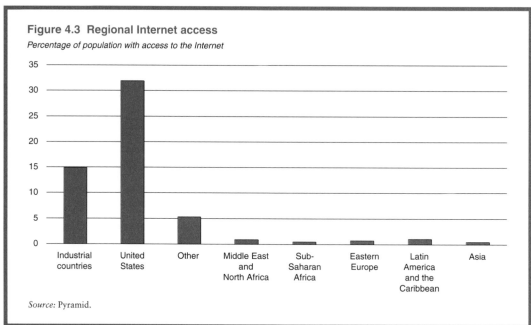

Figure 4.3 Regional Internet access

Percentage of population with access to the Internet

Source: Pyramid.

Internet, a situation that increases the potential for electronic commerce transactions.

Analysis of Internet diffusion

The nascent condition of Internet diffusion in many developing countries reflects the constraints on Internet use, the most important of which is the availability of telecommunications services. Canning (1999) finds strong evidence that the quantity and quality of telecommunications services provided in a country is a significant determinant of the existence of Internet connections and the level of Internet use; to date, almost all Internet users have depended on telephone lines for connection. The trends in "Internet intensity"—the ratio of Internet subscribers to available telephone lines—are remarkably similar across developing and industrial countries, however. Urban density and the policy environment for private sector development are strongly related to growth in Internet intensity.[4] Many developing countries (including, on average, those in Asia, Latin America, and Sub-Saharan Africa) are experiencing much more rapid diffusion of the Internet for the given availability of telephone lines than is the United States. The digital divide results from differential access to telecommunications, not from the use of the Internet after telecommunications are available.

Unfortunately, the gap in telecommunications services between industrial and developing countries is large, so the digital divide is likely to remain wide for some time. The gap is also wide among developing countries, with the poorest countries being particularly disadvantaged. For example, the average OECD country had 70 times, and the average Latin American country had 17 times, the number of telephone mainlines than did countries in Sub-Saharan Africa (excluding South Africa) (figure 4.4). By some indicators, the digital divide is widening. Wilson and Rodriguez (2000) find that an index of between-country inequality in access to communications (the components are personal computers, Internet hosts, fax machines, mobile phones, and televisions) deteriorated substantially during the 1990s.[5]

Prospects for Internet access

Given the enormous investments required for telephone lines (and in some countries the continued dominance of the telephone system by inefficient monopolies), hopes for narrowing the digital divide rest largely on the spread of alternative means of accessing the Internet. The availability of cable, cellular phone, and satellite systems is likely to reduce dependence on telephone lines for access to the Internet during the next decade. Digital cellular telephone systems with Internet access are already spreading rapidly in Japan and Western Eu-

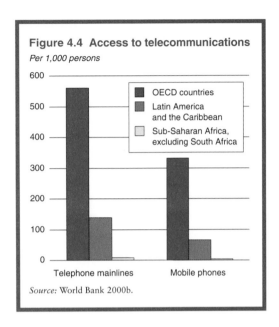

Figure 4.4 Access to telecommunications
Per 1,000 persons

Legend:
- OECD countries
- Latin America and the Caribbean
- Sub-Saharan Africa, excluding South Africa

Source: World Bank 2000b.

rope. Approximately 10 million users in Japan, or 40 percent of total users there, accessed the Internet through mobile telecommunications devices in May 2000 (Reuters 2000). Low-Earth-orbit satellite systems also have potential for reaching areas where telephone service is poor (Wood 1999).[6] Work is underway to investigate the feasibility of Internet transmission through power lines.

All of these links to the Internet will bypass the often inefficient and difficult-to-build telephone networks now used for Internet access and will have substantially higher access speeds, although the forecasts in table 4.1 are speculative. The rapid diffusion of cellular phone and other systems with Internet access will mean that much of the Internet's capacity

Table 4.1 Future Internet access speeds

Platform	Year available	Potential bandwidth
Cellular	1999	144 kilobits
	2000	1.6 megabits
	2003	5.2 megabits
Cable	2000	1–10 megabits
Satellite	2005	64 megabits
Power grid	(?)	2.5 gigabits (?)

Source: Harrow 2000; www.teledesic.com; www.mediafusioncorp.net.

may be available at relatively low cost in many developing countries. Although the most recent experience with wireless Internet access has been disappointing in some respects (witness the slow diffusion of Internet-enabled wireless phones in the United States), over the medium term these alternative Internet platforms are likely to give a significant boost to the spread of the Internet.

Some insight into the implications of new platforms for Internet access and electronic commerce can be gained by looking at the prospects for diffusion of cellular telephones. During the 1990s cell phone diffusion within countries was strongly influenced by per capita income, the change in per capita income, the size of the urban population, and the strength of the policy environment facing the private sector.[7] Assuming future per capita income growth and policy performance will be equal to the 1990s experience, this equation forecasts very rapid growth in cell phone, and hence Internet, penetration during the next decade in all developing regions. Cell phone use in developing countries as a group would quadruple by 2010 compared with 1998.

Cell phone penetration would remain low relative to population, a projected 6 percent in 2010, compared with 2 percent in 1998. However, this figure does not imply that only 6 percent of developing country residents will have access to cell phones, given the potential for multiple use (although privacy concerns may constrain multiple use in some circumstances). For example, hundreds of people have access to the single cell phone provided to each village participating in the Bangladesh Village Pay Phone program.

Increased access to the Internet is only one precondition for effective participation in electronic commerce. Many developing countries, particularly the poorest ones, lack the human capital and complementary services required to make effective use of the latest technologies. There also is concern that developing country firms will face increasing challenges in competing with the leading firms in industrial countries, which have a headstart in using these

new technologies (although at the same time developing-country firms will benefit from lower prices and increased access to services offered by industrial-country firms). Finally, an overly restrictive interpretation of current rules on intellectual property rights could constrain developing countries' access to some of these new technologies, which have largely been developed in the industrial world. One potential issue is the patenting of business processes and methods linked to the Internet; for the time being that practice is found only in the United States. International recognition of such patents could constrain the ability of firms in other countries to compete.

Effects on productivity in industrial and developing countries

Electronic commerce will generate productivity gains by reducing transaction costs. The rapid dissemination of information, the substitution of digital for paper record keeping, and the networking capabilities of the Internet will improve flexibility and responsiveness, encourage new and more efficient intermediaries, increase the use of outsourcing, reduce time to market by linking orders to production, and improve internal coordination. Although the effect of electronic commerce on productivity has probably been small to date (Oliner and Sichel 2000), simulations have indicated that electronic commerce could raise output levels by some 5 percent in the major industrial countries (Mann, Eckert, and Knight 2000; OECD 2000a).[8] Firms can expect productivity gains through improved systems for procurement and inventory control and reduced costs of intermediation and sales transactions, as well as through more rapid diffusion of technology. Consumers also will benefit through reduced search costs, thus increasing competition and reducing prices.

Procurement and inventory control
Firms in developing countries can use the Internet to achieve the kinds of procurement and

inventory savings now enjoyed only by the largest firms that have established EDI systems, simply by purchasing "out of the box" electronic commerce applications (box 4.1). Goldman Sachs (1999) estimates that 30 percent or more of the total cost of intermediate goods typically are "process costs," or the costs of administering transactions and maintaining inventories. The potential for savings can be divided into reduced processing costs of procurement transactions, reduced price of inputs attributable to increased competition, and improved inventory control.

Substituting the Internet for paper-based systems can reduce the cost of processing orders by saving staff time, speeding up the process, and reducing processing errors.[9] Estimates of the savings in processing costs of Web-based procurement are 90–95 percent (Schwartz 2000; U.S. Department of Commerce 1999).

The use of online auctions also can reduce the price of inputs by improving transparency and facilitating competitive bidding. General Electric, for example, has cut the cost of purchased inputs by 10 to 20 percent through online bidding. The potential savings from increased transparency varies with the information content of the good. Goldman Sachs (1999) estimates that the savings from purchasing online may vary from 2 percent in relatively undifferentiated products (such as coal) to 40 percent in highly differentiated ones (some electronic components, for example).

Keeping an electronic inventory and transferring information on replenishment needs over the Internet enables producers and retailers to reduce the time that components and raw materials spend at each processing stage. Even relatively small reductions in inventory holding time in retail trade can mean substantial increases in profits because the average

Box 4.1 Electronic data interchange (EDI) systems

EDI systems provide one view of the potential efficiency gains from relying on the Internet for processing procurement and inventory control. These systems use proprietary software to connect purchasers' and suppliers' computers and to automate the transaction processing and information exchange. EDI is estimated to support about $3 trillion in economic activity in the United States alone (Phillips and Meeker 2000). About 80 percent of the dollar value of intercompany transactions among Fortune 500 companies in the United States is conducted through EDI systems (Bermudez and others 2000). Despite this, only about 100,000 U.S. companies use EDI—out of the 2 million U.S. companies with 10 employees or more. The large investment required to develop proprietary software and the costs involved in integrating new suppliers effectively bars small firms from using EDI. By contrast, a large share of the investment required for similar systems over the Internet has already been made, and interactivity with other computers is automatically provided. Also, it is estimated that operating costs in Internet-based systems are less than 1 percent of EDI systems (Xie 2000).

That large firms are willing to make huge fixed investments and pay high operating costs for EDI systems indicates the substantial gains that firms can capture by transferring from paper-based to electronic systems. The smaller initial investment and lower operating costs in Internet-based systems (along with greater flexibility and transparency of operations) means that small- and medium-size firms can capture these gains.

The migration of EDI systems to the Internet (to reduce operating costs and to improve flexibility) is likely to boost the dollar value of electronic commerce transactions over the next few years. This change will be slow because of the reluctance to abandon the huge fixed costs represented in EDI systems and the cost of conversion to Internet-based systems (Wenninger 1999). Concerns over the lower security of the Internet compared with that of proprietary EDI systems also may limit conversions.

cost to retailers of holding inventory for a year is at least 25 percent of the price, and margins may average only 3–4 percent (OECD 1999). Improved inventory control will enable firms to become more integrated with suppliers, thereby saving time and allowing greater production specialization. Increased production integration has led to a boom in specialized manufacturing firms that produce components for more well-known companies. A famous example is Cisco, whose components are made to Cisco's specifications by suppliers, tested through a connection to the Internet, and then shipped directly to the buyer.

Procurement in most developing countries is slower, less efficient, and more labor-intensive than in industrial countries, so the technical efficiency gains from transferring procurement systems to the Internet could be relatively large (although the lower cost of labor in developing countries means that the economic gains could be more limited than in industrial countries). The savings in working capital from reduced holding of inventories also would be significant in developing countries, where the cost of capital is high and credit is often rationed or unavailable. The lack of reliable telecommunications networks and complementary services—for example, transport facilities—may limit these gains, however. Some limited survey evidence (see annex 4 for description of survey) indicates that North American firms that were better at supply-chain management to begin with are cutting these costs by an even larger amount when using Internet-based inventory systems. This may be because an adequate supply of high-skilled workers and a flexible organization are required to reap the full benefits of these systems.

Reduced intermediary costs

Productivity gains can be derived from eliminating or improving the efficiency of intermediaries involved in marketing and distribution. Middlemen often charge substantial markups because of their knowledge about and contacts with suppliers. By greatly expanding access to information, the Internet has enabled the elimination of retailers, wholesalers, and (in the case of intangible products) even distributors in some sectors. More commonly, existing middlemen have been replaced by new approaches to intermediation made possible by the technology—for example, online auctions and aggregators (firms that represent collections of buyers that can demand lower prices for bulk purchases).

The Internet also can generate significant cost savings in transport. The advertisement and trading of empty truck space over the Web is reducing costs per ton in the U.S. trucking sector (*Economist* 1999). According to one industry estimate, $15 billion to $20 billion annually in cost savings (4 to 5 percent of output in the U.S. trucking industry) may be realized (*Business 2.0* 1999).

Eliminating or transforming intermediary functions will enable developing-country producers to access both domestic and foreign markets at lower cost. By contrast, firms in developing countries whose main purpose is to help domestic companies trade with international markets will be at particular risk. Network externalities, combined with a low marginal cost of adding new users, mean that the market for providing intermediary services offers considerable advantage to the first company on the scene. Thus the later-arriving and less technologically sophisticated firms in many developing countries may have difficulty competing with industrial-country firms as Internet-based intermediaries (UNCTAD 2000). Developing countries also may not be able to capture the cost savings from reduced intermediation in some sectors, such as primary commodity exports, where purchasers are likely to be the major beneficiaries of any cost savings (box 4.2).

Retail transactions

The Internet offers the potential for savings in retail transactions compared with traditional systems. OECD (1998b) suggests that the greater availability of information to the

Box 4.2 The Internet and primary commodity exporters

Electronic commerce may affect relatively homogeneous primary commodities less than it does more differentiated products because most of the necessary information is contained in the product price. Although electronic commerce is likely to provide some benefits to producers by increasing the efficiency of commodity markets, the major benefits will accrue to purchasers.

More timely access to market information about prices could generate benefits to producers. Smallholder farmers in remote areas could check the prices in the nearest market (which could be a considerable journey if done in person) before deciding whether to sell to local middlemen; such a capability could potentially improve the farmers' bargaining position with local and foreign buyers. The Internet also could provide producers with better information about input prices and product availability and easier access to training about best production practices.

Several firms have projected that a large share of commodity trade will occur over the Internet (for example, Forrester Research 1999a), but the efficiency gains will vary depending on the commodity. Commodities already traded on established exchanges (such as wheat), with widely disseminated information on prices and centralized trading, may not be greatly affected. Online auctions will have a greater role in reducing margins for commodities (such as fertilizer) that trade through brokers with limited price transparency. For example, brokerage fees in the sugar trade, which range from 0.5 to 1.0 percent of the value of the commodity, may decline as more trade is done over the Internet.

Producers in developing countries are unlikely to see substantial increases in incomes from lower trading and marketing costs; rather, these gains will accrue to the consumer through lower prices for final products. Lower consumer prices may increase demand only slightly, because the demand for most commodities is price inelastic and the reduction in marketing costs will probably be small.

consumer and savings on providing services could increase the productivity of sales staff in OECD countries by a factor of 10. The evidence on the sale of goods over the Internet so far does not show large savings, however. Preliminary studies found that goods sold on the Internet were priced the same or higher than in stores (Goldman Sachs 1997; Krantz 1998; Lee, Westland, and Hong 2000; OECD 1998a). Other studies estimated that books and compact discs (CDs) were 10 percent cheaper on the Internet (*Economist* 2000; Oliner and Sichel 2000).[10] The potential savings in service transactions are more impressive. For example, the total cost (including investment) of bank transfers over the Internet is half that of existing automated systems and one-eighth that of transactions using tellers (WTO 1998; figure 4.5). Note that a portion of this savings reflects efficiency gains, while another portion reflects the transfer of costs from producers to consumers in the form of time spent searching the Internet.

The lower cost of service transactions is likely to have a less significant effect in developing than in industrial countries because the lower wages paid in developing countries mean that firms have less incentive to undertake the fixed costs involved in setting up electronic systems. Also, poor distribution systems, inadequate protection against credit card fraud, and limited consumer Internet access constrain the potential for business-to-consumer commerce in many developing countries.

Knowledge acquisition and technology diffusion

Easier access to knowledge through the Internet will speed technology diffusion, which is of critical importance to developing countries

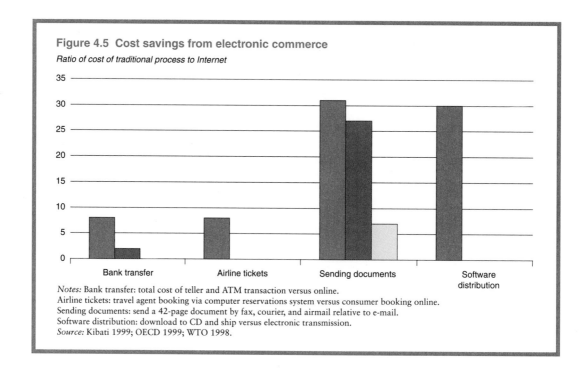

Figure 4.5 Cost savings from electronic commerce

Ratio of cost of traditional process to Internet

Notes: Bank transfer: total cost of teller and ATM transaction versus online.
Airline tickets: travel agent booking via computer reservations system versus consumer booking online.
Sending documents: send a 42-page document by fax, courier, and airmail relative to e-mail.
Software distribution: download to CD and ship versus electronic transmission.
Source: Kibati 1999; OECD 1999; WTO 1998.

because they tend to operate within the technological frontier. Electronic commerce can reduce the costs of communication between geographically distant partners and lower the search-and-compare costs involved in finding potential business partners and technologies. Moreover, the Internet provides a radial structure for interpersonal communication networks. Bulletin boards and news servers allow individuals to exchange information faster and within a wider environment than with networks based on telephone and fax. Connolly (1998) found that differences in communication and transportation infrastructure were significantly related to differences in the rate of product imitation encouraged by foreign direct investment (although this does not necessarily mean that electronic commerce has an independent positive effect). Grossman and Helpman (1991) argue that international contacts enable a country to obtain foreign technologies and adjust them to domestic use, an important channel through which the productivity levels of industrial and developing countries are interrelated. Such international "net-

working" is greatly facilitated by the Internet. Harris (1998) quotes a Neilson survey that found business's primary use of the Internet was for gathering information.

Effects on international trade in developing countries

By opening markets to a wider range of potential buyers and sellers, the Internet is likely to foster a greater volume and variety of trade. The Internet could erode an important advantage now enjoyed by firms in industrial countries: proximity to wealthy customers. For example, the Internet reduces the cost of producing customized products designed for distant markets; consumers in the United States can purchase a hand-sewn suit made by a tailor in Shanghai without ever visiting China (Xie 2000).

Service exports

The Internet will reduce barriers to the sale of services embodying skilled labor (Harris 1998).[11] In the Philippines, for example, companies use the Internet to provide accounting services, process insurance claims, and track credit card defaulters for firms in industrial countries (Jordan and Hilsenrath 2000). In India workers have been transcribing U.S. physicians' oral records into written files since 1996, at one-tenth the cost of U.S. transcription services (Mills 1996).[12] Schuknecht and Perez-Esteve (1999) suggest that financial, insurance, and other business and communication services are likely to see the greatest impact from electronic commerce.

Multinational supply chains

The Internet's impact on access to multinational supply chains by firms in developing countries is uncertain. Increased information on these firms may improve their access to multinationals, which tend to use suppliers with whom they have experience. Goldman Sachs (1999) estimates that, because of poor research, firms' purchasing managers tend to award 90 percent of their procurement contracts to about 20 percent of suppliers. At the same time, suppliers with poor hardware, software, and Internet transmission capabilities may be unable to compete with better-connected companies. It is unclear whether the new online auction systems have resulted in the expansion of supply networks. General Electric, for one example, may be increasing the number of its suppliers through its online bidding site for procurement.

A lack of credibility may make it difficult for firms in developing countries to access online auctions. Purchasers need to have confidence that suppliers will provide input on time and in conformance with specifications, and product quality may not be known ex ante. More than half of 35 large firms using online auction or exchange sites said that they would not do business through online Web sites with firms they did not know (Forrester Research 1999b). Interview results indicate buyers—typically firms in industrial countries—see an especially high risk in purchasing from firms in developing countries. Over time, greater use may be made of certification agencies (such as

the International Standards Organization and the International Electrotechnical Commission) to assess independently the quality of new firms' products and services. However, relatively few small firms, even in industrial countries, use the certification services these bodies provide, because of the cost and fears that certification may not fully address buyers' concerns in the markets where small firms compete (Callaghan and Schnoll 1997).

Online advertisement

New websites are emerging that provide a venue for smaller firms to advertise their goods, and buyers to advertise their product needs.[13] A survey of one of the best-known advertising websites (www.alibaba.com), which has grown to 200,000 subscribers since its April 1999 inception, indicates that the impact has been modest so far, although it is too early to judge the site's full potential. Most participants say they have found only a few new customers so far. Only 13 percent of firms reported that total sales had gone up considerably since posting on the website, whereas 64 percent reported some increase and the rest none (no firm reported a decline in sales). However, 87 percent of the firms viewed the

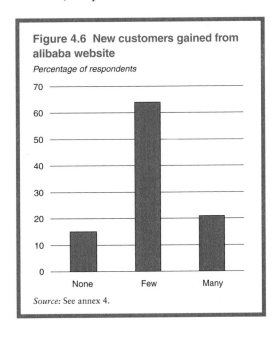

Figure 4.6 New customers gained from alibaba website

Percentage of respondents

Source: See annex 4.

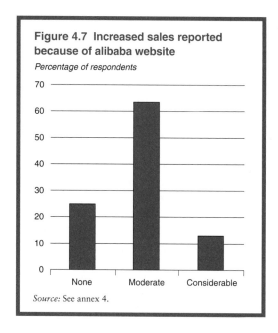

Figure 4.7 Increased sales reported because of alibaba website

Percentage of respondents

Source: See annex 4.

website as helpful or very helpful, with the smaller firms showing the greatest enthusiasm.

Effects on income distribution

The Internet improves access to and use of information, which increases the productivity of capital, thus raising its return relative to labor (Rodriguez 2000). The Internet also increases the demand for skilled labor, particularly in the information technology sector. By contrast, better information will tend to reduce the demand for, and hence the relative return to, unskilled labor involved in the routine processing of transactions and (perhaps) retail sales.[14] There is a risk that this divergence in demand for skilled versus unskilled labor could increase inequality between industrial and developing economies as well as within developing economies.[15] Any rise in inequality may be exacerbated by opportunities for migration as skills shortages in the information technology sectors intensify in industrial countries. Electronic commerce also may increase regional inequality. In many developing nations, Internet services rarely spread beyond the country's capital and a few large urban centers. In Kenya, for example, more than

85 percent of Internet users are in Nairobi (Jensen 1999; Kibati 1999).

Some aspects of electronic commerce could mitigate its impact on inequality, particularly on the poor, in developing countries. The fall in production costs is likely to increase the demand for all workers, despite the fall in the per unit labor input in production. Although inequality may increase, the income of the poor may rise. Also, electronic commerce increases market transparency, thus reducing search costs and reliance on intermediaries. These effects reduce the price of skill-intensive goods, thus raising the real incomes of workers generally, although the poor are unlikely to benefit greatly as consumers because of their limited access.

A direct impact of technological change on inequality in developing countries has been difficult to show empirically, perhaps because the adoption of new technologies has coincided with economywide structural reform (Rodriguez 2000). Studies have shown that, for industrial countries, the recent rise in income inequality has occurred during a period of rapid technological change in the information technology sector.[16]

Impediments to Internet use and the role of policies in developing countries

The presence of network externalities, where all participants gain from each addition to the network, implies that market prices may not fully reflect the total benefit to society from increased Internet access. Thus government has an important role in speeding Internet diffusion. Inappropriate policies and the lack of complementary services, particularly affecting the telecommunications sector, other infrastructure, human capital, and the investment environment severely constrain Internet access in developing countries.

Telecommunications

Poor telecommunications will limit the growth of electronic commerce. Required telecommunications facilities include transmission facilities connecting a country's domestic network to the greater Internet, the domestic Internet backbone, and connections from homes and businesses to the backbone network. The defects of domestic telecommunications services may be less important for the larger firms in developing countries; these firms may find it profitable to invest in telecommunications facilities (such as wireless) that bypass the local network.

State or privatized monopolies that control international connections impose inefficient pricing structures and conditions,[17] which means that many Internet service providers cannot afford to buy enough transmission capacity for electronic commerce applications to function without congestion. This poor state of domestic backbone networks results in a large volume of domestic Internet traffic being sent to the United States before being returned to its region of origin (Cukier 1999). A growing number of African Internet sites are hosted on servers in Europe or the United States because of poor infrastructure (Jensen 1999). Hence,

even traffic that originates and terminates domestically can cost the same as international transmission.

The high cost of Internet access, the lack of local loop infrastructure necessary for basic dial-up modem access, and the poor quality of the local loop infrastructure that does exist all impede connections to the domestic backbone. Country comparisons show a strong relationship between usage price and Internet penetration; for industrial countries the correlation between the Internet hosts per capita and the average cost of Internet access from 1995 to 2000 is $-.73$ (EU Commission 2000; OECD 2000c). Developing countries face much higher costs relative to incomes than do industrial countries (figure 4.8). For example, surveys indicate that some users in Beijing may spend an average of 35 percent of take-home salaries on Internet access charges (Rosen 1999).

Internet use appears to be higher in countries where local phone service is charged at a fixed rate than in those where callers are billed by the minute. For example, in most Latin American countries (Mexico being the major

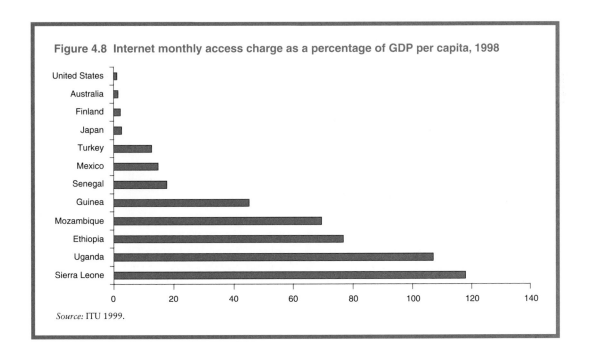

Figure 4.8 Internet monthly access charge as a percentage of GDP per capita, 1998

Source: ITU 1999.

exception), local calls are charged per unit of time (Oxford Analytica 1999), and telephone charges account for 40 percent of monthly access costs (E-Marketer 2000). In the United States the marginal cost of local calls is zero. Note that subsidizing Internet access through flat rate charges for local calls may discourage investment in alternative forms of Internet access that ultimately could be more efficient (EU Commission 2000).

For many developing countries, the most important issue is the lack of telephone service to homes and businesses. Despite increases in rates of telephone line penetration during the 1990s, more than one-third of the 130 developing countries (excluding small islands) with data for 1998 have fewer than 5 telephone lines per 100 inhabitants (figure 4.9). The comparable level in the United States is 66.

The quality of access also is important, as some electronic commerce applications that rely on sophisticated technology and high user interactivity require low congestion and high bandwidth transmission between the user's access device and the host server. The most popular alternatives by which developing countries

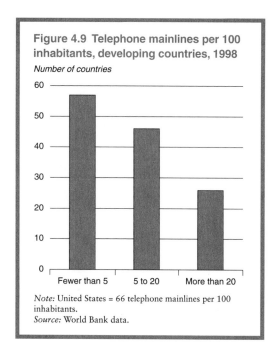

Figure 4.9 Telephone mainlines per 100 inhabitants, developing countries, 1998

Number of countries

Note: United States = 66 telephone mainlines per 100 inhabitants.
Source: World Bank data.

can overcome inadequate local loop infrastructure have been either shared facilities or wireless local loop. Shared facilities, which involve local entrepreneurs selling the use of a computer with Internet access, are a fast and relatively cheap way of increasing Internet use. For example, the number of Internet users on each Internet account in Egypt is estimated to be between 2.5 and 4.5 people (El-Nawawy and Ismail 1999). Public access Internet cafés exist in some 110 countries (Rao 1999).

Wireless and satellite technologies also provide an alternative to the high costs and inefficiencies of many domestic telecommunications systems. Although currently used primarily for voice, mobile phones "soon will be a much better device for many of the usual Internet applications," according to some technologists.[18] Cellular phones in some developing countries have experienced strong growth rates and relatively high penetration, similar to those in industrial countries. In Haiti, for example, poor telephone service (0.9 phone lines per 100 people, less than half Africa's average, and huge waiting lists for new lines) has led to the growth of wireless service (Peha 1999). In 1998, Ecuador, the Slovak Republic, and Western Samoa had ratios of cellular phone subscriptions to regular phone service similar to those of industrial countries (ITU 1998). On average, however, cellular phone penetration remains well below industrial-country levels. Sub-Saharan Africa averages 5 cellular phones per 1,000 people, compared with 265 cellular phones for every 1,000 people in high-income countries (World Bank 2000b).

Impressive increases in penetration can be achieved through increasing competition, although in some cases privatization has meant reducing subsidies to local calls, with a negative impact on Web access, at least in the short term (Zambrano 1999). The relative level of capital spending on communication infrastructure and development of Internet application software generally tends to be higher and more advanced in those industrial countries that liberalized telecommunications markets earlier (OECD 2000a). Perhaps as a result of privatization and liberalization, Africa has recorded its highest annual growth rate in telephone mainlines for a decade (AED 1998a). Figure 4.10 reveals the growing trend of privatization in the telecommunications sectors of developing countries.

Other infrastructure

Poor infrastructure services (other than telecommunications) are an important constraint on electronic commerce. Frequent and long power interruptions can seriously interfere with data transmission and systems performance, so many Bangalore software firms have their own generators (Panagariya 1999). Mail service can be unreliable, expensive, and time-consuming in many developing countries. For example, the unreliability of postal services in Latin America has meant that more expensive courier services must be used to deliver goods ordered over the Internet, and in response, international courier services are setting up special distribution systems in Miami (Lapper 2000; Oxford Analytica 1999).

The lack of safeguards against fraud can severely restrict credit card purchases, the most common means of conducting transactions over the Internet. For example, many Latin American consumers are unwilling to purchase goods over the Internet because credit card companies will not compensate holders for fraudulent use of cards (in many industrial countries, cardholders have only a limited exposure to loss). This lack of security does not make consumer purchases on the Internet impossible. In China, companies are depending on cash payments and local distribution through taxis and bicycles to reach consumers (Fan 2000).

Human capital

A critical mass of highly skilled labor is needed in developing countries to supply the necessary applications, provide support, and disseminate relevant technical knowledge for electronic commerce. The work force in many developing countries lacks a sufficient supply of these skills, and the demand for this specialized labor from industrial countries has further strained the supply of this labor in developing countries. In the mid-1990s North America and Europe had unfilled demand for professionals trained in information technology (figure 4.11). The wages of workers in information technology industries continue to rise more rapidly than those of workers in other

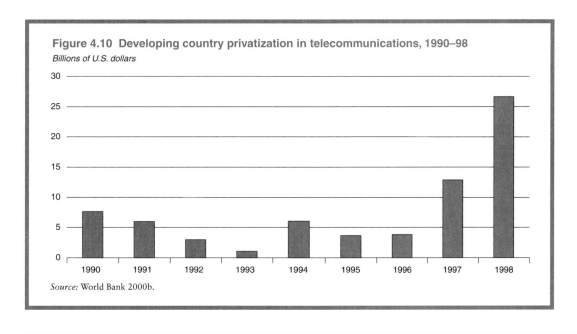

Figure 4.10 Developing country privatization in telecommunications, 1990–98

Billions of U.S. dollars

Source: World Bank 2000b.

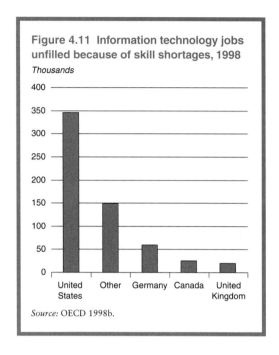

Figure 4.11 Information technology jobs unfilled because of skill shortages, 1998

Thousands

Source: OECD 1998b.

U.S. industries (U.S. Department of Commerce 1999). U.S. firms will be able to fill only half of the estimated 1.6 million positions open in 2000 (ITAA 2000), while the shortfall of information technology workers is estimated at almost 1 million in Japan (OECD 2000b).

At the same time, Harris (1998) notes that the Internet also facilitates the mobility of skilled labor services. Workers can choose to remain in their own country while exporting labor services to higher-paying industrial countries.[19] Developing countries may also reap some benefits from migration. For example, Indians in Silicon Valley have played a role in providing capital, expertise, and business contacts to Indians in the software exporting firms of Bangalore.

Investment environment

Several regulatory impediments to the widespread adoption of electronic commerce exist in many developing countries. Duties and taxes on computer hardware and software and communication equipment increase the expense of connecting to the Internet. For example, a computer imported into some African countries may

be taxed at rates exceeding 50 percent. The overall environment for private sector activities is a significant determinant of Internet service diffusion. An open foreign direct investment regime helps promote technology diffusion, which is important to the growth of electronic commerce. Foreign direct investment also is one channel that could facilitate certification of domestic firms for access to online auctions.

Governments also can play an important role in supporting the certification of firms by providing information on certification procedures, promoting access by domestic firms to international organizations and firms that provide certification, and perhaps subsidizing the costs of certification to demonstrate the kinds of resources available in the domestic market. This role will be particularly important (at least in a transitional sense) as the intermediaries that formerly helped connect developing-country firms to international markets are replaced by Web-based intermediaries that may have less information on developing countries.

Governments must provide a supportive legal framework for electronic transactions, including recognition of digital signatures; legal admissibility of electronic contracts; and establishment of data storage requirements in paper form, intellectual property rights for digital content, liability of Internet service providers, privacy of personal data, and mechanisms for resolving disputes. The U.N. Commission on International Trade Law has a "Model Law on Electronic Commerce" that offers national legislatures legal principles and guidelines for dealing with some of these issues (Price Waterhouse Coopers 1999; UNCTAD 2000).

Governments also have had considerable impact on Internet use through direct interventions. Singapore is providing grants to local companies to encourage participation in electronic commerce (Price Waterhouse Coopers 1999). Malaysia is wiring a zone south of Kuala Lumpur with fast communications (Bickers 1999). The "Wiring the Border" project is providing subsidies to small businesses along the Mexico-U.S. border to finance Internet access. The U.S. Department of Defense played a critical role in developing the initial networking technologies (Goodman and others 1994). The U.S. government also financed the original Internet backbone until increased demand for services led to the creation of commercial backbones; a similar pattern was followed in several other industrial countries (Braga and Fink 1997). Despite some success stories, however, the rapidity of technological change greatly increases the riskiness of government interventions to support Internet access. The expenditure of billions of dollars to connect schools to the Internet through telephone lines could be wasted if wireless or power line technology turns out to be less expensive (Davis and Seib 2000). Furthermore, government investments may crowd out private sector initiatives that could provide services more efficiently.

Finally, government can support the spread of the Internet by switching to online services for its own transactions. Public sector procurement, many aspects of tax and customs administration, the processing of routine applications (such as car permits and real estate licenses) and other governmental functions can often be carried out through the Internet. Decisions on the use of the Internet in public administration should be based on the costs of providing services relative to paper-based processes, the capability of government personnel, and the extent of demand. Nevertheless, greater government use of the Internet can play a role in encouraging public participation.

Language

That most Internet business is conducted in English is currently an important constraint on using the Internet. Estimates of the share of English used on the Internet range from 70 to 80 percent, but only 57 percent of Internet users have English as their first language (ITU 1999; Vehovar, Batagelj, and Lozar 1999). Per capita Internet use averages about 30 percent in those industrial countries where English is common, compared with about 5 percent in other industrial countries (figure 4.12). Famil-

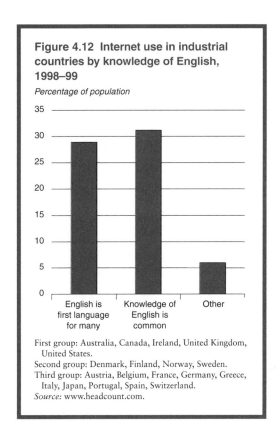

Figure 4.12 Internet use in industrial countries by knowledge of English, 1998–99

Percentage of population

First group: Australia, Canada, Ireland, United Kingdom, United States.
Second group: Denmark, Finland, Norway, Sweden.
Third group: Austria, Belgium, France, Germany, Greece, Italy, Japan, Portugal, Spain, Switzerland.
Source: www.headcount.com.

iarity with English was the principal determinant of Internet use in Slovenia, for all economic groups (Vehovar, Batagelj, and Lozar 1999). Conversely, Internet content is limited in the local language of most developing countries. From a commercial aspect, Schmitt (2000) found that just 37 percent of Fortune 100 websites support a language other than English.[20]

The amount of non-English material on the Web is growing, however. Spanish websites in particular are increasing, in part to serve the large Spanish-speaking community in the United States (Vogel and Druckerman 2000). Improvements in translation services (by people and machines), as well as Web browsers that recognize characters of different languages, should ease language constraints (U.S. Department of Commerce 1999). There is growing recognition that English-only content is insufficient for an international economy.[21]

Challenges to regulatory regimes in developing countries

Electronic commerce will pose difficult challenges for government regulation of tax and financial systems. The growth of electronic commerce will encourage tax competition and may facilitate some forms of tax evasion. Competitive pressures in domestic banking systems will rise, generating substantial benefits to consumers and firms but potentially lowering the franchise value of existing banks.

Tax policy

The growth of electronic commerce will present some challenges to tax enforcement in developing countries and place increased emphasis on improving the technological sophistication of tax authorities and on international coordination of tax collection efforts. The Internet reduces the cost to firms of being physically far away from customers and increases the ability of companies to relocate production, because a substantial share of the work involved in organizing production is carried out by computers that can be located anywhere. Thus multinationals will find it easier to shift activities to low-tax regimes. Governments may find it more difficult to impose desired income tax levels on existing corporations, and competition among developing countries for investment by multinationals may rise. This situation will place a greater premium on efforts to reach agreements among developing countries to limit this kind of competition.

In addition, some of the new transactions conducted through electronic commerce will be difficult to monitor. Governments may not be able to detect the transfer of digitized material and thus know that a taxable transaction has occurred.[22] It may also be difficult to control such transactions through the supplier because companies can easily provide such services from other jurisdictions. Thus effective international agreements to assist with tax enforcement will be important.

The Internet increases the potential for consumer-to-consumer purchases and for barter transactions, which also are difficult to monitor. Barter exchanges using digital money are small now, but the potential for growth could be great when a critical mass of participants is reached (*Washington Post* 2000). Reduced transaction costs also might make it easier for taxpayers to hide potentially taxable activities. The impact of electronic commerce on tax evasion should not be overestimated, however. The sale of domestic goods will still be controlled by monitoring companies' transactions, and imported goods will be controlled at the border.

Tax authorities will require greater expertise in information technology, both to improve the efficiency of tax administration and to enhance government ability to obtain and understand records of electronic transactions. In this respect, the greater transparency and ease of retrieval of electronic transactions (compared with paper processes) could assist tax enforcement.

Financial sector and capital flows

Electronic commerce could pose a significant challenge to government regulation of the financial sector by reducing the franchise value of domestic banks, thus increasing the incentive for banks to undertake excessive risk. At the same time, electronic commerce will generate substantial benefits to consumers and firms that rely on banking services. Competition in domestic banking systems will increase because of reduced costs, greater access by foreign banks, and greater reliance on capital markets by former bank borrowers.

Online banking may reduce banking transaction costs by 15–25 percent compared with regular accounts (Morgan Stanley Dean Witter 1999). Enhanced transparency and competition will mean that a large part of these cost reductions are transmitted to the consumers of banking services. In fact, some degree of price competition among banks is already becoming apparent in the emerging economies (Goldman Sachs 2000).

The Internet will greatly increase the ability of foreign banks to compete in developing countries' domestic markets. The geographic location of the consumer and the service provider will become increasingly irrelevant, eroding the local banks' advantage of having large branch networks. First-mover advantages, economies of scale, and reputational advantages backed by strong supervisory systems will strengthen the competitive position of industrial-country banks. They will be in a better position than domestic banks to offer integrated trade payments systems, in which customers can obtain applications for a letter of credit, care of credit approvals, telegraphic transfers, invoices, and confirmations (Granitsas 2000). One indication of the potential for foreign firms' inroads into developing-country banking systems comes from a 1997 study, which indicated that U.S. and U.K. firms dominated global Internet financial services market because of their reputations, head start, and the predominance of English on the Internet (OECD 1999).

Furthermore, the Internet will reduce the advantage that domestic banks enjoy from having a monopoly on information about their clients. Local banks often are better placed than foreign lenders to monitor the financial position of domestic firms (Eichengreen and Mody 1999). This advantage has enabled domestic banks to play an important role in onlending international capital flows to domestic borrowers; domestic banks accounted for as much as 46 percent of net long-term capital flows to developing countries in 1997 (World Bank 1999). Domestic banks may experience sharper competition for making loans in their own markets, as the Internet makes information about borrowers more accessible to international lenders.

The easier dissemination of credit information made possible by the Internet is likely to strengthen the trend toward greater reliance on bond financing in developing countries, potentially at the expense of domestic banks. The number of firms in developing countries with access to international bond markets increased more than sixfold from 1991 to 1998 (Eichengreen and Mody 1999), and the share

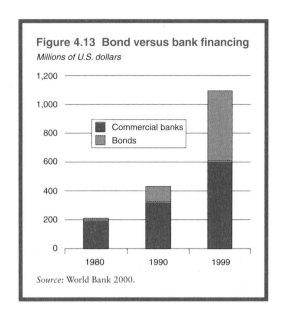

Figure 4.13 Bond versus bank financing
Millions of U.S. dollars

Source: World Bank 2000.

of private source debt that was held in bonds in developing countries rose from about one-fourth in 1990 to more than one-half in 1999 (figure 4.13). Currently, leading rating companies rate only several hundred corporate and foreign bonds. A private initiative is underway to rate millions of companies on the Internet by merging credit management techniques with collecting and organizing information on companies (UNCTAD 2000; www.cface.com). Furthermore, with a huge pool of rated companies, it would become possible to issue guarantees based on estimated default probabilities and to securitize these guarantees through the capital markets.

International coordination

Electronic commerce raises several regulatory issues that should be addressed through improved international coordination. The importance of international cooperation to tax administration was noted earlier. Ensuring open access for the international transmission of goods delivered electronically would facilitate the continued growth of electronic commerce. Members of the World Trade Organization have decided provisionally to exempt such goods from customs duties.[23] A more important contribution to ensuring open access would be to secure agreement on barrier-free treatment of electronically delivered services, by strengthening commitments entered into under the General Agreement on Trade in Services (Mattoo and Schuknecht 2000).

More generally, the rise in the volume of cross-border transactions promised through the spread of the Internet will raise a host of issues requiring international agreement. Examples include improved procedures for allocating domain names used for Internet locations;[24] agreement on privacy standards for data generated through commercial transactions; closer coordination of antitrust reviews to reduce the administrative burden imposed on companies; and efforts to harmonize the laws governing electronic commerce transactions. Electronic commerce will further speed the process of globalization and thus will underline the importance of an effective international framework for cross-border transactions.

Notes

1. See OECD 1999 and UNCTAD 2000 for a more detailed discussion of the definition of electronic commerce.

2. These estimates exclude sales where the Internet is used as an information resource only. In some service sectors, the penetration of electronic commerce is relatively high. In the United States, for example, electronic commerce accounts for some 25 percent of stock trades.

3. These figures vary greatly depending on the definition of electronic commerce used. Projections of trillions of dollars of electronic commerce in part reflect the migration of EDI systems to the Internet. Moreover, these forecasts are extremely speculative. As indicated earlier, estimates of even the *current* size of electronic commerce differ substantially.

4. The regression is $\log(I/T\ 1997) - \log(I/T\ 1990) = -14.76 - 1.04\log(I/T\ 1999) + .86\log(urban\ pop\ 1999) - .10\log(income\ 1990) + .61\log(policy)$. All coefficients are significant except income. Regional dummy variables are also included. R-squared is .97. I/T stands for Internet intensity.

5. Between-country inequality of access to components of this index (such as mobile phones) appears to have declined during the 1990s. Thus trends in the digital divide may differ significantly among different kinds of communications media.

6. Companies such as Teledesic and Skybridge plan to launch satellite systems capable of supporting high-speed Internet access for millions of users. So far the failure of the Iridium system has not derailed these plans.

7. The regression equation is $\log(cell\ 99) - \log(cell\ 90) = -9.16 - .84\log(cell\ 90) + .78\log(urban\ pop\ 90) + 2.12[\log(income\ 99) - \log(income\ 90)] + .78\log(income\ 90) + 1.06\log(policy)$. R-squared is .78. Observations = 99.

8. These studies are by their nature speculative, however, and the results require several restrictive assumptions that may or may not reflect actual events (OECD 2000a).

9. At Cisco the replacement of phone, fax, and e-mail ordering by electronic commerce systems cut the number of orders that had to be reworked from 25 percent to 2 percent (OECD 1999).

10. The use of discounts to increase market share, coupled with the lack of profits, leaves some doubt as to whether these lower prices reflect efficiency gains, however.

11. See World Bank 1995 for an earlier discussion of the potential for long-distance service exports from developing countries.

12. The potential for exports of Internet-based services by developing countries in the medical sector is staggering. About one-third of the cost of health care in the United States, or some $300 billion a year, represents the cost of capturing, storing, and processing information such as records, physicians' notes, test results, and insurance claims (Evans and Wurster 1997).

13. Examples include www.indiaonestop.com; www.in-business.com.ar/mall/;www.maquilamarket. com; and mm.malaysiadirectory.com/b2b/, which focus mainly on markets in India, Argentina, Mexico, and Malaysia, respectively. The World Bank is providing support to the Virtual Souk, an online marketplace for artisans in the Middle East and North Africa, owned by local nongovernmental organizations and cooperatives.

14. Note that the Internet also enables service transactions that would not otherwise have occurred, which increases the demand for literate but not highly skilled workers in developing countries.

15. Inequality is affected by many factors, and the strength of this effect is unknown. Thus, whether the Internet will ultimately have a significant impact on inequality remains uncertain.

16. For example, see Autor, Katz, and Krueger 1998; Bresnahan and Brynjolfsson 1998; Krueger 1993.

17. In Egypt, for example, El-Nawawy and Ismail (1999) report that the cost of an international half circuit can be 2.5 times the international tariff.

18. Helft 2000.

19. Harris (1998) goes further to say that "the Internet can eliminate the scale disadvantage of small

regions in producing services . . . [and] then can potentially lead to in-migration of skilled labor to the region."

20. DePalma, McCarthy, and Armstrong (1998) found that although 49 of 50 companies surveyed had operations outside the United States, and 80 percent print marketing material in other languages, only five said that their multilingual sites were as functionally rich as their English sites.

21. Advertisements have appeared in U.S. business magazines highlighting the need for Internet content to be written in other languages in addition to English. Schmitt (2000) warns businesses that English-only sites are no longer feasible for international companies.

22. According to Bach and Erber (1999), it is virtually impossible to enforce taxes on electronic transactions. This conclusion is uncertain, however, and its accuracy will depend on whether the evolution of Internet technology ultimately favors privacy over government monitoring.

23. The impact of this decision on government revenues should be slight because the tariff lost if no taxes are levied on digitizable goods is less than one-fifth of 1 percent of total revenues in the major developing-country importers (Matoo and Schuknecht 2000).

24. The World Intellectual Property Organization issued a detailed report on the intellectual property issues associated with domain names and has developed an online system to assist in resolving disputes (UNCTAD 2000).

References

AED (*Africa Economic Digest*). 1998a. "African Telecoms: A Renaissance." 19 (10).

———. 1998b. "Roadbuilding on the Information Superhighway." 19 (10).

Autor, Katz, and Krueger. 1998. "Computing Inequality: Have Computers Changed the Labour Market?" *Quarterly Journal of Economics* 113(4): 1169–213 (November).

Bach, Stefan, and Georg Erber. 1999. "Opportunities and Risks of Global Electronic Business Transactions." *Economic Bulletin*. German Institute for Economic Research 36 (4) (April).

Bermudez, John, Bob Kraus, David O'Brien, Bob Parker, and Larry Lapide. 2000. *B2B Commerce Forecast: $5.7T by 2004*. AMR Research (http://www.amrresearch.com).

Bickers, Charles. 1999. "Asia's Race to Go Digital." *Far East Asian Economic Review* July 1 (2).

Braga, Carlos A., and Carten Fink. 1997. "The Private Sector and the Internet." *Public Policy for the Private Sector*. Note No. 122. World Bank, Washington, D.C. July.

Bresnahan and Brynjolfsson. 1998. "Information Technology, Workplace Organisation and the Demand for Skilled Labour: Firm-level Evidence." Stanford University, Palo Alto, Calif. Processed.

Business 2.0. 1999. "Wise Load." (www.business2.com[May1]).

Callaghan, Nancy, and Leo Schnoll. 1997. "ISO 9000 for Small Companies." *Quality Digest Online* (www.qualitydigest.com[August]).

Canning, David. 1999. "Infrastructure's Contribution to Aggregate Output." Policy Research Working Paper 2246. World Bank, Washington, D.C.

Connolly, Michelle. 1998. "The Dual Nature of Trade: Measuring Its Impact on Imitation and Growth." Duke University Working Paper 97–34 (http://www.econ.duke.edu/Papers/Abstracts97/abstract.97.34.html).

Cukier, Kenneth. 1999. "Bandwidth Colonialism? The Implications of Internet Infrastructure on International E-Commerce." (Paper delivered at the annual INET conference sponsored by the Internet Society, San Jose, Calif., (http://www.isoc.org/inet99/proceedings/1e/1e_2.htm).

Davis, Bob, and Gerald Seib. 2000. "Technology Will Test a Washington Culture Born in Industrial Age." *Wall Street Journal*. May 1.

DePalma, D., J. McCarthy, and A. Armstrong. 1998. "Strategies for Global Sites." *The Forrester Report* 3 (3) (May).

Economist. 1999. "A Survey of Business and the Internet." June 16–July 2, 351 (8125) (B1–39).

Eichengreen, Barry, and Ashoka Mody. 1999. "Lending Booms, Reserves, and the Sustainability of Short-Term Debt: Inferences from the Pricing of Syndicated Banking Loans." Working Paper 7113. National Bureau of Economic Research, Cambridge, Mass.

El-Nawawy, Mohamed A., and Magda M. Ismail. 1999. "Overcoming Deterrents and Impediments to Electronic Commerce in Light of Globalisation: The Case of Egypt." (Paper presented at the annual INET conference sponsored by the Internet Society, San Jose, Calif. (http://www.isoc.org/inet99/proceedings/1g/1g_3.htm).

E-Marketer. 2000. "Strong Net Growth South of the Border." March 22. (http:www.emarketer.com).

EU Commission. 2000. *Europe: An Information Society for All*. Progress report for Special European Council on Economic Reforms and Social Cohesion. Brussels. March 23–4.

Evans, Philip B., and Thomas S. Wurster. 1997. "Strategy and the New Economics of Information." *Harvard Business Review* 75(5):70–82.

Fan, Grace. 2000. "Pedicarts Link Shanghai's Streets to the Internet." *New York Times*. March 29.

Forrester Research. 1999a. "Online Energy Industry to Reach $266 Billion by 2004." October. Cambridge, Mass.

———. 1999b. "Managing e-Marketplace Risks." December. Boston, Mass.

Goldman Sachs. 1997. "Cyber Commerce: Internet Tsunami." New York. August 4.

———. 1999. "B2B: 2B or Not 2B? Version 1.1"

———. 2000. *E-Finance in Asia, Part 2: Citibank–an Asian Internet Mandarin in the Making?*

Goodman, S. E., L. I. Press, S. R. Ruth, and A. M. Rutkowski. 1994. "The Global Diffusion of the Internet: Patterns and Problems."

Granitsas, Alkman. 2000. "Tangled in the Web: The Rush into Internet Banking May Not Be Justified by the Number of On-Line Customers in Asia." *Far Eastern Economic Review* May 4.

Grebb, Michael. 2000. "Korea's Digital Quest." *Business Week*. September 25: 68–72.

Grossman, Gene M., and Elhanan Helpman. 1991. *Innovation and Growth in the Global Economy*. Cambridge, Mass. MIT Press.

Harris, R. G. 1998. "The Internet as a GPT: Factor Market Implications.," In *General Purpose Technologies and Economic Growth*, edited by Elhanan Helpman. Cambridge, Mass.: MIT Press.

Harrow, Jeffrey. 2000. "The Rapidly Changing Face of Computing" (http://www.compaq.com/rcfoc/ [April 24]).

Helft, D. 2000. "Latin America Looking to Wireless." *The Standard*. 9 May 2000.

ITAA (Information Technology Association of America). 2000. *Bridging the Gap: Information Technology Skills for a New Millennium*. Arlington, Va.

ITU (International Telecommunications Union). 1998. *ITU Telecommunication Indicators Handbook*. Geneva.

———. 1999. *Challenges to the Network—Internet for Development*. Geneva. February.

Jensen, Mike. 1999. *African Internet Status*.

Jordan, Miriam, and Jon E. Hilsenrath. 2000. "America Talks, India Types Up the Transcript." *The Wall Street Journal*. March 16.

Kibati, Mugo. 1999. "What Is the Optimal Technological and Investment Path to 'Universal' Wireless Local Loop Deployment in Developing Countries." (Paper presented at the annual INET conference sponsored by the Internet Society, San Jose, Calif. (http://www.isoc.org/inet99/proceedings/1c/1c_2.htm).

Krantz, Michael. 1998. "The Internet Economy." *Time* 152 (July 20): 34–41.

Krueger, Anne O. 1993. "How Computers Have Changed the Wage Structure: Evidence from Microdata, 1984–1989." *Quarterly Journal of Economics* 108 (1): 33–60 (February).

Lapper, R. 2000. "Tropical Nets." *Financial Times*. February 3.

Lee, Ho Guen, J. Christopher Westland, and Sewon Hong. 1999–2000. "The Impact of Electronic Marketplaces on Product Prices: An Empirical Study of AUCUNET." *International Journal of Electronic Commerce*. Winter 4(2): 45.

Mann, Catherine L., Sue E. Eckert, and Sarah Cleeland Knight. 2000. *Global Electronic Commerce: A Policy Primer*. Washington, D.C.: Institute for International Economics.

Matoo, Aaditya, and Ludger Schuknecht. 2000. *Trade Policies for Electronic Commerce*. World Bank, Washington, D.C. Processed.

Mills, Mike. 1996. "In the Modem World, White Collar Jobs Go Overseas." *Washington Post*. September 17, p. A1.

Morgan Stanley Dean Witter. 1999. "The Internet and Financial Services." New York. August. Equity Research, North America.

OECD (Organisation for Economic Co-operation and Development). 1998a. "Electronic Commerce: Prices and Consumer Issues for Three Products: Books, Compact Discs, and Software." Paris.

———. 1998b. *The Economic and Social Impact of Electronic Commerce: Preliminary Findings and Research Agenda*. Paris. October.

———. 1999. *The Economic and Social Impact of Electronic Commerce: Preliminary Findings and Research Agenda*. Paris.

———. 2000a. "E-Commerce: Impacts and Policy Challenges." Economics Department Working Paper 252. Paris.

_____ 2000b. *Information Technology Outlook*. Paris.

_____ 2000c. "Local Access Pricing and E-Commerce." Directorate for Science, Technology and Industry, Paris.

Oliner, Stephen D., and Daniel E. Sichel. 2000. "The Resurgence of Growth in the Late 1990s: Is Information Technology the Story?" Finance and Economics Discussion Series 2000–20. Federal Reserve Board, Washington, D.C.

Oxford Analytica. 1999. *Latin America: Electronic Commerce*. September 16. http://www.oxan.com.

Panagariya, Arvind. 1999. "E-Commerce, WTO, and Developing Countries." UNCTAD. Geneva. July (http://www.unctad.org/en/docs/ecwto/pdf).

Peha, Jon M. 1999. "Alternative Paths to Internet Infrastructure: The Case of Haiti." Paper prepared for the annual INET conference sponsored by the Internet Society, San Jose, Calif. (http://www.isoc.org/inet99/proceedings/3f/3f.2htm)

Phillips, Charles, and Mary Meeker. 2000. *The B2B Internet Report*. Morgan Stanley Dean Witter Equity Research. New York. April.

Price Waterhouse Coopers. 1999. *SME Electronic Commerce Study*. Final report, Asia Pacific Economic Cooperation Telecommunications Working Group.

Rao, MaDanmohan. 1999. "Bringing the Net to the Masses: Cybercafes in Latin America." *On the Internet*. 5 (1). (http://www.indialine.com/net.editorial/editorial/70.html).

Reuters. 2000. "It's a Wireless World in Japan." June 20.

Rodriguez, F. C. 2000. "Does Information Technology Raise Inequality?" University of Maryland, Department of Economics. College Park, Md.

Rosen, Daniel H. 1999. "Hype versus Hope for E-Commerce in China." *The China Business Review* (July/August) 26(4): 38–42.

Schmitt, E. 2000. "The Multilingual Site Blueprint." *The Forrester Report* June 2000 (http://www.forrester.com).

Schuknecht, L., and Perez-Esteve, R. 1999. "A Quantitative Assessment of Electronic Commerce." WTO Working Paper ERAD 99–01. World Trade Organization, Economic Research and Analysis Division. Geneva. September.

Schwartz, Nelson D. 2000. "Playing the Internet's Next Gold Rush." *Fortune* 141 (10) 178–82. (May 15).

Suttle, Philip. 2000. "The Digital Economy and the Global Economy." World Financial Markets. Morgan Guaranty Trust Company Economic Research. January 14.

Teo, Pebble. 1999. "Business to Business Electronic Commerce: the Asian Experience." Presentation to OECD Workshop. Oslo, June 17.

UNCTAD (United Nations Conference on Trade and Development). 1999. "Report of the Pre-UNCTAD-X Workshop on Exchange of Experiences among Enterprises in the Area of Electronic Commerce. TD(X)/pc/3." Geneva. September 14.

———. 2000. *Building Confidence: Electronic Commerce and Development*. UNCTAD/SDTE/MISC.11. Geneva.

U.S. Department of Commerce. 1999. *The Emerging Digital Economy II*. (http://www.ecommerce.gov/ede.report.html).

Vehovar, Vasja, Zenel Batagelj, and Katja Lozar. 1999. "Language as a Barrier." (Paper presented at the annual INET conference sponsored by the Internet Society, San Jose, Calif.).

Vogel, Thomas T., and Pamela Druckerman. 2000. "Latin Internet Craze Sets Off Alarm Bells." *Wall Street Journal*. February 16.

———. 1996. *Washington Post*.

Washington Post. 2000. "The Wired Economy: A Special Section." April 5 issue. Washington, DC.

Wenninger, John. 1999. "Business-to-Business Electronic Commerce. *Current Issues in Economics and Finance 5* (10) (June).

Wilson, E., and Rodriguez, F. 2000. *Are Poor Countries Losing the Internet Revolution?* Report prepared for World Bank.

Wood, L., 1999. "Lloyd's Satellite Constellations." (www.ee.surrey.ac.uk/Personal/L.Wood/constellations/overview.html). Report prepared for the World Bank (http://www.infodev.org/library/working.htm.)

World Bank. 1995. *Global Economic Prospects and the Developing Countries 1995*. Washington. D.C.

———. 1999. *Global Development Finance 1999: Analysis and Summary Tables*, Washington, D.C.

———. 2000a. "The Networking Revolution. Opportunities and Challenges for Developing Countries." InfoDev Working Paper. June. Global Information and Communications Technology Department. The World Bank, Washington, D.C.

———. 2000b. *World Development Indicators 2000*. Washington, D.C.

WTO (World Trade Organization). 1998. *Electronic Commerce and the Role of the WTO*. Special Study 2. Geneva.

Xie, Andrew. 2000. Global Economic Forum. Morgan Stanley Dean Witter, New York.

Zambrano, Raul. 1999. "Internet Users in Latin America." Presentation at UNCTAD Workshop on E-Commerce, Lima, August 4–5.

Annex 4:
Firm interviews and website survey

Firm interviews

The interview information included in the chapter is based on conversations with:

- managers or executives from five multinational firms: Ingram Micro, The Gap, Ford, General Electric, and Infosys. These specialize in computer hardware and software distribution; apparel; automobiles; electrical and lighting equipment; and customs software, respectively. The first four appeared on this year's Fortune 200 list, while the last is a major Indian-based multinational software company.
- representatives from: (i) the U.S.-Mexico and U.S.-Philippines Chambers of Commerce; as well as from (ii) the offices of the Commercial or Trade Attaches representing Taiwan (China) and Brazil in the United States.

- participants in a conference on the May 24, 2000, "Wiring the Border" program, including representatives from small-business associations, technology specialists, government officials, and academic experts.

Website survey

The conclusions on the alibaba website are based on a survey of firms via fax, conducted in May 2000. To keep the survey manageable, the firms to be contacted were chosen from selected economic subsectors. Within these subsectors, we included all firms posting offers in the last two weeks of April 2000—whether as sellers or buyers. We received 105 complete replies to our questionnaire from the 800 firms surveyed. A list of all respondents' names and websites (if any) is attached.

Companies Participating in Survey of Alibaba B2B Website Users

China Yangzhou Weiteli Motor-
Manufacturing Co., Ltd.
Tianjin Printronics Circuit Corp.
Horman Company
China National Electric Wire and Cable
I/E Corp. (Xiamen Branch)
Hebei Xin Hua Li Da Sale Department
K.O.G. International Philippines., Inc.
Jiangxi Wire and Cable General Factory
Young Eak Trading Co., Ltd.
Shenzhen Tonghaisheng Investment
Development Co., Ltd.
Jiangsu I/E (Group) Corp. (Heiteng Co.,
Ltd.)
Sinochem Hebei (Shenzhen Toomly)
Import and Export Co., Ltd.
Zhejiang Yongkang Crown Power Tools
Manufacturing Co., Ltd.
Truly Sales Co.
Hongguang Electronics Import and
Export Co. (Guangzhou Office)
Chengdu Guoxin Maida Electronic Co.,
Ltd.
Catic Electronics
H2O Electronics Co.
Dong Young International Corp.
Sinoleather.com Ltd.
Chew The World
Gusung Machinery
Eros Group
Xiangshui Bearing Accessory Co., Ltd.
Shandong Gifts and Decorations Import
and Export Corp.
Dalian F.T.Z. Zhengxing International
Trading Co., Ltd.
Yuyao Kingfan Industry and Trade Co.,
Ltd.

Green Source International Group
Wellmade Industry Corp., Ltd.
Zhejiang Light Industrial Products
Import and Export Corp.
iSquare Design and Development
Shandong Xingfa Foodstuffs
Mideast Mercantile Ltd.
Xiamen Zhongxin Metal Products Co.,
Ltd.
Cintel International
Sandstone International Co., Ltd.
Shanghai Yang Ning International
Trading Co., Ltd.
Pacific Silk Route Pte.
China Shaanxi Techrun Technology
Company
Praphan Ceramica Co., Ltd.
China Tea Import and Export Corp.
Hebei Sanli Cashmere Products Co., Ltd.
Yixing Tanghan Ceramic Co., Ltd.
Xiamen Zhenhua Ind. Corp.
Ningbo Economic and Technical
Development Zone Import and Export
Corp.
Starscom Info-Tech Co., Ltd.
Seanet RS
Cixi Kaida Bearing Co., Ltd.
Kedi Hi-Tech Industrial Co., Ltd.,
Xiamen Office
Shijiazhuang Gulf Semiconductor Co.,
Ltd.
Tao's Inc.
Feidong Foreign Economics and Trade
Corp.
China Dalian Aidi International Trade
Company
Aurora Translation Services
Cixi Fuda Bearing Co., Ltd.
Hanbit Ebenezet
Shen Zhen Xinhaowei Industrial Co.,
Ltd.
G.K. Trading Corp.
Giga Technology Co., Ltd.
On Time Taiwan Ltd.
Suzhou Arts and Crafts I/E Corp.

Belgraver Asia Pte. Ltd.
W. & J. Co., Ltd.
ChangZhou Rui Da Trading Company
Well Hung (Australia) Pte. Ltd.
Renaissance International
Wuhan Zhongbai Group Co., Ltd.
CNACC International Co., Ltd.
Fujian Coal Import and Export Corp.
Tung Kong Handbag Mfy
Ambp Enterprises Co., Ltd.
Software International
Xiamen Gemachieve Enterprise
Shandong Metals and Minerals Import
and Export Corp.
D.P. International
Jitco Group Ltd.
Beijing Orient Sotoma Garment Co., Ltd.
Ishida Co., Ltd.
Ningbo Free Trade Zone Sino-Dubai
International Trading Co., Ltd.
Shriya Impex
Regan (H. K.) Ltd.
Citic Shanghai Import and Export Co.,
Ltd.
Chengde Bearing Co., Ltd.
Manray Concept
Atul Exports
W. H. Enterprises
Guangdong Yangchun Bearing Co. Ltd.
S.L.S. Partnership
Adore International
Dorly International Enterprises Inc.
Shandong Commercial Group
Corporation
Goldsense Technology Ltd.
CV RJR International

Appendix 1
Regional Economic Prospects

East Asia and Pacific

Recent developments

EAST ASIA HAS CONTINUED TO CONSOLIDATE its recovery from the deep crisis-induced recession of 1997–98, albeit with substantial variation across countries in the region. Developing countries in the region registered 6.9 percent growth in 1999, up from a decline of 1.4 percent in 1998. The Republic of Korea experienced the sharpest "V-shaped" recovery, with GDP growth of 10.7 percent in the year. Indonesia, at the other extreme, barely reached positive territory, following its difficult economic performance of 1998. On average, output in the five most affected crisis countries (Indonesia, the Republic of Korea, Malaysia, the Philippines, and Thailand—known as the East Asia-5) recovered smartly at a rate of 6.7 percent from their 1998 crisis decline of 8.2 percent. China suffered a minor dip in output growth in 1999—though still growing at a clip of 7.1 percent—as recovery in exports did not occur until the second half of the year. The newly industrializing economies (NIEs—Hong Kong [China], Taiwan [China], and Singapore), which suffered substantial spillover effects of the crisis, saw a rebound to growth of 4.8 percent in 1999 from 1.1 percent in 1998. And momentum continues to be fairly strong in the region. Data covering the first three quarters of 2000 suggest that the near-term projections published nine months ago in *Global Development Finance 2000* were generally conservative, and we have upgraded the 2000 forecast for most countries. Growth for developing East Asia, in particular, is likely to be nearer to 7.2 percent than to earlier projections for 6.6 percent growth.

A common element across the region over the last 12 to 18 months has been low and stable inflation and interest rates, and these have been strong positive factors in the recovery process. For example, inflation in the East Asia-5 has stabilized at a rate of 1.5 to 2 percent, after a rapid but brief acceleration caused by the devaluation of 1997–98 (figure A1.1). Surging oil prices have translated into mild inflationary pressure in Korea (3.9 percent year on year in September) but have had considerably less impact to date in Malaysia or Thailand. As a result, monetary policy has continued to be largely accommodative, though central bank officials are carefully monitoring the situation. The low-inflation, low-interest rate environment has been particularly beneficial to the process of unwinding the domestic debt problems faced by firms and consumers in the crisis countries. Similarly, governments have been able to limit the growth of public debt (as a share of GDP) below the worst levels initially feared. Indonesia stands out from the other East Asian economies. It has been buffeted by continuing instability—the rupiah dropping 20 percent through October since the beginning of the year—and inflation started a

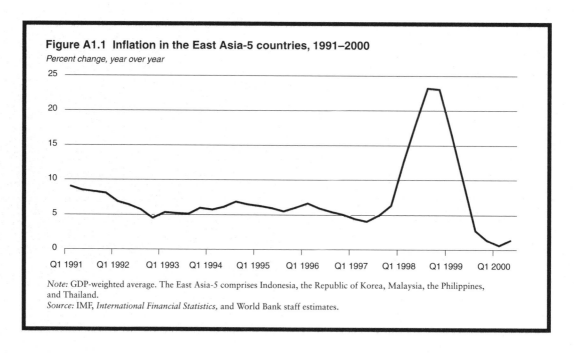

Figure A1.1 Inflation in the East Asia-5 countries, 1991–2000

Percent change, year over year

Note: GDP-weighted average. The East Asia-5 comprises Indonesia, the Republic of Korea, Malaysia, the Philippines, and Thailand.
Source: IMF, *International Financial Statistics,* and World Bank staff estimates.

rapid rise in the third quarter (6.6 percent year on year in September).

In all the crisis countries, real effective exchange rates have stabilized at rates well above crisis troughs, but some 15 to 30 percent below precrisis levels. Thus real devaluation has persisted and facilitated a double-digit boom in exports. Robust export growth and firming export prices have abetted the maintenance of a positive current account balance, though the recovery of imports and higher oil prices has narrowed the balance in many countries. Nonetheless, rising reserves and the improved term structure of foreign debt have led to a substantial improvement in the external position of the region compared to the precrisis position. China's competitiveness—through maintaining stability in its own foreign exchange market—suffered in the wake of the crisis, but ultimately improved as a consequence of price deflation and VAT (value added tax) export rebates. The loss of competitiveness, combined with the sharp import reversals in the crisis countries, including Japan, led to a sharp falloff in export growth—1.7 percent in 1998 (in dollar terms), followed by 5.8 percent in 1999. Weak external demand,

combined with softening internal demand as a result of reforms in the state enterprises and the financial system, led to a deflationary cycle. Deflation effectively yielded a real depreciation of the currency, and export growth has boomed since the second half of 1999, with merchandise exports 35.4 percent above year-ago levels in 2000 (year-to-date through August in dollar terms).

The main weakness in many countries has appeared in the equity markets. On average, stock market indexes in the five East Asian crisis countries declined by over 30 percent (in local currency terms) since the beginning of the year (through early November). Globally, there has been a flight to "quality" instruments, and this has depressed financial markets in almost all emerging markets. Gross financial capital inflows into East Asia appeared to have picked up in the first half of 2000 compared to 1999. However, the flows have been dominated by some large issues, particularly by China. For example, China received $10.4 billion of the regional total of $11.6 billion in equity inflow, and less than $600 million flowed into the equity markets of the East Asia-5 countries. Net flows remain negative, and in particular, commercial banks continue to unwind their local positions.

Near-term outlook

In 2001–02, output for the group is likely to begin a general process of moderating and converging toward longer-term growth paths, with growth easing to 6.4 percent in 2001 and 6 percent by 2002 (table A1.1). Export growth, sizzling in 2000, should ease considerably in 2001 and 2002 in line with slower external growth. External risks for East Asia are similar to what we have assessed over the last 12 months: a hard landing in the United States, a renewal of financial difficulties in Japan, and a weakening of the electronics cycle. But these risks have generally been pushed back in time. And domestic risks in aggregate have diminished from past high levels. Nonetheless, the process of working-out from under the post-crisis financial difficulties is far from finished. Higher interest rates or slower growth could further worsen financial conditions for many firms and consumers still saddled with high debt. The two most vulnerable large countries are Indonesia and the Philippines. These countries also suffer from political weaknesses, civil disturbances, and a perception (from the point of view of investors), that business operating

practices have not changed substantially from earlier, less than transparent modes. Some of the smaller island nations have also suffered from political turmoil (for example, Fiji and the Solomon Islands), whereas newly formed East Timor is in a slow and lengthy process of nation building.

Long-term prospects

Long-term prospects are little changed from earlier projections. Average per capita income grows in our long-term baseline (2003–10) by 5.4 percent per year—somewhat below 1990–2000 per capita growth of 5.9 percent. The factors underlying slower growth vary from country to country. The upper-middle-income countries and NIEs are converging with (or in some cases have exceeded) OECD income levels. They are maturing economies, with already highly educated work forces; and it is likely that GDP growth will ease gradually toward the OECD average over the next several years. The lower-income countries, particularly China, are unlikely to sustain the high growth rates of the past decade. Many of the low-income countries—as well as the crisis-affected middle-income countries—will have to devote resources in order to overcome the legacy of past institutional failures: addressing

Table A1.1 East Asia and Pacific forecast summary

(percent per year)

Growth rates/ratios	1990–2000	1998	1999	Baseline forecast			
				2000	2001	2002	2000–10
Real GDP growth	7.1	–1.4	6.9	7.2	6.4	6.0	6.3
Consumption per capita	5.2	–2.8	5.2	5.9	6.1	6.1	5.8
GDP per capita	5.9	–2.5	5.8	6.1	5.4	5.0	5.4
Population	1.2	1.1	1.1	1.0	0.9	0.9	0.8
Median inflation[a]	5.9	9.2	–1.0	3.8	5.4	5.8	4.8
Gross domestic investment/GDP	31.3	30.1	29.6	30.3	31.1	31.9	32.6
Median central gvt. budget/GDP	–0.8	–2.3	–3.2	–2.8	–2.1	–1.7	–0.8
Export volume[b]	12.2	6.8	6.2	19.4	9.3	8.6	8.5
Current account/GDP	0.3	5.9	4.1	3.3	2.5	2.3	2.1
Memorandum item							
GDP East Asia-5 countries[c]	5.2	–8.2	6.7	6.9	5.5	5.1	5.5

a. GDP deflator.
b. Goods and nonfactor services.
c. Indonesia, Republic of Korea, Malaysia, Thailand, and the Philippines.
Source: World Bank baseline forecast, October 2000.

Table A1.1a Forecast assumptions—East Asia and Pacific

Initial conditions		1988–90	1998–2000
1.	Ratio of real income per capita: industrial / East Asia and Pacific	36.8	23.7
2.	Trade (X+M) / GDP ratio (real)	45.3	67.2
3.	Median inflation rate (percent)	7.4	4.2
4.	Median fiscal balance / GDP	–1.9	–1.7
5.	Investment / GDP (real)	28.3	30.7
6.	Investment / GDP (nominal)	29.0	31.7
7.	Gross national savings / GDP	32.9	36.6
7a.	Gross domestic savings / GDP	34.2	38.3
8.	Current account balance / GDP	–0.1	4.2
9.	FDI / GDP	1.1	3.5
10.	External debt / exports*	107.3	99.7
11.	School enrollment rates Primary (pct of eligible population)	96.0	97.0
	Secondary	55.0	67.0
12.	Illiteracy rate (pct of people 15+ years)	21.0	16.0
13.	Under-5 mortality rate (per 1,000 live births)	55.0	43.0
14.	Life expectancy at birth (years)	67.0	69.0

Exogenous assumptions		1990s	2001–10
1.	Population growth	1.2	0.9
2.	Market's GDP growth	2.9	3.5
3.	Oil price $/bbl (avg.)	18.2	20.2
4.	Market's import growth	7.6	6.7

*Exports of goods and services plus workers' remittances.
Note: Market growth is trade-weighted partner GDP / import growth.
Source: World Bank database, World Bank staff estimates.

nonperforming loans in the financial sector, disposing of distressed assets, and reducing the state's active role in the economy while enhancing its regulatory role and competition.

Initial conditions for sustained high growth in East Asia at the beginning of the millennium appear better than at the beginning of the 1990s, the end-of-decade financial crisis notwithstanding (table A1.1a). Openness increased by more than 20 percentage points over the 1990s and was, if anything, enhanced during the crisis, presenting both an opportunity as well as a challenge. The opportunity comes from the ability to import new technologies, knowledge, and business practices. The challenge comes from increased competition and the need to develop institutions that enhance flexibility and speed of adaptation.

The countries of East Asia—with their ever increasing involvement in the so-called new economy—are well placed to meet the challenge, but they are lagging far behind the more advanced countries. In 1999, the East Asia-5 countries had only half the number of Internet hosts (per 10,000 persons) that Brazil or Mexico had, and only 5 percent compared to the NIEs. And though markets for the Internet and mobile phones have been growing at some 40 percent per year in East Asia, they have been growing at over 50 percent in Brazil and Mexico, in part as a result of deeper reforms and greater competition in the telecommunications sectors of the latter countries. There is also the possibility of reform fatigue or even reversal. Malaysia's recent decision to renege on removing import tariffs on automobiles could signal a weakening of a commitment to regional free trade.

South Asia

Recent developments

GDP growth in South Asia averaged 5.1 percent in 1997–98, as the larger economies—relatively closed to international trade— were successful in mitigating losses of agricultural income tied to commodity price declines in the wake of the East Asian crisis. Output growth accelerated to 5.7 percent in 1999 and is estimated to reach 6 percent in 2000. Better-than-expected agricultural sector performance in Bangladesh, India, and Pakistan has accounted for a fairly large proportion of the recent improvement in growth outturns. In addition, the rate of growth in industrial production in Bangladesh and India climbed to more than 10 percent during the first half of 2000 (figure A1.2). Output in Bangladesh was boosted by the recovery from the massive flooding of 1998. The burgeoning Indian service sector also has maintained strong advances, at rates of more than 8 percent through 1999 and into 2000. Exports of goods and services continue to grow at rapid rates— by more than 10 percent in India, Pakistan,

Figure A1.2 Industrial production in South Asia

three-month moving average, year-on-year, percentage change

Source: IMF, *International Financial Statistics.*

and Sri Lanka. At the same time, manufacturing production has fallen sharply in Pakistan, given financial constraints and other difficulties. And the surge in the oil price and continued weakness in non-oil commodity prices (for example, the prices of Sri Lanka's main export commodities—tea and natural rubber—are now some 20 and 30 percent below recent highs) is exacting a moderate toll from the region's growth momentum.

Recent steps to make South Asian economies more open to capital flows and strengthen the financial system have also supported growth. India eased some restrictions on FDI to encourage foreign flows into the energy sector, where it is most needed. FDI registered $2.2 billion in 1999 and is expected to achieve similar levels in 2000. But foreign investment is broadening in scope across the economy, supplementing domestic investment in such sectors as the software industry, which has achieved remarkable growth of almost 50 percent over the last year. Portfolio flows to India also increased, to a high of $3 billion in 1999–2000, attracted by (and contributing to) the boom in India's stock market. Equity prices increased by more than 50 percent from the first quarter of 1999 to the first quarter of 2000, and capitalization rose to

$210 billion. Recently, however, in tandem with global financial volatility, there was a reversal of portfolio flows, which affected the stock market and exerted some pressure on the rupee. Nonetheless, steps toward improving supervision and restructuring of the banking systems in India, Pakistan, and Sri Lanka have yielded some positive results and have improved confidence in the region to a degree.

Near-term outlook

Average growth for 2001–02 is anticipated to be 5.5 percent for the region (table A1.2). Underlying this aggregate figure, however, are a number of driving and restraining forces shaping the near-term view. Among positive factors are improved prospects for capital inflows, as the Indian government in particular undertakes efforts to boost foreign investment and relax direct exchange controls. And to facilitate the growth of services exports, legislation has been introduced to support the IT sector and develop "e-business." External factors such as continued strong advances in world trade and prospects for an eventual moderate firming of non-oil commodity prices should support growth across countries of the region, especially in Bangladesh and Sri Lanka.

Table A1.2   South Asia forecast summary

(percent per year)

Growth rates/ratios	1990–2000	1998	1999	2000	2001	2002	2000–10
				Baseline forecast			
Real GDP growth	5.4	5.6	5.7	6.0	5.5	5.5	5.4
Consumption per capita	3.5	6.7	3.5	3.7	3.3	3.5	3.6
GDP per capita	3.5	3.7	3.8	4.0	3.7	3.8	3.9
Population	1.9	1.8	1.8	1.8	1.7	1.7	1.5
Median inflation[a]	8.2	8.3	9.8	5.4	5.1	5.0	5.8
Gross domestic investment/GDP	22.2	23.0	23.3	23.7	24.1	24.3	25.0
Median central govt. budget/GDP	–6.9	–5.8	–4.9	–4.7	–4.5	–4.4	–3.7
Export volume[b]	9.9	6.4	4.9	11.5	4.4	8.4	7.9
Current account/GDP	–1.8	–2.3	–1.6	–2.6	–2.9	–2.2	–3.0

a. GDP deflator.
b. Goods and nonfactor services.
Source: World Bank baseline forecast, October 2000.

Recent developments in oil markets will restrain growth in the near term, however. South Asia is one of the more energy import–intensive developing regions, with crude oil and other energy commodities constituting 20 percent of total imports in India and 15 percent in Pakistan (representing 2 percent of GDP in both countries). The 50 percent rise in the oil price over the past year has increased India's import bill by some $4 billion and Pakistan's by $650 million, increasing pressure on balance of payments positions, especially for Pakistan, where external financing difficulties are expected to continue. Moreover, uncertainty generated by the high debt levels and precarious fiscal position of central and state governments is likely to constrain private sector activity.

Long-term prospects

Average GDP growth for South Asia over the 2003–10 period is anticipated to register 5.4 percent, about 0.3 percentage points higher than in projections prepared one year ago. This pace of output growth, combined with declining rates of population growth, should support advances in per capita incomes of close to 4 percent per year over the 2000–10 period, a marked improvement over the 1990s record of 3.5 percent growth (table A1.2). South Asia begins the new decade after having

achieved some progress in a number of areas supportive of longer-term growth (table A1.2a). Although the region remains in large part closed to foreign trade (in part because of the large scale of the Indian domestic economy), median inflation and central government fiscal deficits have declined modestly; external debt ratios have been brought down significantly, and domestic investment and FDI as a share of GDP have increased from generally low levels. Indicators of human capital have also improved, with school enrollment rates rising, illiteracy falling, and life expectancy increasing by three years over the last decade.

Estimates for longer-term growth assume that the region's high potential, as embodied in the initial conditions above, will be fully used. Relative to the 1990s, total factor productivity in India, for example, is expected to continue growing at a slightly higher base (by 0.2 percent) in the next decade. The abundant supply of Indian workers with training in high technology sectors should continue to provide strong momentum to the software industry. Total investment is expected to maintain growth of 8 percent throughout the next decade, with most growth emanating from the private sector. Demand for the region's exports is expected to continue to grow rapidly, with import growth in South Asia's principal

Table A1.2a Forecast assumptions—South Asia

Initial conditions	1988–90	1998–2000
1. Ratio of real income per capita: industrial / South Asia	47.2	39.3
2. Trade (X+M) / GDP ratio (real)	13.6	19.7
3. Median inflation rate (percent)	8.6	7.8
4. Median fiscal balance / GDP	−6.7	−5.4
5. Investment / GDP (real)	20.4	22.7
6. Investment / GDP (nominal)	21.0	22.0
7. Gross national savings / GDP	19.8	19.9
7a. Gross domestic savings / GDP	18.8	19.0
8. Current account balance / GDP	−2.6	−1.5
9. FDI / GDP	0.1	0.6
10. External debt / exports*	311.5	175.8
11. School enrollment rates		
Primary (pct of eligible population)	66.0	73.0
Secondary	52.0	55.0
12. Illiteracy rate (pct of people 15+ years)	53.0	47.0
13. Under-5 mortality rate (per 1,000 live births)	121.0	89.0
14. Life Expectancy at birth (years)	59.0	62.0

Exogenous assumptions	1990s	2001–10
1. Population growth	1.9	1.5
2. Market's GDP growth	2.2	3.2
3. Oil price $/bbl (avg.)	18.2	20.2
4. Market's import growth	6.0	6.2

*Exports of goods and services plus workers' remittances.
Note: Market growth is trade-weighted partner GDP / import growth.
Source: World Bank database, World Bank staff estimates.

export markets rising from 6 percent in the 1990s to 6.2 percent over 2000–10. Intraregional trade and economic integration with the world are assumed to accelerate as an easing of import substitution policies and trade and industrial restrictions takes place. Smaller countries such as Bhutan, Maldives, Nepal, and Sri Lanka will benefit from the reduction in larger-country import barriers. But an important factor likely to restrain growth is the dependency of the region—and especially the smaller countries—on a limited number of export crops, for example, cotton, tea, and rubber. Volatility and secular decline in commodity prices are likely to continue to pressure merchandise export receipts.

However, countries such as India and Pakistan face major challenges in achieving the potential rate of output growth over the next decade. High levels of domestic debt and large fiscal deficits present substantial difficulties in achieving fiscal consolidation while maintaining expenditures that are necessary for growth. A reduction in unproductive subsidies and stepped-up investment in human capital and infrastructure are essential to this effort. Infrastructure bottlenecks and delays in privatization may limit the acceleration of growth in the real and financial sectors. Also, much remains to be done to improve the competitiveness of the region's export industries. The increased focus of the government of India on trade liberalization has coincided with some increases in tariffs and an intensified use of anti-dumping measures. High tariff rates, for example, an average of 40 percent for all goods in India in 1999–2000, limit exporters' access to cheaper, more efficient industrial inputs, and serve in the long term to limit productivity gains.

Latin America and the Caribbean

Recent developments

The economic recovery in Latin America has been broadly favorable, with the region's GDP expected to rise by 4 percent in 2000. Stabilization of global financial markets and the burgeoning of world trade growth have come to support a general resumption of economic activity across the region. As in East Asia, this has been complemented on the domestic front by a steady improvement in most macroeconomic indicators through the course of 2000. Inflation declined or held steady in most countries (Ecuador was a notable exception), allowing interest rates to continue on a falling trend. Unemployment dropped and real wages rose in Brazil, Chile, and Mexico compared with 1999 averages, but unemployment remains high in Argentina and Colombia. Ex-

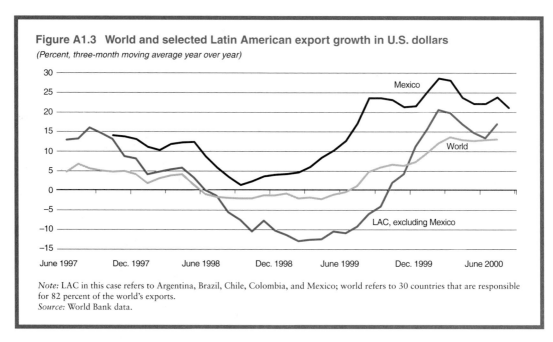

Figure A1.3 World and selected Latin American export growth in U.S. dollars
(Percent, three-month moving average year over year)

Note: LAC in this case refers to Argentina, Brazil, Chile, Colombia, and Mexico; world refers to 30 countries that are responsible for 82 percent of the world's exports.
Source: World Bank data.

change rates stabilized in several countries that experienced periods of freefall during 1999 (such as Brazil and Ecuador), restoring a degree of purchasing power and improving the outlook for private consumption and investment spending.

In real terms, most exchange rates have appreciated in 2000, but they are still low enough to facilitate rapid export growth in countries such as Brazil, Chile, Colombia, and Peru, leading to an improvement in trade balances for most countries (including oil importers). Merchandise exports in dollar terms from the region's largest economies (excluding Mexico) exhibited a sharp recovery from the lows experienced in 1998, growing by over 17 percent year on year during January–June 2000; Mexico's exports advanced by 25 percent (figure A1.3).

Mexico is an exception within the region with respect to the positioning of countries on the recovery and growth cycle. Whereas most Latin American countries experienced negative or slow growth in 1999 because of fallout from the Asian and Brazilian crises, Mexico benefited from its special trading relations through NAFTA with the United States, which remained

the "engine" for world activity through this period. Mexican growth has continued to be buoyed by the U.S. import boom in 1999–2000, with business cycles in the two countries becoming more closely aligned—and likely reaching high points in 2000. In addition, the usual exchange rate difficulties that Mexico experienced with earlier electoral cycles was noticeably absent this time, in part because of prudent macroeconomic policies that helped to restrain inflation under 10 percent for the first time since the 1994 peso devaluation. As Mexico approaches a peak in its growth cycle, while others are escaping the trough, an implication is that near-term growth (2000–01) for Latin America as a whole is unlikely to display the distinct V-shaped pattern of recovery evident in East Asia.

Near-term outlook

Volatility in financial markets and primary commodity prices continues to pose a threat to the recovery in Latin America. Sharply declining equity prices during the first half of 2000 contributed to a period of uncertainty in global financial markets at a time when key commodity price movements for the region also di-

Table A1.3 Latin America and the Caribbean forecast summary

(percent per year)

Growth rates/ratios	1990–2000	1998	1999	2000	2001	2002	2000–10
				Baseline forecast			
Real GDP growth	3.4	2.0	0.1	4.0	4.1	4.3	4.3
Consumption per capita	0.9	0.8	–2.9	1.8	2.3	2.6	2.3
GDP per capita	1.7	0.4	–1.5	2.4	2.5	2.8	3.0
Population	1.7	1.6	1.6	1.6	1.6	1.5	1.4
Median inflation[a]	16.6	7.6	9.3	8.2	9.0	7.0	7.2
Gross domestic investment/GDP	19.4	20.9	19.5	19.8	20.3	20.8	21.7
Median central gvt. budget/GDP	–2.8	–2.3	–2.9	–1.9	–2.0	–2.0	–1.3
Export volume[b]	8.4	7.5	7.0	8.9	7.8	7.3	7.0
Current account/GDP	–2.3	–4.0	–2.9	–2.8	–2.6	–2.6	–2.0

a. GDP deflator.
b. Goods and nonfactor services.
Source: World Bank baseline forecast, October 2000.

verged. The oil price rose sharply, while non-energy commodity prices of importance to the region weakened—particularly coffee, grains, and soybeans. Although most of the large countries experienced strong gains in industrial output in the first quarter of 2000, the recovery appeared to have faltered in the second quarter, except for the oil exporters Ecuador and Venezuela. And private capital inflows fell dramatically. Argentina was particularly hard hit by these developments as they coincided with strong fiscal adjustment and a political crisis that weakened investor confidence and delayed the economic recovery. Nonetheless, consolidation of the region's recovery in 2001–02 is likely, as adjustment in Brazil has been impressive so far, and new governments in Argentina and Mexico appear set to embark on a path of deepened reforms. Global conditions are expected to remain supportive of growth in the region, with above-average world trade growth, gradual recovery in key non-oil commodity prices, declining but still moderately high oil prices, and a modest increase in private capital flows. The Caribbean islands, with their increasing reliance on tourism revenues, are also expected to benefit from moderately strong income growth in North America and Europe over the next two years. Latin American region

Table A1.3a Forecast assumptions— Latin America and the Caribbean

Initial conditions	1988–90	1998–2000
1. Ratio of real income per capita: industrial / Latin America	9.6	10.0
2. Trade (X+M) / GDP ratio (real)	26.7	51.5
3. Median inflation rate (percent)	24.4	6.1
4. Median fiscal balance / GDP	–1.4	–2.3
5. Investment / GDP (real)	18.4	20.2
6. Investment / GDP (nominal)	21.4	19.9
7. Gross national savings / GDP	20.3	17.4
7a. Gross domestic savings / GDP	23.9	19.3
8. Current account balance / GDP	–0.7	–3.6
9. FDI / GDP	0.8	3.9
10. External debt / exports*	279.1	202.5
11. School enrollment rates		
Primary (pct of eligible population)	84.0	94.0
Secondary	58.0	66.0
12. Illiteracy rate (pct of people 15+ years)	15.0	12.0
13. Under-5 mortality rate (per 1,000 live births)	49.0	38.0
14. Life expectancy at birth (years)	68.0	70.0

Exogenous assumptions	1990s	2000–10
1. Population growth	1.7	1.4
2. Market's GDP growth	2.7	3.1
3. Oil price $/bbl (avg.)	18.2	20.2
4. Market's import growth	7.8	6.2

*Exports of goods and services plus workers' remittances.
Note: Market growth is trade-weighted partner GDP / import growth.
Source: World Bank database, World Bank staff estimates.

output growth is expected to reach 4.1 percent in 2001 and to rise further to 4.3 percent by 2002 (table A1.3).

Long-term prospects

Per capita GDP growth over the long term (2003–10) is likely to average around 3 percent, about 0.2 percentage points higher than in projections prepared one year ago. Some of the elements supporting this cautious optimism are highlighted in table A1.3a and include: a definitive movement toward greater domestic macro stability, as median inflation rates dropped from 24 percent to 6 percent over the decade; a two-point increase in real investment as a share of GDP, supported by strong FDI inflows, surging from less than 1 percent to almost 4 percent of regionwide output. And openness to investment flows has been complemented by a remarkable increase in integration with global trade flows—with this measure doubling as a proportion to GDP over the last 10 years. Finally, indicators of human capital have improved, with primary and secondary school enrollment rates rising by some 10 points.

The improved state of initial conditions for the outlook joins with a more definitive trend toward market-friendly policies in the larger countries, such as Argentina, Brazil, and Mexico, and potential for technology spillovers from the United States (particularly for Mexico). Banking and financial sectors in the large economies weathered the global financial crisis of 1997–98, in part because of reforms enacted in many countries following the Mexican crisis. Further strengthening of prudential regulation and supervision should support financial deepening and help to diminish the incentives for capital flight. Finally, the strong inflows of FDI in recent years into areas of the economy that could raise growth of productivity substantially—telecommunications, utilities, ports, and so forth—should produce dividends in the next decade compared with the relatively poor performance of the last 10 years. However, there is need for more progress in financial and

macroeconomic policies to deal with volatility, which may have contributed to the observed cycle of booms and busts in many countries during the 1980s and 1990s. Moreover, vulnerability of the region to swings in external financing is likely to remain a concern in the long run. Low national savings and the persistence of large debt overhangs will require rollover on a continuing basis. And this fundamental exposure to international financial conditions underlines our view that per capita growth potential is unlikely to breach 3 to 3.3 percent over the next decade, which would, nonetheless, be twice as fast as occurred during the 1990s.

Europe and Central Asia

Recent developments

GDP growth in the Europe and Central Asia region (ECA) is expected to accelerate sharply through 2000, after hitting a trough in 1998 and early 1999 following the August 1998 financial crisis in the Russian Federation. Growth in 2000 is anticipated to rise to 5.2 percent, significantly higher than the 1 percent realized in 1999. Notably, for the first time since the onset of the transition and the breakup of the Soviet Union, almost all of the countries in the region are expected to record positive growth. Short-term projections stand well above those prepared for the *Global Economic Prospects* report one year ago, primarily because of the unexpected strength of the rebound in Russia. And a common element supporting near-term growth across the region is a substantial pickup in exports, in large part because of rising import demand from the Euro Area.

In Russia, President Putin's apparent willingness to introduce reforms has eased some political uncertainties and improved business confidence. Russian industry has continued to benefit from the impact of import substitution driven by the sharp devaluation of 1998; this can be witnessed in an industrial production growth rate of close to 10 percent during the first half of 2000. This fillip to growth is diminishing, however, with the recent real appreciation of the ruble. An additional, more recent driver to Russia's unanticipated recovery is the windfall increase in oil and natural gas export revenues. Higher oil prices improved the fiscal balance from –4.2 percent of GDP in 1999 to +1.6 percent during the first half of 2000, and has yielded a primary surplus of 4.8 percent. This has supported continued reductions in government wage arrears, contributing to higher disposable incomes.[1] The current account surplus is expected to register close to $30 billion in 2000, or some 15 percent of GDP, boosting foreign reserve holdings considerably and easing the need for near-term external financing. Ukraine is now registering gains in output, although the political context remains difficult. For several of the hydrocarbon-rich Commonwealth of Independent States (CIS), higher oil and gas prices are providing extraordinary export earnings and contributing to higher output. Oil and gas export volumes should increase as well, as export markets (especially in Western Europe) are expected to achieve stronger growth.

The Central and Eastern European countries (CEECs) are benefiting from growing demand from Western Europe and, to a lesser degree, from Russia. This is boosting growth in Hungary (5.8 percent) and Poland (4.4 percent), in particular. In the Baltic countries, especially Estonia and Latvia, GDP growth of some 4.8 and 3.8 percent, respectively, in 2000 is also largely export-driven. However, high oil prices, combined with the depreciation of the euro, are putting additional pressure on external balances and contributing to higher inflation. Turkey's economy has continued to recover, reaching growth above 6 percent in 2000, up from the sharp 5.1 percent contraction experienced in 1999, because of a rebound in domestic demand tied to marked declines in real interest rates and reconstruction expenditures in the wake of the 1999 earthquake. Business confidence has also improved in response to implementation of an IMF-sponsored stabilization program begun in January 2000. Recent data, however, show that the current account deficit will be larger than targeted, reflecting strong domestic growth, real exchange rate appreciation and higher oil prices.

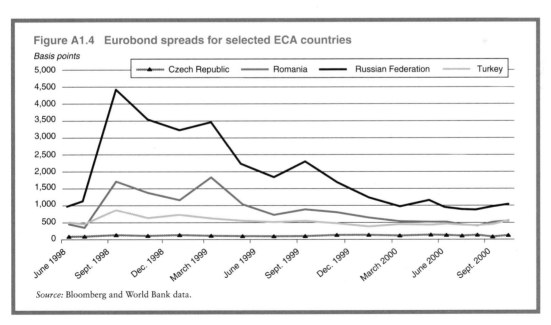

Figure A1.4 Eurobond spreads for selected ECA countries

Basis points

Legend: Czech Republic — Romania — Russian Federation — Turkey

Source: Bloomberg and World Bank data.

Table A1.4   Europe and Central Asia forecast summary
(percent per year)

Growth rates/ratios	1990–2000	1998	1999	Baseline forecast			
				2000	2001	2002	2000–10
Real GDP growth	−1.9	0.0	1.0	5.2	4.3	3.9	4.1
Consumption per capita	−1.7	1.1	1.5	4.9	4.1	3.6	4.2
GDP per capita	−2.0	−0.1	0.9	5.1	4.2	3.8	4.1
Population	0.2	0.1	0.1	0.1	0.1	0.1	0.1
Median inflation[a]	23.3	12.9	8.4	8.0	6.9	5.5	4.6
Gross domestic investment/GDP	25.2	23.0	22.1	22.6	22.9	23.1	23.6
Median central gvt budget/GDP	−3.9	−5.0	−4.5	−4.0	−3.7	−3.5	−3.6
Export volume[b]	0.7	7.1	1.0	8.3	6.5	6.4	6.8
Current account/GDP	−0.1	−1.7	1.6	2.8	1.4	0.6	−1.3
Memorandum item							
GDP Central and Eastern Europe	1.5	2.5	2.5	3.9	3.9	4.2	4.4
GDP CIS states	−4.9	−3.3	2.6	5.9	4.5	3.3	3.5

a. GDP deflator.
b. Goods and nonfactor services.
Source: World Bank baseline forecast, October 2000.

In most ECA countries, exchange rates have broadly stabilized since mid- to late 1999, and inflationary pressures remain largely under control. Early in 2000, several currencies faced upward pressure against the euro, including the Polish zloty, the Czech and Slovak koruny, as well as the Turkish lira following the introduction of a crawling peg regime at the beginning of the year. Interest rates have eased in Turkey and in Russia, where higher fiscal revenues have reduced pressures on central bank financing. Interest rates have been reduced in the Czech Republic and Hungary to stimulate domestic demand, in contrast with rate increases in Poland intended to slow domestic demand and import growth. Investor perceptions of potentially improved prospects for the region, including reduced political uncertainty in Russia, have led to a large decline in spreads on secondary market bonds (figure A1.4).

Near-term outlook

Growth performance for the region through 2002 is expected to remain relatively strong in the aggregate (table A1.4). Output growth is expected to stabilize near 4 percent over 2001–02. The moderate slowdown reflects short-term effects of structural reforms in a

Table A1.4a   Forecast assumptions— Europe and Central Asia

Initial conditions	1988–90	1998–2000
1. Ratio of real income per capita: industrial / Europe and Central Asia	6.9	11.6
2. Trade (X+M) / GDP ratio (real)	27.2	58.3
3. Median inflation rate (real)	43.2	10.5
4. Median fiscal balance / GDP	−2.3	−2.0
5. Investment / GDP (real)	28.4	22.1
6. Investment / GDP (nominal)	27.1	20.7
7. Gross national savings / GDP	29.1	18.7
7a. Gross domestic savings / GDP	28.6	21.9
8. Current account balance / GDP	2.1	−1.2
9. FDI / GDP	0.1	2.3
10. External debt / exports*	128.8	133.7
11. School enrollment rates		
Primary (pct of eligible population)	86.0	93.0
Secondary	83.0	81.0
12. Illiteracy rate (pct of people 15+ years)	4.0	4.0
13. Under-5 mortality rate (per 1,000 live births)	34.0	26.0
14. Life expectancy at birth (years)	69.0	69.0

Exogenous assumptions	1990s	2001–10
1. Population growth	0.2	0.1
2. Market's GDP growth	0.3	3.3
3. Oil price $/bbl (avg.)	18.2	20.2
4. Market's import growth	4.0	5.8

*Exports of goods and services plus workers' remittances.
Note: Market growth is trade-weighted partner GDP / import growth.
Source: World Bank database, World Bank staff estimates.

number of countries; a tightening of policy to avoid overheating in a few Central European countries; and anticipated easing of energy prices, affecting CIS performance. But developments in export markets, policy changes related to European Union (EU) accession, and the highly uncertain path of the oil price will be critical factors in shaping the outlook.

Output among the CEECs is expected to pick up in 2001–02 to 3.9 and 4.2 percent respectively, as export markets remain firm and deeper domestic reforms contribute to improved macro stability and continued dynamism of the private sector. These countries should continue to attract high levels of FDI flows, linked tightly to the EU accession process.[2] Although fiscal and current account pressures will remain high in most of the CEECs, they are expected to ease gradually because of policies that converge more rapidly with Western European norms. In contrast, the outlook for Russia and other hydrocarbon exporters of the CIS is particularly uncertain, given the state of flux in current and prospective oil market developments. Growth in these countries is expected to slow moderately in 2001, with sharper deceleration possible in 2002, as oil prices retreat from current high levels (see the commodities section of this report).

Long-term prospects

The coming decade is likely to be characterized by substantially higher average growth rates than witnessed during the difficult initial transition period of the 1990s. As is apparent, relative performance of countries within ECA has varied tremendously over the last decade, with Poland having re-attained pretransition GDP levels by 1996, while Russia and Ukraine still languish some 40 percent below that level. Despite less-than-satisfactory outturns in a number of transition countries, there has been a degree of underlying progress in strengthening some of the fundamentals for longer-term growth (table A1.4a). Median inflation is now one-quarter of its 1988–90 value, while fiscal balances have been maintained at moderate levels. FDI has risen as a share of regional GDP from 0.1 percent to 2.3

percent (though largely concentrated in the CEECs), and trade openness has doubled, reflecting earlier western reorientation of trade and a nascent recovery of intraregion flows. A principal area of weakness, particularly in contrast with other emerging-market regions, remains the paucity of investment, and there has been a 10–percentage point decline in gross national saving over the period. Despite increasing inequality in Russia and other CIS countries, the basic quality of the labor force remains potentially strong, and it is an asset that, combined with improved physical capital, could sow the seeds for more rapid growth in productivity and living standards.

Given these initial conditions, GDP for the region is projected to expand at a fairly robust 4.1 percent per year for the period 2000–10, contrasted with its decline of –1.9 percent over 1990–2000. But the regionwide forecast again masks expected divergences in growth outcomes at the country level. Countries anchored by the EU accession process have achieved a greater degree of stability and realignment of institutions and markets, positioning them for stronger growth compared to most of the states of the CIS, which have not wholly supported reform as extensively. The current long-term projection for the region is more optimistic than that presented in forecasts of one year ago (3.4 percent average GDP growth for the period 1999–2008)—a revision taking into account three main factors.

The new projections reflect a substantively revised assumption that over the near to medium term, Russia's new administration will be partly successful in improving economic management and in implementing recently proposed social and economic reforms. And growth prospects in the CEECs will begin to reflect benefits associated with the December 1999 Helsinki Accord of the European Commission, a decision to extend invitations for EU membership to Bulgaria, Latvia, Lithuania, Romania, the Slovak Republic, and Turkey. (This is in addition to invitations previously extended to the "early accessors": the Czech Republic, Estonia, Hungary, Poland,

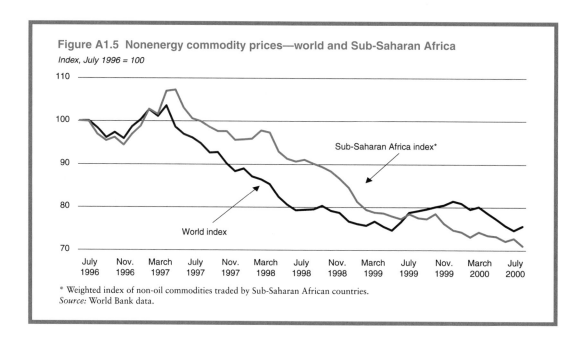

Figure A1.5 Nonenergy commodity prices—world and Sub-Saharan Africa

Index, July 1996 = 100

* Weighted index of non-oil commodities traded by Sub-Saharan African countries.
Source: World Bank data.

and Slovenia.) Finally, the somewhat higher trajectory of growth in world trade and Western European output in the new baseline has a positive impact on expansion in the ECA region.

Despite the upward revision in aggregate growth, there are a number of downside risks. In Russia, risks center on the extent to which the new government will be able to transform the current windfall gains into long-term growth. Policy measures among the EU candidate countries have contributed to increased economic stability and have helped attract substantial foreign capital. But policy mismanagement could expose the CEECs to a sharp reversal of these inflows. There is also a risk that disputes within the European Commission over reforms to its institutions, decisionmaking procedures, and budget and agricultural subsidies—which must be undertaken to accommodate an expanded membership—could delay the accession process, thus deterring foreign investors. Similarly, within the applicant countries, as more contentious reforms are introduced, political support for joining the EU may diminish, potentially slowing the accession process and growth within these countries.

Sub-Saharan Africa

Recent developments

Fallout from the 1997–99 crisis continued to exert a dampening effect on much of the Sub-Saharan African economy in 2000, as non-oil commodity export prices continued to decline over the first half of the year (figure A1.5). But higher oil revenues boosted growth for the region's oil exporters, while South Africa also strengthened modestly to 2.2 percent growth following several years of subdued performance. These and other supporting factors helped to raise GDP growth to an estimated 2.7 percent from 2.1 percent in 1999, and per capita income rose by 0.2 percent.

Substantial variation in performance was apparent across the region. Countries with better policy environments—Botswana, Uganda, and the Communauté Financière Africaine countries (excluding Côte d'Ivoire)—tended to perform better than average, with GDP up 4.4 percent. Oil producers benefited from buoyant export receipts and strong investment and grew by 3.5 percent. In East and southern Africa, many countries lagged behind. The

Table A1.5   Sub-Saharan Africa forecast

(percent per year)

Growth rates/ratios	1990–2000	1998	1999	Baseline forecast			
				2000	2001	2002	2000–10
Real GDP growth	2.1	2.0	2.1	2.7	3.4	3.7	3.6
Consumption per capita	–0.6	–0.6	–1.0	0.3	0.6	0.6	0.8
GDP per capita	–0.6	–0.5	–0.3	0.2	0.9	1.3	1.3
Population	2.6	2.6	2.5	2.5	2.5	2.4	2.3
Median inflation[a]	10.4	5.3	5.1	4.3	3.6	3.5	4.1
Gross domestic investment/GDP	19.5	20.5	19.9	20.1	20.7	21.0	21.9
Median central gvt. budget/GDP	–3.7	–3.3	–3.0	–2.9	–2.4	–2.0	–1.8
Export volume[b]	4.6	0.7	2.4	6.1	5.3	5.9	6.0
Current account/GDP	–1.5	–3.5	–2.3	–2.7	–2.2	–3.1	–3.1
Memorandum item							
GDP major oil exporters[c]	2.5	2.3	3.2	3.5	4.0	3.8	3.8
GDP region × S. Africa/oil-X	2.6	3.6	2.9	3.0	3.6	4.1	4.1

a. GDP deflator.
b. Goods and nonfactor services.
c. Angola, Gabon and Nigeria.
Source: World Bank baseline forecast, October 2000.

weather was partly to blame, as drought in Kenya and Ethiopia, floods in Mozambique and South Africa, and hurricanes in Mauritius contributed to a string of disappointing results. Countries experiencing civil strife or major political disruption—the Democratic Republic of Congo, Ethiopia, Sierra Leone, and Zimbabwe—registered the weakest performances, with GDP falling 1.5 percent during the year.

A strong rise in oil-related export revenue particularly afforded some breathing space to Nigeria's new, democratically elected government. While the country faces enormous short-term problems, a much needed boost to government revenues and strong foreign investment inflows underwrote growth of some 3.1 percent and yielded a sharp improvement in the balance of payments and fiscal accounts. This is helping to tide the country over until a possible resumption of International Monetary Fund lending and hoped-for debt relief. In South Africa, a weak performance by agriculture was the main cause of growth that was somewhat below expectations, though the country also experienced renewed turbulence in financial markets, as investor sentiment turned negative in the fourth quarter of 1999 and remained so through the first half of

2000. Country-specific factors, especially concern over the value of the rand and political developments in the region, were mainly responsible. A conservative fiscal stance helped to reinforce foreign confidence, though a second successive year of declining real public consumption did nothing to counter the weakness elsewhere in the economy.

Near-term outlook

Sub-Saharan Africa should further consolidate its recovery, as growth accelerates to 3.4 percent in 2001 and 3.7 percent in 2002 (table A1.5). Oil exporters will benefit from prices that are expected to remain at high levels through 2002. Further, Angola, Equatorial Guinea, Nigeria, and Sudan are all scheduled to bring additional supplies and exports onstream.[3] However, these gains will in part be offset by terms-of-trade losses to many other countries in the region, especially beverage exporters, who are facing the lowest prices in a generation (see the commodities section of this report). At least, the worst is now likely over, and terms of trade are expected to stabilize or improve modestly as non-oil commodity prices begin to firm. Also, despite the price weakness, privatization and deregulation are promoting

Table A1.5a Forecast assumptions—Sub-Saharan Africa

Initial conditions	1988–90	1998–2000
1. Ratio of real GDP per capita: Industrial / Sub-Saharan Africa	31.4	37.9
2. Trade (X+M) / GDP ratio (real)	39.0	42.9
3. Median inflation rate (real)	10.6	7.2
4. Median fiscal balance / GDP	–3.4	–2.5
5. Investment / GDP (real)	16.9	17.5
6. Investment / GDP (nominal)	17.0	16.7
7. Gross national savings / GDP	15.2	13.5
7a. Gross domestic savings / GDP	17.2	14.8
8. Current account balance / GDP	–1.6	–3.5
9. FDI / GDP	0.5	1.5
10. External debt / exports*	216.9	232.0
11. School enrollment rates Primary (pct of eligible population)	54.0	60.0
Secondary	...	...
12. Illiteracy rate (pct of people 15+ years)	50.0	41.0
13. Under-5 mortality rate (per 1,000 live births)	155.0	151.0
14. Life expectancy at birth (years)	50.0	50.0

Exogenous assumptions	1990s	2001–10
1. Population growth	2.6	2.3
2. Market's GDP growth	2.4	3.0
3. Oil price $/bbl (avg.)	18.2	20.2
4. Market's Import growth	6.1	6.1

... Not available.
*Exports of goods and services plus workers' remittances.
Note: Market growth is trade-weighted partner GDP / import growth.
Source: World Bank database, World Bank staff estimates.

greater supply and export growth in key markets such as cotton and cocoa in west Africa and copper in Zambia. Nevertheless, the impact on real incomes will result in weaker domestic demand and slower growth in the near term. The baseline also assumes a return to more normal weather patterns, which will further boost agricultural production and exports. Trade liberalization, particularly in COMESA, SADC, and the South African-EU FTA, should spur greater trade and regional cooperation. And finally, the Heavily Indebted Poor Countries (HIPC) Initiative is gaining momentum, with nine African countries—Benin, Burkina Faso, Cameroon, Mali, Mauritania, Mozambique, Senegal, Tanzania, and Uganda—now

having received a total of close to $9 billion of relief in net present value terms. Several more African countries are expected to reach decision points in the near future.

Long-term prospects

Despite the growth slowdown of the late 1990s, recent performance continues to support the view that fundamental structural change and institutional strengthening will have a significant impact on Sub-Saharan Africa's prospects. The forecast is for a halt to the region's lengthy decline and marginalization and even for a moderate reversal. The longer term (2003–10) outlook is for sustained GDP growth—around 3.7 percent—with per capita incomes rising 1.5 percent per year. The primary driving force behind the outlook remains better governance and ongoing reforms to the policy environment. Table A1.5a highlights improvements in a number of economic outturns over the last decade that serve as the initial conditions for development into the next 10 years. Median inflation and fiscal deficits have been reduced, while moderate gains in real investment and in FDI have also been achieved. To a degree, these have been countered by a fall in savings rates and a rise in external deficits (characteristic of the secular decline in commodity prices). Increases in school enrollment and the decline in illiteracy rates are more encouraging indicators for the stock of human capital. However, HIV/AIDS is expected to carry substantial negative effects for the future labor force (see below).

Growth is likely to remain modest compared to that of other emerging regions, reflecting a range of negative factors still to be overcome, including poor transportation and communications infrastructure, low savings and private investment rates, and limited access to foreign capital (World Bank 2000). Moreover, without substantial diversification of production, economies in the region will remain overexposed to irregular weather conditions and unfavorable terms-of-trade shocks. Unfortunately, on balance, there seems very little prospect for achieving widespread per capita growth rates on the order of 4 or 5 percent or more, which have characterized East Asia's best performers.

Access to foreign savings may also prove problematic. Apart from the HIPC Initiative, foreign aid is likely to diminish further. The enhanced HIPC Initiative is worth nearly $30 billion in net present value terms, with some 80 percent of the program earmarked for Sub-Saharan Africa. However, even this level of resource transfer—roughly 9 percent of 1998 GDP—is small compared to the region's requirements, and it will be necessary to attract more private capital. The main potential benefit of the HIPC Initiative may be the impetus it gives toward strengthening the policy framework and poverty reduction objectives in the region.

AIDS and the economy. The forecast attempts to factor in more carefully the economic effects of HIV/AIDS—an issue of huge importance for Sub-Saharan Africa. According to U.N. estimates (UNAIDS 2000), Sub-Saharan Africa is home to 24.5 million (or 70 percent) of the 34.3 million existing cases worldwide and 12.1 million of a total of 13.2 million AIDS orphans. Moreover, the epidemic appears to be increasingly concentrated in Africa, where 4 million of the 5.5 million new infections occurred in 1999. Southern Africa is particularly affected, with Botswana, Swaziland, Zimbabwe, Lesotho, Zambia, South Africa, and Namibia having incidence rates in the adult population between 36 percent (Botswana) and 19 percent (Namibia). By contrast, incidence rates in north and western Africa are typically below 3 to 5 percent, though they range up to 8 percent in Cameroon and 11 percent in Côte d'Ivoire. The fact that victims tend to be working adults in the prime of their lives amplifies not only the tragic human impacts but the social and economic disruption as well.

Because the scale of the HIV/AIDS epidemic is unprecedented in recent history, it is difficult to gauge its macroeconomic impacts with pre-cision. Nevertheless, a growing body of survey work has attempted to measure the effects on households and businesses, communities, and governments. Various studies have identified a wide range of costs. These include reduced household savings and labor supply caused by the expenditure of time and money in caring for sick family members or raising orphaned children; lower productivity in the business sector because of illness, absenteeism, skill shortages, and higher training costs; and diversion of government budgets from expenditure on education and infrastructure. The impacts are more severe in sectors such as transportation, construction, and power generation, where male workers live away from their families (UNAIDS 2000, pp. 26–36; Bollinger and Stover 1999). Macroeconomic impacts have been modeled using various approaches at both a regional level and in country-specific studies of Cameroon, Kenya, Swaziland, Tanzania, and Zambia. These studies yield similar estimates of the prospective cost, generally a fall in per capita growth of 1 percent or more annually for countries with high, though not the most extreme, incidence rates (Over 1992; Bollinger and Stover 1999).

Projecting the medium-term economic impact is further complicated by variations in government policy, which can have a major influence on the course of the disease. In Uganda and Zambia, concerted government efforts have helped to lower significantly incidence rates in high-risk populations (see, for example, UNAIDS 2000, p. 10). Nevertheless, until now such interventions have been all too rare. Thus, fairly pessimistic estimates of the impact on population growth and productivity must be factored in, particularly for countries where the incidence is currently high, a category that includes some of Sub-Saharan Africa's consistently strongest performers. In the worst-affected countries, population growth is expected to slow by 1 to 2 percent annually (possibly even to turn negative), while per capita income growth may slow by nearly that much again.

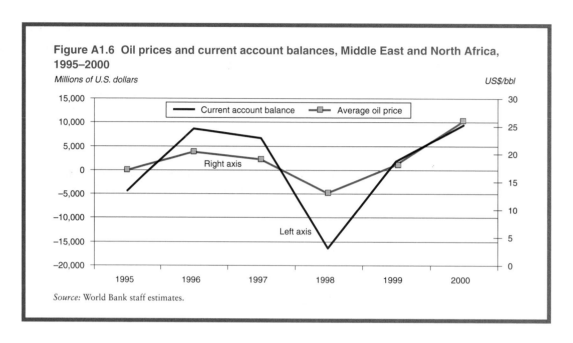

Figure A1.6 Oil prices and current account balances, Middle East and North Africa, 1995–2000

Source: World Bank staff estimates.

Middle East and North Africa

Recent developments

Despite some favorable developments, including higher oil prices, the Middle East and North Africa region's growth prospects remain modest in the short and medium terms. Adverse developments in the Middle East peace process are also casting a renewed pall on prospects for tourism, investment, and trade in the Levant. GDP growth of 2.2 percent was reported in 1999, and growth of 3.1 percent is expected in 2000. Cyclical factors have played a role in the region's recovery, with external factors such as the surge in oil prices, recovery in traditional export markets—especially the Euro Area—and some improvement in weather conditions beginning to relieve drought; these factors are leading to modest improvements in growth outturns. But significant impediments to higher potential growth remain, as the countries in the region face major challenges in the reform of domestic policies affecting trade openness, exchange rates, investment, and the labor force.

Oil prices remained above $30 per barrel for much longer than anticipated in 2000, rais-

ing export revenues and incomes in the oil exporters. As OPEC increased production quotas, export volumes have risen, and most OPEC countries are now producing at peak capacity. The impact on fiscal positions has been favorable; major oil producers had formulated budgets around an assumed oil price of $22 per barrel, and higher revenues have contributed to lower deficits and borrowing requirements. For example, in 1999 Kuwaiti oil revenues grew by 39 percent and public revenues increased by 30 percent. External debt–financing constraints have eased and domestic arrears have fallen. In Saudi Arabia, bank claims on the public sector had grown by 7.7 percent in 1998 and 3.5 percent in 1999, but fell by 8 percent in May 2000. As a result, pressure on exchange rates that were experienced in 1998 and early 1999 in several Gulf countries have eased significantly, and monetary authorities in most oil-exporting countries have built up sufficient foreign reserves to defend their exchange rate pegs. Current account positions have shown large improvement, with a turnaround of over $42 billion between 1998 and 2000, representing about 6 percent of oil exporters' annual GDP (figure A1.6). Increased imports by the Islamic Republic of Iran and Algeria have diminished the magnitude of the region's surplus to a degree.

For the diversified exporters, favorable external conditions have been largely overshadowed by negative domestic effects. Growth rose somewhat to 3.6 percent in 2000 from 3.3 percent during 1999. Strong growth in Europe has fueled a boom in tourism, with record numbers of tourist arrivals and receipts being experienced in many North African and Mediterranean countries. Tourist arrivals increased by 37 percent in the Arab Republic of Egypt, rose to a record 4.8 million in Tunisia, and are rising by 10 percent year on year in Jordan for the first four months of 2000. The economic revival in Europe has also led to gains in some export categories (food and primary commodities, some mechanical goods, and energy), but exports of labor-intensive goods such as textiles and clothing remain flat in value terms. Workers' remittances have also been boosted (75 percent in 1999 in Tunisia) by the improvement in economic activity in the broader Euro-Mediterranean and Gulf regions. The gradual easing of drought conditions in many countries improved agricultural incomes and exports and led to some decline in food imports. But drought conditions have continued in Morocco for the second consecutive year, with a significant impact on overall growth. Price stability in many diversified exporters has been maintained in a time of higher oil prices through energy subsidies to domestic consumers and maintenance of tight monetary policy in support of fixed exchange rate pegs to dollar-dominated baskets. However, there are some troubling elements in the picture for diversified exporters that are limiting GDP growth:

• Exchange rates in many countries are pegged to an appreciating dollar, but these countries' major export markets are in the Euro Area. Prices in the region are rising more rapidly than in the United States, implying that exchange rates are becoming overvalued relative to other currencies. As a result, export growth is generally lower than export market growth would suggest, and several countries, particularly Egypt, are experiencing pressures on their exchange rates.
• Lower confidence in the group stemming from both economic and political factors is a second force restraining growth. Capital

Table A1.6 Middle East and North Africa forecast summary
(percent per year)

Growth rates/ratios	1990–2000	1998	1999	2000	2001	2002	2000–10
				Baseline forecast			
Real GDP growth	3.1	3.3	2.2	3.1	3.8	3.6	3.6
Consumption per capita	0.4	−1.2	−0.3	1.2	1.5	1.3	1.3
GDP per capita	0.9	1.3	0.3	1.1	1.9	1.7	1.7
Population	2.2	2.0	2.0	2.0	1.9	1.9	1.9
Median inflation[a]	...	0.7	4.3	5.2	3.9	3.8	3.6
Gross domestic investment/GDP	21.6	22.0	22.3	22.6	22.8	23.1	23.7
Median central gvt. budget/GDP	−1.6	−3.3	−3.4	−2.0	−1.8	−1.7	−1.2
Export volume[b]	4.6	−2.5	4.2	5.6	4.5	5.1	5.3
Current account/GDP	0.4	−1.0	1.7	1.3	1.0	0.5	0.7
Memorandum item							
GDP oil-dominant economies	2.5	0.9	1.6	3.2	3.3	2.9	3.1
GDP diversified exporters	3.9	5.5	3.3	3.6	4.7	4.9	4.4

... Not available.
a. GDP deflator.
b. Goods and nonfactor services.
Note: Excluding Iraq.
Source: World Bank baseline forecast, October 2000.

markets have responded with disfavor to higher-than-anticipated fiscal deficits in Egypt and Lebanon, with several downgrades undertaken by ratings agencies for Lebanon, large declines in stock market indexes (by 50 percent in Egypt from January to October), and rising spreads. Because of the effects on confidence of the recent conflict in the West Bank and Gaza, and the lower likelihood of a peace agreement in the near future in the Levant, the climate for investment (and tourism) will be poorer and GDP growth will show only modest, rather than strong, recovery in 2000.

Near-term outlook

The recent modest improvement in economic activity in 2000 and the effects of reform programs under way in many countries will influence the near-term outlook for the region favorably. Activity is expected to pick up to 3.8 percent in 2001 and to slow slightly to 3.6 percent in 2002 (table A1.6). For oil-exporting countries, the outlook is conditioned by the expected path for oil prices in the period and the lagged response to higher incomes. With an average price of $28 a barrel for 2000 and $25 in 2001, oil revenues should continue to support income growth in the oil exporters, but large domestic and external arrears and structural budget deficits imply continued need for public sector expenditure restraint and reforms. Improved agricultural conditions in Algeria and the Islamic Republic of Iran, combined with continuing attempts to privatize state industries, and planned investments in the hydrocarbons sector through both domestic and foreign investment, will make positive contributions to growth. Moreover, the gradual reform of the multiple exchange rate regime in the Islamic Republic of Iran is expected to continue, given the success of the "export" rate in recent months. In the Gulf Cooperation Council countries, continued investments in hydrocarbons, reform of investment regimes (particularly the taxation of foreign firms), and a lowering of corporate taxes generally should provide a more favorable

Table A1.6a Forecast assumptions—Middle East and North Africa

Initial conditions		1988–90	1998–2000
1.	Ratio of real GDP per capita: Industrial / MNA region	8.8	9.8
2.	Trade (X+M) / GDP ratio (real)	36.8	37.0
3.	Median inflation rate (percent)	13.4	2.7
4.	Median fiscal balance / GDP	–5.0	–1.0
5.	Investment / GDP (real)	23.1	23.8
6.	Investment / GDP (nominal)	24.8	20.8
7.	Gross national savings / GDP	20.8	19.5
7a.	Gross domestic savings / GDP	20.6	19.2
8.	Current account balance / GDP	–2.1	–1.4
9.	FDI / GDP	0.6	1.2
10.	External debt / exports*	148.9	120.2
11.	School enrollment rates Primary (pct of eligible population)	82.0	86.0
	Secondary	59.0	66.0
12.	Illiteracy rate (pct of people 15+ years)	46.0	37.0
13.	Under-5 mortality rate (per 1,000 live births)	71.0	55.0
14.	Life Expectancy at birth (years)	65.0	68.0

Exogenous assumptions		1990s	2001–10
1.	Population growth	2.2	1.9
2.	Market's GDP growth	2.6	3.2
3.	Oil price $/bbl (avg.)	18.2	20.2
4.	Market's import growth	6.7	6.3

*Exports of goods and services plus workers' remittances.
Note: Market growth is trade-weighted partner GDP / import growth.
Source: World Bank database, World Bank staff estimates.

business climate. And in a reversal of patterns of the 1990s, trade regimes are also expected to become more open, as several countries, such as Saudi Arabia and Oman, seek and gain membership in the World Trade Organization.

The near-term outlook for the diversified exporters indicates that growth will rise to 4.7 percent in 2001 and to 4.9 percent in 2002. Favorable factors assisting growth include the smooth changes in leadership in Jordan, Morocco, and the Syrian Arab Republic, which contributed to lower political uncertainty; the potential for reduction of political conflict in the Western Sahara; and efforts to jump-start the UMA (Arab Maghreb Union). The public sector in several countries will contribute significantly to growth, with bond issues in Lebanon and Egypt to finance higher fiscal expenditures. The recent gradual downward adjustment to the Egyptian pound is expected to continue into 2001, improving the prospects for net exports somewhat. Broadening of privatization programs into areas such as telecommunications, airlines, and the finance sectors in Egypt, Jordan, Tunisia, and Morocco will attract additional foreign investment, helping to deepen equity markets, and improve efficiency in operations of the sectors. However, unfavorable factors persist. The political uncertainty in the Levant appears to be continuing, with significant adverse impacts on confidence and investment. The effects on investment may be felt outside the Levant, particularly because of "wrong neighborhood" effects. Additionally, the pace of reforms in the public sector, privatization programs, and microeconomic reform in the private sector is very slow, suggesting that the gains will not be felt fully in the near term. And with the performance of the large agricultural sectors in many countries heavily reliant on weather conditions, volatility in growth resulting from unpredictable weather conditions will continue.

Long-term prospects

At this juncture, the moderately optimistic near-term picture for the region does not translate into significantly higher long-term growth potential. Despite reforms in many of the countries in the region, much of the improved performance in the recent past owes much to cyclical and external factors such as weather, oil prices, and export market–growth. Significant structural impediments to higher long-term growth remain. Table A1.6a shows that there have been fundamental (and likely secular) improvements in some regional macroeconomic conditions and in the nurturing of the labor force over the last decade. Reduction in inflation and fiscal imbalances, attraction of additional FDI flows, and lowering of external debt ratios are significant. Moreover, considerable improvements in school enrollment, reduction of illiteracy, and better health indicators are positive forward-looking indicators for the future labor force. But the region remains less open to foreign trade than others, with the exception of South Asia, with no change in the ratio of trade to GDP over a 10-year period. And investment has remained stagnant, with little improvement in private capital spending—a critical element in fostering efficiencies and contributing to higher long-term potential growth rates.

Other substantial obstacles to higher long-term growth persist. Public sectors continue to be large and inefficient in delivering services, and the institutional and regulatory capabilities in many sectors are not geared to fostering private sector development. Moreover, the region continues to rely heavily on narrow sources of external revenues, whether they are product or export-market dominated, suggesting the potential for longer-term volatility in export earnings. Overvaluation of exchange rates in several countries will continue to have dampening effects on export growth. And the problem of noncompetitiveness of basic industry will be further exacerbated by the proposed abolition of the Multifibre Agreement (MFA), which will allow greater competition by low-cost producers in traditional export markets for North African textiles and clothing.

Recent political events have cast a pall over confidence in the region, overshadowing the potential for improvements in regional integration resulting from the EU Association Agreements and peace agreements in the Levant. While tensions remain high, prospects for intraregional trade, as well as foreign investment and tourism, will be poor. Even if some form of détente is reached in the Levant, it may result in a "cold peace" where countries may not be in conflict, but the cooperation required for trade relations may be lacking. For oil exporters, the windfalls from higher oil prices are expected to be temporary, and oil prices are expected to fall in the medium term, suggesting that structural changes need to be made to improve fiscal positions and increase the scope of private activity in domestic economies. This implies that while conditions in oil markets and major trading partners are so favorable, the region should take advantage of the current trends to cast a wider net and proceed more quickly with their domestic reform agendas.

Notes

1. The percentage of the population on wages "below subsistence" remains high at 27.6 percent, according to official estimates as of June 2000. However, it has declined significantly from 33.5 percent as of April.

2. The EU market now accounts for 60 to 80 percent of Central and Eastern European countries' exports.

3. Note that Angola, Equatorial Guinea, and Sudan are not OPEC members. For Nigeria, recent crude oil production has been marginally below the OPEC quota of 2.157 million barrels per day. However, the Obasanjo administration has ambitions to increase production well beyond the current quota limit, to 3 million barrels per day by 2003. A warming of relations with Nigeria's foreign joint venture partners and a recent surge in exploration and development activity indicate strongly that an increase of this magnitude will likely be feasible. Less problematic for re-

lations with OPEC, a third liquid natural gas (LNG) train is scheduled to come onstream at Bonny Island in 2002, raising production by 50 percent. The additional output has already been presold. See, further, (http://www.eia.doe.gov/emeu/cabs/nigeria.html).

References

Bollinger, Lori, and John Stover. 1999. "The Economic Impact of AIDS." The Futures Group International, Glastonbury, Conn. Available at (http://www.iaen.org/impact/stovboll.pdf).

Over, Mead. 1992. "The Macroeconomic Impact of AIDS in Sub-Saharan Africa." World Bank. Processed. Available at (http://www.worldbank.org/aids-econ/macro.pdf).

UNAIDS. (Joint United Nations Programme on HIV/AIDS). 2000, *Report on the Global HIV/AIDS Epidemic*. Geneva: Joint United Nations Programme on HIV/AIDS. Available at (http://www.unaids.org/epidemic_update/report/Epi_report.pdf).

World Bank. 2000. *Can Africa Claim the 21st Century?* Washington, D.C.

Appendix 2
Global Commodity Price Prospects

Global commodity prices have followed many different paths since the lows after the Asian crisis, with crude oil prices rising sharply, agricultural prices remaining low, and metals and minerals prices staging a modest recovery. The recovery of non-oil commodity prices lagged behind that of oil prices because supplies of non-oil commodities were slow to adjust to low prices while oil production was significantly reduced by OPEC producers. Producers of non-oil commodities have been left with large inventories that still need to be absorbed before prices can rise significantly. Metals and minerals prices have begun to recover, rising 27 percent since their lows. However, agricultural prices remain near their cyclical lows (after a brief rally that was not sustained), because of continued production increases and large stocks. Rapid global economic growth, which contributed to the sharp increase in crude oil prices in 1999 and 2000, is expected to fuel a recovery in non-oil commodity prices during the next several years.

The near-term outlook is for the divergence in commodity prices to be reduced with declines in energy prices, further increases in metals and minerals prices, and a recovery in agricultural prices (see annex tables A2.1 and A2.3 for nominal price forecasts for individual commodities and indexes). In nominal terms, crude oil prices are expected to decline 11 percent in 2001, relative to 2000, and an additional 16 percent in 2002 as OPEC and non-OPEC supplies increase in response to the surge

in prices in 1999 and 2000. Metals and minerals prices are projected to rise 2.2 and 2.4 percent, respectively, in 2001 and 2002 after rising 13.6 percent in 2000. Agricultural prices continued to fall in 2000, with a decline of 5.2 percent, but are expected to increase 3.9 percent in 2001 and an additional 6.0 percent in 2002 as global stocks begin to fall and demand increases in response to current low prices and rapid economic growth.

Over the balance of the decade, real commodity prices[1] are expected to reverse recent moves as energy and metals prices fall and agricultural prices rise (see annex tables A2.2 and A2.3 for real price forecasts for individual commodities and indexes). Real energy prices are projected to fall sharply from current levels, with real petroleum prices down 47 percent by 2010 compared to 2000 levels as OPEC and non-OPEC supplies increase. Agricultural prices are low by historical comparison, and real prices are expected to rise modestly over the balance of the decade. By 2010, real agricultural prices are projected to rise 9 percent relative to 2000. Metals and minerals prices have already made a significant recovery from the lows of 1999, and by 2010 they are projected to fall 7.6 percent from the 2000 levels. This would still leave metals and minerals prices above the 1999 levels. The long-term decline in real commodity prices, which has been observed for many decades, is expected to continue. However, these trends will largely be dominated during the decade by the reaction of prices to recent extremes, which have seen energy prices rise and agricultural prices fall.

Agriculture

Food

The World Bank's index of nominal food prices has declined by one-third since the recent high in 1997. In real terms, food prices are down by more than half since 1980 (see figure A2.1). The decline in real food prices reflects the combined impact of countries' agricultural policies, improved technology, and changes in demand, which, on balance, have caused food supplies to increase faster than food demand and prices to decline relative to manufactures prices. Despite the price declines, the FAO's index of world food production increased by 20 percent from 1990 to 1999, and per capita production increased by about 5.5 percent. Our forecast is for real food prices to stabilize over the decade following recent declines.

Grain prices are severely depressed, with nominal prices near the lows of the past decade and real prices at all-time lows.[2] Several factors account for current low prices. Consumption growth has slowed over the last few decades, from 2.7 percent per year during the 1970s to 1.7 percent growth during the 1980s and 0.8 percent growth during the 1990s[3], and this has led to nearly stagnant world trade since the late 1970s. While consumption and trade have seen slow growth, world grain yields have been increasing at 1.4 percent per year over the last decade, and an even more rapid 1.7 percent when the countries of the former Soviet Union (FSU) and Eastern Europe are excluded. The yield increases have been rapid enough to meet global demand at declining real prices and still allow total world cropland devoted to grains to fall by 8 percent since the peak in 1981. Among major grain-exporting countries[4], cropland planted to grain has declined 21 percent since the peak. Much of this idled cropland will not likely return to grain production, but it represents substantial capacity that could return if prices rise enough to justify its use. Grain prices are not expected to rise in real terms for any sustained period because of continued yield increases, the surplus production capacity in major exporting countries, and continued moderate demand growth. However, prices are projected to increase over the next several years, as prices recover from current severely depressed levels. This will likely be followed by further price declines be-

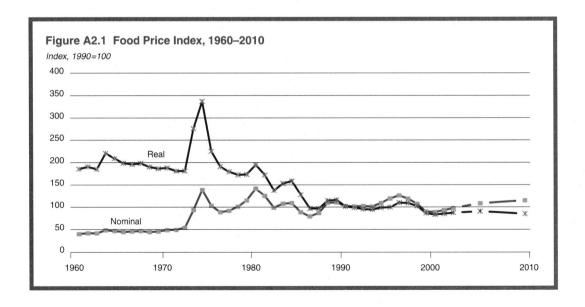

Figure A2.1 Food Price Index, 1960–2010

Index, 1990=100

ginning about mid-decade as production increases exceed demand growth.

Vegetable oil prices remain depressed following the declines in 1999. Prices of major vegetable oils, such as soy and palm, have declined by nearly one-half since their 1998 highs, while prices of other oils, such as coconut and groundnut, have fallen by about one-quarter since their 1999 highs. Unlike most other agricultural commodities, vegetable oil prices increased during the Asian crisis, as Indonesia (a major exporter) imposed export taxes on palm oil in an effort to stabilize domestic prices. These taxes were gradually removed starting in 1999, as the crisis eased, and this caused exports to increase and all vegetable oil prices to fall. Global supplies of vegetable oils are expected to increase 5.0 percent in 2000, compared to the long-term average of 3.5 percent, and this could keep prices depressed for at least another year. Palm oil production has grown by 7.5 percent per year over the past decade, compared to 5.5 percent for soy oil, and this growth is expected to continue as more Southeast Asian and Latin American producers expand palm oil production. Palm oil could displace soy oil as the dominant oil produced within five years, and this would contribute to long-term weakness in the entire vegetable oils complex as palm oil use displaces soy and other oils. Palm oil is already the most heavily traded oil, with a 40 percent market share, while soy oil is second with a 20 percent share. The index of nominal vegetable oil prices fell 8.6 percent in calendar year 2000 and is projected to rise 6.0 percent in 2001. By 2005, nominal prices are projected to increase 30.9 percent from 2000 levels. Real prices are projected to rise less than 3 percent between 2000 and 2010.

Other food prices have been mixed, with beef and shrimp prices strong because of the rapid global economic growth, while banana and citrus prices have remained weak because of large supplies. Sugar prices have recovered from 1999 lows despite large stocks resulting from five consecutive seasons when global production has exceeded consumption. Raw sugar prices averaged 17.6 cents per kilogram in the world market in 2000 compared to an average of 24.5 cents per kilogram during the decade ending in 1998. World production and stocks are expected to fall in 2001, and prices should continue to recover. However, the price recovery is expected to take several years, with prices rising to about 20 cents per kilogram by 2005. Real prices are projected to remain almost unchanged from 2000 to 2010.

Beverages

After falling sharply in 1998 and 1999, the index of nominal beverage prices is expected to increase modestly in 2001 and more rapidly in 2002 (figure A2.2). The decline in prices began as the Asian crisis weakened demand and followed several years of high prices in the mid-1990s, which had stimulated global production. The sharp drop in prices has not yet been reversed despite falling beverage stocks and rising imports. Currency devaluations in the major exporters: Brazil (for coffee), Côte d'Ivoire (for cocoa), and Kenya (for tea) contributed to lower U.S. dollar export prices.[5] Weak currencies in major importers, such as the European Union and the Russian Federation, also weakened import demand. Beverage prices have historically been among the most volatile commodity prices, and a supply disruption in a major producer could quickly reverse the recent price declines. However, barring such an event, prices are expected to be slow to recover because of new capacity added by major exporters. The index of nominal beverage prices is expected to rise 1.5 percent in 2001 and 8.7 percent in 2002. Real prices are expected to increase about 20 percent from 2000 to 2005 and then decline as productivity increases allow supplies to meet demand with falling real prices.

Cocoa prices reached a three-decade low in February 2000, as production increased 6 percent in the 1999 season compared to a decade-long growth rate of 1.4 percent. Cocoa consumption rose in response to lower prices and increased global economic growth, but not enough to keep stocks from rising 12 percent.

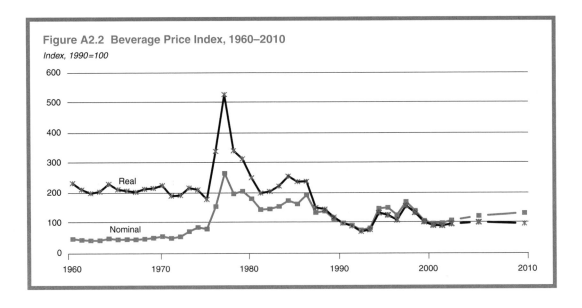

Figure A2.2 Beverage Price Index, 1960–2010

Index, 1990=100

Prices are expected to begin to recover in 2001 as demand increases in major markets accompanying projected strong economic growth. By 2002, nominal cocoa prices are projected to rise 22 percent from 2000 levels. The longer-term outlook is for real prices to rebound from current severely depressed lows. By 2005, real prices are projected to rise 45 percent from the lows of 2000 and then remain about unchanged at that level, but this would still leave real prices at one-third of the 1980 level. One of the factors that should keep prices from returning to previous highs is the 20 percent increase in world cocoa planted areas during the 1990s as low-cost producers such as Côte d'Ivoire, Ghana, and Indonesia expanded production capacity.

Coffee prices declined sharply during 1999 and 2000, with arabica prices down 37 percent and robusta prices down 48 percent. Overproduction, the Brazilian currency devaluation in January 1999, and weak demand in Europe and the United States all contributed to the price declines. Vietnam emerged as the largest robusta producer and exporter, and became the second-largest overall coffee exporter, following Brazil. This contributed to the greater decline in robusta prices compared to arabica prices but also contributed to over-

all weakness in all coffee prices. In response to low prices, Brazil and Colombia, the two largest arabica producers and dominant members of the Association of Coffee Producing Countries (ACPC), agreed to an export retention scheme to withhold 4.5 million bags of production from export during 2000 and 2001. This could support arabica prices and would be more effective if other ACPC countries joined the scheme. However, this will not change the longer-term issues of weak demand growth, excess production capacity, and large stocks, which have been with the industry for many years. Barring a weather-related supply disruption, prices are expected to be slow to recover, with arabica prices increasing only 7.4 percent by 2002 and robusta prices increasing 16.2 percent. Real prices are projected to rise over the next 10 years (from current extremely depressed levels), with arabica prices up 7 percent by 2010 compared to 2000, and robusta prices up 55 percent.

Tea prices have remained the strongest of the three major beverages, with a 10 percent decline in 1999 compared to 1998 and a 2.8 percent increase in 2000. The strength was largely due to poor weather–related growing conditions in Kenya, which reduced quality exports, and the recovery of demand in countries that benefited from increased crude oil prices. Many of the major oil exporters of the Middle East as well as the Russian Federation are major tea buyers. The return of Iraq as a tea importer, following the lifting of U.N. sanctions on food imports, also contributed to the overall price strength. However, supplies are now increasing in major exporters, and nominal prices are not projected to increase significantly over the next several years. Tea yields in Sri Lanka, a major exporter, increased 48 percent from 1990–92 to 1996–98 in response to tea estate privatization in the early 1990s, which led to increased investment and improved management of the tea estates. Nominal prices are expected to rise about 11 percent by 2010 relative to 2000, while real tea prices are expected to fall about 13 percent. There is some prospect that rapid consumption growth in major producing countries, such as India and China, could offset weak demand in industrial countries and provide a firmer price outlook.

Agricultural Raw Materials

The index of nominal agricultural raw materials prices rose by 35 percent during the first half of the 1990s, as the global economy boomed, and then fell sharply by 35 percent in

response to the Asian crisis. Prices are now set to recover from the lows of 1998 and have increased about 5 percent during 1999 and 2000 (figure A2.3). We project a further increase of 4.2 percent in 2001 and 5 percent in 2002. By 2010, real prices are projected to increase 23 percent relative to the 1998 lows, which would still leave the index well below the cyclical highs of the mid-1990s. However, raw materials prices are responsive to global economic conditions and would likely rise further if the global recovery exceeds current forecasts.

Cotton prices have remained around 150 cents per kilogram (nominal) for the past two decades, and there is no reason to think this will change soon. Prices rose 66 percent from 1993 to 1995, from 128 to 213 cents per kilogram, and then fell back to 117 cents per kilogram in 1999. Global consumption rose sharply during the 1980s as clothing fashions favored cotton. However, those trends have changed and global consumption stagnated during the 1990s. Global production has been very erratic in response to wide swings in prices and policy changes in major producers such as China and the United States. Consequently, cotton prices have been volatile, but without a clear trend, since about 1980. Prices have begun to recover from the recent lows, with nominal prices up

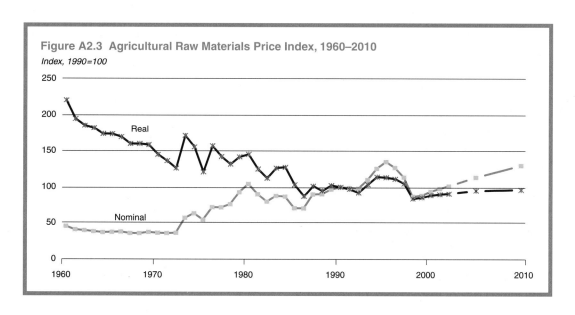

Figure A2.3 Agricultural Raw Materials Price Index, 1960–2010

about 9.2 percent in 2000 and projected to rise about 6.9 percent in 2001. By 2005, nominal prices are projected to rise to 159 cents per kilogram, and by 2010, prices are expected to reach 181 cents per kilogram. In real terms, prices are forecast to rise 24.1 percent relative to the 1999 lows by 2010.

Rubber prices were severely depressed in 1999 because Indonesia, Malaysia, and Thailand (which account for 70 percent of rubber exports) devalued their currencies as a result of the Asian crisis. The price of rubber in U.S. dollars tumbled to a 24-year low in 1999—down 60 percent from the 1995 high. Prices have stopped falling, but the recovery has been modest as record production, weak demand, and high stocks have kept prices near the low reached in 1999. The International Natural Rubber Organization, which was the last U.N.-backed commodity price stabilization body, was formally dissolved in October 1999 after the withdrawal of key members in the wake of the rubber price collapse and currency devaluations. Buffer stocks held by the organization (amounting to 2.5 percent of annual trade) are yet to be liquidated, but they will eventually find their way into the market. Prices are expected to recover slowly and are unlikely to reach the highs seen in the mid-1990s. Our near-term forecast is for nominal prices to rise about 6 percent per year in both 2001 and 2002, following the 12 percent increase in 2000. Real prices are projected to rise 9.2 percent between 2000 and 2010.

Asian tropical timber has been one of the few commodities that have seen rising real prices over the past two decades. However, prices fell following the Asian crisis as demand weakened dramatically. Prices of Malaysian logs have since risen 18 percent from the 1998 lows, and the recovery in Asian economies will likely support further price increases. Malaysian log prices are expected to increase 18.6 percent, in real terms, from 2000 to 2010. African tropical timber is mostly imported into Europe, and prices did not decline as sharply as those of Asian timber did following the Asian crisis. The improving growth prospects in Europe suggest prices of African timber could rise over the next several years as tropical timber becomes scarcer, environmental regulations become tighter, and demand continues to increase. However, real price increases will also be moderated by improved production techniques that allow better use of timber. Real prices of Cameroon log are projected to increase 9.9 percent from 2000 to 2010.

Energy

Crude oil prices have tripled since the lows of early 1999, to well over $35 per barrel, as significant production cutbacks by OPEC (as well as reductions by Mexico and Norway) and strong demand growth, reduced stocks to historically low levels. Product stocks, particularly gasoline and middle distillate, have also been drawn to extremely low levels, and a tight gasoline market is expected to turn into a tight heating oil market this winter. In addition, steep backwardation of futures prices (near-term futures prices lower than distant futures prices) has discouraged stock building above immediate requirements. The U.S. gasoline market has been additionally affected by capacity outages, the introduction of Phase II reformulated gasoline (RFG), the phaseout of methyl tertiary butyl ether (MTBE), and Unocal's RFG patent, which makes it more costly to manufacture gasoline.

OPEC responded to the dramatic price increases by raising production quotas 7.5 percent in April 2000, 2.9 percent in July 2000, and 3.1 percent in October 2000. But these increases were not enough to reduce prices. OPEC also introduced a price band mechanism for its basket of crudes in mid-2000. If the average price of the OPEC reference basket exceeds $28 per barrel each day for 20 consecutive trading days, OPEC production, excluding Iraq's, will increase by 0.5 million barrels per day. If the average price falls below $22 per barrel for 10 consecutive trading days, OPEC production, excluding Iraq's, will decrease by an additional 0.5 million barrels per day. This mechanism was triggered in late October when prices exceeded $28 per barrel for 20 consecutive trading days, and OPEC announced plans to increase production by 0.5 million barrels per day. Saudi Arabia, the largest OPEC producer, has stated that it would like to see prices settle around $25 per barrel. Iraq remains outside the quota system because of U.N. sanctions, but its production has risen to nearly 3 million barrels per day. In response to persistent high prices, the United States released 30 million barrels from its Strategic Petroleum Reserve and set up emergency heating oil inventories in the northeast region.

Inventories are now rebuilding, although stocks will likely remain low in the near term, depending on demand and the severity of winter. OPEC's new price band and accompanying production restraint are designed to stabilize oil prices. However, the impact on prices is expected to be short-lived because oil production costs are substantially below current prices, and advances in technology and improved managerial practices continue to result in ever lower development costs. In addition, the costs of competing fuels and non-conventional energy sources continue to fall and are becoming increasingly competitive when oil prices are high. Non-OPEC oil supplies are expected to continue to increase, despite the significantly slower growth in 1998–99, because of low oil and gas prices. Capital expenditures by the petroleum industry have been relatively modest, despite the rebound in prices, as companies grapple with large merger activities, debt paydown, share buyback programs, and a cautious attitude to the "new" price regime. However, major oil companies have had large earnings increases, and this could eventually lead to significant spending programs, which would result in higher oil production in future years.

Significant advances in oil development technology in recent years, such as 3-D computer seismic, horizontal drilling, and floating production systems, have helped reduce development and operating costs and shifted supply curves outward. New frontiers still remain for substantial oil development, for example, offshore, deepwater, heavy oil, and the Caspian Sea. Large increases in production from offshore West Africa are expected in the next few years, and deepwater advances in the U.S. Gulf

of Mexico and Brazil give promise of similar development in many other locales around the world. The costs of non-conventional oil resources, such as oil sands development in Canada, have fallen significantly in recent years, and new projects have proceeded under the assumption of low oil prices. Several countries have invited in, or back, foreign oil companies, including some OPEC countries, and these actions will result in increased production capacity.

High oil prices will reduce demand and encourage substitution of other fuels for oil, as occurred when prices spiked during the past three decades. For example, world oil demand (excluding demand in the FSU) grew by 2.3 percent in the 1990s compared with global growth of 7.5 percent prior to the first oil price shock in 1973. Efficiency improvements, however, have slowed significantly in recent years as real prices have declined. This has been notable in the United States, with the surge in demand for fuel-thirsty sport-utility vehicles (SUVs). In addition, U.S. corporate average fuel economy (CAFE) standards for conventional automobiles have not been raised since 1990. Thus significant potential exists for improving efficiency in transport and other uses. Higher prices will also encourage the substitution of other fuels, notably natural gas, and also of renewable energy sources. Environmental pressures to reduce local pollution, reduce congestion, and curb greenhouse gas emissions will push policymakers to improve energy efficiency and restrain consumption of oil and other carbon-based fuels. More ominously for oil producers, the development of transport fuel-cell technology[6] looms on the horizon, although the costs remain high and a single preferred fuel has not yet been established.

We expect oil prices to average $28 per barrel in 2000 because of tight underlying market conditions and OPEC's resolve to keep prices within its new price band. Prices are then expected to fall to $25 per barrel in 2001 as higher production from both OPEC and non-OPEC sources allows stocks to rebuild and tilt the market back into surplus. However, most OPEC countries are at or near capacity, with only Saudi Arabia having significant spare capacity. This, along with a delayed non-OPEC supply response, could keep OPEC in firm control of the market for an extended period—perhaps several years. Over the longer term, real oil prices (figure 2.4) are expected to decline because of abundant low-cost global supplies, increasing competition from non-OPEC producers and non-oil fuels, environmental concerns, and technological advances.

Fertilizer

Fertilizer prices, like the prices of many other commodities, have followed very divergent paths over the past several years. Nitrogen fertilizer prices declined from more than $200 a ton to near $60 a ton (for bulk urea), while phosphate fertilizer prices declined only 20 percent (for triple super phosphate, or TSP), and potash fertilizer prices continued to rise. The differences in price behavior were due to the different impact that the economic collapse of the FSU had on fertilizer markets, the different industry market structures, and different export firm behavior. The FSU was both a major producer and a major consumer of fertilizer prior to 1990. When these countries faced severe economic crisis in the 1990s, domestic fertilizer consumption declined along with grain demand, and firms directed their fertilizer production to the export market. This led to aggressive price-cutting and competition for market share in the nitrogen fertilizer market, especially by the Russian Federation and Ukraine. The competition was less intense in the phosphate and potash markets because the FSU countries had smaller market shares and because other major phosphate and potash producers responded to increased exports from the FSU by cutting production rather than by lowering prices and competing for market share. Other factors also contributed to the different price behavior, including the decision by China (the major nitrogen fertilizer importer) to ban nitrogen imports in 1997.

Nitrogen fertilizer prices have increased nearly 45 percent in 2000 compared to 1999 as major producers in Europe and the U.S. cut production. However, the price recovery is expected to slow as the industry faces large excess capacity and continued aggressive export competition. Weak grain prices contribute to weak demand and further delay a significant price recovery, since more than 50 percent of nitrogen fertilizer is used for grain production. Real urea prices are projected to rise 55 per-

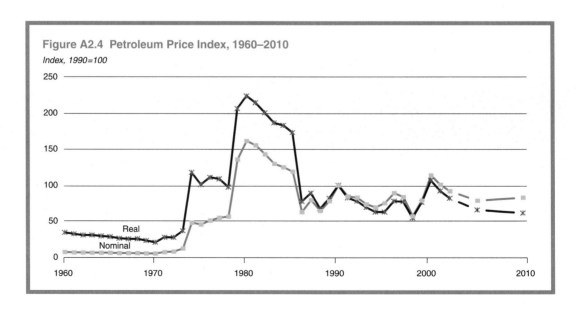

Figure A2.4 Petroleum Price Index, 1960–2010

Index, 1990=100

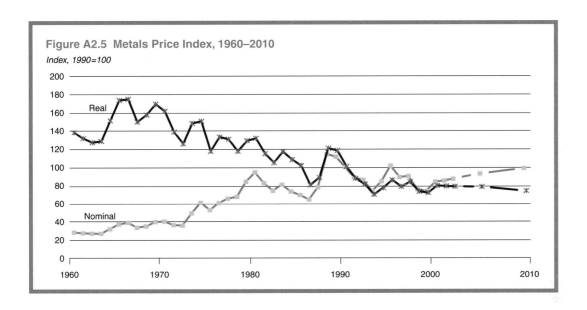

Figure A2.5 Metals Price Index, 1960–2010

Index, 1990=100

cent by 2010 compared to 1999 lows, but still remain 30 percent below the highs of 1996.

Phosphate prices fell less, and will likely reach new highs sooner, than nitrogen fertilizer prices. The industry is faced with surplus capacity, but demand has been strong, as many developing countries have increased imports of phosphate in order to improve the balance of fertilizer applications. After falling 19 percent from 1998 to 2000, TSP prices are projected to increase 7 percent in 2001. Nominal prices are expected to increase an additional 7 percent by 2005 as improvements in world grain prices boost fertilizer demand. By 2010, real prices are expected to decrease as new capacity comes onstream, causing real prices to fall 5 percent from 2000 levels.

Potash prices have increased about 5 percent since 1998, while most other commodity prices fell. This was possible because of strong import demand from developing countries and the willingness of major producers to close production capacity rather than see prices fall. These industry trends are expected to continue and should lead to gradually increasing muriate of potash (MOP) prices. At some point, enough new capacity may be developed to threaten this price stability, but this probably will not occur for several more years. Nominal MOP prices are projected to increase about 1 percent per year until 2005 and then remain about unchanged for the balance of the decade. In real terms, prices will decline, as nominal price increases will not be large enough to offset overall inflation. By 2010, real MOP prices are projected to fall about 19 percent from the 2000 level.

Metals

The World Bank's nominal index of metals and minerals prices has increased nearly 27 percent from the lows in early 1999 because of production cutbacks and strong demand growth (figure A2.5). However, abundant supplies and high stocks have prevented even larger price gains. Much of the increase in the price index has been a result of the more than doubling of nickel prices and the 30 to 40 percent increases in aluminum and copper prices. Other metals prices have failed to move higher because of abundant supplies and in some cases relatively weak demand. Tin prices have risen slightly, while gold and silver prices are relatively unchanged since early 1998. Lead prices have fallen because of weak demand and rising stocks. Many metals prices are poised to increase in the near term in response to demand growth, which accompanies expected strong economic growth, and more favorable supply balances.

Aluminum prices have recovered from the lows of early 1999, but high stocks, rising production, and forward selling by producers have kept a lid on price gains. In mid-2000, the market balance began to tighten because of producer cutbacks in the United States. Nearly 40 percent of the U.S. aluminum capacity is located in the Pacific Northwest, where deregulation of the U.S. power industry, along with strong summer demand, has driven up power prices and led to lower aluminum production. Further production cuts or strong demand growth could lead to a period of higher prices. In the longer term, real prices are expected to weaken because of improved technologies, new lower-cost capacity, and demand-side pressures from substitution of low-cost materials such as plastics. By 2010, real aluminum prices are expected to fall by about 5 percent from 2000 levels.

Copper prices have risen about 40 percent from the lows of early 1999 because of strong demand and significant reductions in high-cost production—much of it in the United States. World copper consumption is expected to grow by more than 5 percent in 2000, and far outstripped global production growth, resulting in a 50 percent decline in London Metals Exchange (LME) inventories. As a result, the market balance has moved into deficit, following large surpluses during the 1997–99. Further shortfalls are anticipated, causing nominal prices to rise by 8.2 percent in 2001 and an additional 3.8 percent in 2002. However, higher prices will bring forth investment in new capacity, along with reactivation of idle plants, which will prevent escalation of real prices over the forecast period. Prices will remain cyclical, with the cost structure of the industry essentially determining the low point in the cycle. New technologies will continue to reduce production costs, leading to declining real prices later in the forecast period. On the demand side, new copper alloys could regain some market share previously lost to aluminum. Although the threat of substitution from new materials exists, it is likely that copper will retain its position in existing applications. Real prices are expected to rise about 3 percent between 2000 and 2010.

Gold has traded between $275 and $300 per troy ounce during most of the past three years because of central bank sales, declining production costs, and forward selling by producers. A number of central banks have been selling gold reserves to exchange their low-interest assets for investments that yield higher interest. The Netherlands, Switzerland, and the United Kingdom are in the midst of large gold sale programs, while other countries are contemplating such actions. In September 1999, 15 European central banks agreed to limit gold sales to 2,000 tons over the next five years and restrict their lending activities, and several producers announced that they would limit or suspend their gold hedging programs. However, this failed to lift prices. Prices are expected to remain under pressure as supplies from all sources will be more than adequate to meet demand. Price movements above $300 per troy ounce will probably face reduced demand, provide greater incentives for producers to sell forward, and encourage central banks to increase sales. Real prices are expected to decline by about 1.7 percent per year between 2000 and 2010.

Nickel prices rose from under $4,000 per ton in December 1998 to more than $10,000 per ton during 2000. Various supply problems contributed to the tight market, particularly technical problems bringing on new capacity in Australia and labor strikes in Canada. Nickel demand has also been very strong because of the strength of the global economic recovery and large growth in steel production. This has depleted stocks, causing LME inventories to fall to the lowest level in nine years. Prices are expected to fall as nickel production increases substantially in the coming years and large amounts of scrap metal are brought to market. The supply deficit is expected to diminish in 2001, and the market is expected to be in better balance going forward. Real prices are expected to decline by nearly 40 percent between 2000 and 2010, mainly reflecting the lofty level of prices in 2000.

Table A2.1 Commodity prices and price projections in current dollars

Commodity	Unit	Actual					Projections				
		1970	1980	1990	1998	1999	2000	2001	2002	2005	2010
Energy											
Coal, U.S.	$/mt	—	43.10	41.67	34.38	33.17	33.00	33.00	33.50	35.00	37.50
Crude oil, avg, spot	$/bbl	1.21	36.87	22.88	13.07	18.07	28.00	25.00	21.00	18.00	19.00
Natural gas, Europe	$/mmbtu	—	3.40	2.55	2.42	2.13	3.80	3.75	3.20	2.75	2.75
Natural gas, U.S.	$/mmbtu	0.17	1.55	1.70	2.09	2.27	4.00	4.00	3.50	2.75	3.00
Non-Energy Commodities											
Agriculture											
Beverages											
Cocoa	c/kg	67.5	260.4	126.7	167.6	113.5	90.0	95.0	110.0	150.0	170.0
Coffee, other milds	c/kg	114.7	346.6	197.2	298.1	229.1	195.0	195.0	209.4	253.5	265.0
Coffee, robusta	c/kg	91.4	324.3	118.2	182.3	148.9	94.8	97.0	110.2	149.9	187.4
Tea, auctions (3) average	c/kg	83.5	165.9	205.8	204.6	183.9	189.0	192.0	192.0	195.0	210.0
Food											
Fats and oils											
Coconut oil	$/mt	397.2	673.8	336.5	657.9	737.1	444.0	500.0	540.0	620.0	650.0
Copra	$/mt	224.8	452.7	230.7	411.1	461.5	310.0	425.0	435.0	460.0	483.0
Groundnut oil	$/mt	378.6	858.8	963.7	909.4	787.7	700.0	740.0	775.0	820.0	850.0
Palm oil	$/mt	260.1	583.7	289.8	671.1	436.0	322.0	340.0	360.0	400.0	450.0
Soybean meal	$/mt	102.6	262.4	200.2	170.3	152.2	185.0	195.0	200.0	215.0	226.0
Soybean oil	$/mt	286.3	597.6	447.3	625.9	427.3	340.0	360.0	380.0	430.0	460.0
Soybeans	$/mt	116.9	296.2	246.8	243.3	201.67	210.0	220.0	230.0	250.0	270.0
Grains											
Maize	$/mt	58.4	125.3	109.3	102.0	90.2	86.0	95.0	110.0	125.0	130.0
Rice, Thai, 5%	$/mt	126.3	410.7	270.9	304.2	248.4	202.0	215.0	235.0	275.0	300.0
Sorghum	$/mt	51.8	128.9	103.9	98.0	84.4	85.0	88.0	100.0	120.0	125.0
Wheat, U.S., HRW	$/mt	54.9	172.7	135.5	126.1	112.0	112.0	120.0	130.0	160.0	170.0
Other food											
Bananas, U.S., new series	$/mt	166.1	377.3	540.9	489.5	373.8	430.5	465.2	490.5	529.1	567.7
Beef, U.S.	c/kg	130.4	276.0	256.3	172.6	184.3	194.0	198.4	202.8	209.4	225.0
Oranges	$/mt	168.0	400.2	531.1	442.4	438.2	365.0	400.0	500.0	565.0	600.0
Shrimp, Mexican	c/kg	—	1,152	1,069	1,579	1,461	1,503	1,515	1,530	1,550	1,590
Sugar, world	c/kg	8.2	63.16	27.67	19.67	13.81	17.84	18.10	18.10	20.00	24.00
Agricultural raw materials											
Timber											
Logs, Cameroon	$/cum	43.0	251.7	343.5	286.4	269.3	275.0	285.0	300.0	330.0	385.0
Logs, Malaysia	$/cum	43.1	195.5	177.2	162.4	187.1	192.0	198.0	210.0	245.0	290.0
Sawnwood, Malaysia	$/cum	175.0	396.0	533.0	484.2	600.8	600.0	620.0	655.0	750.0	900.0
Other raw materials											
Cotton	c/kg	67.6	206.2	181.9	144.5	117.1	127.9	136.7	141.1	158.7	180.8
Rubber, RSS1, Malaysia	c/kg	40.7	142.5	86.5	72.2	62.9	70.6	75.0	79.4	88.2	99.2
Tobacco	$/mt	1,076	2,276	3,392	3,336	3,041	2,985	3,000	3,100	3,250	3,300
Fertilizers											
DAP	$/mt	54.0	222.2	171.4	203.4	177.8	155.0	165.0	175.0	195.0	205.0
Phosphate rock	$/mt	11.00	46.71	40.50	43.00	44.00	43.80	44.00	44.00	44.00	46.00
Potassium chloride	$/mt	32.0	115.7	98.1	116.9	121.6	122.5	124.0	124.0	125.0	127.0
TSP	$/mt	43.0	180.3	131.8	173.1	154.5	140.0	150.0	155.0	160.0	170.0
Urea, E. Europe, bagged	$/mt	48.0	222.1	130.7	103.1	77.8	112.0	120.0	130.0	140.0	150.0
Metals and minerals											
Aluminum	$/mt	556	1,456	1,639	1,357	1,361	1,575	1,600	1,650	1,800	1,900
Copper	$/mt	1,416	2,182	2,661	1,654	1,573	1,825	1,975	2,050	2,200	2,400
Gold	$/toz	36.0	607.9	383.5	294.2	278.8	280.0	280.0	275.0	275.0	300.0
Iron ore, Carajas	c/dmtu	9.84	28.09	32.50	31.00	27.59	29.00	29.50	30.25	32.00	33.00
Lead	c/kg	30.3	90.6	81.1	52.9	50.3	46.0	50.0	55.0	60.0	64.0
Nickel	$/mt	2,846	6,519	8,864	4,630	6,011	8,600	7,500	7,000	6,000	6,800
Silver	c/toz	177.0	2,064	482.0	553.4	525.0	505.0	500.0	510.0	525.0	550.0
Tin	c/kg	367.3	1,677	608.5	554.0	540.4	545.0	550.0	560.0	590.0	610.0
Zinc	c/kg	29.6	76.1	151.4	102.5	107.6	114.0	116.0	117.0	120.0	125.0

— Not available.

$/mt, dollars per metric ton; $/bbl, dollars per barrel; $/mmbtu, dollars per million British thermal units; c/kg, cents per kilogram; $/cum, dollars per cubic meter; $/toz, dollars per troy ounce; c/dmtu, cents per dry metric ton unit of iron (fe).

Note: Projections as of November 14, 2000.

Source: World Bank, Development Economics, Development Prospects Group.

Table A2.2 Commodity prices and price projections in constant 1990 dollars

Commodity	Unit	Actual					Projections				
		1970	1980	1990	1998	1999	2000	2001	2002	2005	2010
Energy											
Coal, U.S.	$/mt	—	59.86	41.67	32.40	32.10	32.70	31.57	30.91	30.13	29.18
Crude oil, avg, spot	$/bbl	4.82	51.21	22.88	12.31	17.49	27.74	23.91	19.38	15.49	14.78
Natural gas, Europe	$/mmbtu	—	4.72	2.55	2.28	2.06	3.76	3.59	2.96	2.37	2.14
Natural gas, U.S.	$/mmbtu	0.68	2.15	1.70	1.97	2.19	3.96	3.83	3.23	2.37	2.33
Non-energy commodities											
Agriculture											
Beverages											
Cocoa	c/kg	268.9	361.6	126.7	157.9	109.9	89.2	90.9	101.5	129.1	132.3
Coffee, other milds	c/kg	456.8	481.4	197.2	280.9	221.7	193.2	186.5	193.3	218.2	206.2
Coffee, robusta	c/kg	364.0	450.5	118.2	171.7	144.1	93.9	92.8	101.7	129.0	145.8
Tea, auctions (3) average	c/kg	332.7	230.5	205.8	192.8	178.0	187.3	183.7	177.2	167.8	163.4
Food											
Fats and oils											
Coconut oil	$/mt	1582.4	935.9	336.5	619.9	713.5	439.9	478.3	498.3	533.7	505.7
Copra	$/mt	895.8	628.8	230.7	387.3	446.7	307.1	406.5	401.4	395.9	375.8
Groundnut oil	$/mt	1508.2	1192.7	963.7	856.8	762.4	693.6	707.9	715.1	705.8	661.3
Palm oil	$/mt	1036.0	810.7	289.8	632.3	422.0	319.0	325.2	332.2	344.3	350.1
Soybean meal	$/mt	408.7	364.5	200.2	160.5	147.3	183.3	186.5	184.5	185.1	175.8
Soybean oil	$/mt	1140.8	830.0	447.3	589.7	413.6	336.9	344.4	350.6	370.1	357.9
Soybeans	$/mt	465.8	411.4	246.8	229.2	195.2	208.1	210.5	212.2	215.2	210.1
Grains											
Maize	$/mt	232.7	174.0	109.3	96.1	87.3	85.2	90.9	101.5	107.6	101.1
Rice, Thai, 5%	$/mt	503.2	570.5	270.9	286.6	240.5	200.1	205.7	216.8	236.7	233.4
Sorghum	$/mt	206.4	179.0	103.9	92.4	81.7	84.2	84.2	92.3	103.3	97.3
Wheat, U.S., HRW	$/mt	218.7	239.9	135.5	118.8	108.5	111.0	114.8	120.0	137.7	132.3
Other food											
Bananas	$/mt	661.7	524.0	540.9	461.2	361.9	426.5	445.0	452.6	455.4	441.7
Beef, U.S.	c/kg	519.6	383.3	256.3	162.6	178.4	192.2	189.8	187.1	180.2	175.1
Oranges	$/mt	669.5	555.8	531.1	416.8	424.2	361.6	382.6	461.3	486.3	466.8
Shrimp, Mexican	c/kg	..	1,600	1,069	1,488	1,414	1,489	1,449	1,412	1,334	1,237
Sugar, world	c/kg	32.8	87.7	27.7	18.5	13.4	17.7	17.3	16.7	17.2	18.7
Agricultural raw materials											
Timber											
Logs, Cameroon	$/cum	171.3	349.6	343.5	269.8	260.7	272.5	272.6	276.8	284.0	299.5
Logs, Malaysia	$/cum	171.8	271.6	177.2	153.0	181.1	190.2	189.4	193.8	210.9	225.6
Sawnwood, Malaysia	$/cum	697.2	550.0	533.0	456.1	581.6	594.5	593.1	604.4	645.6	700.2
Other raw materials											
Cotton	c/kg	269.4	286.4	181.9	136.1	113.4	126.7	130.8	130.2	136.6	140.7
Rubber, RSS1, Malaysia	c/kg	162.2	197.9	86.5	68.0	60.8	69.9	71.7	73.2	75.9	77.2
Tobacco	$/mt	4,287	3,161	3,392	3,143	2,944	2,958	2,870	2,860	2,797	2,567
Fertilizers											
DAP	$/mt	215.1	308.6	171.4	191.7	172.1	153.6	157.8	161.5	167.8	159.5
Phosphate rock	$/mt	43.8	64.9	40.5	40.5	42.6	43.4	42.1	40.6	37.9	35.8
Potassium chloride	$/mt	127.5	160.7	98.1	110.1	117.8	121.4	118.6	114.4	107.6	98.8
TSP	$/mt	171.3	250.4	131.8	163.0	149.5	138.7	143.5	143.0	137.7	132.3
Urea, E. Europe, bagged	$/mt	191.2	308.5	130.7	97.1	75.3	111.0	114.8	120.1	120.5	116.7
Metals and minerals											
Aluminum	$/mt	2,215	2,022	1,639	1,279	1,317	1,560	1,531	1,522	1,549	1,478
Copper	$/mt	5,640	3,031	2,661	1,558	1,522	1,808	1,889	1,891	1,894	1,867
Gold	$/toz	143.2	844.3	383.5	277.1	269.8	277.4	267.8	253.7	236.7	233.4
Iron ore	c/dmtu	39.2	39.0	32.5	29.2	26.7	28.7	28.2	27.9	27.5	25.7
Lead	c/kg	120.7	125.8	81.1	49.8	48.7	45.6	47.8	50.8	51.6	49.8
Nickel	$/mt	11,339	9,054	8,864	4,362	5,819	8,521	7,174	6,459	5,164	5,291
Silver	c/toz	705.2	2866.1	482.0	521.4	508.1	500.4	478.3	470.6	451.9	427.9
Tin	c/kg	1463.5	2329.8	608.5	522.0	523.1	540.0	526.1	516.7	507.8	474.6
Zinc	c/kg	117.9	105.7	151.4	96.5	104.2	113.0	111.0	108.0	103.3	97.3

— Not available.

$/mt, dollars per metric ton; $/bbl, dollars per barrel; $/mmbtu, dollars per million British thermal units; c/kg, cents per kilogram; $/cum, dollars per cubic meter; $/toz, dollars per troy ounce; c/dmtu, cents per dry metric ton unit of iron (fe).

Note: Projections as of November 14, 2000.

Source: World Bank, Development Economics, Development Prospects Group.

Table A2.3   Weighted indexes of commodity prices and inflation

Index (1990 = 100) 2010		Actual				Projections[a]				
		1970	1980	1990	1998	1999	2000	2001	2002	2005
Current dollars										
Petroleum	5.3	161.2	100.0	57.1	79.0	122.4	109.3	91.8	78.7	83.0
Non-energy commodities[b]	43.8	125.5	100.0	99.1	88.0	87.3	90.3	94.8	105.7	115.6
Agriculture	45.8	138.1	100.0	107.8	92.8	88.0	91.4	96.9	110.6	122.3
Beverages	56.9	181.4	100.0	140.6	107.7	89.5	90.8	98.6	121.7	132.9
Food	46.7	139.3	100.0	104.9	87.6	84.2	88.5	93.2	102.3	110.0
Fats and oils	64.4	148.7	100.0	132.8	105.0	96.0	101.8	106.4	116.8	125.7
Grains	46.7	134.3	100.0	101.3	86.4	78.3	84.1	93.2	110.1	117.4
Other food	32.2	134.3	100.0	84.1	74.0	77.9	80.0	82.4	86.2	93.0
Raw materials	36.4	104.6	100.0	87.3	88.5	91.8	95.7	100.5	113.0	130.3
Timber	31.8	79.0	100.0	90.9	111.8	112.0	115.7	122.3	140.4	168.2
Other raw materials	39.6	122.0	100.0	84.8	72.7	78.1	82.1	85.6	94.3	104.4
Fertilizers	30.4	128.9	100.0	122.1	114.1	106.9	111.9	114.3	116.7	123.3
Metals and minerals	40.4	94.2	100.0	75.5	73.7	83.8	85.6	87.6	92.7	98.6
Constant 1990 dollars[c]										
Petroleum	21.1	223.8	100.0	53.8	76.5	121.3	104.5	84.7	67.7	64.6
Non-energy commodities	174.7	174.3	100.0	93.4	85.2	86.5	86.4	87.4	91.0	90.0
Agriculture	182.4	191.8	100.0	101.6	89.8	87.2	87.5	89.4	95.2	95.1
Beverages	226.6	252.0	100.0	132.4	104.2	88.6	86.8	91.0	104.8	103.4
Food	186.0	193.4	100.0	98.9	84.8	83.4	84.6	86.0	88.1	85.6
Fats and oils	256.4	206.5	100.0	125.2	101.7	95.1	97.4	98.2	100.5	97.8
Grains	186.1	186.5	100.0	95.4	83.6	77.5	80.4	86.0	94.8	91.4
Other food	128.4	186.6	100.0	79.3	71.6	77.1	76.5	76.0	74.2	72.3
Raw materials	145.1	145.2	100.0	82.3	85.7	91.0	91.6	92.7	97.3	101.4
Timber	126.6	109.7	100.0	85.7	108.2	111.0	110.7	112.8	120.8	130.8
Other raw materials	157.7	169.4	100.0	79.9	70.3	77.3	78.5	78.9	81.2	81.3
Fertilizers	121.1	179.0	100.0	115.0	110.4	105.9	107.0	105.5	100.5	96.0
Metals and minerals	160.8	130.8	100.0	71.1	71.3	83.0	81.9	80.8	79.7	76.7
Inflation indexes, 1990 = 100[d]										
MUV index[e]	25.10	72.00	100.00	106.14	103.31	100.93	104.54	108.38	116.18	128.53
Percentage of change per year		11.11	3.34	0.75	−2.67	−2.30	3.58	3.68	2.35	2.04
U.S. GDP deflator	33.59	65.93	100.00	119.32	121.11	123.89	126.87	129.91	138.54	152.96
Percentage of change per year		6.98	4.25	2.23	1.50	2.30	2.40	2.40	2.17	2.00

[a]Commodity price projections as of November 14, 2000.
[b]The World Bank primary commodity price indexes are computed based on 1987–89 export values in U.S. dollars for low- and middle-income economies, rebased to 1990. Weights for the subgroup indexes expressed as ratios to the non-energy index are as follows in percent: agriculture 69.1, fertilizers 2.7, metals and minerals 28.2, beverages 16.9, food 29.4, raw materials 22.8, fats and oils 10.1, grains 6.9, other food 12.4, timber 9.3, and other raw materials 13.6.
[c]Computed from unrounded data and deflated by the MUV index.
[d]Inflation indexes for 2000–10 are projections as of November 3, 2000. MUV for 1999 is an estimate. Growth rates for years 1980, 1990, 1998, 2005, and 2010 refer to compound annual rate of change between adjacent endpoint years; all others are annual growth rates from the previous year.
[e]Unit value index in U.S. dollar terms of manufactures exported from the G-5 countries (France, Germany, Japan, the United Kingdom, and the United States) weighted proportionally to the countries' exports to the developing countries.

Description of Price Series in Commodity Price Tables

Aluminum (LME) London Metal Exchange, unalloyed primary ingots, high grade, cash price.

Bananas (Central and South American), import price, free on truck (f.o.t.) U.S. Gulf.

Beef (Australian/New Zealand); frozen boneless; 85 percent chemical lean; cost, insurance, and freight (c.i.f.) U.S. East Coast.

Coal (U.S.) thermal, free on board (f.o.b.) Hampton Roads/Norfolk.

Cocoa (ICCO), International Cocoa Organization daily price.

Coconut oil (Philippines/Indonesian), bulk, c.i.f. Rotterdam.

Coffee (ICO), International Coffee Organization indicator price, other mild Arabicas, average New York and Bremen/Hamburg markets.

Coffee (ICO), International Coffee Organization indicator price, Robustas, average New York and Le Havre/Marseilles markets.

Copper (LME), grade A, cathodes and wire bar.

Copra (Philippines/Indonesian), bulk, c.i.f. N.W. Europe.

Cotton ("Cotton Outlook A Index"), c.i.f. Northern Europe.

Crude oil, average spot price of Brent, Dubai, and West Texas Intermediate, equally weighed.

DAP (diammonium phosphate), bulk, f.o.b. U.S. Gulf.

Gold (U.K.), London afternoon fixing.

Groundnut oil (any origin), c.i.f. Rotterdam.

Iron ore (Brazilian), Companhia Vale do Rio Doce (CVRD) Carajas fines, contract price to Europe, f.o.b. Ponta da Madeira.

Lead (LME), refined, settlement price.

Logs (West African), sapele, high quality (Loyal and Marchand LM), f.o.b. Cameroon.

Logs (Malaysian), meranti, Sarawak, Tokyo import price.

Maize (U.S.), no. 2, yellow, f.o.b. U.S. Gulf ports.

Natural Gas (Europe), import border price.

Natural Gas (U.S.), Henry Hub, Louisiana.

Nickel (LME), cathodes.

Oranges (Mediterranean exporters), EEC indicative import price, c.i.f. Paris.

Palm oil (Malaysian), bulk, c.i.f. N. W. Europe.

Phosphate rock (Moroccan), 70 percent BPL, contract, free alongside ship (f.a.s.) Casablanca.

Potassium chloride, f.o.b. Vancouver.

Rice (Thai), 5 percent broken, white rice, milled, indicative survey price, f.o.b. Bangkok.

Rubber (Malaysian), RSS 1, f.o.b. Kuala Lumpur.

Sawnwood (Malaysian), dark red seraya/meranti, select and better quality, kiln dry, cost and freight U.K.

Silver (Handy and Harman), refined, New York.

Sorghum (U.S.), no. 2 milo yellow, f.o.b. Gulf.

Soybean meal (any origin), c.i.f. Rotterdam.

Soybean oil (Dutch), crude, f.o.b. ex-mill.

Soybeans (U.S.), c.i.f. Rotterdam.

Sugar (world), International Sugar Agreement daily price, raw, f.o.b. Caribbean ports.

Tea, average of quotations at Calcutta, Colombo, and Mombasa/Nairobi.

Tin (LME), refined, settlement price.

TSP (triple super-phosphate), bulk, f.o.b. U.S. Gulf.

Urea, (varying origins), bagged, f.o.b. Eastern Europe.

Wheat (U.S.), no. 1, hard red winter, export Gulf.

Zinc (LME), special high grade, settlement price

Notes

1. Real prices are obtained by deflating nominal prices by the unit value index in U.S. dollar terms of manufactures (MUV) exported from the G-5 countries (France, Germany, Japan, the United Kingdom, and the United States) weighted proportionally to the countries' exports to the developing countries.

2. Grains account for 55 percent of the world's food supplies (calories) and occupy nearly one-half of the world's cultivated cropland (FAO). Grains prices are important as an indicator of overall food prices because of the close substitutability of grains with other food crops in production and consumption. Sugar and vegetable oils account for about 10 percent each of the world's total calorie supplies while animal products and fish account for about 16 percent. The remaining roughly 10 percent of world food supplies come from fruits, nuts, pulses, roots, tubers, and vegetables.

3. However, the growth during the 1990s was reduced by a 40 percent decline in grain consumption in the FSU countries and smaller declines in Eastern Europe. When these countries are excluded, world grain consumption grew by 2.0 percent per year during the 1990s. Growth rates in China and India, with 46 percent of developing-country populations, has been 1.9 and 1.5 percent, respectively, during the 1990s.

4. The five largest grain exporters are Argentina, Australia, Canada, the European Union, and the United States. Together, these entities account for about 85 percent of world exports.

5. For example, the Brazilian real depreciated 68 percent from 1997 to 1999, the CFA franc depreciated 9 percent, and the Kenyan shilling depreciated 16 percent (IFS, August 2000)

6. Fuel cells convert energy stored in a fuel directly into electricity and heat without combustion. Using hydrogen as fuel, they emit only water and heat as waste products.

Appendix 3
Global Economic Indicators

Table A3.1 Growth of real GDP, 1971–2010

(GDP in 1995 prices and exchange rates—average annual percentage growth)

	1999 GDP (current billions of U.S. dollars)	1971–80	1981–90	1991–99	1999	Estimate 2000	Forecast 2000–10
World	**20,215**	**3.6**	**3.0**	**2.4**	**2.8**	**4.1**	**3.4**
High-income economies	**23,665**	**3.3**	**3.1**	**2.2**	**2.7**	**3.8**	**3.0**
Industrial	23,135	3.2	3.0	2.1	2.7	3.7	2.9
G-7	19,895	3.3	3.1	2.1	2.5	3.6	2.8
United States	8,710	2.8	3.2	3.0	4.2	5.1	3.3
Japan	4,395	4.5	4.0	1.3	0.3	2.0	2.2
G-4 Europe	6,050	2.9	2.3	1.6	1.9	3.1	2.8
Germany[a]	2,080	2.7	2.3	1.7	1.4	3.1	2.8
Euro Area	6,375	3.2	2.4	1.8	2.4	3.4	3.0
Other industrial	3,240	3.1	2.6	2.4	3.5	4.0	3.2
Other high-income	735	7.9	5.5	5.3	4.2	6.3	5.3
Asian NIEs	530	9.5	7.4	5.9	4.8	6.9	5.9
Low- and middle-income economies	**6,555**	**5.3**	**2.7**	**3.2**	**3.2**	**5.3**	**5.0**
Excluding Eastern Europe and CIS	5,175	5.5	3.4	4.7	3.3	5.3	5.2
Asia	2,490	5.4	6.8	6.7	6.6	6.9	6.1
East Asia and Pacific	1,895	6.6	7.2	7.1	6.9	7.2	6.3
China	990	5.3	9.1	10.4	7.1	7.5	...
Korea, Rep. of	405	7.6	7.7	5.8	10.7	8.7	...
Indonesia	145	7.9	5.6	4.1	0.3	4.4	...
South Asia	595	3.1	5.8	5.4	5.7	6.0	5.4
India	445	3.0	5.9	5.7	6.2	6.4	...
Latin America and the Caribbean	2,055	5.9	1.1	3.2	0.1	4.0	4.3
Brazil	750	8.5	1.5	2.4	1.0	4.1	...
Mexico	485	6.7	1.9	3.1	3.7	6.8	...
Argentina	280	3.0	-1.5	5.1	-3.1	0.8	...
Europe and Central Asia	1,095	4.9	1.2	-2.3	1.0	5.2	4.2
Russian Federation[b]	400	4.8	-0.3	-5.8	3.2	7.2	...
Turkey	185	4.2	4.0	3.7	-5.1	6.2	...
Poland	155	5.0	-0.3	3.9	4.1	4.4	...
Middle East and North Africa	505	6.6	2.4	3.1	2.4	3.1	3.6
Saudi Arabia	140	10.3	0.4	2.1	0.4	2.9	...
Iran, Islamic Rep.	110	1.8	2.7	3.8	2.5	2.1	...
Egypt, Arab Rep.	90	6.6	5.5	4.3	5.9	5.3	...
Sub-Saharan Africa	330	3.3	1.8	2.0	2.3	2.7	3.6
Republic of South Africa	130	3.5	1.3	1.4	1.2	2.2	...
Nigeria	35	4.7	1.1	2.5	4.1	3.1	...

a. Data prior to 1991 covers West Germany.
b. Data prior to 1992 covers the former Soviet Union.
Source: World Bank data and staff estimates.

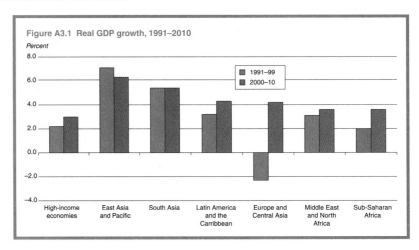

Figure A3.1 Real GDP growth, 1991–2010

Table A3.2 Growth of real per capita GDP, 1971–2010

(GDP in 1995 prices and exchange rates—average annual percentage growth)

	1999 GDP per capita (current U.S. dollars)	1971–80	1981–90	1991–99	1999	Estimate 2000	Forecast 2000–10
World	5,055	**1.7**	**1.3**	**1.0**	**1.5**	**2.7**	**2.3**
High-income economies	26,560	2.4	2.4	1.6	2.2	3.2	2.7
Industrial	27,545	2.4	2.4	1.5	2.2	3.2	2.6
G-7	28,920	2.5	2.5	1.5	2.0	3.1	2.5
United States	31,915	1.8	2.2	2.0	3.2	4.1	2.5
Japan	34,725	3.3	3.4	1.0	0.2	1.9	2.3
G-4 Europe	23,465	2.6	2.1	1.3	1.8	2.9	2.8
Germany[a]	25,370	2.6	2.1	1.4	1.4	3.1	3.0
Euro Area	21,865	2.7	2.1	1.5	2.2	3.3	3.0
Other industrial	21,320	2.3	2.0	1.9	3.1	3.7	3.0
Other high-income	17,165	5.2	3.7	3.6	2.6	4.6	4.1
Asian NIEs	16,565	7.2	5.9	4.6	3.6	5.6	5.0
Low- and middle-income economies	1,290	3.2	0.8	1.6	1.7	3.7	3.7
Excluding Eastern Europe and CIS	1,230	3.2	1.3	3.0	1.7	3.6	3.7
Asia	810	3.2	4.9	5.1	5.2	5.4	4.9
East Asia and Pacific	1,030	4.5	5.6	5.8	5.8	6.1	5.4
China	790	3.4	7.5	9.2	6.2	6.6	...
Korea, Rep. of	8,685	5.7	6.4	4.7	9.7	7.8	...
Indonesia	690	5.4	3.7	2.4	–1.1	2.7	...
South Asia	450	0.6	3.5	3.5	3.8	4.0	3.9
India	450	0.7	3.6	3.8	4.3	4.5	...
Latin America and the Caribbean	4,035	3.4	–0.9	1.5	–1.5	2.4	3.0
Brazil	4,470	5.9	–0.4	1.0	–0.3	2.8	...
Mexico	4,965	3.6	–0.2	1.3	2.0	5.1	...
Argentina	7,745	1.3	–2.9	3.8	–4.3	–0.4	...
Europe and Central Asia	2,300	3.9	0.4	–2.5	0.9	5.1	4.1
Russian Federation[b]	2,740	4.2	–0.9	–5.7	3.5	7.5	...
Turkey	2,885	1.8	1.6	2.2	–6.5	4.6	...
Poland	3,985	4.1	–1.0	3.7	4.0	4.3	...
Middle East and North Africa	1,975	3.6	–0.6	0.9	0.3	1.1	1.7
Saudi Arabia	6,505	5.1	–4.8	–1.3	–2.8	–0.4	...
Iran, Islamic Rep.	1,760	–1.4	–0.7	2.2	0.9	0.5	...
Egypt, Arab Rep.	1,430	4.4	2.9	2.3	4.2	3.6	...
Sub-Saharan Africa	515	0.5	–1.2	–0.6	–0.3	0.2	1.3
Republic of South Africa	3,115	1.2	–1.2	–0.6	–0.5	0.5	...
Nigeria	285	1.7	–1.9	–0.4	1.5	0.7	...

a. Data prior to 1991 covers West Germany.
b. Data prior to 1992 covers the former Soviet Union.
Source: World Bank data and staff estimates.

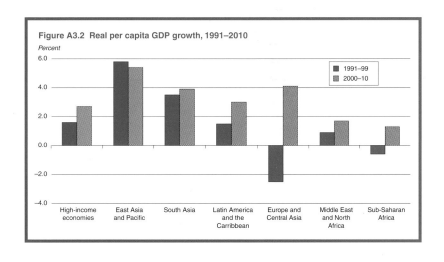

Figure A3.2 Real per capita GDP growth, 1991–2010

Table A3.3 Inflation: GDP deflators, 1971–2010

(percentage change[a])

	1971–80	1981–90	1991–99	1999	Estimate 2000	Forecast 2000–10
World	8.0	6.4	5.1	2.9	2.8	2.5
High-income economies	7.2	5.8	2.8	2.0	2.1	2.0
Industrial	7.2	5.8	2.6	2.0	1.9	2.0
G-7	7.0	5.7	2.5	2.0	1.8	2.0
United States	5.7	6.5	2.3	1.5	2.1	2.1
Japan	8.1	3.4	1.1	–0.9	–1.5	0.3
G-4 Europe	6.3	7.2	4.1	2.0	1.8	1.7
Germany[b]	5.3	3.6	3.9	0.9	0.0	1.2
Euro Area	7.0	6.7	3.9	1.2	1.2	1.7
Other industrial	8.9	6.9	3.7	3.1	2.0	2.1
Other high-income	7.7	6.2	4.9	4.2	5.0	3.8
Asian NIEs	6.7	6.1	4.1	2.0	3.0	2.9
Low- and middle-income economies	11.2	8.7	14.1	6.7	5.8	4.8
Excluding Eastern Europe and CIS	11.6	10.0	9.6	6.2	5.2	4.7
Asia	12.2	7.1	8.3	6.5	4.9	5.2
East Asia and Pacific	11.0	5.7	6.4	1.4	3.3	5.0
China	2.2	5.6	7.1	–2.2	2.1	...
Korea, Rep. of	23.4	7.1	5.6	–1.6	0.4	...
Indonesia	22.9	8.9	16.9	17.2	3.3	...
South Asia	12.2	8.8	8.9	8.8	5.4	5.7
India	9.1	8.4	8.8	5.5	5.4	...
Latin America and the Caribbean	14.3	24.0	19.0	6.5	8.2	7.0
Brazil	40.9	562.9	637.2	9.0	8.1	...
Mexico	22.5	67.4	19.1	15.9	12.0	...
Argentina	138.7	765.3	16.1	–2.0	0.9	...
Europe and Central Asia	3.0	4.5	177.2	7.5	11.4	5.3
Russian Federation[c]	0.3	10.3	345.1	56.3	43.3	...
Turkey	42.3	47.2	74.5	52.2	53.7	...
Poland	6.5	101.5	25.8	6.9	7.8	...
Middle East and North Africa	14.9	8.0	4.8	8.7	5.5	3.6
Saudi Arabia	26.9	–2.7	1.9	12.8	5.5	...
Iran, Islamic Rep.	20.9	15.7	25.2	11.8	14.1	...
Egypt, Arab Rep.	11.2	13.3	9.4	5.6	6.1	...
Sub-Saharan Africa	10.1	9.3	9.4	5.1	4.4	4.5
Republic of South Africa	13.4	15.1	10.4	6.9	6.4	...
Nigeria	14.0	17.7	34.7	11.9	19.7	...

Note: Deflators are in local currency units: 1995=100.
a. High-income group inflation rates are GDP-weighted averages of local currency inflation. Low- and middle-income groups are medians. World is GDP-weighted average of the two groups.
b. Data prior to 1991 covers West Germany.
c. Data prior to 1992 covers the former Soviet Union.
Source: World Bank data and staff estimates.

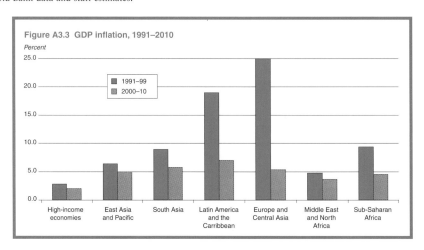

Figure A3.3 GDP inflation, 1991–2010

Table A3.4 Current account balances, 1970–2010

(percentage of GDP)

	1999 current account (billions of U.S. dollars)	1970–80	1981–90	1991–99	1999	Estimate 2000	Forecast 2000–10
World	−130.1	0.1	−0.4	−0.1	−0.5	−0.8	−0.4
High-income economies	−152.4	0.1	−0.2	0.1	−0.8	−1.1	−0.5
Industrial	−194.1	0.0	−0.5	−0.1	−1.0	−1.3	−0.6
G-7	−220.4	0.2	−0.4	−0.1	−1.1	−1.5	−1.0
United States	−331.5	0.0	−2.0	−1.7	−3.7	−4.6	−3.6
Japan	106.9	0.7	2.4	2.5	2.5	2.5	2.2
G-4 Europe	6.5	0.2	0.3	0.1	0.1	0.0	0.4
Germany[a]	−19.3	0.5	2.6	−0.7	−1.0	−1.0	−0.4
Euro Area	21.8	0.0	0.4	0.5	0.5	0.7	1.1
Other industrial	26.3	−0.9	−0.9	0.4	−0.2	0.4	1.4
Other high-income	41.7	7.2	9.8	3.9	5.9	4.3	2.6
Asian NIEs	37.6	0.1	6.8	5.0	7.2	4.8	3.3
Low- and middle-income economies	22.3	0.0	−0.8	−1.1	0.3	0.2	−0.2
Excluding Eastern Europe and CIS	22.2	−0.6	−2.1	−1.5	0.2	−0.3	−0.3
Asia	73.3	−1.1	−1.4	−0.3	3.0	1.3	1.0
East Asia and Pacific	79.0	−1.4	−1.1	0.1	4.1	3.3	2.1
China	15.7	−0.4	0.1	1.5	1.6	0.4	...
Korea, Rep. of	24.5	−6.1	0.7	0.7	6.1	2.6	...
Indonesia	5.8	−1.4	−3.1	−1.0	4.1	4.5	...
South Asia	−5.7	−0.5	−2.0	−1.7	−1.6	−2.6	−3.0
India	−2.8	0.3	−1.7	−0.2	0.6	−2.0	...
Latin America and the Caribbean	−55.6	−2.6	−1.8	−2.5	−2.9	−2.8	−2.0
Brazil	−25.1	−4.1	−1.6	−1.8	−4.4	−3.8	...
Mexico	−14.2	−3.1	−0.7	−3.8	−2.9	−3.1	...
Argentina	−12.3	−0.3	−2.1	−3.1	−4.3	−3.8	...
Europe and Central Asia	0.2	0.5	2.2	0.2	1.6	2.8	−1.3
Russian Federation[b]	25.0	2.0	3.6	2.1	6.7	8.4	...
Turkey	−1.4	−2.0	−1.3	−0.6	−0.7	−3.0	...
Poland	−12.5	−0.9	−1.4	−2.5	−7.5	−7.0	...
Middle East and North Africa	13.3	6.6	−3.5	−2.2	−1.7	1.3	0.7
Saudi Arabia	−1.7	19.8	−7.2	−1.4	−1.3	2.3	...
Iran, Islamic Rep.	5.5	2.4	−0.4	0.6	2.5	2.7	...
Egypt, Arab Rep.	−1.6	−4.9	−3.4	1.1	−3.1	−1.5	...
Sub-Saharan Africa	−8.9	−1.9	−2.8	−1.9	−2.3	−2.7	−3.1
Republic of South Africa	−0.5	−1.7	0.6	−0.2	−0.4	−1.2	...
Nigeria	0.5	0.8	−0.7	−0.9	1.2	−0.2	...

a. Data prior to 1991 covers West Germany.
b. Data prior to 1992 covers the former Soviet Union.
Source: World Bank data and staff estimates.

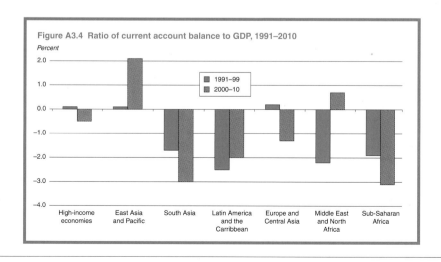

Figure A3.4 Ratio of current account balance to GDP, 1991–2010

Table A3.5 Exports of goods, 1998

(percent)

	Merchandise exports (US$ millions)	Average annual growth 1989–98	Effective market growth 1989–99[a]		Merchandise exports (US$ millions)	Average annual growth 1989–98	Effective market growth 1989–99[a]		Merchandise exports (US$ millions)	Average annual growth 1989–98	Effective market growth 1989–99[a]
World	5,357,268	6.4	7.7	**Latin America and the Caribbean** (continued)				**Middle East and North Africa** (continued)			
All developing countries	1,274,662	8.4	7.9	Uruguay	2,829	8.8	11.5	Tunisia	5,724	7.4	5.5
				Venezuela	17,564	4.4	8.2	Yemen, Rep.	1,501	14.1	9.1
Asia	577,029	12.5	8.5	**Europe and Central Asia**	246,594	5.5	7.2	**Sub-Saharan Africa**	71,047	3.1	6.8
East Asia and Pacific	524,083	12.7	8.6	Armenia	229	..	4.6	Angola	3,767	5.2	8.2
China	183,529	15.2	8.5	Azerbaijan	678	..	6.6	Botswana	2,061	2.9	..
Fiji	393	4.3	6.8	Belarus	7,135	..	4.0	Cameroon	1,800	1.5	6.9
Indonesia	50,371	9.9	7.9	Bulgaria	4,194	–1.4	7.1	Côte d'Ivoire	4,575	5.7	6.2
Korea, Rep.	132,122	12.8	9.5	Czech Rep.	26,395	..	6.7	Ethiopia	568	4.7	6.9
Malaysia	72,517	10.2	8.4	Estonia	2,690	..	6.0	Gabon	2,322	8.1	6.9
Myanmar	1,134	13.5	8.9	Georgia	300	..	..	Ghana	2,091	9.7	6.3
Papua New Guinea	1,773	5.6	7.7	Hungary	20,747	5.2	6.3	Kenya	2,013	5.0	6.3
Philippines	29,496	13.7	7.7	Kazakhstan	5,871	..	6.4	Madagascar	538	5.5	6.0
Thailand	52,747	13.1	8.2	Kyrgyz Rep.	535	..	10.7	Nigeria	8,971	3.7	6.9
Vietnam	9,365	..	9.4	Latvia	2,011	..	6.6	Senegal	1,100	2.9	6.7
				Lithuania	3,962	..	6.6	South Africa	29,234	1.5	6.8
South Asia	52,946	10.2	7.5	Moldova	644	..	3.8	Sudan	596	14.2	6.9
Bangladesh	5,141	13.7	6.9	Poland	32,467	10.5	6.2	Zambia	874	–3.7	7.2
India	34,076	11.1	7.6	Romania	8,302	2.2	6.6	Zimbabwe	1,924	3.3	7.1
Nepal	482	10.3	6.2	Russian Federation	74,888	..	8.3	**High-income economies**	4,082,606	5.8	7.6
Pakistan	8,512	5.8	7.8	Slovak Rep.	10,720	..	7.9				
Sri Lanka	4,735	11.5	6.6	Tajikistan	586	..	..	**Industrial**	3,625,472	5.6	7.4
				TFYR Macedonia	1,322	..	4.0				
Latin America and the Caribbean	285,435	8.2	8.0	Turkmenistan	614	..	..	**G-7**	2,622,063	5.2	7.7
Argentina	26,441	7.8	9.6	Turkey	31,220	10.6	6.1	Canada	217,374	6.4	6.8
Bolivia	1,104	6.4	9.3	Ukraine	13,699	..	..	France	300,665	5.6	6.8
Brazil	51,136	4.4	8.9	Uzbekistan	2,888	..	..	Germany	539,743	5.2	6.8
Chile	14,831	6.9	8.3					Italy	242,092	5.4	7.2
Colombia	11,493	7.2	7.4	**Middle East and North Africa**	94,557	3.5	7.2	Japan	375,299	2.5	9.1
Costa Rica	5,547	16.0	7.1	Algeria	10,265	2.5	6.6	United Kingdom	271,806	5.2	7.0
Dominican Rep.	4,981	10.0	6.5	Bahrain	3,270	–1.0	7.5	United States	675,084	6.7	8.6
Ecuador	4,203	6.1	8.0	Egypt, Arab Rep.	4,403	4.0	6.7				
El Salvador	2,451	11.9	8.1	Iran, Islamic Rep.	12,982	3.1	7.1	**Other industrial**	1,003,409	6.6	6.6
Guatemala	2,847	9.1	8.5	Iraq	7,848	–3.2	10.4	Australia	76,083	6.5	7.8
Jamaica	1,613	9.2	6.4	Jordan	1,802	5.7	7.1	Austria	63,922	8.4	6.5
Mexico	117,459	11.7	6.9	Morocco	7,144	6.3	6.4	Belgium[b]	159,548	4.8	6.2
Panama	6,325	9.3	7.6	Oman	5,508	6.1	8.9	Denmark	47,908	4.4	7.0
Paraguay	3,723	16.3	11.4	Saudi Arabia	38,822	2.5	7.4	Finland	43,393	7.7	7.2
Peru	5,735	8.1	8.2	Syrian Arab Rep.	3,135	4.5	6.9	Greece	9,493	4.8	6.5
Trinidad and Tobago	2,258	4.7	8.0					Iceland	1,927	–1.6	6.4

Table A3.5 Exports of goods, 1998 (continued)
(percent)

	Merchandise exports (US$ millions)	Average annual growth 1989–98	Effective market growth 1989–99[a]		Merchandise exports (US$ millions)	Average annual growth 1989–98	Effective market growth 1989–99[a]		Merchandise exports (US$ millions)	Average annual growth 1989–98	Effective market growth 1989–99[a]
Other industrial (continued)				Other high-income	457,135	7.6	9.1	Other high-income (continued)			
Ireland	63,513	16.4	6.2	income				Singapore	110,591	8.8	10.0
Netherlands	172,795	4.6	6.4	Brunei	1,894	0.2	8.7	Taiwan,			
New Zealand	12,271	2.8	7.6	Hong Kong,				China	110,046	6.3	8.9
Norway	40,637	7.9	6.4	China	175,784	9.3	9.2	United Arab			
Spain	109,690	10.4	6.7	Israel	22,972	6.6	7.1	Emirates	27,059	0.7	6.8
Sweden	83,369	7.1	6.6	Kuwait	9,618	3.2	8.6				
Switzerland	92,845	5.0	6.9	Qatar	4,377	2.7	7.4				

.. Not available
a. Effective market growth is a weighted average of import volume growth in the country's export markets.
b. Includes Luxembourg
Source: See technical notes.

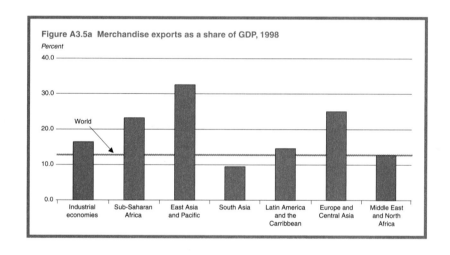

Figure A3.5a Merchandise exports as a share of GDP, 1998

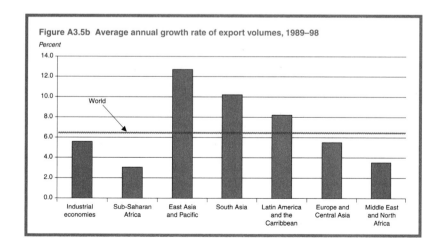

Figure A3.5b Average annual growth rate of export volumes, 1989–98

Table A3.6 Imports of goods, 1998

(percent)

	Merchandise imports (US$ millions)	Average annual growth 1989–98	Merchandise Imports/GDP
World	5,281,525	6.4	18.4
All developing countries	1,251,828	8.0	21.3
Asia	452,912	9.0	18.8
East Asia and Pacific	384,220	9.3	20.7
China	136,915	11.3	14.5
Fiji	612	4.3	38.8
Indonesia	31,942	8.4	33.9
Korea, Rep.	90,495	6.0	28.5
Malaysia	54,469	12.7	75.1
Myanmar	2,480	15.8	10.1
Papua New Guinea	1,078	-2.8	29.0
Philippines	29,524	13.4	45.4
Thailand	36,706	6.9	32.8
Vietnam	10,351	21.9	38.1
South Asia	68,692	7.4	12.3
Bangladesh	6,716	9.6	15.7
India	44,828	8.0	10.4
Nepal	1,239	6.4	25.9
Pakistan	10,607	3.7	16.7
Sri Lanka	5,302	10.2	33.8
Latin America and the Caribbean	323,048	13.0	16.4
Argentina	29,558	19.1	9.9
Bolivia	1,760	10.5	20.6
Brazil	57,739	14.1	7.4
Chile	17,347	12.9	22.7
Colombia	14,007	11.0	13.6
Costa Rica	5,791	15.0	55.3
Dominican Rep.	7,597	16.7	47.9
Ecuador	5,198	11.5	26.4
El Salvador	3,717	13.4	31.3
Guatemala	4,256	10.5	22.6
Jamaica	2,710	7.6	42.2
Mexico	125,374	15.3	30.6
Panama	7,696	11.6	84.2
Paraguay	3,942	13.8	45.3
Peru	8,200	10.5	13.1
Trinidad and Tobago	2,999	10.4	47.0

	Merchandise imports (US$ millions)	Average annual growth 1989–98	Merchandise Imports/GDP
Latin America and the Caribbean (continued)			
Uruguay	3,601	11.4	17.3
Venezuela	14,816	1.2	15.6
Europe and Central Asia	302,686	5.6	30.3
Armenia	806	..	42.4
Azerbaijan	1,724	..	41.9
Belarus	8,569	..	33.4
Bulgaria	4,574	-7.5	37.3
Czech Rep.	28,989	..	51.4
Estonia	3,805	..	73.1
Georgia	1,060	..	20.4
Hungary	23,101	9.0	48.3
Kazakhstan	6,672	..	30.4
Kyrgyz Rep.	756	..	46.4
Latvia	3,141	..	49.1
Lithuania	5,480	..	51.0
Moldova	1,043	..	64.5
Poland	45,303	12.9	28.8
Romania	10,927	3.4	28.6
Russian Federation	57,791	..	20.9
Slovak Rep.	13,071	..	64.2
Tajikistan	731	..	41.1
TFYR Macedonia	1,722	..	51.1
Turkmenistan	1,137	..	42.0
Turkey	45,552	12.8	22.9
Ukraine	16,283	..	38.4
Uzbekistan	2,716	..	16.1
Middle East and North Africa	91,390	3.1	19.0
Algeria	865	-18.7	1.8
Bahrain	3,299	3.5	61.7
Egypt, Arab Rep.	14,617	4.7	17.7
Iran, Islamic Rep.	13,608	2.2	11.9
Iraq	1,205	-18.7	0.5
Jordan	3,404	3.2	46.0
Morocco	9,463	7.9	26.6
Oman	5,217	7.0	34.9
Saudi Arabia	27,535	2.7	21.4
Syrian Arab Rep.	3,307	5.4	19.0

	Merchandise imports (US$ millions)	Average annual growth 1989–98	Merchandise Imports/GDP
Middle East and North Africa (continued)			
Tunisia	7,875	7.9	39.5
Yemen, Rep.	2,201	3.6	36.7
Sub-Saharan Africa	81,791	5.2	26.8
Angola	2,079	3.8	27.7
Botswana	1,983	6.7	40.7
Cameroon	1,452	1.4	16.4
Côte d'Ivoire	2,705	4.3	24.8
Ethiopia	1,042	0.8	15.9
Gabon	765	-0.9	16.1
Ghana	2,897	10.8	38.8
Kenya	3,029	4.9	26.2
Madagascar	693	7.9	18.5
Nigeria	9,211	7.3	22.3
Senegal	1,245	2.5	26.6
South Africa	27,216	4.2	20.3
Sudan	1,732	6.4	16.2
Zambia	1,022	3.8	30.5
Zimbabwe	2,019	4.9	31.9
High-income economies	4,029,697	5.9	17.7
Industrial	3,589,067	5.6	16.3
G-7	2,622,338	5.6	13.9
Canada	204,554	5.7	34.4
France	279,506	4.6	19.6
Germany	459,188	6.0	21.8
Italy	202,782	4.7	17.2
Japan	251,254	4.1	6.6
United Kingdom	305,730	4.9	22.0
United States	919,324	6.8	11.0
Other industrial	966,729	5.5	30.2
Australia	83,433	5.3	17.0
Austria	67,988	6.1	32.9
Belgium[a]	149,230	5.1	56.2
Denmark	44,021	5.5	25.4
Finland	30,903	3.7	24.6
Greece	19,173	4.8	15.9
Iceland	2,279	4.5	28.8
Ireland	41,896	12.9	48.6

Table A3.6 Imports of goods, 1998 (continued)
(percent)

	Merchandise imports (US$ millions)	Average annual growth 1989–98	Merchandise Imports/ GDP		Merchandise imports (US$ millions)	Average annual growth 1989–98	Merchandise Imports/ GDP		Merchandise imports (US$ millions)	Average annual growth 1989–98	Merchandise Imports/ GDP
Other industrial (continued)				Other high-income	440,629	8.8	61.5	Other high-income (continued)			
Netherlands	152,247	4.8	40.5	Brunei	1,718	12.0	35.4	Qatar	3,322	10.1	30.8
New Zealand	11,334	5.0	21.5	Hong Kong, China	183,503	10.6	112.6	Singapore	95,781	8.2	115.7
Norway	39,070	5.1	26.6					Taiwan, China	98,949	7.4	37.4
Spain	127,740	7.9	22.9	Israel	26,197	6.6	21.0	United Arab Emirates	24,995	12.0	52.9
Sweden	66,237	3.9	29.1	Kuwait	7,714	1.6	30.5				
Switzerland	92,882	2.5	35.4								

.. Not available
a. Includes Luxembourg
Source: See technical notes.

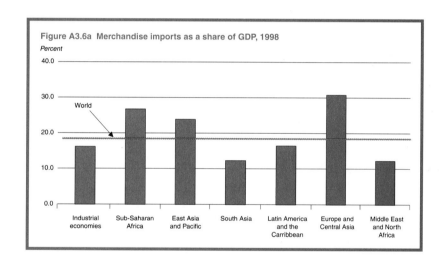

Figure A3.6a Merchandise imports as a share of GDP, 1998

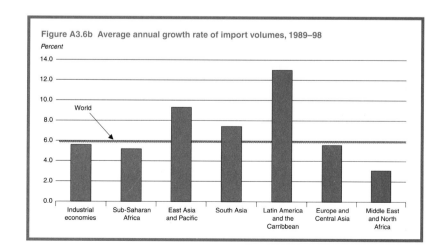

Figure A3.6b Average annual growth rate of import volumes, 1989–98

Table A3.7 Direction of merchandise trade, 1998[a]
(percentage of world trade)

Source of exports	High-income importers							Low- and middle-income importers							World
	United States	EU-15	Japan	Other indus-trial	All indus-trial	Other high-income	All high-income	Sub-Saha-ran Africa	East Asia and Pacific	South Asia	Europe and Central Asia	Middle East and North Africa	Latin America and the Carib-bean	All low- and middle-income	
High-income econ.	12.1	29.7	3.1	13.8	52.0	5.5	57.4	1.0	6.1	0.7	3.8	1.7	4.7	17.9	75.3
Industrial	10.0	28.3	2.3	13.0	47.3	4.3	51.6	0.9	3.8	0.5	3.7	1.6	4.5	14.8	66.4
United States	...	2.8	1.2	1.3	7.6	1.2	8.8	0.1	1.1	0.1	0.2	0.3	2.8	4.8	13.5
EU-15	3.4	22.2	0.7	10.2	28.7	1.3	30.1	0.6	1.0	0.2	3.2	1.0	1.1	7.0	37.1
Japan	2.5	1.4		0.7	4.2	1.4	5.6	0.1	1.4	0.1	0.1	0.2	0.4	2.2	7.8
Other industrial	1.1	9.6	0.5	3.4	12.2	0.6	12.8	0.2	0.6	0.1	1.0	0.3	0.4	2.5	15.3
Other high-income[b]	2.1	1.4	0.7	0.8	4.6	1.2	5.8	0.1	2.3	0.2	0.1	0.1	0.2	3.1	8.9
Low- and middle-income economies	6.1	6.0	2.0	2.6	14.9	2.9	17.8	0.5	1.8	0.5	2.0	0.6	1.5	6.9	24.7
Sub-Saharan Africa	0.2	0.4	0.0	0.2	0.8	0.1	0.8	0.2	0.1	0.1	0.0	0.0	0.0	0.4	1.2
East Asia and Pacific	2.2	1.6	1.5	1.0	5.7	2.4	8.1	0.2	1.2	0.2	0.2	0.2	0.3	2.4	10.4
South Asia	0.3	0.3	0.1	0.1	0.6	0.1	0.8	0.0	0.1	0.1	0.0	0.1	0.0	0.3	1.0
Europe and Central Asia	0.3	2.4	0.1	0.8	2.9	0.1	3.0	0.0	0.1	0.0	1.6	0.1	0.1	2.0	4.9
Middle East and North Africa	0.2	0.6	0.2	0.2	1.0	0.2	1.2	0.0	0.3	0.1	0.1	0.1	0.0	0.6	1.8
Latin America and Caribbean	2.9	0.7	0.1	0.3	3.9	0.1	4.0	0.0	0.1	0.0	0.1	0.1	1.1	1.4	5.4
World	18.2	35.7	5.0	16.4	66.8	8.4	75.2	1.5	7.9	1.2	5.8	2.3	6.2	24.8	100.0

a. Expressed as a share (percent) of total world exports. World merchandise exports in 1998 amounted to some $5,360 billion.
b. *Other high-income* group includes the Asian newly industrializing economies, several oil exporters of the Gulf region, and Israel.
Source: IMF, *Direction of Trade Statistics.*

Table A3.8 Growth of current dollar merchandise trade, by direction 1989–98

(average annual percentage growth)

Source of exports	High-income importers							Low- and middle-income importers							World
	United States	EU-15	Japan	Other indus-trial	All indus-trial	Other high-income	All high-income	Sub-Saha-ran Africa	East Asia and Pacific	South Asia	Europe and Central Asia	Middle East and North Africa	Latin America and the Carib-bean	All low- and middle-income	
High-income economies	6.1	4.0	3.8	3.3	4.6	8.0	4.9	2.9	8.6	3.1	11.8	4.7	12.0	9.9	5.7
Industrial	5.9	3.8	3.5	3.0	4.4	7.1	4.6	2.6	7.0	1.0	11.7	4.7	11.9	9.6	5.3
United States	...	5.4	4.4	4.2	6.4	7.5	6.5	6.1	8.8	1.8	6.7	6.9	12.9	10.8	7.7
EU-15	6.2	3.7	4.5	2.9	3.9	8.1	4.1	2.4	8.2	0.1	13.5	4.4	11.8	11.0	4.8
Japan	2.9	2.5	...	2.0	2.5	6.3	3.4	-0.5	5.6	0.2	-0.4	3.8	8.9	5.6	3.8
Other industrial	5.1	3.2	3.0	2.4	3.4	6.2	3.5	2.5	7.8	-0.1	10.8	2.5	10.8	9.6	4.1
Other high-income[a]	6.9	8.2	4.7	8.2	6.8	12.0	7.7	5.8	12.0	10.3	17.7	5.6	14.8	11.6	8.9
Low- and middle-income economies	12.1	10.5	6.2	9.5	10.4	11.0	10.5	12.3	17.6	12.1	13.0	7.8	15.9	16.7	11.4
Sub-Saharan Africa	5.9	4.1	8.5	2.5	5.2	28.4	5.9	14.1	21.3	26.1	2.9	12.0	11.6	15.8	7.8
East Asia and Pacific	11.0	12.1	6.9	14.3	10.3	11.5	10.6	10.3	20.1	12.8	12.2	8.1	23.7	17.3	11.6
South Asia	12.9	8.9	1.6	6.8	9.4	13.0	9.9	17.0	14.5	13.7	-3.2	8.7	32.4	14.3	9.7
Europe and Central Asia	13.7	10.1	-1.9	8.5	9.9	13.4	10.0	4.2	4.7	-2.6	6.1	3.2	8.8	12.6	8.0
Middle East and North Africa	1.7	2.8	5.1	0.4	2.8	3.2	2.8	15.6	18.5	8.1	0.3	7.2	2.7	10.5	4.6
Latin America and Caribbean	14.5	3.4	1.4	2.0	10.4	6.4	10.3	5.1	6.0	9.4	-0.5	6.3	15.0	12.5	10.6
World	7.7	4.5	4.5	3.8	5.5	8.9	5.8	4.9	9.9	5.4	9.3	5.1	12.8	10.9	6.5

a. *Other high-income* group includes the Asian newly industrializing economies, several oil exporters of the Gulf region, and Israel.
Note: Growth rates are compound averages.
Source: IMF, *Direction of Trade Statistics*

Table A3.9 Structure of long-term public and publicly guaranteed (PPG) debt, 1998
(percentage of long-term PPG debt)

	Concessional	Non-concessional			Concessional	Non-concessional	
		Variable	Fixed			Variable	Fixed
All developing economies	**25.7**	**35.1**	**39.2**	**Europe and Central Asia** (continued)			
				Bulgaria	2.1	84.9	13.0
Asia	**37.1**	**31.4**	**31.5**	Czech Republic	1.1	43.4	55.6
East Asia and Pacific	**26.6**	**37.7**	**35.7**	Estonia	12.7	62.8	24.5
China	27.0	35.1	37.9	Georgia	58.9	11.2	29.9
Indonesia	41.6	38.6	19.9	Hungary	3.3	23.0	73.6
Korea, Rep.	0.1	54.2	45.7	Kazakhstan	8.7	62.0	29.3
Malaysia	12.9	24.8	62.4	Kyrgyz Republic	67.8	23.8	8.4
Myanmar	88.1	0.0	11.9	Latvia	18.6	78.5	2.9
Papua New Guinea	59.9	19.9	20.2	Lithuania	9.6	52.7	37.7
Philippines	40.5	32.6	26.9	Moldova	24.5	48.1	27.4
Thailand	26.9	31.5	41.6	Poland	22.5	58.7	18.8
Vietnam	22.2	16.5	61.3	Romania	8.3	34.8	56.9
				Russian Federation	1.9	54.9	43.2
South Asia	**60.3**	**17.6**	**22.1**	Slovak Republic	7.2	36.5	56.2
Bangladesh	99.0	0.1	0.8	Tajikistan	88.2	9.2	2.6
India	48.0	19.3	32.7	Turkmenistan	6.8	79.1	14.1
Nepal	98.5	0.0	1.5	Turkey	11.6	21.6	66.9
Pakistan	64.6	27.6	7.8	Ukraine	2.9	59.6	37.5
Sri Lanka	89.7	5.8	4.6	Uzbekistan	19.0	55.2	25.9
Latin America and				**Middle East and**			
the Caribbean	**7.7**	**42.4**	**49.9**	**North Africa**	**48.6**	**29.8**	**21.6**
Argentina	2.9	34.0	63.1	Algeria	11.5	53.8	34.7
Bolivia	74.8	10.2	15.0	Egypt, Arab Rep.	84.8	4.4	10.8
Brazil	1.6	53.5	44.9	Jordan	52.1	28.2	19.7
Chile	7.6	78.1	14.2	Morocco	33.6	38.3	28.2
Colombia	5.3	39.7	55.0	Oman	24.9	45.0	30.1
Costa Rica	23.0	25.0	52.1	Syrian Arab Republic	92.4	0.0	7.6
Dominican Republic	43.6	36.5	19.9	Tunisia	28.3	25.1	46.6
Ecuador	15.4	54.2	30.4	Yemen, Rep.	90.3	2.2	7.5
El Salvador	48.5	26.8	24.7				
Guatemala	44.3	23.2	32.6	**Sub-Saharan Africa**	**51.9**	**13.1**	**35.0**
Jamaica	34.1	23.4	42.5	Angola	27.3	12.8	59.9
Mexico	1.5	37.3	61.1	Botswana	58.2	11.4	30.4
Panama	7.2	49.1	43.7	Côte d'Ivoire	45.8	39.0	15.2
Paraguay	58.2	19.9	22.0	Cameroon	54.5	13.4	32.1
				Ethiopia (excludes			
Peru	18.9	42.1	39.1	Eritrea)	91.6	0.2	8.2
Trinidad and Tobago	0.9	52.2	47.0	Gabon	24.7	14.2	61.1
Uruguay	4.7	43.8	51.5	Ghana	82.9	0.4	16.7
Venezuela	0.3	54.7	45.1	Kenya	73.5	4.7	21.8
				Madagascar	70.9	5.7	23.3
Europe and				Nigeria	6.8	19.7	73.5
Central Asia	**8.1**	**46.9**	**45.0**	Senegal	78.8	11.6	9.7
Armenia	56.3	22.9	20.8	Sudan	51.0	14.6	34.4
Azerbaijan	74.5	25.5	0.0	Zambia	68.6	13.4	18.1
Belarus	11.5	67.7	20.9	Zimbabwe	45.5	16.2	38.3

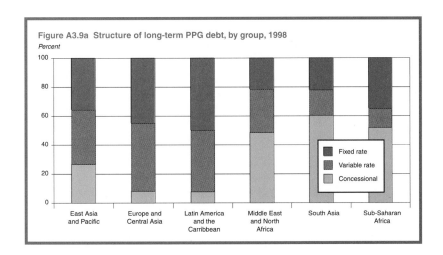

Figure A3.9a Structure of long-term PPG debt, by group, 1998

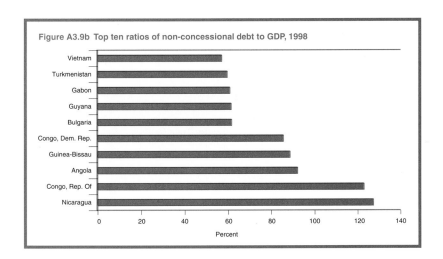

Figure A3.9b Top ten ratios of non-concessional debt to GDP, 1998

Table A3.10 Long-term net resource flows to developing countries, 1998
(millions of U.S. dollars)

	Total	Percentage of GDP	Private				Official		
			Total	Debt flows net	FDI	Portfolio	Total	Official development assistance	Other
All developing countries	318,325	5.13	267,700	81,191	170,942	15,567	50,625	37,310	13,315
Asia	95,424	4.25	74,830	–2,349	67,821	9,358	20,594	11,543	9,051
East Asia and Pacific	82,838	4.94	67,249	–5,919	64,162	9,007	15,588	6,857	8,732
China	45,230	4.78	42,676	–2,349	43,751	1,273	2,554	1,360	1,194
Indonesia	–808	–0.86	–3,759	–3,653	–356	250	2,951	1,618	1,333
Korea, Rep.	13,201	4.16	7,644	–1,867	5,415	4,096	5,557	–19	5,576
Malaysia	8,529	11.77	8,295	2,703	5,000	592	235	66	169
Myanmar	272	..	153	83	70	0	119	120	–1
Papua New Guinea	418	11.23	230	120	110	0	188	229	–41
Philippines	2,764	4.25	2,586	419	1,713	454	178	481	–303
Thailand	8,987	8.02	7,825	–1,458	6,941	2,341	1,162	355	807
Vietnam	2,150	7.91	832	–368	1,200	0	1,318	1,304	14
South Asia	12,586	2.23	7,581	3,571	3,659	351	5,005	4,686	319
Bangladesh	1,303	3.05	288	–23	308	3	1,015	1,026	–11
India	7,604	1.77	6,151	3,174	2,635	342	1,453	1,010	443
Nepal	253	5.28	–1	–13	12	0	253	253	0
Pakistan	1,871	2.94	806	306	500	0	1,066	1,179	–113
Sri Lanka	818	5.21	325	126	193	6	493	488	5
Latin America and the Caribbean	136,972	6.71	126,854	55,783	69,323	1,748	10,118	3,522	6,595
Argentina	19,553	6.56	18,899	12,699	6,150	50	654	–165	818
Bolivia	1,194	13.96	860	–12	872	0	334	445	–111
Brazil	59,393	7.63	54,385	21,930	31,913	542	5,008	106	4,902
Chile	9,189	12.04	9,252	4,526	4,638	87	–62	47	–110
Colombia	3,797	3.69	3,630	566	3,038	26	168	30	138
Costa Rica	796	7.59	800	241	559	0	–5	–30	25
Dominican Rep.	807	5.09	771	6	691	74	36	42	–6
Ecuador	838	4.25	584	–247	831	0	254	152	102
El Salvador	428	3.60	242	230	12	0	186	109	77
Guatemala	897	4.76	621	–52	673	0	276	173	103
Jamaica	534	8.32	586	217	369	0	–52	29	–81
Mexico	22,428	5.47	23,188	12,220	10,238	730	–760	–31	–730
Panama	1,600	17.50	1,459	253	1,206	0	141	–14	155
Paraguay	305	3.51	236	–20	256	0	69	20	50
Peru	3,024	4.82	2,724	620	1,930	174	299	204	95
Trinidad and Tobago	733	11.48	761	31	730	0	–28	7	–35
Uruguay	696	3.34	496	332	164	0	201	6	195
Venezuela	8,008	8.43	6,866	2,367	4,435	64	1,142	13	1,129
Europe and Central Asia	59,562	5.94	53,342	26,089	24,350	2,904	6,220	5,791	429
Armenia	321	16.91	232	0	232	0	89	99	–9
Azerbaijan	1,178	28.62	1,081	58	1,023	0	97	65	33
Belarus	216	0.84	122	–27	149	0	94	3	91
Bulgaria	673	5.49	498	32	401	66	175	95	81
Czech Republic	3,197	5.67	3,331	648	2,554	129	–135	100	–235
Estonia	780	15.00	714	80	581	53	66	56	11
Georgia	207	3.97	57	7	50	0	150	164	–14
Hungary	3,815	7.98	4,683	2,488	1,936	259	–869	97	–965
Kazakhstan	2,337	10.63	1,983	825	1,158	0	353	95	258
Kyrgyz Republic	293	17.95	108	–2	109	0	185	178	7
Latvia	530	8.29	366	5	357	4	164	70	94
Lithuania	1,183	11.02	983	57	926	0	200	86	114

Table A3.10 Long-term net resource flows to developing countries, 1998 (continued)

(millions of U. S. dollars)

	Total	Percentage of GDP	Private				Official		
			Total	Debt flows net	FDI	Portfolio	Total	Official development assistance	Other
Europe and Central Asia (continued)									
Moldova	100	6.22	62	–23	85	0	39	12	27
Poland	9,716	6.18	9,653	2,319	6,365	969	62	319	–256
Romania	1,825	4.78	1,826	–247	2,031	42	–1	227	–228
Russian Federation	20,142	7.28	19,347	16,286	2,764	296	796	12	784
Slovak Rep.	1,691	8.30	1,480	918	562	0	211	70	141
Tajikistan	70	3.91	–3	–21	18	0	72	72	0
Turkmenistan	601	22.20	473	343	130	0	128	75	54
Turkey	1,584	0.80	1,641	–179	940	880	–57	–219	163
Ukraine	2,438	5.75	2,087	1,344	743	0	351	133	219
Uzbekistan	732	4.35	592	392	200	0	140	162	–22
Middle East and North Africa	**11,472**	**1.94**	**9,222**	**3,290**	**5,054**	**878**	**2,249**	**4,067**	**–1,818**
Algeria	–1,427	–3.01	–1,321	–1,328	5	2	–106	62	–167
Egypt, Arab Rep.	2,458	2.97	1,385	–186	1,076	494	1,073	1,258	–184
Iran, Islamic Rep.	–325	–0.28	588	564	24	0	–913	–5	–908
Jordan	632	8.56	207	–114	310	11	425	377	48
Morocco	936	2.63	965	470	322	174	–29	373	–401
Oman	–248	–1.65	–214	–330	106	10	–34	–29	–5
Syrian Arab Rep.	143	2.12	76	–4	80	0	67	104	–37
Tunisia	619	3.10	694	4	650	40	–76	–17	–59
Yemen, Rep.	6	0.10	–210	0	–210	0	216	233	–17
Sub-Saharan Africa	**14,895**	**4.46**	**3,452**	**–1,621**	**4,394**	**679**	**11,444**	**12,387**	**–943**
Angola	249	3.31	40	–320	360	0	209	238	–30
Botswana	107	2.19	91	–5	95	0	16	40	–24
Cameroon	238	2.68	1	–49	50	0	237	368	–131
Côte d'Ivoire	729	6.67	181	–260	435	6	548	719	–171
Ethiopia	500	7.64	6	2	4	0	494	495	–2
Gabon	–64	–1.36	–57	–7	–50	0	–8	37	–45
Ghana	579	7.74	42	–29	56	15	537	571	–35
Kenya	149	1.29	–57	–72	11	4	206	301	–94
Madagascar	414	11.08	15	–1	16	0	399	417	–18
Nigeria	598	1.45	1,028	–25	1,051	2	–430	–143	–287
Senegal	341	7.28	24	–16	40	0	317	350	–33
Sudan	558	5.21	371	0	371	0	187	188	–1
Zambia	281	8.37	40	–32	72	0	241	289	–49
Zimbabwe	68	1.08	–217	–296	76	3	285	216	69

Source: World Bank data.

Technical Notes

The principal sources for the data in this appendix are the World Bank's central databases.

Regional aggregates are based on the classification of economies by income group and region, following the Bank's standard definitions (see country classification tables that follow). Debt and finance data refer to the 137 countries that report to the Bank's Debtor Reporting System (see the World Bank's *Global Development Finance 2000)*. Small economies have generally been omitted from the tables but are included in the regional totals.

Current price data are reported in U.S. dollars.

Notes on tables

Tables A3.1 through A3.4. Projections are consistent with those highlighted in Chapter 1 and Appendix 1.

Tables A3.5 and A3.6. Merchandise exports and imports exclude trade in services. Imports are reported on a c.i.f. basis. Growth rates are based on constant price data, which are derived from current values deflated by relevant price indexes. Effective market growth is the export-weighted import growth rate of the country's trading partners. The IMF's Balance of Payments database is the principal source for data through 1998; in some cases these data

have been supplemented by UNCTAD and UN Comtrade databases or by World Bank staff estimates. Trade figures for countries of the former Soviet Union reflect the total of non-CIS and intra-CIS exports and imports.

Tables A3.7 and A3.8. Growth rates are compound averages and are computed for current dollar measures of trade.

Table A3.9. Long-term debt covers public and publicly guaranteed external debt but excludes IMF credits. Concessional debt is debt with an original grant element of 25 percent or more. Nonconcessional variable interest rate debt includes all public and publicly guaranteed long-term debt with an original grant element of less than 25 percent whose terms depend on movements of a key market rate. This item conveys information about the borrower's exposure to changes in international interest rates. For complete definitions, see *Global Development Finance 2000.*

Table A3.10. Long-term net resource flows are the sum of net resource flows on long-term debt (excluding IMF) plus non-debt-creating flows. Foreign direct investment refers to the net inflows of investment from abroad. Portfolio equity flows are the sum of country funds, depository receipts, and direct purchases of shares by foreign investors. For complete definition, see *Global Development Finance 2000.*

Classification
of Economies

Table 1 Classification of economies by income and region, July 2000

Income group	Subgroup	Sub-Saharan Africa		Asia		Europe and Central Asia		Middle East and North Africa		Americas
		East and southern Africa	West Africa	East Asia and Pacific	South Asia	Eastern Europe and Central Asia	Rest of Europe	Middle East	North Africa	
Low-income		Angola Burundi Comoros Congo, Dem. Rep. of Eritrea Ethiopia Kenya Lesotho Madagascar Malawi Mozambique Rwanda Somalia Sudan Tanzania Uganda Zambia Zimbabwe	Benin Burkina Faso Cameroon Central African Republic of Chad Congo, Rep. of Côte d'Ivoire Gambia, The Ghana Guinea Guinea-Bissau Liberia Mali Mauritania Niger Nigeria São Tomé and Principe Senegal Sierra Leone Togo	Cambodia Indonesia Korea, Dem. Rep. of Lao PDR Mongolia Myanmar Solomon Islands Vietnam	Afghanistan Bangladesh Bhutan India Nepal Pakistan	Armenia Azerbaijan Georgia Kyrgyz Republic Moldova Tajikistan Turkmenistan Ukraine Uzbekistan		Yemen, Rep. of		Haiti Nicaragua
Middle-income	Lower	Namibia Swaziland	Cape Verde Equatorial Guinea	China Fiji Kiribati Marshall Islands Micronesia, Fed. Sts. of Papua New Guinea Philippines Samoa Thailand Tonga Vanuatu	Maldives Sri Lanka	Albania Belarus Bosnia and Herzegovina Bulgaria Kazakhstan Latvia Lithuania Macedonia, FYR[a] Romania Russian Federation Yugoslavia, Fed. Rep. of[b]	Turkey	Iran, Islamic Rep. of Iraq Jordan Syrian Arab Republic West Bank and Gaza	Algeria Djibouti Egypt, Arab Rep. of Morocco Tunisia	Belize Bolivia Colombia Costa Rica Cuba Dominican Republic Ecuador El Salvador Guatemala Guyana Honduras Jamaica Paraguay Peru St. Vincent and the Grenadines Suriname
	Upper	Botswana Mauritius Mayotte Seychelles South Africa	Gabon	American Samoa Korea, Rep. of Malaysia Palau		Croatia Czech Republic Estonia Hungary Poland Slovak Republic	Isle of Man	Bahrain Lebanon Oman Saudi Arabia	Libya Malta	Antigua and Barbuda Argentina Barbados Brazil Chile Dominica Grenada Mexico Panama Puerto Rico St. Kitts and Nevis St. Lucia Trinidad and Tobago Uruguay Venezuela, Rep. Bol. de
Subtotal	157	25	23	23	8	26	2	10	7	33

Table 1 Classification of economies by income and region, July 2000 (continued)

Income group	Subgroup	Sub-Saharan Africa		Asia		Europe and Central Asia		Middle East and North Africa		Americas
		East and southern Africa	West Africa	East Asia and Pacific	South Asia	Eastern Europe and Central Asia	Rest of Europe	Middle East	North Africa	
High-income	OECD			Australia Japan New Zealand			Austria Belgium Denmark Finland France[c] Germany Greece Iceland Ireland Italy Luxembourg Netherlands Norway Portugal Spain Sweden Switzerland United Kingdom			Canada United States
	Non-OECD			Brunei French Polynesia Guam Hong Kong, China[d] Macao, China[e] New Caledonia N. Mariana Islands Singapore Taiwan, China		Slovenia	Andorra Channel Islands Cyprus Faeroe Islands Greenland Liechtenstein Monaco	Israel Kuwait Qatar United Arab Emirates		Aruba Bahamas, The Bermuda Cayman Islands Netherlands Antilles Virgin Islands (U.S.)
Total		25	23	35	8	27	27	14	7	41

a. Former Yugoslav Republic of Macedonia.
b. Federal Republic of Yugoslavia (Serbia/Montenegro).
c. The French overseas departments French Guiana, Guadeloupe, Martinique, and Réunion are included in France.
d. On 1 July, 1997, China resumed its exercise of sovereignty over Hong Kong.
e. On 20 December, 1999, China resumed its exercise of sovereignty over Macao.
Source: World Bank data.

Definitions of groups

For operational and analytical purposes, the World Bank's main criterion for classifying economies is gross national product (GNP) per capita. Every economy is classified as low-income, middle-income (subdivided into lower-middle and upper-middle), or high-income. Other analytical groups, based on geographic regions and levels of external debt, are also used.

Low-income and middle-income economies are sometimes referred to as developing economies. The use of the term is convenient; it is not intended to imply that all economies in the group are experiencing similar development or that other economies have reached a preferred or final stage of development. Classification by income does not necessarily reflect development status.

This table classifies all World Bank member economies, and all other economies with populations of more than 30,000. Economies are divided among income groups according to 1999 GNP per capita, calculated using the World Bank Atlas method. The groups are: low-income, $755 or less; lower-middle-income, $756–$2,995; upper-middle-income, $2,996–$9,265; and high-income, $9,266 or more.

Table 2 Classification of economies by income and indebtedness, July 2000

Income group	Sub-group	Severely indebted	Moderately indebted	Less indebted		Not classified by indebtedness

Low-income		Afghanistan Mali
		Angola Mauritania
		Burkina Faso Mozambique
		Burundi Myanmar
		Cameroon Nicaragua
		Central Niger
		   African Nigeria
		   Republic Rwanda
		Comoros São Tomé
		Congo, Dem. and Principe
		   Rep. of Sierra Leone
		Congo, Rep. Somalia
		Côte Sudan
		   d'Ivoire Tanzania
		Ethiopia Uganda
		Guinea Vietnam
		Guinea- Zambia
		   Bissau
		Indonesia
		Lao PDR
		Madagascar
		Malawi
			Bangladesh
			Benin
			Cambodia
			Chad
			Gambia, The
			Georgia
			Ghana
			Haiti
			India
			Kenya
			Kyrgyz Republic
			Moldova
			Mongolia
			Pakistan
			Senegal
			Togo
			Turkmenistan
			Yemen, Rep. of
			Zimbabwe
				Armenia
				Azerbaijan
				Bhutan
				Eritrea
				Korea, Dem. Rep. of
				Lesotho
				Nepal
				Solomon Islands
				Tajikistan
				Ukraine
				Uzbekistan
						Liberia

Middle-income	*Lower*	Bolivia
		Bosnia and
		   Herzegovina
		Bulgaria
		Cuba
		Ecuador
		Guyana
		Iraq
		Jordan
		Peru
		Syrian Arab
		   Republic
			Algeria
			Belize
			Colombia
			Equatorial
			   Guinea
			Honduras
			Jamaica
			Macedonia, FYR[a]
			Morocco
			Papua New
			   Guinea
			Philippines
			Russian
			   Federation
			Samoa
			St. Vincent and
			   the Grenadines
			Thailand
			Tunisia
			Turkey
				Albania
				Belarus
				Cape Verde
				China
				Costa Rica
				Djibouti
				Dominican
				   Republic
				Egypt, Arab
				   Rep.
				El Salvador
				Fiji
				Guatemala
				Iran, Islamic
				   Rep. of
				Kazakhstan
				Kiribati
				Latvia
				Lithuania
				Maldives
					Namibia
					Paraguay
					Romania
					Sri Lanka
					Suriname
					Swaziland
					Tonga
					Vanuatu
					Yugoslavia,
					   Fed. Rep. of[b]
						Marshall Islands
						Micronesia, Fed. Sts. of
						West Bank and Gaza

	Upper	Argentina
		Brazil
		Gabon
			Chile
			Hungary
			Lebanon
			Malaysia
			Mauritius
			Panama
			Uruguay
			Venezuela, Rep. Bol. de
				Antigua and
				   Barbuda
				Bahrain
				Barbados
				Botswana
				Croatia
				Czech
				   Republic
				Dominica
				Estonia
				Grenada
				Korea, Rep.
				Libya
				Malta
					Oman
					Poland
					Saudi Arabia
					Seychelles
					Slovak
					   Republic
					South Africa
					St. Kitts and
					   Nevis
					St. Lucia
					Trinidad and
					   Tobago
						American Samoa
						Isle of Man
						Mayotte
						Palau
						Puerto Rico

Table 2 Classification of economies by income and indebtedness, July 2000 (continued)

Income group	Sub-group	Severely indebted	Moderately indebted	Less indebted	Not classified by indebtedness	
High-income	OECD				Australia Austria Belgium Canada Denmark Finland France[c] Germany Greece Iceland Ireland Italy	Japan Luxembourg Netherlands New Zealand Norway Portugal Spain Sweden Switzerland United Kingdom United States
	Non-OECD				Andorra Aruba Bahamas, The Bermuda Brunei Cayman Islands Channel Islands Cyprus Faeroe Islands French Polynesia Greenland Guam Hong Kong, China[e] Israel	Kuwait Liechtenstein Macao, China[d] Monaco Netherlands Antilles New Caledonia N. Mariana Islands Qatar Singapore Slovenia Taiwan, China United Arab Emirates Virgin Islands (U.S.)
Total	207	46	43	59	59	

a. Former Yugoslav Republic of Macedonia.
b. Federal Republic of Yugoslavia (Serbia/Montenegro).
c. The French overseas departments French Guiana, Guadeloupe, Martinique, and Réunion are included in France.
d. On 20 December ,1999, China resumed its exercise of sovereignty over Macao.
e. On 1 July, 1997, China resumed its exercise of sovereignty over Hong Kong.
Source: World Bank data.

Definitions of groups

This table classifies all World Bank member economies, and all other economies with populations of more than 30,000. Economies are divided among income groups according to 1999 GNP per capita, calculated using the World Bank Atlas method. The groups are: low-income, $755 or less; lower-middle-income, $756–$2,995; upper-middle-income, $2,996–$9,265; and high-income, $9,266 or more.

Standard World Bank definitions of severe and moderate indebtedness are used to classify economies in this table. *Severely indebted* means either: present value of debt service to GNP exceeds 80 percent or present value of debt service to exports exceeds 220 percent. *Moderately indebted* means ei-

ther of the two key ratios exceeds 60 percent of, but does not reach, the critical levels. For economies that do not report detailed debt statistics to the World Bank Debtor Reporting System (DRS), present-value calculation is not possible. Instead, the following methodology is used to classify the non-DRS economies. *Severely indebted* means three of four key ratios (averaged over 1996–98) are above critical levels: debt to GNP (50 percent); debt to exports (275 percent); debt service to exports (30 percent); and interest to exports (20 percent). *Moderately indebted* means three of the four key ratios exceed 60 percent of, but do not reach, the critical levels. All other classified low- and middle-income economies are listed as *less indebted.*